T0197106

Aaronsohn's Maps

AARONSOHN'S MAPS

The Man Who Might Have Created
Peace in the Middle East

Patricia Goldstone

COUNTERPOINT
BERKELEY, CALIFORNIA

Library of Congress Cataloging-in-Publication Data is available

ISBN 978-1-61902-559-2

Cover design by Kelly Winton

Interior design by VJB/Scribe

COUNTERPOINT

2560 Ninth Street, Suite 318, Berkeley, CA 94710

www.counterpointpress.com

Printed in the United States of America

To Aaron and Sarah Aaronsohn

Contents

Preface

> Through this forest of special pleading the historian gropes
> his way, trying to recapture the truth of past events and find
> out "what really happened." He discovers that truth is subjec-
> tive and separate, made up of little bits seen, experienced, and
> recorded by different people. It is like a kaleidoscope; when
> the cylinder is shaken the countless colored fragments form a
> new picture. Yet they are the same fragments that made a dif-
> ferent picture a moment earlier. This is the problem inher-
> ent in the records left by actors in past events. That famous
> goal, "wie is wirklich war," is never wholly within our grasp.
>
>   — Barbara Tuchman, *The Guns of August*

> When a man rubs out a pencil-mark, he should be carful
> to see that the line is quite obliterated.
>
>   — Graham Greene, *The Ministry of Fear*

Aaron Aaronsohn was always in a hurry. To be in a hurry was to him the harbinger of progress, and the fury of perpetual motion suited him well. The two-seater De Havilland 4 in which he took off from the Royal Air Force base at Kenley on the afternoon of Thursday, May 15, 1919, was only quicker by some hours than train and steamship, but it suited him to soar above the intricately patchworked fields of the Kent countryside, gliding down currents of warm air like a hawk or a gull — or a god. Depending on prevailing winds and weather conditions, the journey from Kenley, just south of London, to Buc, near Paris, averaged two hours and thirty-eight minutes, the duration of a trip on the Eurostar today. For military VIPs and delegates to the Paris Peace Conference like Aaron, it amounted to the same thing, a comparatively quick and comfortable means of transport with the added cachet of the new.

It is comical to imagine Aaron cramming himself into the refurbished mail plane, which is what the DH-4 was. It looked like a bumblebee with its stumpy wings, and too small to fly as far as London, let alone France. He was a big man, built like a tank: it was said that he could lift a full-grown horse onto his broad back and throw it to the ground. A photograph taken in 1918 shows Aaron literally bulging out of the backseat of a sleek roadster parked in front of Fast's Hotel in Jerusalem, the premier destination for colonial nabobs. He is natty in blazer and boater (as is his Arab driver), looking self-assured and eminently clubbable save for his pugnacious jaw. With his crisp, russet hair, slightly hyperthyroid eyes, and tendency to corpulence, he bears a distinct resemblance to the young Orson Welles.

Aaronsohn was only forty-three years old in 1919, but he was the product of big events and big changes. In fact, he was one of the most extraordinary figures of World War I and its aftermath, the formation of the modern Middle East. Scientist, diplomat, and spy, he was a warrior-intellectual of prodigious energy and talent and the one man who, according to William "Champagne Billy" Bullitt, President Woodrow Wilson's special envoy to the Paris Peace Conference, might have engineered a workable solution to the thorny issue of Palestine's boundaries. During the war, he ran the most successful network of native spies in the Middle East and enabled the British general Edmund Allenby to capture Jerusalem – a decisive factor in winning the war, the facilitation of which made Aaron T. E. Lawrence's rival for the laurels of the Near East campaign.

Aaron's dandyism hid a Nietzschean will, the equivalent of what Lawrence called the ability to "dream in broad daylight" – to make his dreams real. "To see me," Aaron once wrote a friend, "one would conclude that I am soft, indolent, and jovial. But I know how to want, to want with tenacity and perseverance, to want with all the optimism of our race, and to sometimes transform my will into power." What this superman wanted was an independent Palestine, free from debt and Great Powers – and grounded in an egalitarian working relationship between Jews and Arabs. "If we fail, we alone shall suffer," he wrote in his diary. "But if we succeed, at least we shall not be indebted to anyone, and we shall have the right to say that our own efforts and merits have overcome all obstacles."

The De Havilland carried Aaron, his military pilot and escort, Captain Elgie Jefferson, and several bales of Aaron's documents, including the unique geological maps of Palestine he had created out of many years of youthful exploration. These, as two French newspapers would remark the next day, "were of considerable interest to the Paris Peace Conference." Carefully wrapped in waterproof material to preserve them in the not-unlikely event of an air catastrophe, these maps defined Aaron's "maximum boundary," the largest territory for the new Palestine among the several plans being presented in Paris. Israelis today would recognize it as the outline for Greater Israel, the territorial manifesto of the Likud Party based on Old Testament claims to Samaria and Judaea. Taking the Litani River in Lebanon as its northern border, it included the Sinai, a large swatch of Transjordan containing the fertile plains east of the Jordan River, and a chunk of Syria where the Jordan headwaters were located.

Aaron was not an ideologue but a pragmatist; water resources rather than biblical manifest destiny were the key to his maps. In this, as in so many other ways, he was ahead of his time. Where Winston Churchill and others saw oil as the defining commodity of the twentieth century, Aaron saw beyond them into the twenty-first, when water would become the most critical resource in the Middle East. Prewar Palestine was a dusty satellite of Syria that could not, in the eyes of great imperialists like Lord George Nathaniel Curzon, the former viceroy of India, feed the hordes of European Jews who wanted to relocate there. But Aaron also foresaw the conflict that such an influx could unleash, and cautioned against allowing unfettered immigration until the resources of the country could be built up to support both the Arab and Jewish populations. Scientifically managed in vast carrying systems that could irrigate an entire country, water, in Aaron's view, could support a vital new population in the millions and restore Palestine to the land of milk and honey described in the Song of Songs, "a fountain of gardens, a well of living waters and streams from Lebanon." Sufficient water would make the new Palestine economically independent and prepare it for a modern development boom. From his perspective, these waters should have included all of the headwaters of the Jordan River as well as the Litani River — waters that were the mains of the region and already a source of conflict between the new entities of Palestine, Lebanon, Syria, and the Great Powers that backed them, Britain and France.

Aaron proposed that with European technology and Jewish

engineering skills, these waters could be developed under a single management to provide for the needs of all three Middle Eastern countries. Properly managed – by himself, of course – such a water system would provide the foundation for cooperation between Arab and Jew. Without such cooperation, Palestine had no economic future and would be doomed to constant water wars. In the maps and plans he carried with him from London were the outlines of just such a venture that, had it succeeded, would have altered the course of modern history. But executing this vision required far more than maps. It required an almost superhuman agility at political maneuvering between the rocks and whirlpools of the Paris Peace Conference.

Aaron, so brilliant in so many ways, had the fatal flaw that makes the tragic hero. His hubris led him away from science, where he excelled, and into politics, where he did not. It led him to believe he could beat the Great Gamesmen at their own game to win the best deal he saw for the new Palestine. To triumph over all odds is the job description of a hero, but the odds against success in the creation of the modern Middle East at the Paris Peace Conference were almost insurmountable, even for the Great Powers, namely Britain, France, Germany, Russia, and, to a lesser extent, Italy, which had been jousting for the past century to control approaches to the vast wealth of the Indian subcontinent. Britain, France, and Russia (which had withdrawn from its wartime commitments when the czarist government fell and was consequently excluded from representation) had entangled themselves in a series of secret alliances that endlessly complicated the drawing of postwar boundaries. Britain, in order to pursue a war for which it was undermanned, had further compromised itself by bartering vague promises of territory and sovereignty in exchange for intelligence and insurgencies to undermine the Ottoman axis of the Central Powers, and, belatedly, for Jewry to swing the United States into the war. These ephemeral guarantees, issued freely to the rival dynasties of Sharif Hussein of Mecca and Ibn Saud of Riyadh, to the Zionists of Europe and America, and even to a select few of the Turkish enemy, made carving up the Ottoman carcass a recipe for future conflict, particularly as Britain, France, and America commenced quarreling immediately over the future of the oil contained within the old Ottoman territories.

It would have taken a Ulysses to negotiate these perils, and Aaron, by the time he put himself on the plane to Paris, had lost both the patience and the cunning of the mythical survivor of the Trojan War. Chaim Weizmann, who emerged from the Paris Peace Conference as leader of the world Zionist movement and eventually became the first president of the modern state of Israel, possessed these qualities in abundance, along with considerable sangfroid; furthermore, he was unwearied by battle. Aaron was bruised and exhausted.

In spite of his prodigal talents, Aaron suffered from a very thin skin. He collected injustices and often avenged them with bursts of incandescent temper. Even Sarah, his favorite sister, who ran his intelligence-gathering operations in Palestine during the war, had feared her brother's not-infrequent explosions. His American friends and patrons often described him as a "new kind of Jew," a frontiersman free at last of the physical and mental restraints of the ghetto wall. Two qualities still tethered him to that wall: a longing to be all things to all men, and a stubborn need to belong. He burned to prove himself on the field of battle the equal or the superior of the British, for whom he had harvested the only reliable intelligence in Palestine. This need made him peculiarly vulnerable to the manipulations of others. Not only had he allowed himself to work unpaid and unrecognized, but he had allowed Sarah to be sacrificed for the British victory. Forsaking the pursuit of knowledge for that of politics had cost him all he had. Still, he felt, the leaders of the Great Powers looked down on him, and now, just as he was poised to reap the only reward that could make his life meaningful, he was excluded from their councils. His boundary proposal was in part a form of revenge for, or at least acknowledgment of, Sarah's loss – but revenge, as his British masters might have told him, makes a dish that is best served cold.

Aaron Aaronsohn never reached his destination. Legend has it that the De Havilland 4 was lost in fog over the English Channel. Felix Frankfurter, the Supreme Court justice and ardent Zionist who was his friend, attempted a biography of him in 1939, when Europe was once more engulfed in war, and wrote portentously of the "bloodstained hand" that had swept him from life. Frankfurter never specified to whom the bloodstained hand belonged, nor did he finish his book.

More than eighty years after Aaron's death, I traced my way through the tight rows of small white crosses in the Quartier Anglais of Dunkirk Town Cemetery. I was trying to find what was left of him. It was the end of a long journey that had taken me not only to the Middle East but down the rabbit hole of the Public Record Office in London, wherein lie the remains of the secret diplomacy of World War I. I first stumbled across a mention of the Aaronsohns while researching a book on water and conflict in the Middle East. Here was a lost leader with the stature to foresee the problems of the present day, a Jew who loved Palestine but did not hesitate to criticize the fractious politics of Zionism, detested all ideologies as forms of incompetence, and did not see a future without Arab-Jewish cooperation. Moreover, he defined the fundamental issue of the future state's relations with its neighbors as the quintessentially pragmatic one of water resources, which could have been solved, at least early on, by means that did not involve the loaded weaponry of race, religion, or culture.

Why was so little generally known about Aaron and Sarah Aaronsohn, whose perils seemed made for the big screen? In the Public Record Office, where Foreign Office, War Office, Cabinet, and other official records are kept, I found myself deep in a thicket of the yellow notes thoughtfully left behind by scrupulous archivists to indicate where pages of a sensitive nature have been removed. The gaps in the documents — and the curiously spun, often self-contradictory nature of what I had read in libraries elsewhere — hinted at an historic injustice — a great crime, as Zola might have put it, on which a nation was built.

Aaron, born in Romania, bred in Palestine, educated in France, sponsored by Germany and Turkey, adopted by America, and employed by the English, was a citizen of the world. Though his heart unquestionably beat for Palestine, his instincts were cosmopolitan, and he frequently and vehemently railed at the narrowness of his fellow Jews. He kept his diaries in French, in penny notebooks the size of a small woman's hand, and on his person at all times. Although he was an exhaustive annotator of facts, he was not someone who wanted his innermost thoughts to be known, and he interspersed his French with Hebrew, Arabic, German, English, and even Turkish, all languages he spoke fluently. Because he cultivated the habit of secrecy from an early age, and because of the loss or destruction of certain documents, there are elements of his identity that will always remain a mystery.

I have filled in the gaps left by official censorship with two years of cross-referencing, comparing the documents of the Public Record Office with military records, private papers and diaries, newspaper accounts, fiction and nonfiction sources, and other documents held in American, French, and Israeli archives. Some sources, like the last two months of Aaron's meticulous diaries – which perhaps shed too much light on what really happened at the Paris Peace Conference – are believed to have been destroyed. His vital water maps also mysteriously vanished in the fog of his last plane journey, after being rescued by a British military plane.

With the passage of years and recent pressure within the British intelligence services to declassify more documents, it has become possible to reconstruct the Aaronsohns and to do their remarkable story justice, Sarah no less than Aaron. There is significant new evidence to suggest that Sarah, known at the time as the Jewish Joan of Arc, was the real "S.A.," the mysterious, erotic figure to whom Lawrence dedicated his war memoir, *Seven Pillars of Wisdom,* and one of the great literary enigmas of the twentieth century:

> I loved you, so I drew these tides of men into my hands
> and wrote my will across the sky in stars
> To earn you freedom, the seven-pillared worthy house,
> that your eyes might be shining for me
> When we came.

But Aaron was the real actor, the mover of profound and profoundly troubling events that reverberated far beyond his time. Despite or even because he is almost unknown today, the fragments of Aaron Aaronsohn's life form a new picture of *wie is wirklich war*, "how it really was." They open a way into what happened behind the scenes at the Paris Peace Conference of 1919 and into the big issues behind World War I, issues that still bedevil the world today. Reassembling Aaron's short but eventful life is to piece together a novel view of World War I as a war that began not in the Balkans but in the Middle (at that time the "Near") East; and certainly not in the effort to, as Woodrow Wilson so famously put it, make the world "safe for democracy," but in the great European railway race, which began almost fifty years before the outbreak of hostilities in 1914. Reconstructing Aaronsohn shows how Zionism was used by the great European powers, particularly Britain and Germany, to advance their aims in what historian Niall Ferguson calls "Globalization I" — the fierce economic competition to build the first international banking, transport, and telecommunications systems. It is also the story of how the Zionists, in turn, learned to use the Great Powers to their benefit, and of how the propaganda campaign in which Aaron played a leading role set the stage for World War II, with terrible results for the Jews. His life presents the rarest of opportunities to study the full consequences — personal, political, and global — of the first great exercise in spin.

I began my work on this book during the run-up to the 2003 Iraq war. Like other researchers, I was denied access to the main body of British archival material relating to Aaron's activities for the Eastern Mediterranean Special Intelligence Bureau on the grounds that the same methods are still in use today. The war fought to control the riches of the Middle East has never ended, and Aaron is still at the heart of the matter.

It is therefore time to resurrect Aaron Aaronsohn, if only to measure the degree of his relevance to the events of our own day. Although he intended it to serve a peaceful purpose, the maximum boundary for which he fought before his death in 1919 became the basis for all subsequent Zionist territorial demands — and military campaigns — up to the present day. It is, in fact, the rock on which the 1990s peace process initiated by Bill Clinton foundered. Aaron's maps make it possible to understand why Israel and Syria cannot agree on the Golan Heights; how their disagreement led to war with Iraq; and how the only comprehensive Middle East solution put forward to resolve it — a 5,000-mile-long "Peace Pipeline" that would bring water from Turkey to Saudi Arabia — looks increasingly like the Berlin-Baghdad Railway that caused so much conflict a hundred years ago.

Although he is relatively obscure today, in his lifetime Aaron was a figure of notoriety, admiration, and considerable envy. Though many saw him as a selfish and unscrupulous opportunist who was using

Zionism to feather his own nest, he sacrificed more than any other leader to secure the best deal for Palestine and was a contender for the leadership of the new nation. When his name does come up in Israel today, it is generally as an icon of the far right and the author of plans to resettle West Bank Palestinians in Iraq; but the richness and strangeness of his personality (and his strong pro-Arab views) make him an unlikely spokesperson for any ideological perspective. I have spent a great deal of time over the past three years wondering just what he would have accomplished if he had lived. When he died in that flimsy plane in 1919, just entering his prime, President Woodrow Wilson's special envoy to the Paris Peace Conference wrote:

> He was the greatest man I have ever known. He seemed a sort of giant of an elder day . . . like Prometheus. It is not easy to express his greatness in lifeless words; for he was the quintessence of life, of life when it runs torrential, prodigal and joyous . . . The Jewish race had many brilliant leaders but when Aaron died I believe that it lost the man who, before all others, could kindle the hearts and minds of other nations to active sympathy. And not Zion alone will suffer for his loss.

The Jew in the Bathchair

> The Jew is everywhere, but you have to go far down the backstairs to find him. But if you're on the biggest kind of job and are bound to get to the real boss, ten to one you are brought up against a little whitefaced Jew in a bathchair with an eye like a rattlesnake. Yes, sir, he is the man who is ruling the world right now and he has his knife in the empire of the Tzar, because his aunt was outraged and his father flogged in some one-horse location on the Volga.
>
> — John Buchan, *The Thirty-Nine Steps*

In the autumn of 1882, a tattered delegation of Romanian Jews arrived in Constantinople and landed in front of the American minister, Lew Wallace, a Civil War general famous as the author of *Ben Hur.* They were led by an Englishman, Laurence Oliphant, a gentile Zionist who petitioned Wallace to intercede with the Turkish Sultan Abdul Hamid II to allow the Jews to settle in that part of Abdul Hamid's empire called Palestine. Among the convoy were Ephraim Fischel Aaronsohn, an entrepreneurial farmer from Falticeni, in the foothills of the Carpathian Mountains, and his pious young wife, Malkah. Eager for a home that would allow them to realize their ambitions, they had made the long, dangerous journey by train, diligence, and ferry with their only child, a robust and curious six-year-old boy named Aaron.

The Aaronsohns' journey was set in motion by the great turning point in the modern history of the Jews, the pogroms of 1881. Imperial Russia's revival and extension of the Ignatieff Decrees, stifling Jewish economic activities in the Pale, created a tidal wave that sent Russian Jews spilling over the border into Romania, Romanian Jews pouring into Austria, and Jews from all parts of Eastern Europe crowding into the slums of the cities of the West. Hundreds of thousands of Jews in the isthmus of Europe between the Black Sea and the Baltic were driven from areas they had inhabited for years by Romanian and Serbian nationalist peasant leaders engorged with new liberties and power as their provinces slipped away from Ottoman control. The Aaronsohns became part of the wave of predominantly bourgeois Zionists who came to the Holy Land before 1885 that was known as the First Aliyah. Like the word *haj* in Arabic, *aliyah* means pilgrimage.

Unique among the arrivals of the First Aliyah, Ephraim Fischel was not only skilled at agriculture but modestly knowledgeable about hydrology as well. In his native Romania, he had parlayed his success as a farmer into owning a prosperous inn and had managed the holdings of a number of great landowners before his prosperity invited persecution. The pious Malkah was a beauty, not without a streak of coquetry, and her upwardly mobile husband was inordinately proud of her. Malkah could claim a lineage going back to King David. Her revered father, Rabbi Samuel Galatzanu (who fled Russia for Falticeni, which lies close to the Russian border), had been tortured by the Romanian authorities when a Christian child in his community disappeared during Passover. The child was later found safe and the accusations of child sacrifice retracted, but Galatzanu died of his injuries and his death hastened the Aaronsohns' departure. They sought opportunity as well as sanctuary. With the notable exception of the BILU, a small but impassioned group of young intellectual nationalist pioneers from Russia who were dedicated to the concept of tilling biblical soil with their own hands, the vast majority of European Jews at that time viewed the Holy Land as an extension of America and would have settled in the United States – or any place that would let them live free of the strangulations of the Pale – as happily as in Palestine.

General Wallace, a militant evangelical, was touched by their plight and cabled U.S. Secretary of State F.T. Frelinghuysen: "Refugee Jews starving here. Delegates ask good offices with Sultan to colonize Syria. May I act?" Frelinghuysen gave him leave to use his good offices in an unofficial capacity, as the United States government was reluctant to be perceived by the Turks as encouraging independent colonization.

Laurence Oliphant's Zionism only thinly concealed an imperial streak. Oliphant had been one of the most celebrated agents for Queen Victoria's Secret Service, a career cut short by his publicly denouncing the British Foreign Office's betrayal of nationalist aspirations throughout Europe in the illustrious pages of *Blackwood's Magazine*. His associate in acting as agent for societies of Romanian Jews – described by Wallace in his dispatches as a "respectable gentleman," though he was known only as "Mr. Alexander" – was also acting as agent for Sir Edward Cazalet, a British railway entrepreneur. Like Wallace and Oliphant, as well as other hardheaded British military men such as General Edmund Allenby, Richard Meinertzhagen, and even future prime minister David Lloyd George, Cazalet was a gentile Zionist who professed the belief that returning the world's wandering Jews to Palestine, their biblical homeland, would hasten the Second Coming of the Messiah and a new Christian dawn. However these men were also stimulated by commercial interests. Oliphant was a commercial adventurer. Cazalet had already invested considerable money and effort in railway networks in Romania, which, until the opening of the Persian oil fields, was Europe's chief petroleum source. Now, like many other would-be railway kings in Europe, he was eager to expand the railway network, which already stretched from London to Bucharest, to include Turkey, Palestine, and the rest of what imperial geographers called the "historic highway" connecting Europe with Asia, in what we now call the Middle East. Cazalet was keen to protect his investment by returning friendly Europeans, i.e., Jews, to Palestine to settle alongside his railroad tracks and thus provide a buffer against potentially hostile Arabs. Oliphant's plan to settle the Romanian contingent in the rich agricultural area of western Syria, where the Jordan rises, would give the colonists a solid economic base as well. Cazalet and Oliphant lobbied the British Parliament to make Zionism a political reality, a convenient packaging of purposes not uncommon in the annals of British imperial policy. When bundled with the Admiralty's voracious need for oil as it converted its battleships from steam power to outstrip Germany's in an increasingly vicious naval race, it would shape the course of the twentieth century.

The Aaronsohns were fleeing the frying pan for the fire by applying for asylum to Abdul Hamid, a melancholy man (bearing an unfortunate physical resemblance to Rasputin) who was placed on the throne when his older brother succumbed to insanity. At least early in his reign, Abdul Hamid was a perspicacious economic planner who wished to see his country benefit from modernity, and ushered in the development of modern telecommunications, transport, and women's education in Turkey. As his rule progressed, however, his dependence on Europe drew increasing hostility from nationalist groups. He retreated into paranoia and the seclusion of his palaces, where his spies furnished his only link to the outside world, and became known as the Red Sultan for presiding over the slaughter of almost 2.5 million Armenians between 1894 and 1908.

For the greater part of four centuries, the Ottomans had treated non-Islamic populations with relative tolerance, allowing them to practice their religions as long as they paid their poll taxes, and to govern their own communities as long as they reported to the local bey. In their dispatches to the State Department, American envoys to the Near East described Jews under the old Turkish rule as fortunate compared to those subjected to the caprices of Romanian and Serbian nationalists in the Balkan Ottoman provinces. But Turkey was still crushed under a debt incurred during the Crimean War in 1854, when France and England came to Turkey's aid against Russia. Foreign investment was the most expeditious way out, and had to be courted with liberal concessions. As Abdul Hamid's foreign debt spiraled out of control, he came under increasing attack from Islamic nationalists already enflamed by the Capitulations, a series of trade agreements enacted by Europe earlier in the century, which had handed a near monopoly to Armenian Christians, Jews, and other European minorities residing in the Ottoman Empire in such choice areas as banking and import-export: the slaughter of the Armenians in part originated in their favored status. Granting concessions to build Turkish railroad infrastructure, Abdul Hamid's best means of courting foreign investment, fueled the nationalists' other chief source of irritation – the growing invasion by Western, primarily female, tourists, led by the British travel giant Cook's Tours.

After the British conquest of Egypt in the 1870s, the Turks were opposed to foreign control of Turkish land. Zionism, though it would not fully emerge as an organized worldwide political movement until the Basel Congress of 1897, already presented a threat. Although they were officially prohibited from settling in Palestine, it was not unusual for Jews to enter under the guise of making *aliyah*, and then to disappear into existing settlements. When General Wallace called on the

Turkish minister of affairs to espouse the Jewish cause, he was told that the Aaronsohns and their coreligionists could come whenever they wanted and settle in groups of two hundred or two hundred and fifty families in any unoccupied lands in Mesopotamia, around Aleppo or around the Orontes River in Syria — as long as they became Ottoman subjects.

The Aaronsohns had no choice but to accept the sultan's terms and were now newly minted Ottoman citizens. However, like many other Jews at the time, they entered their Promised Land by an arduous route. After a miserable journey of forty days by boat, yawing from port to port in the heavy seas of winter, they were allowed by the local authorities to land at Jaffa. Then it was another ordeal, this time by pack mule, through wilderness territory where mudslides and quicksands and sudden raids by Bedouin bandits were commonplace, before they reached Haifa. From Haifa, they endured yet another grueling journey to the settlement of Zichron Ya'akov. What they found there was far from a land of milk and honey. Though beautiful, Palestine had been eroded by four centuries of not-so-benign neglect. It was a land of typhus and malaria, of marshes and mosquitoes and stinging black flies. It would take years of unremitting hard work to build a successful life there, and the biggest obstacle would be their fellow Jews.

There was great hatred and little room in nineteenth-century Palestine, just as there was in Yeats' Ireland. The land was poor, resources limited, and almost all the Jewish population subsisted on the *Halukah,* alms collected from Jews on all five continents to encourage their coreligionists in the Holy Land to pray for them. Sectarian strife was unavoidable. The two main groups of combatants were the Sephardim, primarily descendants of those Jews received by the sultan after being expelled from Spain in the fifteenth century, their numbers augmented by stray migrants from North Africa, Italy, Greece, Persia, and Afghanistan; and Ashkenazic Jews from Central and Eastern Europe. (*Sepharad* means Spain in Hebrew; *Ashkenaz* means Germany.) The Sephardim had strict rules governing how *Halukah* was to be apportioned and for the most part abided by them. The Ashkenazic sects were another matter entirely. Reluctant to place themselves under the authority of the Sephardic chief rabbi, they initiated some of the bitterest infighting in the Jewish homeland by overriding the central

Halukah distribution system created by the older Sephardic community, collecting charity directly from their hometowns in Europe. This reduced the funds available to the dominant group and furthermore embedded centuries-old doctrinal conflicts between the Prushim and Hasidim of Poland and Lithuania in the only extant foreign-aid channel for the Jews.

Charity was for the majority not only a way of life but the only way of life. Recipients of the dole were enrolled at birth and could only be removed by order of the rabbi, who thus enjoyed almost unlimited power as the threat of excommunication carried with it the threat of loss of livelihood. Rabbis administered justice with an iron hand. Heavy corporal punishment such as the lash was applied to miscreants, including women, and a form of stocks — where the guilty were vigorously pelted with stones by the entire congregation — was erected to serve as a model to the community. Conformity was enforced by the encouragement of tale-telling. Letters dispatched to the comptrollers of the *Halukah* in Europe destroyed the reputations and livelihood of pious dissenters. The spreading of false rumor became a favored form of social vendetta. The Jews of Jerusalem resembled in many respects the early Puritan settlements of New England that inspired the Arthur Miller play *The Crucible.*

Entrepreneurial Jews like the Aaronsohns represented a different class of people. Ephraim Fischel sought a better life for his family than the squalid conditions created by dependence on *Halukah,* which recreated the ghettos the Jews had fled in Europe. Although the Lovers of Zion, who deplored "modern influences" and the emigration of Jews to America rather than to Palestine, had made it possible for him to leave Romania, Ephraim Fischel's aspirations suggest he may have been happier in the New World. He certainly passed on a rugged sense of independence to his young son Aaron, along with his talent for hydrology and a taste for the finer things in life.

Already more prosperous than their neighbors, Ephraim built Malkah a neat stucco farmhouse with high stone gates and an ornate tile roof, set suitably aloof at the end of an avenue of tall pines in Zichron Ya'akov, near the beautiful slopes of Mt. Carmel. They had three more boys, Samuel, Tzvi, and Alex, and two girls, Sarah and Rivka, and expanded their compound to three dim, cool dwellings, curtained in brocade and furnished in heavy dark wood that Aaron later embellished with lavish inlaid pieces from Damascus.

Many years after Aaron's death, his youngest brother, Alex, wrote a biographical note for a volume of Aaron's early scientific explorations, describing an idyllic childhood inspired by Arcadian vistas of Mt. Hermon and the Mediterranean and the friendship of the humble Arab *fellahs* who worked in the Jewish settlement. It was a childhood of riding, swimming, and dancing parties, harvest festivals and hard work in the fields that still left time for intensive scholastic studies by day and Torah studies by night. The touch of the sun seemed to work miracles on Europe's pallid children. Young Aaron was a prodigy who mastered four languages by the time he was twelve, although his academic career was somewhat tarnished by his habit of lecturing his schoolmasters, particularly on the subject of botany. The font of his knowledge was the marvelous classical library given to this tiny village of eighty houses by His Grace, the Baron Edmond de Rothschild, whose name, according to Alex, "could never be pronounced in Zichron Ya'akov without adding the benison 'God give him long life.'"

Zichron cultivated an air of distinction, even of eccentricity. It was known early on as a "little Paris," a center of fashion and intellectual life. However exaggerated this description might be, it suited the young Aaronsohns, whose neighbors described them from the beginning as snooty, and stuck not only on themselves but on one another – Malkah, a typically doting mother, regarded her children as royalty and treated them accordingly. Isolated by their own abilities and by being a cut above their fellow villagers, the young Aaronsohns drew in on themselves, developing their own amusements and special language, corresponding voluminously throughout their lives, and, in Alex's case, drawing extensively on their siblings for literary inspiration. Sarah, the family beauty, was also its *belle lettriste*, and apparently as precocious as Aaron. With her little sister, Rivka, as her obliging sidekick, she carried on a spirited correspondence with local intellectual lights such as the writer and lexicographer Eliezar Ben Yahuda, who led the fight to revitalize the Hebrew language, before she was twelve years old. At twelve, she finished her formal education in the village school but continued to study at home and read both widely and deeply and with equal ease in Hebrew, German, Yiddish, and French. For entertainment, Alex, in whom vigilanteism mingled with an irresistible urge to self-dramatize, taught her how to shoot pistols and defend herself from brigands and marauding Turkish soldiers.

Aaron was a proto-*sabra,* thin-skinned, fiercely independent, and just as apt to settle an argument with his fists as with his tongue. From an early age he had little patience for the fears and constraints of the ghetto. He grew up alongside the Arabs who tended and protected Jewish fields and vineyards. He learned their language, responded to their friendship, and entered their homes to partake of their holidays. His view of them was by no means sentimental, but the conviction that Arabs and Jews could live and work side by side came to form the foundation of his views and reverberated throughout his career.

But life in Zichron Ya'akov was far from idyllic. The Jewish community's divisions of class and culture would make internal division as much a threat as invasion from without through the years. The Aaronsohns were to become a lightning rod for these conflicts, for the family did not fit neatly into one division or the other. At a time when the rabbis kept close track of religious practices for the assignation of *Halukah,* the Aaronsohns were almost impossible to define in religious terms. Ephraim Fischel and Malkah were traditionally Orthodox. Aaron grew up studying Talmud, but as an adult he was defiantly irreligious, and Sarah, a freethinker who had no reason to love rabbis, followed his example. Little has been written of the middle Aaronsohn brothers, Tzvi and Samuel (or Shmuel), but the slender evidence suggests they identified with the more conservative element of the *Yishuv* and disapproved of their flamboyant siblings. Alex, on the other hand, became more British than the British themselves.

But the ghetto and its bonds were hard to escape. The very closeness of the family unit teetered on the incestuous. The distribution of talent among the children was far from even, and the family festered with jealousies that mirrored those of the larger community. Aaron and Sarah, the two stars, formed a natural unit, and throughout Aaron's life Sarah was the one person he trusted. Shmuel, second to Aaron in the hierarchy of age but not in ability, resented the favoritism he showed to Sarah. Tzvi, the family ne'er-do-well, resented everyone. Alex, in many ways the most complex of the six children, both worshipped his formidable oldest brother and desperately tried to outdo him. Rivka, who had little identity of her own, became Alex's puppet and a surrogate Sarah.

When Aaron was ten years old, Ephraim Fischel applied for a grant from Baron Edmond de Rothschild, known in Palestine as M. le Baron or simply, *Le Patron,* to drill for water at the nearby settlement of Rishon-le-Zion (First in Zion). Aaron's father got more than he bargained for. Once the Baron took over the reins of financial responsibility, every new settler in one of his colonies had to sign an agreement "to submit myself totally to the orders that the administration shall think necessary in the name of M. le Baron in anything concerning the cultivation of the land and its service and if any action shall be taken against me I have no right to oppose it." What Ephraim Fischel Aaronsohn, dedicated to building a better life for his family, thought of this has gone unrecorded; it must have disheartened him to flee oppression in Romania only to find it at the hands of his coreligionists in Palestine. However, he won permission to drill, and so began his son's training in hydrology.

The tyranny of the Ashkenazic rabbis was not the only medieval relic exported to Palestine. Another was the patronage of the Rothschilds, who, though secular benefactors, ran up to twelve settlements as feudal fiefdoms, with their fellow Jews as serfs.

The clash of empires that ushered in the nineteenth century hid another epic struggle, that of the ancient landed aristocracy versus the new lords of international finance. The *Finanzbonaparten*, as the Rothschilds came to be called, emerged from the Napoleonic wars with the British government in their debt, having bankrolled the Duke of Wellington's famous victory at Waterloo. They then became bankers to the Holy Alliance of Christian Monarchs (established among the emperors of Russia and Austria and the king of Prussia to help resettle Europe's boundaries after Napoleon's fall) and fanned out to Paris,

Vienna, Naples, Frankfurt, and London to direct the flow of funds. In 1817, the Rothschilds advanced their first major state loan, to Prussia, for five million pounds. Others followed in rapid succession until it might reasonably be said that the Rothschilds acted as the world's first development bank. Between 1815 and 1914, the five houses of Rothschild bailed out the governments of Naples, Portugal, South Africa, Uganda, Brazil, and Palestine, and underwrote the construction of the Suez Canal, for a total of 1.6 billion pounds sterling in loans.

By 1845, the Rothschilds were the richest family in the world, perhaps in all of history. Their five international banking houses comprised one of the first multinational corporations. Not only did they issue bonds, they discounted bills and dealt in commodities (especially gold and silver), insurance, and private banking services, using their multinational structure to engage in arbitrage on a hitherto-unseen scale. To archconservatives like John Buchan, the popular novelist who parlayed his literary skills into a seat in the British Parliament and a governor's mansion in Canada (and whose sardonic description of "the Jew in the bathchair" resembles popular caricatures of Alphonse de Rothschild in the British magazine *Vanity Fair*), they were anarchists in that their greatest contribution to economic history, the creation of a truly international bond market, overturned the social order by destroying the preeminence of land as an asset. Scarcely fifty years after the Rothschilds and others of the mighty "Cousinhood" of wealthy Jewish families connected by marriage had settled into their newly created baronies in England and France, the development of Zionism – with its emphasis on land – as an independent force in world politics superceded the Rothschilds' carefully nurtured role as the voice of the Jewish people.

Edmond's older brother Alfonse de Rothschild was a formidable politician known as the best-informed and most beautifully mustachioed man in Europe. A brilliant businessman, he was heavily invested in Russian oil at least forty years before William Knox D'Arcy began tying up Persian oil concessions for the British. Russian oil, which in the 1860s was already emerging as the European rival to the American monopoly Standard Oil, was the Baron's pet project. By the early 1880s, almost two hundred Rothschild refineries were at work in Baku on the oil-rich Aspheron Peninsula, a spur of the Caucasus Mountains projecting into the Caspian Sea. Working conditions were atrocious. Most workers lived without their families, and the average working day ran to fourteen hours, with two hours of compulsory overtime. Little wonder that Baku soon became a revolutionary hotbed.

Largely because of Baku's oil fountains, Russian production rose tenfold between 1879 and 1888, until it equaled 23 million barrels, more than four-fifths of American production. By the mid-1880s, the Rothschilds were poised to become the chief oil supplier, not only to Europe but to the Far East. But the Baku-Batum railroad was already proving inadequate to transport the volume of oil being produced. Another route was needed, and came in the form of the recently opened Suez Canal, which shortened the journey to the Far East by four thousand miles. Palestine was suddenly of interest to the Rothschilds as it provided access to the Suez.

The Rothschilds were leaders of the Jewish community worldwide and a bulwark against anti-Semitism. Their emissaries had actively intervened in persecutions such as the infamous Damascus Affair of 1840, in which scores of Syrian Jews were rounded up, tortured, and threatened with execution for the so-called ritual murder of a Capuchin monk and his servant. However, their attitude toward Zionism was highly equivocal. They valued their Judaism but equally valued their assimilation, and initially found the idea of a Jewish homeland unsettling because of the threat it might pose to their already-established national identities.

The English Rothschilds were in fact as alarmed as any squire from the Shires might be by the flood of Central European Jews entering England between 1885 and 1895 to escape persecution in Czarist Russia and Romania. They were doubly alarmed when the socialist tendencies of the emigrés contributed to a massively disruptive tailors' strike in the East End of London in 1888. A young Georgian communist who would become known to the world as Joseph Stalin was already organizing laborers to strike at the Rothschild oil interests in Batum. With the example of Russia before them, the Rothschilds feared that the new Jewish arrivals' politics might unleash a wave of persecutions in Britain, and moved swiftly to invent strategies to forestall such upheaval.

One strategy was to restrict immigration; however, the Cousinhood agreed that "exclusion" was uncomfortably close to "expulsion." The alternative was to get as many newcomers as possible to move on, as quickly as possible. Palestine became the obvious solution.

That Edmond, whom his statesmanlike brother regarded as a child, too immature to enter the banking business at age twenty-five, was given the family brief for Palestine speaks volumes for the Rothschild ambivalence toward Zionism. Edmond's first love was art. He then interested himself in viniculture, and, in the 1880s, established some forty agricultural settlements, industries, and schools in Palestine. He was ultimately to spend over twelve million pounds sterling to try, unsuccessfully, to make them viable. He regarded the settlements as his personal fiefdom. Theodor Herzl, the Viennese journalist and playwright who founded the European Zionist movement on the principle of the independent Greek nation-state, approached him for sponsorship in 1895, but Edmond said that he regarded Herzl's plan of founding a state in Ottoman territory as a threat to his own colonization scheme. He actively encouraged his settlers to seek Ottoman citizenship. Despite Herzl's handsome offer to make him the "first prince of Palestine," Edmond looked askance at Herzl's socialist agenda, and at the anarchic threats with which the nation-builder alternated his blandishments. Herzl, for his part, dismissed Edmond as a lightweight, a "decent, goodnatured, fainthearted man who utterly fails to understand the matter and who would like to call it off as a coward tries to call off an imperative operation," as the Viennese wrote in his diaries. "I believe he is now disgusted that he ever began with Palestine, and he'll perhaps run to Alphonse and say 'You're right, I should have gone in for racing-horses rather than wandering Jews.'"

The young students who aspired to become the pioneers of colonization in Palestine in the early 1880s were largely urban products who knew neither agriculture nor the country, nor the language and customs of the native Arabs. Adept at political ideology, they were woefully inept at farming. Like the earliest Pilgrims in America, they faced starvation in their first years in Palestine, compounded by epidemics of malaria from the swamps they were trying to farm. They were saved by Edmond de Rothschild, who assumed financial responsibility for the four settlements in direst straits in exchange for full transfer of ownership of their real estate. His declared intention was to work toward a time when the settlements would become economically independent. Under his patronage, they never did. It remains unclear whether Edmond ever fully intended to make his settlements autonomous; certainly he fostered a culture of dependency that became one of the first and most pressing problems of the Jewish homeland.

The Baron set up a top-heavy administrative bureaucracy resembling nothing so much as a feudal hierarchy: himself at the top in Paris; countrywide "inspectors" located in Beirut and at the farm school at Mikweh-Israel; "senior commissioners" for the big regional colonies at Rosh-Pinna, Zichron Ya'akov, and Rishon-le-Zion; and scores of "junior commissioners" for the small local colonies. The commissioners, at all levels, were French-speaking Jews, largely originating from Alsace. Nonetheless, they were expected to deal with such complex local matters as the distribution of welfare to settler families and relations with the Arab neighbors and Ottoman bureaucrats. Only a few were qualified agronomists, and this, combined with language limitations and a certain amount of graft, augured ill for the Baron's success in business.

In 1897, the Rothschild machine in Paris made an arbitrary decision to eliminate the highly diversified farming that flourished without irrigation in Palestine and make the wine industry the central factor in the Jewish agricultural economy. The Baron invested huge sums of money in the massive planting and irrigating of vineyards and in the building of state-of-the-art winepresses, billed in company literature as the "largest and most modern in the world." His managers imported choice species of French vines, destroyed almost immediately by plant lice that typically infest European grapevines. By the time the Palestinian vineyards finally became productive, the price of wine in European markets had fallen so low that the settlers' rented plots no longer yielded a net profit sufficient to support their families. The Baron's administration was forced to buy up the wine at a price high enough to allow his colonists to live. The deficit resulting from this subsidy became so enormous that around the time that Herzl castigated him for his faintness of heart, Edmond concluded an agreement through the Jewish Colonization Association to turn the colonies over to the settlers. As soon as the leash was loosed, the settlers collectivized into syndicates such as the Cooperative Society of Vine-Planters of the Great Cellars of Rishon-le-Zion and Zichron-Ya'akov, took over the Baron's cellars and winepresses, and cut production by two-thirds in order to boost the price of their exports. Ephraim Fischel Aaronsohn, by now the leading farmer of Zichron Ya'akov, was prominent among the organizers.

The Baron's repressive tendencies accorded ill with Ephraim Fischel's oldest son. Aaron brought himself to the attention of the Baron's commissioners from his earliest school days by his singular genius for botany. When he was twelve, it was decided to train his talent to some useful purpose. He was taken out of school and sent to travel, alone on horseback, among the farmers of the Rothschild colonies, to transmit instructions from the commissioners to the colonists, and check the number of laborers employed against wages paid. The Baron was clearly grooming him for a high position in his bureaucracy, where the boy's knowledge of Arabic, as well as of agriculture, would make him a unique asset. But Aaron had a mind of his own and used his missions to store up a trove of information for his own later explorations.

It became increasingly apparent that Aaron was not retainer material. Deference was never part of his vocabulary. At age seventeen, he was sent by his patron to study for two years at the famous agricultural school at Grignon, near Paris. This was in 1893, at the height of the Dreyfus affair, which whipped anti-Semitism to witch-hunt proportions in France and frightened even the Rothschilds. Aaron expressed sadness and anger about the political climate in a letter to his parents. When the school registrar asked the strapping seventeen-year-old to state his nationality, Aaron unhesitatingly answered in a loud voice: "Juif." His defiance earned him respect. (One Paris newspaper drolly referred to him as "the only Jew in France.") He improved on it with a talent for making as many friends as he made enemies.

At the end of two years, the Baron rewarded Aaron's achievements by sending him home as agricultural specialist in charge of Metulla, a new colony in Northern Galilee. The Syrians claimed Northern Galilee, the largest cereal-producing region of Palestine, for themselves, and naturally, wished to reserve its choicest parcels. Aaron rewarded the Baron's investment in him by unceremoniously telling him the truth. The Druse sheikhs who sold the land to the Rothschilds had done them out of a great deal of money by selling them terrain that was infertile and useless; furthermore, it was the fault of the Baron's managers for not informing him. The Baron, shocked at Aaron's impudence, told Aaron he had been sent to Metulla to concern himself with agricultural matters, not to question the wisdom of his employer. The managers, who had probably benefited nicely from *baksheesh* in the transaction of the sale, blackened the young whistle-blower's name to his benefactor. *Le Patron* retained an essential fondness for his tempestuous prodigy, and Aaron for him (throughout his life, he referred to Edmond as "The Good Old Gentleman"). But Aaron was unable to come up with the proper show of humility necessary to put himself back into Edmond's good graces, and though Aaron wrote several letters demanding his attention, the Baron shut him out of his confidence for many years.

If Aaron Aaronsohn had risen in the employ of Baron de Rothschild, he might have ended up in Paris as one of his highly paid and well-traveled stewards, and the fate of Palestine might have been very different. But, just as Palestine was not destined to remain a colony for long, Aaron was not destined to be an employee. He packed his bags and left the Baron's comfortable serfdom to find work in agricultural research on a large and prosperous estate near Smyrna in Anatolia, where his seemingly limitless energy made his Turkish employers call him Shaitoun — the Devil. The young man was acquiring a brilliant if troublesome reputation, as well as many introductions among highly placed Turks and German engineers. These led him to his life's work, accomplished during six years of solitary wandering throughout the length and breadth of Syria and Palestine: the first and perhaps still the best comprehensive survey of Palestine's waters.

2.

The Spies of Moses

> And Moses sent them to spy out the land of Canaan,
> and said to them, get you up this way south-
> ward, and go up into the mountain:
>> And see the land, what it is; and the people that dwell-
> eth therein, whether they be strong or weak, few or many;
>> And what the land is that they dwell in,
> whether it be good or bad . . . fat or lean . . .
>> So they went up, and searched the land from the wil-
> derness of Zin unto Rehob, as men come to Ha'math.
>> — Numbers, chapter 13

In the years in which Aaron Aaronsohn began his scientific explorations, England and Germany's competition to link Africa, Europe, and Asia via the long-forgotten land of Palestine became the run-up to war. Abdul Hamid's bankrupt and decaying Ottoman Empire was the last staging ground in what banker James de Rothschild called an *"affaire gigantesque,"* before which the great financiers of Europe trembled in anticipation. The nineteenth century was the age of consolidating and connecting the empires established in the preceding age of exploration with European centers of power. Railway bonds were its preeminent financial instrument. From the 1840s onward, each of the five imperial powers — France, Italy, Russia, Britain, and, belatedly, Germany — schemed to extend its railway systems all the way to the gold and diamonds of South Africa and to the fabled markets of India and China. Turkey was considered by most imperial geographers to be the confluence of three continents, Europe, Africa, and Asia, "a meeting-place and nothing more," as one blithely put it. Turkey in fact commanded a high ground of tremendous strategic and commercial importance, the path over which generals from time immemorial had marched to conquer the world.

The Ottoman Empire, like many before it, was created by seizing control of the world's oldest and most developed trade routes. An enormous transit trade passed through the narrow waterways of the Bosphorus, the Sea of Marmara, and the Dardanelles; up and down the Tigris, Euphrates, and Nile rivers; and across the ancient Silk Road to India and China. The empires of the Nile and Mesopotamian basins, of the Syrian strip, and of the Hittite mountain region had waxed fat since recorded history began by seizing and guarding the arteries of West Asiatic traffic: the original Suez Canal was developed by the pharaohs in the nineteenth century BC. The short-lived prosperity of the Jewish empire at the time of Solomon was attained immediately after it had become sole mistress of the international routes through Syria and Mesopotamia by extending its boundaries from the Red Sea and the Mediterranean to the Persian Gulf. Assyria took these land routes from Judaea in the eighth century BC, only to lose them a century later to the Chaldeans. In another century the Persians moved in. Cyrus the Great conquered from the Aegean to the Persian Gulf in the sixth century BC, and his son Darius added Egypt and India to the Persian Empire, only to be conquered in turn by Alexander the Great. All of these generals saw Palestine, the long-forgotten corner of the Ottoman Empire in which the Aaronsohns had sought sanctuary, as the hub of conquest.

The European railway race began as a drive to connect these trade centers by commercial rather than military means. It was the beginning of the phenomenon we now call globalization, led by a handful of financial players that notably included the international, family-owned banking House of Rothschild. The ballooning scale and cost of conflict between France and the rest of Europe between 1789 and 1848 presented undreamed-of opportunities to the Rothschilds and other ambitious risk takers who could capitalize on the borrowing needs of the combatant states, along with the disruption of their national patterns of trade and banking. The Jews, who had mastered the art in secrecy in order to transact business throughout several centuries of discriminatory legislation across Europe, held a distinct advantage in spiriting money offshore. The extended and widely dispersed family networks through which this was accomplished were one reason why the term *cosmopolite* was to carry such opprobrium in the British Parliament in the nineteenth century. The Houses of Rothschild became known to their competition (chiefly to the House of Barings, bankers to the Queen) as the "Jew[s] in the bathchair," in John Buchan's memorable phrase — leaders of a new cartel that increasingly controlled the world's finance, commodities, and transport trade.

Banks proliferated rapidly all over Europe in the 1850s, and it is difficult to determine whether the wildfire expansion of the banking business drove the wildfire expansion of the railway system or vice versa. Certainly the banks' most important source of business from the 1850s onward was the financing of railway lines and the emerging telecommunications business, both voracious consumers of capital. So prodigious were the railways' needs for infusions of capital that no one nation could afford them and money was raised, some through the first public bond issues, across the Continent and England. For the first time, the power of international financiers eclipsed that of governments, which, understandably, resented them. The ministers of Napoleon III urged His Imperial Majesty to purge himself of the tutelage of James de Rothschild, who, said his finance minister, Achille Fould, "reigns in spite of you."

The battle between the Rothschilds, with their legendary troves of private capital, and Napoleon's favorites, the Pereires brothers, who put together Crédit Mobilier with the first publicly raised share capital, created the banking business as we know it. The battle between the Houses of Rothschild and the House of Barings created the pan-European transportation system. The growth of banking and railway networks in turn fed the growth of colonial empires, or "markets," and governments, attempting to spend their way out of a period of political instability, created expansionary credit policies to feed them all. This public-private alliance was a peculiarly symbiotic relationship, creating debt that then had to be serviced by the purchase of more infrastructure. The investors came, and the tracks were laid — across Belgium, Spain, Northern Italy, Austria, the Balkans, Russia, and last of all, Turkey, which had become a political hostage to its ever-increasing debt.

By the 1860s, largely by cross-investing in banks, James de Rothschild of the family's Paris house secured a railway network that would one day lead all the way from the Belgian ports of Ostend and Antwerp, via Berlin, to Constantinople and the Black Sea. At the same time, the

Crimean War ushered in an era of upheaval that made railway ownership a matter of national security as well as financial interest. The
French and, ten years later, the Prussians won military victories by
mobilizing their railways; and commercial battle lines were redrawn
according to nationalist sentiments. After the Franco-Prussian War
of 1870-71, the only train allowed to roll across all of Europe was
the famous Orient Express, owned by a crafty Belgian banker named
Georges Nagelmackers, who won his concessions by trading on his
country's neutrality. Twenty years later, as animosity grew between
Britain and Germany, English investors declined to put money in German railways. In the years preceding World War I, a small handful of
international players scrambled to consolidate their networks, and
the great European railway race came down to the finish line: the Berlin-Baghdad Railway, the last and crucial link connecting Constantinople, the gateway to Europe, with Basra in Mesopotamia, or what is
now Iraq, the gateway to India.

From its inception in 1898, the opening of the Baghdad Railway was
considered more momentous than the opening of either the Suez or
Panama canals, which preceded it by almost fifty years. The creation
of a railway from Constantinople under European control became a
symbol of the dissolution of the Ottoman Empire and of the invasion
of the East by the spirit of Western enterprise. The oil trade was as yet
only a whisper compared to the hubbub surrounding the opening of the
markets of the Orient to the manufacturing centers of a newly indus-
trialized Europe. Nonetheless the British, in particular, were alert to
the possibility of a train link through Basra to the Persian oil fields
and thence to India, the jewel in their imperial crown. At the same
time they planned another transcontinental imperial railway, one that
would link Basra with the colonial fiefdom built by Cecil Rhodes out of
the gold and diamonds of South Africa.

In the last years of the nineteenth century political tensions had
already been kindled where railway networks crossed borders in the
Piedmont-Lombardy region of Northern Italy and in the Balkans. It
was the Baghdad Railway, however, that was to prove the tinderbox of
the world's first phase of globalization, and the core of the Near Eastern campaign of World War I.

Generals very often study old campaigns to plan new ones. First

Napoleon and then Bismarck had studied the legendary campaign of Alexander the Great. Thus Napoleon, vying with Britain for global control, conquered Egypt in 1798 as the preliminary step in a grand plan to make himself master of Syria, thereby cutting a crucial link out of the chain of the Asia Minor highway to threaten Britain's position in India. Egypt, in Napoleon's view, was merely a passageway to Palestine. The legendary general recognized that a successful attack on the Constantinople-Baghdad axis would spell the end of Ottoman domination of the East: a half century later, French architect Ferdinand de Lesseps built the Suez Canal, over which the British gained control in 1875 by reconquering Egypt and buying out France's shares in the Canal. Bismarck saw the highway as a means of establishing rapid overland access to India and superseding British control of the Suez. Even more, he saw Turkey, and the verdant delta of the Tigris and Euphrates rivers, as the future breadbasket of an expanding Europe.

And Europe was expanding. In 1871, Wilhelm I of Prussia was proclaimed first emperor of Germany, and Bismarck his "iron chancellor." Bismarck, who originated the idea of a German empire, realized that Germany, essentially a land power, had arrived too late to magnify itself by naval might, as Britain had. Instead, he envisioned its expansion by commercial means. A German-controlled line of trade traffic starting at Hamburg, crossing the Bosphorus, and strategically connecting with the mineral and agricultural riches of the East via rail would mean that a passage to India could take as little as eight days, thereby eclipsing the British-controlled Suez Canal and overcoming Germany's relative naval weakness. Bismarck's realization initiated Germany's famous *Drang nach Osten*, or "drive toward the East," which wiped out the boundaries of recalcitrant Balkan nations to open a path for the Baghdad Railway.

While Bismarck saw the railway primarily as a commercial venture, military planners like Helmut von Moltke saw otherwise. Von Moltke, general chief of staff for Wilhelm I, believed that it could play a vital role in transporting troops as well as travelers and thus was essential to long-range military strategy. Up to the reign of France's Louis XIV, European wars were largely fought to obtain or safeguard routes between east and west, and between north and south. Frederick the Great of Prussia was famous for his dictum that more and better roads

would only facilitate invasion, but as early as 1830, German econo-
mists predicted the advantages that railways would bring to the army
possessing them. By the Franco-Prussian War of 1870-71, von Moltke
was able to hand Wilhelm a decisive victory by seamlessly mobilizing
the transborder railroads almost before a single shot was fired. European generals remembered von Moltke's overwhelming victory for
generations. The integration of the national railway systems with one
another was seen as an ominous event. Every great power had sunk
years of work and untold sums of money into perfecting its railway system, and military planners demanded increasing involvement. As the
tracks stretched farther toward their distant destinations, the stage
was set for global railroad investment to transform into global conflict.

Global railroad investment was a competition in which Germany, being
a land power, had a natural edge. In 1898, one year after initiating the
naval buildup many historians believe caused World War I, Kaiser Wilhelm II paid a state visit to his fellow monarch, Sultan Abdul Hamid
II. His travel arrangements, made by the British travel agent Thomas
Cook and Sons, were a measure of how far the first phase of globalization had advanced. Germany and England enjoyed amicable relations
at the time, due in part to coinvestiture in the projected railway and in
part to British distaste for French and Russian influence in the region.

Superficially, the visit was a courtesy from one monarch to another,
but beneath the pomp and circumstance Kaiser Wilhelm pressed the
sultan to allow Georg von Siemens of the Deutsche Bank to finance
construction for the Berlin-Baghdad railway. Abdul Hamid's dilemma
was that by opening his country to the economic development it desperately needed, he also made it a pawn in the great railway game. To
extend the railway system as far south as Basra, German engineers
planned to blast more than twenty tunnels through Turkey's traditional bulwark against invasion – the towering Anatolian plateau. The
fears of nationalists like the Young Turks were awakened, but Abdul
Hamid was too deeply in debt to turn back. He had developed a preference for German engineers, who could also advise him on modernizing
his army, and thus favored German railway projects above all others.

Unlike the other Great Powers, Germany devoted considerable resources to developing agriculture in Abdul Hamid's empire. Bismarck's idea was to make Turkey into the garden of Europe by enhancing its tremendous potential to grow fruits, cereals, and cotton, which could be loaded onto the new trains and shipped without delay to Berlin, Hamburg, and Ostend. In addition to sinking over $200 million into laying track from Constantinople to Basra, Germany invested commensurate amounts in vast irrigation projects in Anatolia. One of these would one day employ the skills of a young agronomist named Aaron Aaronsohn.

Abdul Hamid granted Deutsche Bank the concession in order to repay his Crimean War debts, and a year later signed another convention granting von Siemens the right to extend his Anatolian Railway all the way to Basra, the entry to the Persian oil fields and to the Indian Ocean, where Britain struggled to maintain its sphere of naval influence. In the last years of the nineteenth century, the first well-substantiated reports of Persia's fabulous oil potential snared the interest of a British solicitor by trade and gambler by nature, one William Knox D'Arcy, who had just hit the jackpot with an Australian gold-mining syndicate. On May 28, 1901, D'Arcy signed an historic agreement with the Persian Shah Muzaffar al-Din for a concession that would last until 1961 and cover three-quarters of the country. In essentially bribing the elderly and childlike figurehead of the crumbling Qajar dynasty with extra monies for his costly amusements, D'Arcy received considerable support from the British government. Any means of fortifying Persia against the relentless nineteenth-century Russian drive of expansion and annexation in Central Asia was "a sort of premium on the Insurance of India" and made the defenseless country, as Lord Curzon, who dominated Britain's foreign policy at the time, remarked in Parliament, one of "the pieces on a chessboard upon which is being played out a game for the domination of the world."

By 1903, sufficient oil had been discovered in D'Arcy's patch to make Persia a priority to the British Admiralty. Britain and Germany had gotten along well up to this point and had even co-invested in the railway system that was too vast for any one nation to finance. But Britain, overstretched by its imperial reach, was showing the first signs of manufacturing fatigue at the same time that Germany was marshalling its industrial might. England's mastery of the world's sea-lanes was the single most important source of its disproportionate power, and an impassioned debate broke out between the Sea Lords of the British Admiralty over the comparative virtues of domestically extracted coal versus far-off foreign oil to power faster ships.

In May 1903, Foreign Secretary Lord Lansdowne made an historic statement in the House of Lords: the British Government would "regard the establishment of a naval base or a fortified port in the Persian Gulf by any other power as a very grave menace to British interests, and we should certainly resist it with all the means at our disposal." This statement was seized upon by Lord Curzon as "our Monroe Doctrine in the Middle East," meaning that the transference of any territory in that part of the world from one European power to another would be viewed with hostility, and possibly armed intervention, by Great Britain. The reference to the German beachhead at Basra was obvious. British investors led by Sir Ernest Cassel and Lord Revelstoke, head of Barings, pulled their money out of the Baghdad Railway because of public outcry over German co-investment.

Public outcry may have subsided were it not for one important event. In 1905, amiable Georges Nagelmackers, who had charmed his way through the previous century's minefields of inter-European disputes to create the Orient Express, died of a sudden heart attack. Davison Dalziel, a newspaper magnate who also happened to be heavily cross-invested in the British Pullman Company and whose only daughter, Elizabeth, was married to Nagelmackers' only son, Rene, took over as chairman of Nagelmackers' *Wagons-Lits Compagnie*. Dalziel, who was to become a staunch supporter of the war minister, Lloyd George, merged with Thomas Cook's and, later that year, presented Parliament with a Napoleonic scheme to extend Nagelmackers' luxury line through the Near East, via Baghdad, Aleppo, Basra, and Damascus, and linking up with the *Wagons-Lits* service from Cairo to Palestine. Parliament vetoed his plan for reasons of military security, but Dalziel was a dog with a bone and close political ties to Alfred Harmsworthy, Lord Northcliffe, the media emperor of his day, who also cross-invested heavily in railroads. Along with Northcliffe and James Henry Dalziel, another newspaper entrepreneur to whom Davison Dalziel was to trade the influential *Pall Mall Gazette* and who appears to have been a distant cousin, Davison Dalziel formed a strong base of support for the war minister and future prime minister, Lloyd George, who would support their commercial aims with his Near Eastern campaign in World War I.

Britain's main imperial interest, inspired by political geographers such as the formidable David "D.G." Hogarth, was to establish a land bridge controlled by British forces. It would extend from its pivotal base in Egypt, guarding the mouth of the Suez Canal, to the crown colony of India and beyond, to British possessions in Southeast Asia. The Southeast Asian territories would also connect with East African territories subject to British control, i.e., Uganda, Sudan, Kenya, Tanganyika, the Rhodesias, and South Africa. An imperial railway network running from London to Constantinople was designed to link Haifa to Alexandria and thence to South Africa; and through Persia, all the way to Shanghai. Thus Britain hoped to ensure an uninterrupted flow of raw materials to its mills, and of grains, cereals, fruits, and stimulants to its masses. The hub of this grand plan was Palestine and Mesopotamia, known today as Iraq, where the British considered developing a major center for wheat and cotton production as they had already done in Egypt and Sudan, and where Herzl had considered settling the Jews as an alternative to Palestine.

The Berlin-Baghdad Railway was a major obstacle to the British plan. Lying athwart the Asia Minor peninsula, it would divert all such traffic from London to Berlin and provide a shortcut to India that beat the British sea route by eight days. If diplomatic relations between Britain and Germany were to sour, it would also provide rapid access to the Near East for German troops.

Political observers in Britain — which had neglected the building of the Suez Canal and ignored the opportunity to help run the Trans-Siberian Railway — watched the Baghdad Railway's progress with envy and frustration. An Edinburgh University political scientist who advocated "internationalizing" the railways in the Middle East as a thinly disguised pretext for annexing them, declared of the Basra concession: "Germany has secured, with one stroke of the diplomatic pen, what England and Russia have striven for generations to obtain ... The Holy Land will become a German province." More dire predictions soon followed.

> Should the Baghdad Railway be destined to remain German
> property the line is destined to become the backbone of
> German supremacy in western Asia. Germania, helmeted
> and carrying sword and shield, will ride over its rails to
> conquer Palestine and to wrest the wealth of the Nile and
> Ganges from British grip. But the foreign interests of every
> European nation are affected by the construction of this
> celebrated railway. It is the most direct route to Asia for all
> of Europe. The question of its internationalization is
> therefore one of the problems of European democracy.

Professor Otto Warburg of the University of Berlin, an interested observer of these debates, traveled to Anatolia and the Levant in 1900. Warburg was one of the outstanding botanists of his time and a founder of *Das Deutsche Kolonialwirtschaftekommittee*, the German Committee for Colonial Economy. He was also a family member of the Jewish, Hamburg-based Warburg banking dynasty that, almost as famously as the House of Rothschild, had helped to fund railway expansion in Europe and had a particularly strong connection to American financial circles through Otto's cousin Paul Warburg, a member of the Federal Reserve Board. On the boards of dozens of German companies that were involved in the worldwide German colonial expansion, Warburg had advised Theodor Herzl on the agricultural potential of Palestine, helped to found the Jewish National Fund, and, from 1911 to 1920, served as head of the Berlin Zionist Organization. He was an expert in the field of colonization. Appointed to Otto von Bismarck's Prussian Colonization Committee in 1901, he worked closely with Georg Augustus Schweinfurth, Kaiser Wilhelm's protégé, political geographer, and an ardent searcher for the origins of biblical wild wheat.

Yet another race was on. The world's basic grain stocks were fast being depleted by rapid population growth. The original wild wheat, which had flourished on the Beisan plain before Christ was born and had given Palestine the name "the land of milk and honey," had to all intents and purposes vanished from the planet, selected out by centuries of cultivated crops.

The biblical wild wheat was distinguished by a fragile rachis (the principal stem of a flower cluster). On a spear of wheat, the rachis holds the glumes, the husks of precious grain. A fragile rachis ensured that the grain would be widely disseminated by errant winds; but this characteristic, so useful to the plant itself, was a drawback for man. Wheat with a brittle rachis must be harvested before complete maturity and is difficult to handle, requiring the use of mills rather than simple flails. Man, over the centuries, had chosen to develop forms of wheat that were easier to harvest, leading to its evolutionary extinction.

The scientific community raised the alarm: the world's food supplies were at grave risk. Scientists all over the world, but most particularly German scientists, joined in the search for wild wheat.

As with the railway race and its espousal of Zionism by some of its investors, the biblical aspects of wild wheat gave economic competition a warm, evangelical glow. But as the Berlin-Baghdad argument heated up, the gentle study of botany came to resemble war by other means. The original wild wheat was linked to the origins of civilization as we know it. "Aryo-centrists" (who were Slavophiles) argued that Southern Russia was the cradle of human culture, while "Germano-centrists" claimed that distinction for the shores of the Baltic Sea. This "scientific" debate reflected the struggles for cultural and racial superiority that emerged along with nationalist struggles in Central Europe in the late nineteenth century and, later still, fed the preoccupations of Adolph Hitler (who, in *Mein Kampf,* cited German concerns about food sources as one of the justifications for World War I). The ranks of supporters of yet another theory, which held that agricultural civilization originated with the Semites, in Mesopotamia, the eastern Mediterranean, or ancient Egypt, contained a surprising number of German gentile Zionists.

German botanists in particular linked the *Urweizen,* the primordial wild wheat known as *emmer* in Hebrew and *Triticum diccocoides* in Latin, to a sweeping historical quest for the primordial forms of culture, of language, even to questions like the geographical whereabouts of the Garden of Eden. But Warburg's interest in *Urweizen* was intimately related to his interest in railroads. Along with Bismarck, he believed that Palestine would be a central intercontinental crossroad, and that its ports and railroads must be highly developed. A railway company that received a concession from the Turkish state and sectors of state land – a concession bearing in fact a strong resemblance to the Baghdad Railway—would provide the engine of settlement. The company would settle Jews in colonies in wide areas on both sides of the track through private capital raised to purchase land. One of his models was the German colonization project in the Polish province of Poznán, where Bismarck wanted, through bloodless economic, legislative, and administrative means, to obtain German ownership over most of the land and to create a German majority among the population.

In Palestine, Warburg met a group of energetic young Zionists headed by Dr. Selig Soskin, Aaron Aaronsohn, and the hydraulic engineer Joseph Treidel. Soskin was a former Jewish Colonization Association official in charge of the draining of the Haderah swamps on the Mediterranean coast between Haifa and what is today Tel Aviv. He and his wife, Sonia, were Aaron's closest friends; the three were inseparable despite the fact that Aaron avowed an undying if platonic love for Sonia, and had gone so far as to carpet a room with roses for her to walk on. His feelings did not appear to interfere with his working relationship with Sonia's husband. Along with Treidel, the two set up the shoestring Technical Agricultural Office, which they titled propitiously in German the *Technische und Landwirtschaftliche Buro fur Palastina*, to advise would-be farmers on the purchase of arable land.

According to Alex Aaronsohn, Sonia Soskin was the only woman Aaron ever loved, although his correspondence, as we shall see, reveals his seductive nature. The choice of an unattainable woman, while Aaron was in the vigor of his young manhood, is a revealing one. Aaron's appetite for sensual pleasures such as the best food and other luxuries was, like everything about him, outsized. If his diary notations on the charms of hotel chambermaids are any indication, he was an intensely sexual man as well. On the one hand, triangulated relationships were far from unusual in intellectual circles at the time. Aaron delighted in showing off, and his flamboyant displays of affection for Sonia were a convenient way of flouting the rabbis, whose despotic rule he despised. On the other hand, this choice of an unattainable woman bespeaks an early realization on Aaron's part that the ordinary joys of family life were not for him, perhaps even a premonition that his own life would not be long. Throughout his life, he was prone to black, even suicidal moods that could only be avoided by focusing his volcanic energies on the pursuit of an obsession. One woman was too small and too fragile, and, ultimately, too unimportant for Aaron to pursue. The obsession of his life was the creation of an economically independent Palestine where Jews like himself could prove themselves equal to, or better than, any European.

In the kitchens of the *Yishuv,* it was whispered that Aaron's real passion was reserved for his sister Sarah. While this prurient tidbit smells of overheated imagination, it is true that Sarah also fell in love with an unattainable man, her sister Rivka's fiancé, the revolutionary poet Absalom "Absa" Feinberg. But Sarah was as much of a show-off as Aaron and, in her own way, burned with the desire to prove herself a "new kind of Jew." Loving Absa was a means of liberating herself from the stultifying conventions of the *Yishuv*. Free of the restrictions imposed by husband and children, Sarah could join her brother in his revolutionary life's work.

But first Aaron would suffer on his own after leaving the employ of Baron de Rothschild. At Smyrna, his capacity for hard work – and the relationships with high Turkish functionaries created by his facility with languages – encouraged the two French brothers who employed him to give their raw young overseer carte blanche in experimenting with his radical notions of agriculture. Intoxicated by his good fortune, he hired a Palestinian comrade who then went after his job. There were dark whispers of bribes taken, and Aaron abruptly left his employer. This cycle of euphoric enthusiasm followed by extreme disillusionment would repeat itself throughout his life. Though suspicious by nature (and scrupulously honest with money), Aaron naively expected his achievements to be rewarded with adulation rather than with *schadenfreude*.

At Haifa, on the Mediterranean about thirty kilometers north of the Aaronsohns' home at Zichron Ya'akov, was a prosperous German colony known as the Temple, established in 1868 by Christoph Hoffman and Georg David Hardegg, who broke from Lutheranism to gather in God's country to anticipate the Second Coming of Christ. The industrious ex-Lutherans, now known as the People of God or Templers, made a tidy living from farming, and the colony became a model of reform for the deplorable condition of Palestinian agriculture under the Ottomans.

Aaron attached himself as a salesman to a Templer importer of agricultural machines by the name of Duck, who took him to Paris for the World's Fair of 1900. Upon his return to Palestine, Aaron put his theories of scientific agriculture to work in improving Arab techniques of dry farming, or breaking up surface soil to irrigate it with nothing more than Palestine's heavy dew. But Duck, at Aaron's recommendation, also bought five American harvesters to use on Arab farms where no machine had ever been seen. The shiny new machines broke in the stony fields. The men and horses Aaron had hired out of his own pocket stood idle. The enterprise lost money and Aaron and Herr Duck soon parted ways, to cries of exploitation on Aaron's part.

Aaron's next venture was the Technical Agricultural Office that he had formed with Treidel and Soskin. Supplied with nothing but enthusiasm, Aaron embarked on the initial stages of what was to become his most enduring legacy. In 1901 he made the first of many forays on his sturdy mare Fahra into the deserts of the Sinai and the Negev, wrapped in the traditional *abba*, or woolen coat, of an Arab. In his diaries he jotted his findings of plants, mineral deposits, and, above all, water sources, traveling by night and subsisting largely on chocolate, a habit his rival, T. E. Lawrence, would imitate. He noted the luxuriant growth of *Esyphus spina-christi*, or Christ-thorn, a thorn tree with a small edible fruit tasting of dried apples that thrives in excessively alkaline soil, as a sure sign of once-cultivated fields. He searched out species like *Pistachia atlantica*, *Prunus cerasia*, the wild date, and the Jaffa orange, which could be made tastier and more durable for export through grafting. He noted where the dry crust of topsoil could be pulverized with a harrow, a tool unfamiliar to the Arabs, until it was as fine as ash and ready to yield rich crops of sesame. And, with the natural though untrained eye of a political scientist, he remarked how, as he was later to write, the "peculiar methods of cultivation which have been brought about by political conditions – the vicissitudes of war, the continual migrations of tribes, and of colonization – all acting through such long periods of time," developed an extraordinary range of cultivated plant varieties and made the country an exceptionally promising one to study. These jottings became the cumulative basis for what Aaron longed to create: the first complete botanical and geological survey of Palestine, and a comprehensive map of its surface water and groundwater. But such a survey was far beyond the resources of the minuscule Technical Agricultural Office, and Aaron's next obsession became funding his ambition.

A number of important clients from Germany, Britain, and even America began visiting the humble bureau, and not all of them confined their interest to agriculture. In the first steps of an intricate minuet, Aaron's footsteps in the desert crisscrossed those of such "travelers" who came with diplomatic *irades* (a Turkish document signifying that it is the will of an important personage that the bearer be allowed safe passage) in search of esoterica like the biblical paradise or the vanishing oryx or the equally elusive Druse. This was an era when the word *traveler* had more than one meaning, when even the wealthy and well educated often undertook the "Grand Tour" for the convenience of their governments. Aaron's footsteps intersected those of Douglas Carruthers, Gertrude Bell, T. E. Lawrence, and even the celebrated German secret agent Wilhelm Wassmuss, who was building his reputation as much on his Adonis-like looks as on his talent for harrying the British flank in Persia, and for whom the gentlemen of the back office of the British War Ministry affectionately named their pet mouser.

German surveyors were already a familiar sight throughout the Ottoman Empire. The Germans had been given forestry and mining rights and had commenced drilling a series of twenty-two long and treacherous tunnels through the Taurus Mountains to connect the Baghdad Express with the Mesopotamian plain. But their presence was not quite so well established in Palestine, where, from 1865 onward, the Queen's Palestine Exploration Fund, partnered with the British War Office, had sent archaeologists, biblical scholars, and the Royal Engineers to obtain an accurate map of the country by doing, as the Fund loftily declares in its official history, "at leisure and systematically that which has hitherto been entirely neglected, or done only in a fragmentary manner by the occasional unassisted efforts of hurried and inexperienced travellers."

Aaron was neither hurried nor inexperienced, nor hampered by European allegiances – the surveyors of the first attempt to map the region in 1801 could only go where they were protected by the French army. In addition to being a resident of Palestine, with a resident's knowledge and close relationships with the local Arabs, Bedouin, and

Druse, he spoke Hebrew as fluently as he spoke Arabic, and was an accomplished Torah scholar as well. This was a particular asset in tracking strategically important biblical sites whose names were, in the late nineteenth and early twentieth centuries, still mapped in Arabic. However, the Palestine Exploration Fund disdained local input. Its charter, laid out by the Archbishop of York in 1865, stipulated that the society should be politically and religiously neutral in all matters; but to ensure that, in the words of the official history, "the work should be faced in the same spirit of fearless investigation into the truth as obtains in scientific research," the principal task of surveying was allotted to the British War Office, which oversaw the Royal Engineers.

War Office representatives often scorned biblical knowledge and had a strong preference for modern railway maps. Money, and therefore time, was always short as the Fund's royal sponsors kept a tight hand on the purse strings. Nor were the findings of the Royal Engineers beyond question. Even Lieutenant-Colonel Horatio Herbert Kitchener, First Earl Kitchener (known to his familiars as K of K), who surveyed Galilee in the late 1870s and early 1880s for the Palestine Exploration Fund before going on to glory as sirdar, or commander in chief, of the British army in Egypt and governor general of Eastern Sudan, worked in penury and under conditions of great pressure. Many years later, Kitchener admitted to a colleague and fellow surveyor, Colonel Stewart Newcombe, that much of the mapping he did of the stretch from Beersheba to Akaba just as the railroad frenzy was reaching its peak was "inaccurate and not worth attention." This stretch of the Sinai and Negev deserts, known in the Old Testament as the Wilderness of Zin, where the Israelites under Moses spied out water sources for the flight from Egypt, assumed tremendous strategic significance in the run-up to World War I. In 1913, Kitchener, as part of the war preparations, commissioned a new mapping of the area to be carried out by Newcombe, assisted by two young archaeologists, Leonard Woolley and T. E. Lawrence, who did their entire survey in a matter of months. The survey, and subsequent publication of their account of their adventures, *The Wilderness of Zin,* established Lawrence's career as the consummate Arabist. But despite Lawrence's later iconic status as the burning-eyed young Englishman in the white burnoose who led the Arabs to independence from their Turkish oppressors, his information was incomplete. Newcombe, in his correspondence, acknowledged his debt to Aaron Aaronsohn, who preceded Lawrence and Woolley by a decade, and had spent six years exhaustively surveying the same territory.

In 1902, the Technical Agricultural Office went bankrupt. Joseph Treidel left to look for work in America and Selig Soskin to seek medical treatment, apparently for tuberculosis, in Germany. Soon after the Soskins' arrival in Berlin, Warburg had him appointed a member of the German Committee for Colonial Economy and, later, a member of the Prussian Colonization Committee. He then invited Aaron to Berlin, where he introduced him to "Herr Lieber Professor" Georg Augustus Schweinfurth, recommending Aaron to the task of collecting more wild wheat specimens that could shed light on the origins of cultivated plants in his homeland.

Like T. E. Lawrence's mentor, D. G. Hogarth, Schweinfurth was a formidable Renaissance intellect who used an esoteric discipline as a basis for the thoroughly modern science of political geography. Between 1863 and 1888, Schweinfurth explored extensively in eastern and equatorial Africa and Arabia and as an anthropologist became famous for establishing the existence of the African Pygmies. He then applied his knowledge to advising Bismarck on building German colonies in Africa.

It is easy to see why a young man of Aaron's talents, well known to the German scientific community in both Turkey and Palestine, would have been of intense interest to Schweinfurth. Otto von Bismarck, Schweinfurth's employer, had invested heavily in agricultural development throughout the Ottoman Empire because of his plan to ship produce via the Berlin-Baghdad Railway.

It is also easy to see why Aaron would be interested in Schweinfurth's sponsorship. The German scientific community was revered throughout the world. If he discovered the *Urweizen,* the attendant notoriety would lift all his other boats, while the funding he received would attract other funding – and not only from Germany – to help him realize his dream of developing Palestine into an economically self-sufficient country.

Aaron proposed to revolutionize wheat growing by producing in Palestine hardy new races of *emmer* that could be adapted to the semiarid regions of Algeria, Tunis, Syria, Egypt, Turkestan, and America (an experiment still being attempted in Israel today). He calculated that he could increase the yield of wheat by at least one bushel per acre in these vast areas and thus vastly increase the world's food supplies. His proposal evidently met with Schweinfurth's approval, for he sent the young man to study colonial administrative structures in North Africa for two months, "with an eye to finding a suitable patron for Palestine."

Aaron returned to Palestine fully funded by his German sponsors and, for the first time, basking in prestige. In January 1903, Warburg recommended to Theodor Herzl that Aaron and his colleagues, Soskin and Treidel, join a geological survey in the Dead Sea region headed by the well-known German geologist Max Blanckenhorn and commissioned by Sultan Abdul Hamid. Blanckenhorn was struck by the young man's ability to observe and note geologic formations, and with his grasp of geognosy – the science of soil conditions – particularly in terms of assessing potential arability in the light of scientific improvements in irrigation. Aaron, for his part, resented the senior geologist's preemption of credit for his own discoveries, with an irritated sensitivity that was to become altogether too frequent for his own good.

From 1903 to 1908, Aaron crisscrossed the Transjordanian deserts continually, sometimes with Blanckenhorn, sometimes alone on his own botanical mission. Always Aaron maintained an immaculate diary in French, which was then the international language of diplomacy. Even at this early date, Aaron wrote as though he intended his diaries to be seen by others. A poor sleeper throughout his short life, each morning he rose two hours before dawn and meticulously noted the barometric pressure and other meteorological observations, along with the distance he had traveled. He was traveling toward a goal of his own as well: the accumulation of information to fill in his map of Palestine.

For those whose senses were sharpened with land lust, the arid, alkaline soil of Palestine was like the body of a virgin, waiting to be awakened to the joyous fecundity of the Song of Songs: *A garden enclosed is my sister, my spouse; a spring shut up, a fountain sealed* . . . Aaron traveled the length and breadth of Palestine, for the most part alone on his Arab mare, taking note of every conceivable way in which the land could be made fruitful. Farthest south, the Gaza plain was ideal for barley growing. Toward the middle part of the coast, around Jaffa, the great plain of Sharon, with its soil of mingled clay and chalk, was ripe for orchards of orange trees and almond trees; to the north, the plain of Esdraelon, whose soil, of basaltic origin, rich in humus, waited to be plowed with abundant crops of sesame. The plain of Beisan was famous in biblical times for its fields of wheat; the mountains of Judea, for their rich, terraced crops, their vineyards, and their orchards of olive and fig trees. *Awake, O north wind; and come thou south; blow upon my garden, that the spices thereof may flow out. Let my beloved come into his garden, and eat his pleasant fruits.* Even the "desert" of Judea was really a steppe where numerous flocks of sheep and goats could find, even in the dry heat of summer, a natural, abundant pasturage. The valley of the Jordan, a gigantic natural rift whose southern portion, falling 1,200 feet below the level of the Mediterranean, makes it one of the lowest places on earth, was lush with tropical flora owing to its hothouse temperatures. Away to the north the mountains of Gilead, with their forests of oak and pine, rivaled those of Lebanon; and still farther north, the fertile volcanic tableland of Hauran offered yet another wheat bowl. All that it lacked was water. *A fountain of gardens, a well of living waters, and streams from Lebanon . . .*

By the end of his journeys, Aaron had obsessively documented the plant life and mineral deposits of the Syrian and Jordanian deserts; correctly positioned a number of townships wrongly placed on British, French, and German maps; and drawn the water supply available from rivers, springs, aquifers, and ancient artesian wells, or *qanats.* For their services, Aaron, Blanckenhorn, and Treidel each received the Turkish *Liakat d'or* or medal of merit directly from Sultan Abdul Hamid, who invited them to Constantinople to present their findings.

It seemed Aaron was at last to be a prophet with honor in his own country, but in 1905 he entered a collision course with events that would lead to World War I and beyond. In January 1905, Warburg instructed the Palestine Commission in Berlin to set up a *Landesbureau* as a go-between for land purchases for the Jewish National Fund (JNF). Warburg's plan was to prepare for large-scale Zionist immigration all over Palestine; given his connections to Bismarck's Poznán project in Poland, it is reasonable to assume that the bulk of the immigration would be German. Warburg chose Aaron as his chairman.

The *Landesbureau* collapsed within months of its inception, faced with intense antagonism from non-German members of the *Yishuv*, the Jewish community in Palestine, who viewed it as an invasion and a threat to their own acquisitions. The *Yishuv* vented sharp criticism against Aaron and his fellow workers, whose relatively high salaries came from public funds before, it was argued, the JNF had acquired even one parcel of land. The real problem arose from the *Landesbureau*'s autocratic method of operating – the *Yishuv* accused its members of trying to reinvent themselves as Rothschilds.

Alex Aaronsohn habitually attributed his famous brother's continual brawling with his fellow Jews to envy of Aaron's successes. Certainly *schadenfreude* played no small part in Aaron's difficulties, but there were deeper reasons. Aside from their religious differences, there were already vast political divides between the Jews of the First Aliyah and those of the Second, who arrived after 1885. The émigrés of the early years of the twentieth century, when Aaron was beginning his travels, were predominantly socialists who grew up in the revolutionary movement in Russia (many took part in the first revolution in 1905), but who no longer believed that overthrowing the Czarist regime would improve the lot of the Jews. That could only be accomplished by uprooting the largely urban Jews of the diaspora and rehabilitating them as an agricultural people in Palestine, creating another revolution there. The settlers of the Second Aliyah clashed repeatedly with the settlers of the First Aliyah who, like the Aaronsohns, were for the most part bourgeois in their aspirations, and had led the agricultural movement. They also had first claim on the land.

The new arrivals were willing to fight for an independent life in Palestine. In this they should have been able to make common cause with Aaron rather than with the rabbis. But they were steeped in dogma of another kind – the endless committeeism that was to make the bureaucracies of the Soviet Union such a nightmare. The philosophers, journalists, and politicians among them characteristically regarded their word as the last word, and the more pragmatic views of a rare man of science like Aaron as heresy. Aaron felt strongly that the Arab *fellahs* of Palestine had a knowledge of farming that the newcomers lacked, and should continue to work the land they had worked for centuries. But the *chalutzim* (settlers) brooked no interference from the pioneers of the First Aliyah, whom they thought weak and cowardly and insufficiently assertive in their Jewish identities. They believed that above all the Jews must avoid again becoming an economically dependent section of the population, at the mercy of unfriendly circumstances and regimes. It was not enough to be colonists in Palestine, dependent on native labor like the French colonists in Algeria, whose administrative structure Aaron had favorably observed. To fulfill its function, Palestine had to change the whole economic structure, the very psychology of the Jewish people. They must become workers in every branch of the national economy, dependent on no one's labor but their own. They must rediscover their peasant roots. Even without the necessary skills, they held physical labor on the land as their highest ideal and vigorously debated the need for a Jewish "conquest of soil." Led by a bantam, redheaded, twenty-three-year-old Polish Marxist named David Ben-Gurion, they united to fight, tooth and nail, the older, bourgeois settlers.

Ben-Gurion arrived in Palestine in 1907, a member of the Social-Democratic Jewish Workers' Party, Poale Zion. From the age of eleven he had dedicated himself to promoting emigration to the Holy Land by tithing his schoolmates' pocket money. He held the Jewish right to work the land, to settle in uninhabited reaches and make them blossom, as the highest of all values. Early in his career, Ben-Gurion at least nominally admitted the need of Jews to employ Arabs, but in 1907, speaking at a Poale Zion gathering in the Galilee, he first articulated the doctrine of *Avodah Ivrit* — the demand that Jews employ only Jews — that was to create such hardship.

By this time, the Jewish population of Palestine had swelled to seventy to eighty thousand, three times its number in 1882, when the Aaronsohns arrived. Having been less than 5 percent when the Ottomans imposed their first entry restrictions, it was now over 10 percent of the total population of close to 650,000. Moreover, Jews sought to acquire land, which stirred the nationalist resentments created by the Capitulations, the European trade agreements that favored the Jewish and Armenian minorities.

Many of the newly arrived émigrés, believing they were coming to a barren, uninhabited land, were genuinely taken aback to find so many Arabs living in Palestine (approximately 95 percent of the population in 1882 was Arab). Lacking any knowledge of Arabic, or the desire to acquire it, they established their own colonies and institutions in a manner distinct from the Old Settlers. Moving very much within their own environment, they acquired the adeptness of their Orthodox Jewish neighbors at insulating themselves within walls of their own making and in so doing, quickly projected much of the sense of oppression they had felt within the Pale in Poland, Romania, and Russia onto their new neighbors.

Ben-Gurion spent three years pioneering in the Galilee and in Zichron Ya'akov. Before his arrival, the question of Arab-versus-Jewish labor was never an issue in the Galilee, and relations between Jew and Arab were remarkably harmonious. Within a year of his arrival, violence broke out. In the bloody Purim incident of February 1908, a nasty brawl between Arab and Jewish workers ended in one Arab's death. When two Arabs shot and killed a Jewish watchman in retaliation in 1909, an endless cycle was born. By 1911, Ben-Gurion could speak of "Arab hatred that is growing still more intense":

> This hatred originates with the Arab workers in Jewish settlements. Like any worker, the Arab worker detests his taskmaster and exploiter. But because this class conflict overlaps a national difference between farmers and workers, this hatred takes a national form. Indeed the national overwhelms the class aspect of the conflict in the minds of the Arab working masses, and inflames an intense hatred towards the Jews.

This convenient use of Marx left the door open to a solution that would set Ben-Gurion squarely at odds with Aaron Aaronsohn. Socialism would eradicate Arab hatred by liberating the Arab worker from his servitude, i.e., from his job, and thus from the grip of the Islamic clergy who "incited the people to rise up against the Jews, to take their land, pillage their property, and threaten their very lives."

Aaron was an autocrat by nature and had scant patience for what he called the "committee-sickness" of socialism: temperamentally he was more akin to the great empire builders (or robber-barons) of the American frontier. Not being an ideologue, he did not oppose socialism, but had no particular use for it, either. As an agricultural leader, he rebelled against the proposals of the new political coteries to employ exclusively Jewish labor, largely unskilled, at nearly two and a half times the cost of skilled Arab farmhands. As a politician, he foresaw disaster in excluding the Arabs by "liberating" them from working the land they looked on as their own. He was bound to clash with the newcomers, as each party was convinced that they, and they alone, knew the method and should control the means for building the new Jewish national home.

In 1906, bruised from infighting and stung by his failure to find Kotschy's wild wheat, Aaron returned to Berlin, where Schweinfurth convinced him that his research was important enough to resume. Aaron undertook yet another journey home. On June 18, 1906, he was walking with Moses Bermann, a fellow agronomist, in the vineyard of the Jewish agricultural colony at Rosh-Pinna, formerly under the control of Baron Rothschild. The two scientists were deep in an abstruse discussion of the Eocene origin of the ground (the Eocene era, when the Central Valley of California was formed and mammals became dominant, is characterized by formations of limestone, sandstone, lignite, and, in some areas, oil-producing shale). Suddenly, Aaron spied, in a crevice of fossilized limestone, a sprig of what looked at first like barley but proved, as he grasped it in his hand and shook its brittle spine, to be the wild wheat of his dreams. As he later described his find in a United States Department of Agriculture bulletin:

> I could hardly believe that it was really the plant for which I was looking. The development of the head and grains was so perfect — so nearly like the forms produced under cultivation at the present day — that I could scarcely believe this was their wild prototype, though, to be sure, if it had not been so well-developed primitive man would not have noticed it, or at least would not have appreciated the importance of its cultivation to such an extent as he did.

Within months of this discovery, Aaron achieved a worldwide reputation as a scientist. The doors and windows of the *Yishuv*, which had cramped and suffocated him, were flung open, and he was free to take advantage of what the world could offer and indeed, to bring it home. His chief publicist was none other than Georg Augustus Schweinfurth, who made sure that his findings were published in leading international scientific journals — and who furnished him with impeccable introductions in Washington.

Here Aaron appears to have struck a Faustian bargain that would haunt him for the rest of his life. Like the nuclear physicists of a later era, he made the decision to subordinate his pure and necessary scientific research to the uses of realpolitik. He was intent on proving that the new kind of Jew was the most able colonist, and this move must have seemed the most expedient way to further his researches, given the plethora of economic and strategic resources that could be made available for developing his emerging country by playing off the great powers. It was a decision that would cost him dear.

3.

Flying the Zionist Kite in America

Friday, March 25, 1910

Katzman, etc. came. They are full of distrust of Aaronson [*sic*]. Want to know how he persuaded men like Schif-
fand Rosenwald to go into a nationalistic venture. Lipsky
calls him a clever politician who turns out that side of his
scheme that happens to suit his patron. American wheat
improvement to the patriotic Schiff, Jewish Palestine to Marshall, scientific interest to Loeb, nationalism to me.

— Henrietta Szold diaries, March 25, 1910

In 1909, the year that Aaron arrived in America, the gentle and
indomitable Henrietta Szold suffered the second great heartbreak
of her life. Seven years earlier, the death of her adored father, the Hungarian-born rabbi Benjamin Szold, who headed a prosperous congregation in Baltimore, had toppled her into a catastrophic depression.
The woman who would found and lead Hadassah, the women's wing
of the Federation of American Zionists; who would organize medical
relief for a devastated Palestine after the First World War and repop-
ulate the country with thousands of German and Russian children in
the Second World War; who would eventually lead the federation itself
and become a powerful force in world politics, had spent the first forty-
two years of her life as her father's amanuensis, too consumed by her
duties to find a husband.

Upon her father's death of heart failure, Szold took a leave of
absence from the Jewish Publication Society, which, as its secretary,
she largely ran. She enrolled in a course of rabbinical studies at the Jewish Theological Seminary in New York. The rabbinical hierarchy at the
time did not allow women to become ordained, but condescended to
allow her to pursue her studies on the grounds that they would improve
her work with the Jewish Publication Society. At the seminary she
met an ambitious young professor, Louis Ginzberg, who even more

satisfyingly filled the void left in her soul. Thirteen years Ginzberg's senior, Szold dropped back into the role she had played for so many years with her father, editing Ginzberg's work, listening to and commenting on his speeches, mentoring and mothering him. A deeply passionate woman who had put off her biological urges far too long, she also introduced him to what she described in her journal as the "cosmic mystery of sex." In March 1909, en route to a lecture tour in Europe, her protégé announced to her that he was engaged to marry a young woman who could give him children.

Cramped by the conventions of her time, Henrietta took a long sea voyage in the company of her mother, first to Europe and then to Palestine. In a spirited exchange of letters with Dr. Cyrus Adler, head of the Jewish Publication Society and future president of the Jewish Theological Seminary, she demanded and received six months paid leave at the munificent salary of two thousand dollars, and an additional gift of five hundred dollars toward what she described with bitter irony as her "honeymoon." She found her way unerringly to Zichron Ya'akov (Jacob's Memorial), the village where the Aaronsohns were leading citizens, by that time prosperous enough to boast its own hotel. There, although Aaron was by this time in America, she met his family and became a convert to the Zionist cause that would provide new meaning for her life.

Szold subsumed her deepest longings for love and children into her work, a flame that burned more ardently with advancing age. Pictures show her metamorphosing from a plain girl into a remarkably beautiful older woman, her youthful stolidity melting away to reveal a delicate bone structure dominated by the intelligence of her huge dark eyes. She was not without vanity, brushing her striking white hair five hundred strokes a night to make it shine, and keenly appreciative of any compliment to her fine ankles. The French would have adored her as that beacon of the salon, *une femme spirituelle*, who made her wit and passionate interest in the affairs of the world a form of feminine attractiveness. Though she was never to risk another Louis Ginzberg, she remained a kingmaker in search of a king and throughout her long life adopted men much younger than herself, often married or otherwise out of reach, men such as the artist Saul Steinberg and the single-minded Palestinian agronomist Aaron Aaronsohn.

.•. .•. .•.

In the winter of 1908, Georg Schwemfurth sent a clipping from a Munich newspaper describing the remarkable discovery of his young protégé to David Fairchild, head of an obscure division of the United States Department of Agriculture called the Section of Foreign Seed and Plant Introduction. They had met at a hotel in Tunis on a North African botanizing expedition. Fairchild was a pillar of the nascent military-industrial complex; his skills, in addition to classifying seeds, included laying mines in the Potomac for the navy to prevent any Spanish battleships from reaching the capital at the onset of the Spanish-American War. He was also the son-in-law of the fabled inventor Alexander Graham Bell. Though a professional cynic, Fairchild was, true to his name, fair-minded and generous about the achievements of others. He admired Schweinfurth wholeheartedly for the depth of his erudition. "How can a human mind retain the images of over 40,000 species of plants with such clearness that, when dried fragments of any of them are laid before him, he will, without a moment's hesitation, give the scientific name, the name of the botanist who first described them, and often the date when they were named?" he wondered in a 1939 memoir.

Their subsequent friendship is a poignant reminder of the close relations that existed between the United States and German governments at this time. In 1909, the British War Office issued a report projecting that in the event of war the United States would ally itself with Germany. In six years, Fairchild's division, which along with the entire Department of Agriculture was a great source of unofficial contacts, would come under the scrutiny of the Creel Committee on Public Information, an extragovernmental propaganda agency named for the jingoist journalist George Creel and infamous for its anti-German witch hunts during World War I, which extended to renaming sauerkraut "liberty cabbage."

But in 1909, Fairchild was rolling in funds and riding high on the crest of America's last frontier movement. It was the end of the cowboy era. The wealthy cattle owners who wanted the great ranges of the Midwest and Southwest left untouched and unfenced were defeated in state legislation that allowed their holdings to be broken up by farmers. The

first transcontinental railroad – which had inspired Georges Nagelmackers to build his Orient Express – was crowding the big farmers in
turn, bringing in new populations every day that threatened to break
up their grip on the land. Cities like San Francisco were expanding at
an exponential rate. More people meant more food had to be grown.
As a result of this increased demand, large numbers of farmers were
appealing to the government for experimental crops, particularly for
crops adapted to irrigation, a new system of agriculture in the United
States.

In 1909, Fairchild's sister department, the United States Geological Survey, sounded a piercing alarm. The operation of hydroelectric
generators, of railway and trolley cars, of factory machinery, internal
combustion engines, battle and merchant ships – of all the machinery that made the new frontier – was made possible by one product
and one product alone: petroleum. At the same time that demand was
bursting all bounds, the traditional fields of New York and Pennsylvania, the cradle of Standard Oil, were in decline, as were the fields of
Appalachia, Indiana, and Illinois. The survey projected that the United
States had already used up half of its maximum supply of domestic oil
in its frenzy to reach the Pacific. The projected shortage of oil was the
reason strategists predicted war with Britain, in terms that recalled
Britain's saber rattling over the Baghdad Railway. Mark Requa, chief
engineer of the U.S. Bureau of Mines, wrote: "We must either plan for
the future or we must pass into a condition of commercial vassalage,
in time of peace relying on some foreign country for the petroleum
wherewith to lubricate the highways of commerce, in time of war at the
mercy of the enemy who may either control the source of supply or the
means of transportation; in either event our railways and factories will
cease operation, our battleships will swing helplessly at anchor, and
our country will resound with the martial tread of a triumphant foe."

As a scientist whose researches furthered military goals, Fairchild
was interested in exactly those same areas of the United. States that so
interested the Geological Survey. His newly established bureau was
charged with advising immigrants to the underpopulated Southwest
United States on what to plant. He wanted to grow coconuts, mangoes,
and pineapples on the Texas Gulf Coast, where growing numbers of

oil workers also needed food. He was eager to stabilize the unprecedented number of Armenian immigrants – fleeing fresh persecutions
in Armenia and western Turkey – by importing *emmer* and sesame,
the ancient crops of the Middle East, to the American Midwest, and by
introducing Middle Eastern fruit production to California. When Fairchild heard from Aaron himself, in a letter that described the writer's
talents in no uncertain terms and offered his services to the United
States, he found Aaron's brash approach engaging. Aaron, bringing
"ex Oriente lux" – "light from the East," in his own self-conscious
Latin phrase – was writing enthusiastically on breeding new strains of
drought-resistant wheat and importing fruits that flourished in desert
climes, and on how the Sultan date and the Shamouti, or Jaffa, orange
might be introduced to America. The young Palestinian's ideas perfectly fit the bill. Aaron was already developing a sure sense of how to
please his prospective masters, and observations on oil deposits in Palestine could not fail to be appreciated as well. Fairchild wrote back to
Schweinfurth to tell his young man that if he had any notion of exploit-
ing his wild wheat, he should come over to America and give Fairchild's
wheat breeders a good look at some specimens.

"Early in June," Fairchild wrote in his memoir, "a short, light-com-
plexioned Jew walked into my office and introduced himself in broken
English as Aaron Aaronsohn from Palestine . . . We resorted to German
and I soon discovered that I was in the presence of a remarkable man."

Everything about Aaron astonished Fairchild, from the speed with
which he picked up English to his encyclopedic knowledge of California, sight unseen. Within a week of Aaron's arrival, Fairchild over-
heard the young man carrying on lengthy technical discussions in
English comparing the flora of Palestine and California. Requested to
show off his erudition in a lengthy dissertation – in English – for the
departmental bulletin, Aaron was more than happy to oblige.

Within months, Aaron was delivering addresses before large crowds
at a dry-farming congress in Wyoming, a botanists' convention in
Washington, and at the University of California at Los Angeles. Fairchild was not a man to bandy about words like "genius," but he seemed
to recognize that he was in its presence. "His was one of those rare pio-
neer minds which quickly leap to the essentials . . . No foreigner had

ever been in my office who had so keen an understanding of the soils, climates, and adaptability of plants to their environments as had this friend of Schweinfurth's."

For his part, Aaron was quick to see the similarities between California and Palestine. Many a joint research project between Israel and California, from the development of their citrus industries to that of large-scale water-moving, has since been based on his observations: "Passing from west to east, we have in Palestine the coast zone, extending along the Mediterranean, similar to the littoral region of the Pacific, and the zone of hills and plateaus of the mountains of Judea and Galilee, forming, so to speak, the backbone of the country and being similar to the foothill region of California. Farther east we have the valley of the Jordan, the diversified parts of which are similar in soil, climate, and agricultural possibilities to the San Joaquin, Imperial and Death valleys."

The nascent citrus industry in Palestine, dominated at that time by the Rothschilds and by Arab entrepreneurs in the area of Jaffa, was to be the country's economic backbone in the Mandate period after the war (so-called because of the British mandate to administer); it would be based on the California free-enterprise model rather than on the collective farming methods of the Labor Zionist movement. Studying the free-enterprise model naturally appealed to Aaron. But California pioneered a model for water use that was to be even more important in his work.

During the Gold Rush of 1849, California miners established a tradition of water use with far-reaching ramifications in order to divert water from foothill streams and rivers for flushing gold out of the earth. These diversions violated the age-old English doctrine of riparian rights, which specifies that water diverted from a stream for non-domestic use (domestic use meaning urban and residential) must be returned to that stream undiminished. Though minor in themselves, they became the basis for a more convenient doctrine of "appropriation and beneficial use," which allowed the diversion of water for the benefit of enterprise without returning it to its source. This doctrine was taken up en masse by farmers and used to justify the Wright Act of 1887, a law that permitted California farmers to bond together in what are known as irrigation districts, pool their resources, and bring water from where it was to where it was needed – probably the single most important contribution to the growth of California agriculture, but one that created conflict with its neighboring states and Mexico. By the end of the nineteenth century, water-moving on an increasingly massive scale had become an integral part of the state's development. Plans to divert the Colorado River to California's Imperial Valley began as early as 1849, and the Imperial Canal, which cut a sixty-mile bypass into the Colorado River, was completed by 1900.

Aaron was not slow to observe that California's water problems were almost identical to Palestine's, and so was its soil. Like Palestine, California contained vast tracts of arable land in its arid southern portion, while two-thirds of its water resided in the north. Like that of Palestine, the desert soil of the south was highly alkaline and therefore, with the help of scientific irrigation, able to "blossom like the rose." He could also see that California was a model for others – like Palestine – that aspired to absorb population at an unprecedented rate. People followed water: between 1890 and 1900, the population of Los Angeles alone more than doubled, from 50,000 to 102,000. By 1904 it trembled at the 200,000 mark, and there it seemed fated to stay, for there simply was not enough water to support a larger population. Palestine, which experienced a similar influx at the time of the Second Aliyah (1885-1919) and anticipated yet more from the Zionist movement, could learn from Los Angeles, where Aaron spent a good deal of his time in California.

He was there to observe the fanfare attending the opening of the Los Angeles Aqueduct, begun in 1905 and completed in 1913. It was California's second major water project, and it drew international attention. Only the Panama Canal, declared the *Los Angeles Times*, matched it for size, magnitude, and cost. The most ambitious water project since Roman times, it was a 223-mile gravity-fed canal designed to bring the waters of the Owens River, a tributary of the Colorado, southwest to Los Angeles. This single act, driven by Los Angeles water czar William Mulholland – the model for Noah Cross, John Huston's megalomaniac character in Roman Polanski's *Chinatown* – transformed Los Angeles from a sleepy pueblo in a barely habitable strip of coastal desert to the water-guzzling metropolis of many millions that it is today.

Aaron made several trips back and forth from Palestine to California between 1909 and 1912, which allowed him to observe the aqueduct's progress. He had a megalomaniac streak in his own character, and probably would have liked nothing better than to be known as Palestine's water czar. Only a few years later, he drew up plans, strongly resembling Mulholland's diversion of the Owens River, to divert the waters of the Litani River, at the time of this writing the main thrust of a full-scale Israeli invasion of Lebanon. Instead of building an aqueduct, Aaron planned to siphon off the Litani into the Jordan, to bring down enough water to irrigate the Negev Desert, a fertile region very similar to Southern California or the Imperial Valley before the Los Angeles Aqueduct or the Imperial Canal existed. Although his intention was to build a base for peaceful coexistence in long-term water development, he would in fact embroil Palestine, like California, in water wars that would last for generations and continue to this day.

Aaron amused Fairchild as much as he amazed him, and the older scientist's appraisals of his restless character are highly illuminating: he suspected him of spending his talent on his scientific endeavors while reserving his genius – if not his real ambitions – for more worldly pursuits, like that of politics, diplomacy, or even espionage. Although Fairchild enjoyed his brashness, he feared for Aaron as well. Over the long run, he regretted that his prodigally gifted protégé was, perhaps like his own younger self, tempted by ego and the brilliant lights of the world stage to use his "assiduous application to his botanical studies" only to "[throw] his watchers off their guard." Unlike Aaron, Fairchild had been born into power, and he foresaw that the young man's provincial assertiveness in expressing his will to power might dangerously alarm those same "watchers"; that his craving for action might drive him to prostitute his introductions and antagonize the very people who could help him the most, and that the visas he was granted for scientific travel might lead him down paths from which there was no return.

As a quid pro quo for his success in bringing light from the ancient East to the American Southwest, Aaron asked Fairchild, who had excellent connections in government circles, to introduce him to the wealthy Jews of America. Fairchild commented dryly: "I was curious to know why Aaronsohn wanted these introductions, and he explained to me that if he went himself with his story of the wild wheat, they would not believe him, but would immediately ask what the Department of Agriculture thought of his discovery. I was of course much interested in this wild wheat, but when Dr. Adler and Mr. Straus inquired whether its introduction would revolutionize wheat-growing (which was rather the inference to be made from some of Aaronsohn's claims) I had to hedge, and throw the burden of proof onto the shoulders of the wheat breeders and let it rest there."

However, Fairchild was no stranger to mixing politics with science, or even with military science. Dr. Adler was Cyrus Adler, Henrietta Szold's employer at the Jewish Publication Society and known as the most influential Jew in America. Mr. Straus was Oscar Straus, the first Jew to serve as a Cabinet secretary. These were the only two Jews of Fairchild's acquaintance, and he introduced them to Aaron regardless of his protégé's bombast, noting that "these were the early days of the Zionist movement about which little was known as yet in America."

The conclusion of the Spanish-American War had forced the United States to give up its opportunities for oil exploration in the Philippines; and Mexico, the "great oil field of the world," according to the alarmist report published by the United States Geological Survey in 1909, was already dominated by the British-controlled Aguila Company. Securing alternative sources of oil became a matter of the highest diplomatic priority. Fairchild's work for the Section of Foreign Seed and Plant Introduction placed him in a prime position to observe the world, which is why others connected to his office thought it "highly desirable" to have an experiment station and plant-breeding garden "somewhere at the eastern end of the Mediterranean," where oil was being discovered. In 1910, the American consul at Beirut reported to the U.S. State Department on the first discovery of petroleum and iron in Syria. In 1913, America's biggest energy company, Standard Oil of New Jersey, formed a partnership with two local Arab landowners, Selim Ben Ayoub and Ismail El Husseini, and purchased a twenty-five-year concession from the Ottoman authorities to explore the vicinity of the Dead Sea for oil, phosphates, and bitumen, just as Aaron had done eight years before in the company of the German geologist Blanckenhorn. Standard Oil's agent in Jerusalem — then described as being part of Syria — was an ambitious twenty-nine-year-old engineer named William Yale, who was to become one of the most acute American analysts of the Middle East and to have close contact with Aaron.

Although the United States government could not or would not fund such a station for fear of raising the threat of resource wars with Britain, Fairchild "hoped that Aaronsohn would make friends with prominent Jews and secure their support for such a garden in Palestine." Increasingly America saw such Jews as assets in its struggle to stake an oil claim in the Ottoman territories, against the machinations of the English and the Germans, who had been haggling with Abdul Hamid over rights and concessions for several years. Beginning with Grover Cleveland's first presidency in 1885, a long string of Jews became ambassadors to Constantinople at a time when Jewish ambassadors were a diplomatic rarity.

Fairchild and his colleagues at the United States Geological Survey overestimated Zionism's value as a unifying political force, even for Jews like Aaron (who, though strongly nationalistic in opposing foreign rule in Palestine, also opposed large-scale Jewish immigration because he believed it would unsettle the Arab population). In 1909, the Zionist movement represented only a tiny fraction of American Jews and did not even approach Jewish socialism in strength or influence. Although the Federation of American Zionists, founded in 1898, endorsed Theodor Herzl's Basel protocol establishing the tenets of world Zionism, it was a loose coalition of individuals and societies and could never raise the financial resources for educational and organizational work that would have cemented a strong union. American Zionism reflected the *Yishuv* in its inner divisions between the religious Zionists, or *Mizrachi,* and Poale Zion, the Labor Zionists; between recent immigrants, Yiddish in language and culture and with a strong adherence to traditional Judaism, and Americanized Jews – particularly the prominent ones – who saw Zionism primarily as a refuge for the persecuted Jews of Europe. Orthodox Jews in both Europe and America for the most part opposed it as a heresy, ungrounded in Torah. Reform rabbis, who spoke to a large segment of the German-Jewish population, regarded America as their Zion; and Zionism as a threat to assimilation. *Aliyah,* to a distant country notoriously ill-ruled, was a remote and appalling objective to hundreds of thousands of Jews who had already uprooted themselves from Europe and were just beginning to enjoy the comforts of their new home. Not until the end of World War I, with the Balfour Declaration stating British support for a national Jewish homeland in Palestine, and the emergence of new leaders like Judah Magnes and Louis Brandeis, a prominent German-Jewish labor lawyer who worked closely with banking titan Jacob Schiff and who reconciled Zionism with American loyalties by declaring it heir to the Pilgrim experience, would Zionism become a significant force in American Jewish life.

The resourceful Aaron had already, in 1907, made the acquaintance of Rabbi Judah Leon Magnes, head of the preeminent German-Jewish Reform Temple Emanu-El in New York. His congregation included the families of Jacob Schiff and Paul Warburg, who created the structure of the U.S. Federal Reserve; Julius Rosenwald, president of Sears, Roebuck and Company; Louis Marshall, one of the most prominent labor lawyers of his day; and Judge Julian Mack, president of the World Zionist Organization. A charismatic young rabbi who had visited Zichron Ya'akov on a fact-finding tour for his fund-raisers, Magnes shared Aaron's vision of an expansionist national home for the Jews, one built on firm working relations with the Arabs. In America, Magnes served as unofficial consul general for European and Palestinian Jews and their missions, and introduced Aaron to those members of his congregation who could provide the most practical support for an experiment station for the advancement of agricultural science — Schiff, Rosenwald, Marshall, and Mack. Cyrus Adler, in turn, introduced Aaron to "Miss Szold," a title Henrietta by now wore proudly, not only as the heartbeat of the American Zionist movement but its social center as well.

Aaron's natural charm and ebullience blossomed as he became the center of a wide circle of influential Jewish leaders in New York and Chicago, many of whom regarded him as the first of the *sabras*, a two-fisted frontiersman pleasingly like an incarnation of their younger selves. They were German Jews, the elite of the most successful migration at that point in United States history — now entrenched in the legal, medical, and engineering professions, and, in the aftermath of the Civil War, on Wall Street — and they had not lost all of their rough edges.

Many of these Jewish American leaders whose patronage Aaron now enjoyed had arrived in the 1840s, when revolution roiled the patchwork of states that was Germany; and were consequently known as

Forty-Eighters. Because so many had been peddlers in the old country, they soon strapped on their packs and set out for the frontier of the "goldenah medinah," the golden place of opportunity. Levi Strauss headed for the California gold rush with a roll of heavy denim on his back. When a miner complained that his jeans wore out too quickly, Strauss made him a pair with copper rivets reinforcing the pockets, and an empire was born. Jewish peddlers went from door to door in the West and South, selling clothes, food, and household utensils. The most assiduous soon expanded operations, to stocking other peddlers from open warehouses that, in the cities, became the foundations of great department stores – Gimbels, Thalheimer's, Abraham & Straus.

Even the most influential Jew in America, the formidable Jacob Schiff, owed his eminence to the rag trade: his firm, Kuhn, Loeb, opened its New York retail bank in 1867 on the strength of a fortune made selling uniforms to Yankee soldiers in Cincinnati. Despite the origins of his firm's wealth, Schiff had arrived in America already a patrician who, many Russian Jews thought, looked down on them from a haughty Germanic perch. A Frankfurt native and, originally, an Orthodox Jew, he came from a family that had befriended the Rothschilds and included six centuries of prominent scholars, rabbis, and businessmen. In 1875 he accepted an invitation to join the new banking house of Kuhn, Loeb in New York and immediately cemented the alliance by marrying Solomon Loeb's daughter, Therese. In the next generation, he would consolidate his international reach by marrying their daughter, Frieda, to Felix Warburg of the Hamburg-based banking clan.

Schiff amassed both fortune and political influence by venturing into financial terrain where other Jews then feared to tread. Railroad financing was the most lucrative part of Wall Street, and the most jealously guarded turf of gentile banks. Though the more cautious Solomon Loeb opposed him, by 1877, Schiff had won Chicago & Northwestern Railroad as a client and, by 1880, pushed his father-in-law into retirement.

By 1894, Schiff was second only to J. Pierpont Morgan in wielding power on Wall Street, and M. M. Warburg and Company was marketing Kuhn, Loeb railroad securities in Germany. His best friend was London banker Sir Ernest Cassel, known familiarly as Windsor

Cassel because of his close ties to the Prince of Wales. Another German Jew, Cassel had moved to England as a teenager and amassed a fortune in banking, then converted to Catholicism. He served as Kuhn, Loeb's foreign agent, worked with Lord Revelstoke of Barings to organize English investors for the Baghdad Railway, and was knighted for his efforts. The Warburgs joined the venture in raising finance for Deutsche Bank, the railway's creator.

"Court Jews" who had found their niche in banking because seventeenth-century church prohibitions forbade wealthy German noblemen to lend money at interest, the Warburgs, like the Rothschilds, grew from working as money changers and pawnbrokers to arbitraging currencies among the three hundred kingdoms, principalities, city-states, and duchies that made up Germany before 1870. Due to their protected status, they never suffered early persecutions and often mediated between the Jewish population and the local prince, developing a hybrid status, neither gentile nor Jew, but, according to historian Ron Chernow, secure in their loyalty to the German state.

In 1798, the main branch of the family moved to the important Hanseatic port of Hamburg and expanded the money-lending business into the bank of M. M. Warburg and Company. Warburg's primary business was foreign exchange and trade bills. The Warburgs, in association with the Frankfurt-based Rothschilds, replenished the city's silver stocks after the departure of Napoleon's forces in 1814, and thereafter the two houses maintained a close relationship. When Europe destabilized in the 1840s, the Warburgs' prosperity grew along with that of Hamburg, which became the crossroads of a profitable new human commerce in emigrants taking ship for England or America. And when the First German Reich was created by the end of the Franco-Prussian War in 1870, the Warburgs, newly emancipated along with the rest of Germany's Jews, participated in the second loan that allowed France to pay its enormous war reparations to Germany. These reparations, arranged by Alphonse de Rothschild, were to have fateful repercussions at Versailles in 1919 when France took its revenge on Germany, and the Rothschild enterprises, in which Aaron was once more involved suffered accordingly.

.·•. .·•. .·•.

When Wall Street took over from London as the world's banker in the early twentieth century, the American German-Jewish banking elite took over the Rothschild role in protecting suffering Jews everywhere. Like England's Rothschilds – and like the white Anglo-Saxon Protestant ruling class, doling out charitable relief to potentially unruly new-comers and working to maintain the status quo – they, too, wished to help their poor and persecuted fellows, but they also wished to stem the tide of undesirables they felt threatened their privileged position. Their arrival in the United States had coincided with the birth of the nativist Know Nothing Party, and they feared the backlash that a new flood of associated "foreigners," whose socialist leanings raised the specter of labor unrest, could create. Their fears were justified when, after the Civil War, social clubs, hotels, private schools, and benefit committees began excluding some of the most conspicuously success-ful German Jews of the Gilded Age.

From the 1870s onward, prominent spokesmen for the German-Jewish establishment tried to limit Jewish immigration from Eastern Europe. The secretary of the Hebrew Emigrant Aid Society, for exam-ple, repeatedly wired his European counterparts to stop sending more Jews and took the position that "as American Israelites we have a duty to the community in which we live, which forbids us to become parties to the infliction of permanent paupers upon our already overburdened cities." In 1891, Jacob Schiff and Oscar Straus met with President Ben-jamin Harrison to urge him to protest to Russia about the anti-Semitic decrees that "forced groups of its people to seek refuge in another country, and that country our own." When the Kishinev pogrom of 1903 again made the American Jewish community fear the kind of con-tagion an influx of destitute Russian Jews might bring, Schiff again suc-cessfully petitioned a U.S. president, this time Theodore Roosevelt, to protest to Russia. In 1904, Schiff boasted to Lord Rothschild: "I pride myself that all the efforts, which at various times during the past four or five years have been made by Russia to gain the American market for its loans, I have been able to bring to naught."

In 1905, Schiff intervened in an unprecedented way when he suc-cessfully led a banking consortium to back Japan's war against Russia.

He thereby ensured Japan's military victory, which broke czarist power in the Far East and Persia and realigned the board of the Great Game. But his newly aggressive tactics were to have unforeseen consequences: while he may have aided Turkey by removing Russia from the table, Schiff also removed the last significant barrier to war between Britain and his beloved Germany.

Schiff was still far from any form of commitment to Zionism, although that year new pogroms led him, in consort with Adler and Mack, to create the first Jewish-American relief committee to support Jews worldwide. Schiff and Felix Warburg had regarded Palestine as a spiritual home for Judaism rather than a future nation-state, and, with Louis Marshall, believed unreservedly that "political Zionism places a lien upon citizenship" and would create "a separateness that would be fatal." In 1906, Schiff warned in the *New York Times*: "It is quite evident that there is a serious break coming for those who wish to force the formation of a distinct Hebraic element in the United States, as distinct from those of us who desire to be American in attachment, thought, and action."

Adler from the start disparaged the idea of a Jewish state in the Holy Land but recognized the need for a haven from persecution. As early as the First Zionist Congress at Basel in 1897, he wrote Theodor Herzl a proposal to find a refuge for Jewry in Mesopotamia (a proposal that was to be revived by right-wing Jewish lobbyists in 2003, after the United States invasion of Iraq, with one slight twist — Iraq was to be used as a haven for persecuted Palestinians run out of Israel).

Schiff, for his part, assiduously avoided Herzl's many efforts to enlist him in the Zionist cause, right up to the founder of Zionism's death in 1904. But in February of 1910, Schiff's interest in Zionism suddenly awakened. A prolonged series of strikes among the young Jewish girls of the International Ladies' Garment Workers' Union soon spread to the male Cloakmakers Union and thence to the American Federation of Labor, where it became a massive and well-organized effort to create a scandal for the goyim.

In fact, the scandalous aspect was the German Jews' treatment of their fellow Jews. By the time the East European émigrés entered the United States in the 1880s, most of the opportunities for peddling had dried up. Instead, they gravitated to the garment sweatshops of the

Lower East Side, where many of their bosses were German Jews. Most of the new workers were young and energetic socialists who vociferously protested their atrocious working conditions, but when they banded together to demand higher wages for their eighteen-hour days, their fellow Jews turned hired goons on them. The strikes dragged on for seven months. Finally Schiff and Louis Brandeis negotiated a fifty-hour week, higher wages, and a preferential union shop the socialists called "a scab shop with honey." The simmering ill-feelings reignited in the tragic Triangle Shirtwaist Factory fire, which, on March 25, 1911, killed 146 young women workers when flames broke out on the eighth floor of the Asch Building. Factory owners had secured the exits as a means of controlling their workers and preventing access to union organizers.

Schiff joined forces with another prominent German-American Jew, Henry Morgenthau, to ensure that such a tragedy would never happen again, and also to reunite a badly fractured community. A high-minded Committee for Safety was created, headed by Morgenthau, who had made his fortune in real estate after graduating from Columbia Law School with his rival, Oscar Straus. Schiff, Morgenthau, and other German-Jewish leaders now thought that Zionism as a strong sense of cultural, rather than political, identity might reunite the community.

Aaron found himself courted by worldly, powerful, self-made, self-determining men like Brandeis and Schiff. Before long, Aaron was inviting Fairchild to join him for lunch with Julius Rosenwald at Delmonico's in New York, to persuade Rosenwald and his friends to fund an experiment station at Haifa for the advancement of agricultural science.

Schiff found young Aaron Aaronsohn and his proposed experiment station uniquely persuasive in furthering his goals. The idea of a Jewish scientific laboratory and plant-breeding garden in Palestine, closely connected to the American scientific establishment and run by a charming and articulate spokesperson like Aaron, could provide a focal point of pride for the American Jewish community. But having contributed with his usual heavy-handed generosity to Palestinian institutions such as the Technical Institute of Haifa, Schiff emphatically did not want to be considered "the tail to the Zionist kite," as small and precarious as it was.

•◆• •◆• •◆•

The many factions that made up the body of the "Zionist kite in America chattered loudly with envy in Miss Szold's salon at how the upstart Aaronsohn gained the ear of the most influential Jew in America. Aaron Aaronsohn was thirty-three when he finally met Henrietta through Cyrus Adler upon her return to the United States from Palestine. She was forty-nine. Their meeting was to unsettle her new and hard-won tranquility.

An undated letter written by Aaron reveals that he was not only aware of the womanly side of her personality, but highly responsive to it:

> My dear friend
>
> To stay a full two months in the States and to have so little opportunity to see you and talk to you is one of the many unhappy events of my trip. In your sweet modesty you completely ignore the inspiration the saint you are is for those fortunate enough to know you, and to get the benefit of your tender friendship. You may feel surprised at that, but it is a fact. And I hoped, I hoped very much, to have a good chance of spending hours and hours in your company. Fate or the "Organization," equally cruel, inhuman things, decided it otherwise, decided against us. We should have rebelled. But what is the use of kicking, now, when it is too late.

Although undoubtedly he sincerely warmed to Henrietta's wit, vision, and affectionate guidance, Aaron was not without opportunism. He was, after all, a politician as well as a scientist, a fact Szold – herself a politician albeit one who worked behind the scenes – appears to have recognized. To Szold, the tempestuous Aaron personified Zionism's nationalist ideal. Not even the lure of money, to which most Jews in America had already succumbed, could deflect him.

On February 10, 1910, the Jewish Agricultural Experiment Station became the only Palestinian company to be incorporated under New York State law. The board of directors read like a Who's Who of

American Jewry: Julius Rosenwald was president, Professor Morris
Loeb of Columbia University was vice president, Paul Warburg trea-
surer, and Szold secretary. Schiff, as was his wont, played silent partner, though he, along with Otto Warburg, supplied the bulk of the
funding. The meetings took place at Henrietta's cavernous apartment
across the street from the Jewish Theological Seminary on Manhat-
tan's Upper West Side

Both Schiff and Warburg were at that time strongly pro-German
and favored making the experiment station into a hub for a Bismarck-
style network of benign colonization. Aaron, by now too accustomed
to his leading role as first *sabra*, and to the deference of the rich and
powerful, loudly announced his opposition to any foreign control of
Palestine, even that of his American patrons. Aaron's resistance was
strengthened by the fact that Schiff insisted on interrogating him about
whether he was an agnostic or a practicing Jew. When Schiff and Warburg objected, in the manner of money the world over, at losing control
to the "Zionist kite," Aaron threatened to walk out. Since his knowledge of Palestinian botany was key to a successful experiment station,
the threat was effective. Szold, who cordially detested Schiff's patronizing Germanic ways, approved tacitly of Aaron's insistence on fighting his own fight, no matter what it might lose him. Her diary shows
that her attraction to him deepened:

> MONDAY, MARCH 28, 1910
> For me it suffices that he is a thorough scientist and that he
> seems to be an idealist besides, not a talking but a working
> idealist. I like him better and better.

> TUESDAY, MARCH 29, 1910
> The man is symmetrically developed and he demonstrates
> anew that if a man has something to say he knows how to
> say it.

On Sunday, April 4, 1910, Szold's lengthy diary entries are all about
Aaron, who had come to say good-bye before departing for Palestine.
"After supper Aaronson [*sic*] came and the stimulating talk I had
with him on this farewell occasion will remain in my memory. He is
distinctly a personality, a rigorous worker, and at the same time not

devoid of strong sentiments . . . I felt impelled to urge him to get married. He is 34, he ought not to wait. A woman would be made happy by him, his energy, his big plans, and his idealism."

Aaron was, in other words, exactly the kind of man that would have made Szold happy. In his brawling she sensed a passion as powerful as her own, an openness and a physicality that set him in a class apart from the ghettoized intellectuals of her circle "I believe Aaronson is a whole man," she wrote that night. "I hope he is successful. He himself anticipates bitter opposition in Palestine . . . That is one of the many things I felt in all my intercourse with Aaronson, that my mind is vague and flabby. He is a specialist and individualist . . . I shall miss his stimulating presence. He is a scholar, a gentleman, a man of the world."

Sitting alone together in the deepening twilight of her comfortable parlor, she noted wistfully, "We talked of nothing but dry-farming."

4.

Minuet

In 1909, a slight, even delicate-looking Englishman barely five-foot-five in his socks, with a girlish giggle and a kit full of irritating pretensions like wearing his Oxford school tie as a sash for his baggy, none-too-clean white shorts, arrived in Beirut on board the *SS Mongolia*. The barely twenty-one-year-old T.E. Lawrence, who would make the title "of Arabia" uniquely his own, spoke less than a hundred words of Arabic at the time. He was armed with a Baedeker, some maps in need of updating given to him by another young archaeologist working for British Naval Intelligence, and a camera equipped, unusually for the time, with a telephoto lens, courtesy of his Oxford mentor, David Hogarth.

For a recent undergraduate, Lawrence's letters of introduction were quite extraordinary. His *irades* were signed by none other than Lord Curzon, formerly the all-powerful British viceroy of India whose mastery of bureaucracy and effulgent sense of his own importance personified the Raj. Curzon had just shifted his gravitas into the seat of chancellor of Oxford – a post that, though honorary, was scarcely less important in perpetuating the colonial legacy by nurturing generations of Foreign Office administrators-to-be. The move was not entirely voluntary on Curzon's part; though a consummate infighter, he had just fallen victim to the machinations of his longtime enemy, K of K (which also stood for Kitchener of Khartoum, the Sudanese siege which had made Lord Kitchener an undefeatable legend in his own time). Kitchener had launched a campaign to shift the locus of political power in the imperial hierarchy from India to the Middle East.

Just finished with his scholarship exams, Lawrence was traveling on an Oxford fellowship to sketch and photograph Crusader fortifications, inspect the archaeological site of Carcemish in Syria, and buy Hittite coins for Hogarth, an archaeologist and traveler descended from a long line of Anglican ministers who, like Schweinfurth, was more interested in imperial geography than in sarcophagi. At first glance Lawrence was an unlikely candidate for the straitlaced atmosphere of the Foreign Office, but Hogarth was prized for his acumen – particularly by the directors of intelligence at the Admiralty, where he had strong unofficial connections, and who needed exceptional young scholars for less conventional activities.

Despite his bohemian dishevelment, Lawrence was aware of his advantages, which came not from social class but from genuine and untiring scholarship. Aaron Aaronsohn was later to refer to him as "that little snot" because of his aptitude for dismissing the opinions of others with withering and excessive scorn. For all his conceit, Lawrence was a welter of insecurities, as uncertain of his manhood as he would be of his later achievements. He was, literally, a bastard and – what was worse at the time – a poor boy in a school for rich men's sons. He was a class-jumper in a caste-bound age who would never feel at home in the company to which he aspired; later he rejected the Order of the Garter from the King of England's own hand and used one of his other honors for a dog collar. Despite his obvious brilliance, he was more than a bit of a faker who would develop a habit of misleading his chroniclers. He was perhaps not above appropriating the achievements of others to embellish his own myth. The foreword to his most famous work, *Seven Pillars of Wisdom,* condescends to his more obscure fellow intelligence officers as "the un-named rank and file: who miss their share of credit as they must do, until they can write the dispatches." Yet for all his faults and perhaps even because of them, Thomas Edward Lawrence was a hero of the twentieth century, a modern knight-errant in whom the chivalric impulse to break one's young body in the service of an ideal metamorphosed into the impulse to break one's youthful ideals in the service of a public image.

Lawrence's youthful ideals were in fact formed by chivalric literature such as Sir Thomas Malory's *Le Mort d'Arthur*, a work that accompanied him on all his later military campaigns. From its pages he absorbed an intense admiration for and understanding of medieval warrior codes that later translated to an immediate affinity for the Arabs, a desire to serve rather than to lead, and an eccentric asceticism that could be used to draw attention to himself. It was clear from an early age that Lawrence, as he remarked in *Seven Pillars of Wisdom*, suffered from "a craving to be famous, and a horror of being known to like being known."

Much has been made of Lawrence's alleged homosexuality, particularly as the source of his well-documented masochism. The source of this particular facet of the Lawrence legend is the famous Deraa incident described in chapter 80 of *Seven Pillars of Wisdom*, where Lawrence volubly describes his erotic arousal after being raped, whipped, and pierced with a bayonet by his fiendish Ottoman captors. Lawrence later admitted that his account of the Dera'a incident was false, and his later biographers have discredited it. The possibility that a wildly insecure and ambitious young man, having passed through the sexual ordeals of the British public-school system, in flight from his lowly social standing and puritanical upbringing, might be inclined to masochism without being homosexual has gone unexamined, not to mention the fact that bisexuality is hardly unknown among honorable British schoolboys.

In fact, during his time at Oxford it seemed axiomatic that the higher the intelligence, the hazier the sexuality. The affectation of homosexuality was a form of protective coloration, or even a card of admission into certain enviable circles. It was the era of Bloomsbury, of marriages like that between diplomat Harold Nicolson and novelist Vita Sackville-West, both of whom had homosexual affairs. At Oxford, Lawrence was known both for his priggishness and for his close friendship with Vivyan Richards, an aesthete with whom he explored the Pre-Raphaelite twilight and the byways of medieval chivalry. Richards made no bones about the nature of his affection for Lawrence but made equally clear that it was unrequited. Richards, perhaps to console himself, felt that Lawrence was in fact as asexual as his Pre-Raphaelite ideal:

> He had neither flesh nor carnality of any kind; he just did not understand. He received my affection, my sacrifice, in fact eventually my total subservience, as though it was his due. He never gave the slightest sign that he understood my motives or fathomed my desire. In return for all I offered him — with admittedly ulterior motives — he gave me the

purest affection, love, respect that I have ever received
from anyone . . . a love and respect that was spiritual in
quality. I realize now that he was sexless – at least that he
was unaware of sex.

Another gay friend who cherished the most heated admiration for
Lawrence for many years, the poet and physician Ernest Altounyan,
also insisted Lawrence had no real interest in homosexuality, although
Altounyan made his best efforts to cultivate one in him. Lawrence did
write nostalgically of the mud of the docks in Alexandria, where he
spent some youthful nights sleeping rough in the company of well-built
Arab stevedores, but in mature works such as *The Mint* he expresses
only the squalor of the exclusive company of men. In *Seven Pillars*,
he professes an aesthetic admiration for the "clean love" of youth for
youth, slaking the need for physical passion in the hot sands of long
journeys. This admiration was fashionable by the standards of the secret
Uranian Society of Lawrence's youth at Oxford, which included Lord
Alfred "Bosie" Douglas – Oscar Wilde's lover – and the equally notorious Baron Corvo (the writer F. W. Rolfe), but he also describes his need
to be with a woman, albeit in typically ambiguous, even tortured terms:

> The lower creation I avoided, as a reflection upon our
> failure to attain real intellectuality. If they forced them-
> selves on me I hated them. To put my hand on a living thing
> was defilement; and it made me tremble if they touched me
> or took too quick an interest in me. This was an atomic
> repulsion, like the intact course of a snowflake. The
> opposite would have been my choice if my head had not
> been tyrannous. I had a longing for the absolutism of
> women and animals, and lamented myself most when I saw
> a soldier with a girl, or a man fondling a dog, because my
> wish was to be as superficial, as perfected; and my jailor
> held me back.

Lawrence's "jailor," his tyrannous superego, prodded him merci-
lessly to succeed, to revenge himself on the class that had rejected him
while he was still a vulnerable schoolboy – the class of his aristocratic

and disdainful cousin Robert Vansittart. Vansittart was deeply embarrassed by Lawrence's undergraduate showing-off, which included such tricks as firing revolvers in the sewers of Oxford. But Lawrence's only weapons were those of his scholarship and extreme eccentricity. Only by appearing to scorn the aristocracy completely could he penetrate their ranks; to become, as playwright Joe Orton might put it, "a better class of person." Like Orton, Lawrence enjoyed slumming, an activity that relieved the stress of his aspirations and may have included the attentions of lower-class women as well as lower-class men. (A "Mrs. Jennings" was put under treatment for "nerve strain" after insisting in a series of letters to Lawrence, his mother, and the War Office that Lawrence make an honest woman of her following their first encounter in 1919.)

At that time in his life when impressionable young men are most likely to formulate their ideals, Lawrence crossed paths with Sarah Aaronsohn. It is difficult to imagine that having met her, he would not overcome the prohibitions of his "jailor."

Lawrence's official assignment was to sketch, photograph, and measure a series of Crusader fortifications, which allowed him not only to travel to remote parts of Palestine and the Levant but also to examine in detail the points of entry by which the Crusaders sought access to the fabled trade routes of the Far East. Unofficially, he was there to report on the progress of the Baghdad Railway. The intricate etiquette governing agents of Great Powers, following one another's footsteps across the desert sands, gathering information in the bars and smoking rooms of Shepherd's and Fast's, and always maneuvering for commercial advantage, demanded that any such contacts with other "travelers" like Gertrude Bell, Douglas Carruthers, and the Aaronsohns go unrecorded. An entry in Aaron's diaries, *"Causer et causer avec les anglaises,"* which translates to "Lots and lots of argument with Englishwomen," suggests an encounter with Bell. A map of their journeys shows such contacts were inevitable, particularly as Lawrence's footsteps overlapped Aaronsohn's and may indeed have followed them in an elaborate, almost courtly minuet.

In the first phase of what was to be a three-part journey, Lawrence made his way alone and on foot from Southern Lebanon to Northern

Palestine via Lake Tiberias, where he visited Aaron's friend and colleague, the Scottish medical missionary and Christian Zionist Dr. D.
W. Torrance. There Lawrence developed a hitherto unsuspected interest in botany. He then traveled to Athlit, located on the slopes of Mount
Carmel overlooking Haifa, where Aaron was to build his Jewish Agricultural Experiment Station in 1910. Here Lawrence sketched the
Castellum Peregrinorum, fortified by the Knights Templar in 1218
and famous for being the northernmost Crusader castle in Palestine,
but he neither described his visit nor any contact with the Rothschild
colony just a few miles down the road at Zichron Ya'akov, where the
Aaronsohn family, the most prominent in the village, received distinguished foreign visitors like Henrietta Szold.

Lawrence would not have been able to avoid the Aaronsohns. The
stretch of Bedouin turf that lay between the Jewish colony at Lake
Tiberias and Athlit was a particularly dangerous one for a non-Arabic
speaker. In a sparsely populated and often hostile region, the European bastion of Zichron Ya'akov would have been an inevitable port-
of-call for the young Lawrence, given his lack of Arabic and his need
for introductions to local luminaries like Dr. Torrance. The Aaronsohn
family was already well known to intelligence circles through Aaron's
scientific activities. They were Europhiles, and native Arabic speakers.
Aaron was one of the few Europeans who could count on safe conduct
through Bedouin territory, due to a long-ago favor in settling a dispute
for a Bedouin chief. He was still in America at the time of Lawrence's
visit, but Sarah was in Palestine and in charge of her absent brother's
affairs. She rode, could shoot, and knew her way through the wilds to
Dr. Torrance's station as well as any man and would have been a logi-
cal choice to provide Lawrence with an interpreter and safe conduct.

Lawrence's Foreign Office biographer, Sir Anthony Nutting, denied
the young adventurer ever met Sarah Aaronsohn with the assertion
that she was not in Palestine at the time of his arrival, having been married off to an elderly Turkish Jew; and that even if she was in Palestine,
she was still a child. But Sarah did not marry until 1914. She was still in
Palestine in 1909, and, at nineteen years old, only two years younger
than Lawrence himself, with a stature and temperament that could not
fail to fascinate a repressed young Edwardian male.

Later accounts written by Alex or commissioned by Rivka to

perpetuate myths about the Aaronsohns as the first family of the Israeli Right depict Sarah as a conventional Jewish maiden, content to mind the house and look after the family needs. This picture ill-accords with the actions of the girl who became known as the Jewish Joan of Arc.

As a child, Sarah had all Aaron's mettle, along with his challenging stare. Competing with the boys at horse-racing or swimming interested her far more than hearth and home. She was in her element exploring the desert with her oldest brother. At puberty, Sarah's parents expected her to fall meekly into her mother's path, not an easy one for a young woman who not only grew up as her brothers' intellectual equal but was accustomed to being a celebrity from a very early age. Aaron, who wanted his sisters to see the world, sent her off instead on a Grand Tour of Germany, Switzerland, and Italy, from which she returned with a high-fashion finish. An accomplished dressmaker, she whipped up creations for herself and her younger sister, Rivka, to display on summer-evening postprandial promenades through Zichron Ya'akov that would not have been out of place on the boulevards of Paris. In the burgeoning cafe society of Haifa, people would often stop by the Aaronsohns' table for a sighting of the glamorous Sarah. A photograph taken when she was a young girl shows her, self-aware and sensuous, flirting under the deep brim of a dramatic hat. By age sixteen she was already a full-bosomed, broad-shouldered young Diana, who "might have been the leader of a Hebrew return with glory," Lawrence later remarked, according to Jerusalem's police commissioner, Douglas Valder Duff.

Sarah was in many ways the most rebellious of the Aaronsohn children, a free spirit who would not have been out of place in the 1960s. Through her reading and her correspondence, Sarah could easily tap the spirit of Jewish feminism that was stirring in Europe. By 1912, the year of her mother's death, the membership of the Bund Deutscher Frauenverein, Germany's largest feminist organization, had doubled, from 132,000 to 235,000. By the 1920s it would number almost one million, and would be disproportionately Jewish. Because of their comfortable, middle-class status and concentration in urban areas, Jews were among the first religious groups in Germany to practice birth control, which increasingly freed Jewish women from the confinement of domestic responsibility. At the same time, they still faced the antifeminism of Jewish men, and for the most part applied their new-found freedom to charitable rather than political activities.

Back in Zichron Ya'akov, Sarah's letters and journals rang with her impatient longing to be free of social constraints and to be truly equal with her brothers. Aaron indulged that spirit, both to flout the rabbis and to demonstrate his favorite sister's exceptional status; if there were rumors in the *Yishuv*, he did nothing to dispel them. In 1908, the year before Lawrence's arrival in Palestine, Sarah accompanied Aaron on one of his trips into the wild hills of Rosh-Pinna and Lake Tiberias. They were not alone, sleeping under the stars; their third companion was the handsome revolutionary poet Absalom Feinberg, known as Sheikh Salim among the Arabs for his skill as a desert traveler. Absalom, known affectionately as Absa, was a *Biluim*, one of an early group of Russian Marxists who emigrated in the Second Aliyah and set up an agricultural colony at Gadera. The inexperienced farmers nearly starved on the fruits of their labors, and Aaron and his father came to their rescue on many occasions. At age twenty, Aaron adopted Absa, a child of ten, as a protégé.

One night, when all were grown up, Sarah and Rivka encountered Absa on a moonlight ride back from a dance at a neighboring village. Both young women were equally smitten, and Sarah began a flirtation with Marxism as well. Sarah gravitated naturally toward cosmopolitan intellectuals resembling her adored older brother. She was irresistibly drawn to the fiery, black-browed Absa though she refused to allow him to get away with his Byronic moods. Both were high-spirited and enjoyed competing with each other, whether in racing horses or swimming or arguments over definitions of the proletariat, the new woman, and the concept of free love. Sarah's eagerness to compete at sports, unusual for a woman at the time, was a sure sign of her progressive politics; she was equally reluctant to fend off Absa's advances for fear of being thought old-fashioned. Like Henrietta Szold, Sarah allowed herself to believe that their heady preoccupations lifted them outside the realm of social convention, at the same time that she hoped Absa's heated desire for a muse involved a deeper commitment. But Absa's revolutionary principles did not extend to the sexual sphere. Shortly after they began an affair, he transferred his affections to her shy and mouselike sister, Rivka, a colorless young girl, quaint rather than attractive and quite overshadowed by her more glamorous sibling. He asked Rivka to marry him, and, in an undated letter, petitioned Sarah for a "quieter happiness":

> Sarati — In spite of everything, here we are, still friends, and I love you with all the strength of my heart. But you make me furiously angry, and for that you are a naughty girl, Sareleh, my darling. I would like to enjoy a quieter happiness, so I ask you to send me quickly, in a registered parcel, your little sister. We will talk about you here, I promise you, and think of you when the sun goes down. In the moonbeams we will see something of your dreaming eyes, and in the flame of the setting sun your ardent heart.

What the ardent Sarah thought of such a request has gone unrecorded, but it coincided with Lawrence's visit to Palestine.

Sarah's anarchist soul, intellectual curiosity, and (for her time) flamboyant sexuality outraged the Puritan element of the *Yishuv*. Tongues wagged at her relationship with Absa, which continued to smolder platonically after he announced his engagement to Rivka, and burst into open flames again once the war began. During Sarah's brief lifetime, the *Yishuv* threatened more than once to cast her out. It was rumored that her relations with her brother were unnatural; that a later lover, Yussuf Lishansky (who was also a married man), bumped off Absa in order to enjoy Sarah's favors; and, much later, that Sarah had been the plaything of a wealthy Turk in Constantinople between the ages of twelve and sixteen. There is no documentation to support this last lurid claim, and it makes little sense either logistically or in terms of her pious upbringing. One thing is clear: like Szold and other early feminists who broke into the realm of politics, Sarah was a liberated woman, fond of the company of men. That would have been a revelation to Lawrence, uncertain of his sexuality and hagridden by a domineering religious mother.

But Sarah Aaronsohn's most powerful attraction for Lawrence was more than physical. The young devotee of chivalric ideals, as he tells us in *Seven Pillars*, was in love with the unattainable, and Sarah was the one thing Lawrence was not. She was instinctively, unflinchingly brave. Unlike Lawrence, who confessed to having a typically Edwardian divided spirit and a morbid fear of pain, Sarah Aaronsohn did not know what fear was. "She is so simple in her greatness," Aaron wrote in his diaries "and so unconscious of the nobility of her soul."

However, Sarah's love affairs were incidental and limited to men who bore a strong resemblance, physically or spiritually, to her brother. They seemed predestined to fail. Like many ambitious people who put their stamp on the Middle East – like Lawrence, like Gertrude Bell, like Aaron himself – Sarah lusted only for what she could not have and so kept her life unencumbered for her work.

If Freud had encountered the Aaronsohns and Lawrence, perhaps even the self-effacing Miss Szold, and undoubtedly the self-dramatizing Miss Bell (who preferred to be seen in billowing white raiment, galloping full tilt on her favorite black stallion through the Iraqi countryside), he would have declared work to be the perfect form of sublimation. For those with personalities – and appetites – larger than the norm, for the Nietzschean and the eccentric, the talented and the misfit, imposing order on the Asian Near East or the American West or the African Congo was a compelling means of taming the wildness within themselves – of achieving, as historian Christopher Lasch puts it, "a fragile triumph over the id." For the European Jew in particular, conditioned by years of oppression in the ghetto, the biblical homeland represented not only an opportunity to build a new society free of feudal inhibitions, but a temptation to throw off civilization altogether and revert to a savagery that could be conveniently directed at the natives whose lands they wished to acquire. Those who were civilized feared their own hearts of darkness and worked relentlessly to subdue them.

By 1909, the year of Lawrence's arrival in Palestine, civilization was itself coming off the rails – and threatening to become an enormous train wreck. That year, Britain ratcheted up the great European railway race from fierce competition to open aggression. German diplomats wrung yet another concession out of Abdul Hamid to grant harbor privileges in Kuwait, an Ottoman vassal ruled by an Arab sheikh, and an important point of entry to the Indian Ocean. Britain, engaged in its own negotiations with. Abdul Hamid, promptly invoked its version of the Monroe Doctrine and sent a gunboat to Kuwait to discourage the venture.

Abdul Hamid massed an army to oppose the British on the borders of Kuwait but was deposed later in 1909 when he tried to plot a counterrevolution against the Young Turk insurrection. Observers remarked that the Red Sultan might have kept his throne with the support of the United States had he given a retired American rear admiral, Colby Chester, what he had so patiently sought. For years Chester had haggled with Abdul Hamid to gain America a footing in the oil race by granting Chester drilling concessions to the *vilayets* (districts) of Baghdad and Mosul. Instead, the Sultan sold the package of rights to the Germans in the Anatolian railway concession of 1904, and was preparing to sell them again to the British in 1909 when he was unceremoniously ousted.

The Young Turk revolution fueled expectations that the new Turkish government would undergo the thorough reforms promised by its leaders: Talaat Pasha, Enver Pasha, Djemal Pasha, and their part-Jewish financial vizier, Djavid Bey. In practice, the upsurge of Turkish nationalism and the breakdown of central authority resulted, predictably, in the maltreatment of all foreigners who had attracted envy and hatred during the years of the Capitulations. The fact that the fiercely chauvinistic Young Turk leadership was still tied to the apron strings of the great oil powers exacerbated preexisting xenophobia.

Abdul Hamid had been bad enough in his later, paranoid years, but Djemal Pasha, the despot who now governed Syria and Palestine, was infinitely worse. Where Abdul Hamid's darker nature was held in check by an apparently firm grasp of political realities, Djemal Pasha answered only to his ambitions. A squat, powerful figure of a man with a sadistic sense of humor, he was animal-like in both his ferocity and cunning. He was also treacherous and deeply corrupt, a warlord who swung with any power who would support him. Responsible for decimating the intellectual elite of Syria to quell the threat of insurrection, he was completely unpredictable in his persecutions of both Armenians and Jews. For two years he was, in fact, married to a Jewess.

When the marriage ended in 1909, over her complaints against his many infidelities, Djemal Pasha's attitude toward his Jewish subjects took a decided turn for the worse.

Aaron returned to Palestine in 1910. He was thirty-four years old and at the height of his powers. His trip to America had won him funding, acclaim, political power, and, most important, had solidified his unbridled egotism into true self-confidence. Over the next four years he built up the Jewish Agricultural Experiment Station at Athlit into an international showcase of the beginnings of "a type of experimental agriculture which would be epoch-making," David Fairchild wrote in the *Journal of Heredity*.

Athlit was an unprepossessing stretch of sand dunes interspersed with malarial marshes. Its dreary hillocks hid the bones of populations past, but to Aaron these grim relics were testimony to his assumption that the seemingly barren earth could support large settlements. The massive ruin of the Crusader castle sketched by Lawrence loomed up from the coastline. Near the harbor of Athlit was a huge mound that had been a city more than two thousand years before the Knights Templar built their last outpost. The alleyways of the Roman port of Caesarea snaked under the coastal sand dunes south of the experiment station, and, even more ancient, the Phoenician port of Dor lay buried in between.

In the four years that preceded the war, this desolate spot was the busiest in Palestine. In selecting Athlit for his experiment station, Aaron was bent on proving to the world — or, more specifically, to those who could fund large-scale immigration — that there was no such thing as worn-out soil. His German mentors had excited audiences in Berlin with their declaration that the land of Palestine had once supported six million people and could do so again; he seized this message as the key to nation building. He set his Jewish Agricultural Experiment Station in a grove of palms, joined it to the main highway by the only strip of macadamized road in the entire country, and made it a showcase for year-round cultivation. In four short years, he succeeded in his main objective: introducing and improving the cultivation of cereals and other plants that could resist bad weather, disease, and parasites. He created a new strain of sesame that yielded twice the harvest of any other strain grown in the country, as well as five new strains of sirocco-resistant barley and gluten-rich wheat, a table grape that ripened earlier than any other grape in the Egyptian market, mulberries that leafed earlier than those of Palestine's competitors in textiles, and local olives that could outproduce foreign ones in oil. In a remarkably early display of environmental consciousness, he designed more than forty plant species to keep the dunes from shifting. In addition, his investigations into Palestine's geology resulted in the country's outstanding collection of specimens and a profound modification of theories on the structure of its soil – all in all, not bad for an institution that only three years later would be known chiefly as a cover for espionage.

Aaron always maintained that he used no fertilizer and the same primitive tools and the ancient techniques of dry farming as did the Arab farmers. Dry farming is used to raise crops, primarily cereals, in regions of low rainfall, where irrigation is impractical. It relies on such practices as harrowing and crop rotation, and is most successful where the annual rainfall is between ten and twenty-two inches a year. Among its other innovations, the Jewish Agricultural Experiment Station pioneered the use of windmills to generate electrical power.

Aaron's American sponsors came to visit, inspect, and report back his progress. Among them was Nathan Straus, brother of Oscar, who introduced pasteurized milk into the United States to combat tuberculosis. Aaron persuaded Straus to help him set up a health center next door to the experiment station, where they began the first scientific research into causes and control of malaria, the scourge of Palestine.

Here, with one of the tactless blunders with which he sabotaged his successes throughout his career, Aaron unified his enemies and probably sacrificed his main chance for the leadership of the *Yishuv*. Dr. Hillel Yoffe, a fellow scientist, was one of the *Yishuv*'s original leaders and had recommended that Aaron be sent to Grignon to complete his education. Yoffe's sister, Rachel, a university-trained botanist some years older than Aaron, worked with Aaron at the experiment station and cherished a deep infatuation for the dynamic young scientist. Her brother hoped to make a match between royal families that would have cemented Aaron's political aspirations. But Aaron had his sights set elsewhere, and with bullish candor made that clear. The disappointed matchmaker was further wounded when Aaron failed to support him as director of the malaria station, and so from being an early admirer of Aaron's he became a longstanding and vindictive enemy. Personal grudges made fertile soil for political hostilities in a small and too-intimate community, and much of Aaron's later misfortune can be traced to his cloddish treatment of the Yoffes.

In Aaron's absence, Ben-Gurion had become the head of an anti-Arab vigilante group known as *Hashomer* — literally "Watchman," in memory of the Jewish watchman murdered by Arabs in 1909. Hashomer foreshadowed the Israel Defense League and was one of the building blocks of the Irgun, a paramilitary group under the British Mandate that became one of the principal draws for the Israeli Army. It gave some of the most damaged spirits out of Central Europe a formula for exorcising their evil memories of the Pale; Manya Wilbushewitz, one of its founding members, was long remembered "fanatic and mad," in the words of Israeli historian Tom Segev, galloping on horseback over the Galilee like a Cossack dressed in Arab garb. With the threat of Turkish persecutions and war on the horizon, the *Yishuv,* under Yoffe's leadership, made Hashomer responsible for protecting the community. Aaron feared Hashomer more than he feared the Turks and warned his family repeatedly of the possibility of betrayal.

In 1912, Aaron left for another extended trip to the United States. It was to further distance him from the *Yishuv.* This time he was partly subsidized by the French Jewish Colonizing Association, "to study the best agricultural methods practised in California, Texas, and Florida." While visiting his friends Juhan and Jessie Mack at their summer camp in the Adirondacks, he met Ruth, their seventeen-year-old daughter.

Ruth Mack was royalty, the only child of one of the German-American Jewish first families. From a modest mercantile background, Judge Julian Mack became, in the opinion of Judge Learned Hand, "one of the most distinguished judges of his time: incisive, swift, at ease in every subtlety." He was renowned for adjudicating cases of exceptional legal and financial complexity, including the criminal prosecutions of separatist and folk hero Marcus Garvey, Harry M. Daugherty (President Harding's attorney general, who was implicated in the Teapot Dome scandal), and a number of important antitrust suits.

When Ruth met Aaron Aaronsohn she was wise beyond her years —

and slight, vivacious, passionate, funny, and emancipated to boot. She set her cap at Aaron with all the determination her privileges afforded her. "Dear sweet brother," she wrote "Lel" (Alex Aaronsohn, who followed his older brother to the United States):

> I am very disappointed and – don't tell, please – hurt at not having heard from Aaron. I know he's been busy and blue but he has written other letters. And he means so awfully much to me. I don't think I've ever liked and admired any one man or woman as much – it's hard, you know, to find an extremely likeable and admirable person. And I think Aaron is "all things To [*sic*]" – well, not all men perhaps, but to our family in general and to me in particular. Of course you agree!

So did Ruth's parents, who welcomed Aaron, Alex, and eventually Rivka into the family with open arms. Aaron addressed the Macks as "Momsie" and "Popsie" in his many letters and was a frequent house-guest in the Adirondacks. The Macks were well aware that their precocious daughter had a lively attraction to the opposite sex – her letters to Alex have a distinctly flirtatious tone – and, like proper parents of the time, insisted on reading her correspondence with men. "It's so hard to keep on just writing letters and not tell any real thoughts!" Ruth complained to Alex in 1913. Two years later, she wrote, "Oh, my dear, if only I could tell you everything that I want to, instead of writing these silly platitudes! There is so much to say that it's hard to say anything at all, don't you think?"

For his part, Aaron appreciated pretty girls – to the point of noting any attractive hotel maids in his diaries – but clearly Ruth's tender age and status gave him pause. She was not only a highly desirable young woman but offered the potential of a union that would put him on an equal footing with the Schiffs and Warburgs. He exercised unusual restraint, and possibly a certain amount of calculation. His letters to her are those of a loving older brother. Hers, both to and about him, imply a good deal more. "Everyone else seems small and insignificant beside him that I can't really like and enjoy people."

Rather than a royal marriage and what it might bring him in the New Zion, Aaron's sights were on the coming war and how it might help him set his stamp on Palestine. In 1913 he returned home, no doubt thanking his lucky stars that he had not seduced Ruth Mack. Lawrence and Woolley were completing their explorations of the Wilderness of Zin. Although there is no record that Aaron met Lawrence at that time, the two were dreaming along parallel lines, one for Jewish independence and one for Arab independence.

In early 1914, another member of German-American Jewish royalty came to visit Aaron at Zichron Ya'akov. His guest was none other than Henry Morgenthau, who had put his considerable fortune behind Woodrow Wilson's presidential campaign in 1912 and accepted the prize post of ambassador to Turkey in 1914. (Morgenthau protested for some time before accepting the post that the Turkish ambassadorship was the only diplomatic post to which a Jew could aspire, owing to the interest of American Jews in the welfare of the Jews of Palestine; however, the post was increasingly influential because of America's oil interests.) Rabbi Stephen Wise had met Aaron in America and arranged for Morgenthau to visit the now-fabled agronomist as the climax of Morgenthau's first trip to Palestine.

The two men hit it off immediately, according to Morgenthau's son's memoir. Morgenthau, an archassimilationist, even started using Yiddish in his letters home: "Such a *jontefdick* [holidaylike] dinner I have not had in a long time . . . I have never in my life seen Jewish men and girls look as fine, robust, honest, self-reliant and independent as these people did. They showed the result of honest toil and open air; and the way they danced, the decency thereof, puts to shame the gilded youth of America."

On the same visit, Morgenthau had a "very long conference with some of the leaders of the colony," who told him "they might eventually have to drive out the Arabs." Morgenthau equivocated on this subject, "one of the most troublesome questions in connection with the development of Palestine," but it is clear that even at this early entry point, Morgenthau and the United States were nowhere near as neutral as the Wilson doctrine was to suggest.

Six months later, according to documents in the U.S. State Department petroleum files, Morgenthau, who had strong connections to Standard Oil through James Stillman (president of Rockefeller-controlled National City Bank of New York, a Rockefeller family member, and a member of Morgenthau's board of directors), was instructed by the State Department upon the advice of Standard Oil to "interpellate" [*sic*] the Turkish government on the subject of a proposed government petroleum monopoly: "Establishment of a petroleum monopoly would very adversely affect the interests of this company in the entire Ottoman Empire and doubtless other American interests would be similarly affected."

Poor, unlucky Colby Chester had been sidelined once again. Faced with a common threat, the British and Germans had united to form the Turkish Petroleum Company in 1912 and compelled the Young Turks to recognize all the rights Abdul Hamid had withheld. This last Anglo-German joint diplomatic effort was settled by 1914, and cut Chester, and America, out of the competition.

Morgenthau presumably carried out his instructions, which were to urge that the monopoly not be consummated "without full opportunity being first accorded the United States Government for examination and diplomatic discussion." This diplomacy, however, was soon to be carried out by other means. Almost immediately upon shaking hands on the Turkish Petroleum Company, the British tried to force the Germans out of the company and vice versa. This and all other Anglo-German business disagreements smoldered until August 1914, when they ignited in World War I – a conflagration that, ironically, would end with the United States in a position of unprecedented power. Aaron, Ruth, Sarah, Lawrence, and indeed their entire generation, who had been flirting with destiny up to that point, would find themselves rushing toward it, into the furnace that was engulfing the world – and in which flirtations, harmless and otherwise, along with personal alliances and archaeological extravagance and even the higher aims of science would soon be lost.

5.

The Locust Hunter

The years from 1910 to 1914, though marked with triumphs for Aaron, were not happy ones for Sarah. In 1912, Malkah Aaronsohn, age sixty, died the "death of kissing." According to Felix Frankfurter's unfinished biography of Aaron, the "death of kissing" refers to euthanasia and is attributed in the Midrash to Moses, "over whom no angel of death would have power, whose soul the Lord gently took from him by a divine kiss." Malkah, in the words of her son Alex, had the gift of prophecy and foresaw the clouds of world war gathering. Her father had died of torture in a Romanian pogrom, and it is possible that what she foresaw was a new terror in her adopted homeland: "Her great heart, full of tender love and yearning, suddenly stopped beating." The family record is silent as to whether her despair drove her to suicide, a death abhorrent to pious Jews and one for which euthanasia might have been a euphemism. Sarah, twenty-two years old and already considered overripe for marriage, was called on to take Malkah's place as the keeper of the hearth.

Increasingly unhappy, Sarah looked for liberation. Every day she was confronted with the spectacle of her former lover, Absa, paying court to her little sister. According to Jewish tradition, Rivka, the younger sister, could not marry before Sarah, the older. Family legend recounts that Sarah married a wealthy, traditional Jewish merchant of Turkish descent and German education to clear the way for Absa and Rivka. The facts are somewhat different. Haim Abrahim, her husband, was a close friend to Aaron, who had apparently arranged the match. Abrahim had many high-level German commercial connections and traveled to Germany frequently on business. Sarah was eager to leave Palestine. In March of 1914, she went to live with Abrahim in Constantinople.

The marriage was not a happy one. From being head of the Aaronsohn household, she was demoted to the ménage of her inlaws, over whom she had no particular authority. Her independent ways were subject to constant correction by her rigid, Germanic husband. She wrote constantly, bemoaning her sad fate, to Absa, who, from the vantage of hindsight, realized that Sarah, not Rivka, was the woman he loved – and wooed her safely from a distance.

A mystery is here. If, as Felix Frankfurter suggested in his 1939 manuscript – written after the 1936 annexation of Austria by Hitler – Aaron had observed the German expansion eastward with deep misgivings and warned his friends in the United States about its relentless imperial drive, why did he marry his most cherished sister to a man whose deepest sympathies lay with the Kaiser?

In the light of the strategies that preceded the guns of August 1914, Sarah's move to Constantinople was opportune in more ways than one. For ten centuries Russia had lusted after Constantinople, the Black Sea exit it rechristened Czargrad, and for the year-round warm-water portage afforded by the Dardanelles. Although Britain had been Turkey's protector for the past hundred years, in 1914 a young First Sea Lord, Winston Churchill, turned down Turkey's request for a permanent alliance because of his disdain for the nation, the so-called Sick Man of Europe. In July 1914, Germany, anxious to secure the only ally who could close the Black Sea exit and cut Russia off from Britain and France, and their supply lines, stepped into the void by accepting Turkey's offer for a defensive alliance to become operative in the event of either party going to war with Russia.

The new government established by the Young Turks, who now styled themselves the Committee of Union and Progress, was determined to recover the pan-Islamic empire of Ottoman glory and believed neutrality offered the best chance of achieving this. There was, however, considerable division among the leadership of the committee. Enver, the handsome war minister and the Young Turks' romantic hero, saw Germany as the wave of the future. Talaat, the committee's political boss and its real ruler, believed that Turkey would become no more than a German vassal if the Central Powers won. Although Talaat, a profound realist, believed that Turkey would also lose its possessions if the Entente Powers – France, England, and Russia – won, still others within the Turkish government preferred an Entente alliance if Russia could be bought off. The third of the Young Turkish proconsuls, Djemal Pasha, counted himself in this camp, but he was also a warlord whose loyalties were for sale to the highest bidder.

In the eyes of the American ambassador, Henry Morgenthau, who had the dubious pleasure of shaking his hand, Djemal was the very image of a wicked fairy-tale vizier: "His eyes were black and piercing; their sharpness, the rapidity with which they darted from one object to another, taking in apparently everything with a few lightning-like glances, signalized cunning, remorselessness, and selfishness to an extreme degree. Even his laugh, which disclosed all his white teeth, was unpleasant and animal-like . . . He was undersized, stumpy, and somewhat stoop-shouldered; as soon as he began to move, however, it was evident that his body was full of energy. Whenever he shook your hand, gripping you with a vise-like grip and looking at you with those roving, penetrating eyes, the man's personal force became impressive."

Djemal Pasha was no primitive, but a highly sophisticated political opportunist whose memoir is a cynic's model of self-serving revisionism. From humble beginnings, he had risen to the position of military governor of Constantinople, in which assassination and juridical murder were his chief duties. Through a reign of terror remarkable and chilling for its efficiency, he achieved a cabinet position as marine minister, from which vantage he attempted to manipulate the fortunes of war.

Two days before the British War Cabinet dispatched its legendarily terse telegram, "War, Germany, act," to the army chief of staff in the early hours of August 5, 1914, the German Admiralty had wired its own instruction to its commander in the Mediterranean, Admiral Wilhelm Souchon: "Alliance with Turkey concluded August 3. Proceed at once to Constantinople."

Souchon's command consisted of two fast new battle cruisers, the *Goeben* and the *Breslau*. Both the British and the French admiralties were convinced that Germany's only two battleships in the Mediterranean constituted the chief menace to the French troop transports from North Africa that would decide the opening engagements of the war. On August 3, after Souchon heard on his radio that war had been declared on France, he headed for the Algerian coast and opened fire on the ports of Philippeville and Bône, under the guise of a Russian flag. He then broke for Constantinople. Under the impression that Souchon's two ships were continuing west and not east, two British dreadnoughts, the *Indomitable* and the *Indefatiguable*, chased the *Goeben* and the *Breslau* back into the Adriatic. A third British battleship, the *Gloucester*, engaged the *Breslau* as the two ships ran the gauntlet for the entrance to the Dardanelles, but could not hold them. Incredibly, Churchill had totally misread Souchon's real intent, which was to compel the Turks, by force if need be, to spread the war against their ancient enemy, Russia, into the Black Sea.

On August 6, with the German assault on Liege, the center of railroad and communications networks between Belgium and Germany, Europe entered what Helmuth von Moltke called "the struggle that will decide the course of history for the next hundred years." The First World War had begun. When Souchon, after much maneuvering, finally obtained permission from Enver Pasha on August 10 to let his ships through the heavy mines that had been laid in the Dardanelles, Turkish neutrality was effectively violated. Long after the fact, Churchill acknowledged his mistake in not securing an early alliance between Britain and Turkey, for the *Goeben* and the *Breslau* brought with them, as he wrote in his history of the war, "more slaughter, more misery and more ruin than has ever before been borne in the compass of a ship." Disguised as a sale to the Turkish government and rechristened with Turkish names, the two German dreadnoughts entered the Black Sea in October and shelled the Russian ports of Odessa, Sevastopol, and Feodosia. Only Djemal Pasha, in his capacity as marine minister, opposed Turkey facilitating Germany's ruse, though for his own reasons.

On November 4, Russia declared war on Turkey, followed by Britain and France the next day. Not only was Turkey, which at that time covered most of what we now call the Middle East, drawn into the war as Germany had desired, but it also drew in its neighbors, Bulgaria, Greece, Romania, and Italy; thereafter, in the words of historian

Barbara Tuchman, "The red edges of war spread over another half of the world." (Tuchman deserves her own voice in this narrative. She was related to the Warburgs by marriage, and was Henry Morgenthau's niece.)

Even as Britain went to war with Turkey, it sought to divide and conquer. Immediately following the pursuit of the *Goeben* and the *Breslau*, Sir Louis Mallet, then British ambassador to Constantinople, privately advised his government to draw off its fleet and assure the Turks that Britain did not intend to treat them harshly. Djemal Pasha received these assurances and adjusted them to his own interests – the overthrow of his cohorts, Talaat and Enver.

Through her window in Constantinople, barred in harem fashion though it was, Sarah was uniquely positioned to report back on all these interesting events. She did so with infinite resourcefulness in coded letters home, writing in French, the family language, and concealing news of the first Armenian massacres under the stamps.

A few months later, Aaron sent Rivka to Beirut to maintain close contact with the American consul there, and Alex made his way to British headquarters in Cairo. The Aaronsohns were busy transforming themselves into the true cosmopolitans they envisioned themselves to be – and getting as far from the shtetl as they could. Like the Rothschilds a century earlier when they had fanned out across Europe to gain control of the banking world, the Aaronsohns were now rising to prominence in the emerging world of intelligence. For Sarah, this difficult and dangerous work provided a status independent of social mores and a challenge to her mettle. For Aaron, whose search for a patron for Palestine had turned, over the summer, into a far more urgent search for a protector, it was the new coin of the realm. Despite the rarefied accomplishments of their highly educated recruits, all of the intelligence services were soon to find themselves in desperate need of the encyclopedic practical information he could best furnish them, and disposed to make any kind of deal in order to get it With a wealth of knowledge at his fingertips, Aaron found himself in a position where, with luck and daring, he might not only declare independence from the Rothschilds but, in terms of influence, be considered their equal.

.-. .-. .-.

Early in 1915, David Fairchild, still working at the United States Department of Agriculture, received a telegram from Aaron that, he drily noted, was "our first intimation of trouble." In his telegram, Aaron begged Fairchild to help him prevent the Turkish forces from destroying his enterprise at Athlit. Fairchild, who had been in constant communication with Aaron regarding his scientific work, obligingly consulted Paul Warburg (Otto's cousin) of the Federal Reserve. Warburg in turn persuaded the State Department to dispatch Admiral Decker, commander of the American fleet in the eastern Mediterranean, to rescue "Aaron Aaronsohn, a collaborator of the United States Department of Agriculture, and his valuable collections." But after putting so many high-ranking officials to so much trouble, Aaron, refusing to come onboard Admiral Decker's man-of-war, inexplicably rejected the assistance he himself had solicited. Fairchild was mystified, the more so when he did not hear from Aaron for many months.

Instead of choosing to be rescued from the Turks, on February 18, 1915, Aaron wrote to "His Excellency Djemal Pasha, Marine Minister and Commander of the 4th Army" on the recommendation of the Reverend Dr. Otis Glazebrook, the American consul at Jerusalem. Introducing himself, his scientific explorations, and his American contacts, Aaron brazenly solicited the favor of an interview. He had more than one reason for his actions. He hoped, intermittently, to come to terms with the Turks — perhaps, even, that the Turkish desire for neutrality would align with the official position of the United States, a goal his friend Henry Morgenthau was actively pursuing. That hope had been badly shaken when, in December 1914, the Ottoman governor of Jaffa, a bitter anti-Zionist named Beha ad Din, brutally expelled the Russian Jewish population. At that point, Aaron, Absa, and Alex formed their vigilante organization, the Gideonites, and reorganized the Jewish Agricultural Experiment Station into a station for espionage operations against the Turks in Palestine. Thus was born the spy ring NILI (a Hebrew acronym taken from Samuel 15:29: *Nezah Ysrael Lo Yeshakker*, meaning "the strength of Israel shall not lie"), which would garner both acclaim and controversy during the war. Aaron the scientist, by his own admission, became Jasoos the spy, with Djemal Pasha himself a prime target of his observations.

Aaron, though an egotist, was not driven by selfish motives. His life had become entirely focused on his impetuous desire to secure the best deal for Palestine: nothing less than the emancipation of the *Yishuv* under the benign rule of a Great Power would satisfy that desire. Trusting nothing but his own genius, Aaron was profoundly autocratic and almost childishly confident of his ability to manipulate others to reach his goal. In Djemal Pasha he met his match, but Djemal, with no altruistic motives to recommend him, was one of the unsung villains of World War I.

Shortly after his self-serving objection to the Turks' purchase of the *Goeben* and the *Breslau,* the former marine minister was exiled to the provinces by Talaat and Enver, who feared his unpredictable temperament and were not unaware of his duplicity. They could not afford to demote him because he enjoyed the allegiance of the security forces. His new position as military governor of Syria and Palestine and commander of the Fourth Ottoman Army in Egypt gave him considerable power; and he played a lone hand in ruling an area today comprising Syria, Lebanon, Israel, and Jordan as his personal fiefdom. He ardently espoused the cause of the Jews in Palestine, to whom he referred as "our Ottoman brothers," and was the only one of the Young Turk proconsuls to distance himself from the Armenian massacre that took place in 1915.

However, this was not because Djemal Pasha had discovered within himself a concern for human rights, but because he wished to keep open a back door to the Allied powers. Throughout 1915 and 1916, under the aegis of Prime Minister Herbert Asquith and his Foreign Secretary, Sir Edward Grey, the British Foreign Office put out feelers through its ambassador, Sir Louis Mallet, and others for a separate peace with Turkey, motivated by the desire to isolate Germany militarily but also, it may be conjectured, to preserve good relations with the geopolitical entity that controlled the future of oil. Djemal, who hoped to snatch the Sultan's turban as his share of the spoils, had many contacts with Grey.

By 1914, the Ottoman Empire was a carcass ripe for the picking, and all of the Great Powers were circling like buzzards. Djemal's piercing gaze was focused on finding the most suitable patron among them. Aaron was hunting for a suitable patron for Palestine. The question of who offered the most advantageous alliance was by no means clear for the Palestinian Jews in 1915. Headquartered in Berlin, the Zionist leadership had strong attachments to Germany and expressed loyalty to the Ottoman Empire. The United States was still neutral, and in many quarters sympathetic to Germany. The U.S. ambassador to Turkey, Henry Morgenthau, was, in the words of Sir Cecil Spring-Rice, British ambassador to the United States, "undoubtedly closely connected with Germans in the United States and has some influence in the White House as he organized the financial side of the Presidential campaign." When the Armenian massacres began in Turkey, Morgenthau worked closely with his German counterpart in Constantinople, Hans von Wangenheim, to help the victims. Worldwide outrage against the massacres was fanned by such propaganda efforts as Liberal statesman and jurist Lord James Bryce's 1916 report, which damned Talaat and Enver's government to further the British objective of dismembering the Ottoman Empire as expeditiously as possible. This caused the first of many breaches between the Turks and the Germans. The Germans tried to distance themselves as best they could – not least because the loyal Zionist leadership in Berlin feared the Jews of Palestine might be next. Morgenthau, although American, became a go-between for the Asquith government, a position that, if successful, might have paid off in the most coveted ambassadorial honor, an appointment to the Court of St. James.

Great Britain offered increasingly rosy prospects for the benign rule Aaron sought. In the first months of 1915, Sir Herbert Samuel, a pillar of Anglo-Jewish society, confided to Foreign Secretary Edward Grey his conviction that Britain "ought to play a considerable part in the formation of such a [Jewish] state, because the geographical situation of Palestine, and especially its proximity to Egypt, would render its goodwill to England a matter of importance to the British Empire." He embroidered this thesis in a memo that would become famous, advising that Britain annex Palestine to the Empire.

Grey was reluctant to thus partition Turkey on the grounds that it would play into Russia's plans for expanding its territories, provoke France into demanding its share of the spoils, and set off a territorial gold rush among the Entente Powers. But the weakness in his argument was Germany, which, as Grey told the War Council on March 10, 1915, was eager to isolate England by concluding a separate peace with

Russia and France – thus preparing the way through Turkey for a strike at the Empire's jugular, the Suez Canal.

Field Marshal Kitchener reasoned that with Alexandretta, Mesopotamia, and the all-important Baghdad Railway under British rule, the Suez Canal, Egypt, and, most important, India would be safe. (Alexandretta, on the southern Mediterranean coast of modern Turkey, was considered a major troop-landing site, for it was the junction for the Hedjaz railway and the Anatolian railway systems.)

He was backed in his desire to invade Turkey by the Admiralty, notably Churchill, who was itching, as he announced to the War Cabinet, to "make a clean sweep" of the "inefficient and out-of-date Turkish nation, which has long misruled one of the most fertile countries in the world."

General Edmund Barrow, Military Secretary of the India Office, opposed Kitchener and Churchill. Such an acquisition campaign, he argued, would set Britain on a collision course with its allies and mire her in "enormous and unprofitable expenditure" for generations to come. He was seconded in his misgivings by Prime Minister Herbert Asquith, in words that appear prophetic today: "Taking on Mesopotamia . . . means spending millions in irrigation and development with no immediate or early return; keeping up quite a large army white & colored in an unfamiliar country; tackling every kind of tangled administrative question, worse than we ever had in India with a hornet's nest of Arab tribes."

Barrow recommended that Britain champion Islam and support Turkey as an Asiatic buffer state against Russian incursions. At the same time, Britain could consolidate its oriental empire by maintaining control over Mesopotamia and Egypt. Barrow's view of Palestine as an indispensable geopolitical link between Mesopotamia and Egypt remained a staple in British strategic doctrine until the country's final withdrawal from India and Palestine in 1948.

To reach Britain, Aaron had to pay toll to Djemal Pasha. When Aaron first approached him in February 1915, the satrap had nearly succeeded in taking control of the Suez Canal, Britain's passage to India. Twenty thousand Turkish soldiers had crossed the supposedly waterless Sinai

Desert in six days, dragging heavy artillery and pontoons to be used in crossing the Canal. Djemal's Fourth Army made it all the way to the Canal and even launched a pontoon across it, then was routed in a hail of Maxim gunfire in a surprise counterattack by the British. "Just what took place in the attack is known to very few," noted Aaron's brother Alex, commissioned by the American magazine *Atlantic Monthly* to stir hearts and minds. Rumors circulated that Djemal Pasha had been bought by the British, and that the defeat at Suez had been planned by him. In any case, he was able to beat it back to Beersheba with his main force intact. "It is not clear why it was allowed to escape," wrote John Buchan, the author of *The Thirty-Nine Steps,* who was then working as director of information for the British Ministry of Defense, in his 1922 official chronicle of the war. "With 130 waterless miles to cover, there seemed no reason why a beaten and dispirited force should ever have succeeded in reaching Beersheba." The secret of their rapid advance – and equally rapid retreat – was a series of wells which Djemal had sunk in the desert on a line from Beersheba to the Canal.

In March 1915, Churchill spurred the Allies to launch a campaign to gain control of the Dardanelles, capture Constantinople, and establish contact with the Russians through the Black Sea: the aforementioned invasion of Turkey, by way of Gallipoli. Thousands of Allied soldiers were slaughtered in what became one of the worst military and political debacles of the war. Sarah's loveless marriage enabled her to report in her coded letters on Churchill's next epic blunder, the disastrous British campaign on the Gallipoli Peninsula in the following months, which resulted in the deaths of thousands of British and Australian soldiers.

In March, the British in Egypt also used commanding officer J. W. Oman of the *USS Carolina* (the American battleship that in June 1915 carried Alex and Rivka to safety in New York, where they could be of help raising funds for Palestine) to sound out Djemal Pasha on a peace pact, hinting strongly at a partition of the Ottoman Empire that would enthrone him as king of an independent Syria. Later that month, the Turkish government reversed its Jewish policy and instructed its satraps to seek the cooperation of the Jews, but gave no guarantees that the Jews would escape the Armenians' fate.

The idea of a Judeo-Turkish alliance was by no means new to the

Foreign Office. In the British Embassy in Constantinople before the war, it was commonly believed that the Young Turk movement originated in the Jewish community of Salonika, and that Jews had shaped it, even as an instrument of terror. That belief led straight back to the financial capitals of Europe, i.e., to the Rothschilds – hence John Buchan's pugnacious assertion that the war itself was created by Jewish capitalists for their own anarchic reasons. However, by early 1916, British diplomats like Hugh O'Beirne and Gerald Fitzmaurice began to believe that if the Jews were offered an appealing deal for Palestine, they would withdraw their support from the fractious Young Turk government – and thus cause its collapse.

In May 1915, Djemal Pasha sent Armenian intermediaries to neutral Copenhagen and Stockholm to make contact with British agents with a modest proposal that his role be expanded to that of Sultan over a caliphate composed of Syria, Palestine, Mesopotamia, and Arabia. In return, he announced his willingness to cede autonomy to an Armenian state governed by a Christian prince with European advisors – and to forever renounce Constantinople and the Straits. He further announced his willingness to turn the Turkish Fourth Army against his rivals, Talaat and Enver, and send it to march on Constantinople reinforced by British troops from Egypt. The Foreign Office was entranced.

Shortly after Djemal's return from Egypt, in the early summer of 1915, Syria was visited by a plague of locusts that recalled the scourges of biblical times. The sky turned black with the dreaded insects, which, after forty years' absence, were flying north from Sudan to lay their eggs. The ground was covered with the heavy bodies of the females, burrowing into the soil to deposit their egg packets that, if hatched, would destroy every crop. In July, to avert a catastrophic famine that would overwhelm soldiers and civilians alike, Djemal summoned Aaron to Damascus and entrusted him with saving Northern Palestine, the breadbasket of Syria. Although the threat was real enough, locust hunting was a convenient and thus common cover for intelligence gathering; at times, in the history of the Middle East, it has seemed that there were more locust hunters than there were locusts.

.–•. .•–. .•–.

The locust campaign took more than two months. Aaron was given an office in Damascus, under Djemal Pasha's nose if not his thumb. He had direct access to the highest military and civil authorities in Palestine, Syria, and Lebanon, and even to the Porte, the Ottoman court at Constantinople. Galvanized by the threat of a large and starving army, Djemal issued a military order giving Aaron's dispatches priority over those by ordinary government officials. Aaron had the power to mobilize companies and battalions against the insect foe, and to recruit anyone necessary to assure success. Thousands of Arab troops were put at his disposal, and he set them to digging trenches, into which the hatching locusts were driven and destroyed before they got their wings.

The two autocrats enjoyed a testy relationship. Aaron complained to Djemal Pasha's face about his lazy and inefficient agricultural policies. Djemal cordially threatened to have him hanged. Aaron, according to Alex, invited him to try it. "The weight of my heavy body will crack the wood [scaffold] so loudly that the sound of it will be heard in America."

Bluffing aside, both Aaron and Djemal played their cards carefully. Changes in Constantinople reflected a disintegrating Ottoman Empire and the increasing power of Djemal's enemies, Talaat and Enver. Germany's position was weakened by the increasingly vitriolic disputes between its envoy, Baron von Wangenheim; General Liman von Sanders; and the German Foreign Office. At the same time, intelligence circles in Damascus were electrified by news of a plot to unseat the Ottomans.

In the autumn of 1915, while Aaron was still residing in Damascus, a mysterious young Arab named Mohammed al-Faruqi emerged from obscurity to maneuver the British into promising support for Arab independence in the Middle East. To this day, not much is known about al-Faruqi's background or affiliations. He claimed to be a member of a secret society of Arab-speaking Ottoman army officers called al-Ahd ("The First," or, as it later became known, "The Covenant"), which formed in protest over the Young Turks' preferential advancement of Turkish-speaking officers and grew to a potential insurrection in the ranks. Al-Faruqi was stationed in Damascus early in 1915, when Emir Feisal, son of Sharif Hussein of Mecca and later the close companion of Lawrence of Arabia, stopped there on the first of several visits. The reason for Feisal's visit was to test support among the plethora of anti-Ottoman Arab secret societies embedded in Damascus for his father's plans to incorporate the majority of Arab Asia as an independent kingdom under his rule – plans very similar to those Djemal Pasha was harboring. Hussein had discovered that the Young Turkish government was planning to depose him after the war. The discovery prompted him to consider opposing Turkey in the war, though he feared such a betrayal might isolate him within the Arab world.

Hearsay suggests the secret societies were disposed to set up a bidding competition between Britain and Turkey for Arab loyalties. They advised Feisal to counsel his father not to join the Allies unless Britain pledged to support his bid for independence. With such a pledge in hand, they could nudge the Ottoman government to match it. However, Djemal Pasha beat them to it. Scenting a plot, he crushed the secret societies, arrested their leaders, and sent the three divisions under their command to almost certain death on the Gallipoli Peninsula, where their blood would mingle with that of Churchill's troops. He then initiated his own bidding war, offering to deliver an insurrection of Arab officers to Britain if it would guarantee him the Sultan's throne.

Al-Faruqi had been one of the young officers marched off to die at Gallipoli. He deserted instead and crossed over to Allied lines in autumn 1915. Claiming to have important information for British intelligence, he was promptly sent to Egypt for interrogation by military officers and the germ of what was to become the Arab Bureau, that league of nation-building archaeologists, lepidopterists, unicorn hunters, and other Oxbridge gentlemen that included T. E. Lawrence and his mentor, D. G. Hogarth. He told them what he had heard from the remnant of conspirators who remained in Damascus, of their plan to support Hussein in an "Arab revolt" against the Ottoman Empire should Britain support the Damascus Protocol, their program for Arab independence. If Britain did not support them, the Arab movement would throw all its weight behind Germany and the Ottoman Empire.

Britain, which had derisively dismissed previous overtures from Hussein, now entertained them, with the idea that the Arabs, far from being independent, would be proxies for British rule. These overtures became the basis for Kitchener's plans to incite a "revolt in the desert," famous for its association with Lawrence of Arabia. The so-called Arab Revolt was meant to divide the Ottoman Empire and deter any Pan-Islamic rally to the cause of Germany, Turkey's ally. Kitchener also saw it as a means to bring the Baghdad Railway under British control — not only securing India but placing the India Office at Simla under the thumb of his own agency, which was to become the Arab Bureau in Cairo.

Meanwhile, Djemal Pasha's promised insurrection was heavily, if secretly, encouraged by British Foreign Secretary Sir Edward Grey. Soon after al-Faruqi's desertion from the Turkish lines at Gallipoli, the Mediterranean group of the British Secret Service began to transmit reports of high-level defections among Arab officers in the Turkish army, and even in the High Command. Russian intelligence, aware of the movement, was anxious to exploit it. On December 29, 1915, the Russian Foreign Minister, Sergei Sazanov, wired Grey: "We learn from Armenian circles at Constantinople that Jamal [*sic*] Pasha would be prepared to lead an open rebellion against the Turkish government and the Germans provided the Allies accept the following terms."

These terms were to guarantee the independence and integrity of Turkey in Asia. Included were the autonomous provinces of Syria, Palestine, Mesopotamia, central Arabia, Yemen, Armenia, Cilicia (that region of southeast Turkey formerly known as Little Armenia, into which the Kurds moved in force once the last of the Armenians emigrated), and Kurdistan, under Djemal Pasha's sovereignty. If the Allies accepted the terms, Djemal would guarantee the downfall of the Young Turks and the dethronement of the Sultan, and would launch a campaign against them that would ensure the Allies' entry into Constantinople with arms and supplies. Sergei Sazanov concluded: "Even in the event of Jamal's failure to overthrow the Government and dethrone the Sultan, any internal disturbance in Turkey would serve to weaken her and thus serve our common purpose, and it would therefore be desirable to enter into secret negotiations with Jamal through trusted Armenian agents."

The next day, Count Benckendorff, the Russian ambassador to England, called at the Foreign Office in London to ask Grey what he thought about encouraging Djemal's revolt. Grey allegedly replied that he "did not think very much would come of it, but we wish to encourage it for all it was worth." However, in a secret memo to the War Department, Grey was much more explicit in suggesting Djemal Pasha's overtures offered a unique opportunity to double-cross the French, who had staked out a claim to Syria (which at that time included Palestine) and Cilicia in an earlier agreement with Russia. The Russians, he wrote, should be encouraged to negotiate with Djemal Pasha and assured that the British would not let their own claims stand in the way of such negotiations. However, Grey cautioned that his government had already offered to support Arab claims to Arabia and "some adjoining districts in the south" if the Arabs broke with the Turkish government, and was thus obliged to honor its promises (this disclaimer could refer equally to promises made to King Hussein of Mecca and to Ibn Saud of Riyadh). Once the war was safely won and European alliances no longer essential, everything would be up for grabs; or rather, in Grey's more diplomatic phrasing: "In discussions with the Arabs we have carefully abstained from any discussions on or giving any opinion in regard to the Caliphate, which we consider is a matter exclusively for Moslems to settle among themselves."

France, a colonial presence since the Crusades, understood perfectly well that whoever put the Caliphate in power would control it after the war. A vitriolic protest from the French Foreign Ministry reminded its erstwhile allies in London and St. Petersburg that Syria and Cilicia should be auctioned off, not to Djemal Pasha but to France. Meanwhile, Djemal Pasha's demands became increasingly insatiable, and further negotiation with the tyrant was effectively scuttled. Count Sazenov, red in the face, insisted that Russia had no intention of cheating a faithful comrade-in-arms, i.e., France, and had never taken Djemal Pasha seriously; but the French continued to blame Grey for attempting to sideswipe them. In an attempt to keep France in the increasingly shaky alliance that formed the Entente, negotiations for what became known as the Sykes-Picot Agreement commenced soon thereafter. Needless to say, the boundaries marked by Djemal Pasha conflicted with both those the British promised to the French and those they promised to the Arab nationalist leader Sharif Hussein of Mecca. The seeds of disaster at the Paris Peace Conference were already sown.

.•. .•. .•.

At the same time that al Faruqi went over to the Allies, Aaron was plotting his own escape from Damascus. In October, he sent Absa Feinberg to Egypt to make contact with British military intelligence. Leonard Woolley, in charge of what would later be called "hum-int" (human intelligence, as opposed to "sig-int," or signal intelligence) and counterintelligence for the Arab Bureau, had scented unreliability in Alex. Absa made a more convincing presentation. At Port Said, where Woolley was headquartered, the two shook hands on a perilous bargain. NILI was to remain small and carefully concealed – gathering intelligence for the British, who would monitor their activity via the *Zaida,* a motorized yacht volunteered for service to the Crown by its owner, Archibald Primrose, the Earl of Rosebery, and which was already in touch with Arab spy rings at Haifa and Tyre. Like Sir Henry MacMahon and Sir Mark Sykes, Woolley left no exact record of his commitments behind – and Absa, in a long letter to Henrietta Szold that is the only surviving documentation of this meeting, was also careful not to pin himself down. But in Aaron's mind, the only compensation for the extreme danger to Sarah in organizing what amounted to a Jewish insurgency against the Turks was an independent Palestine. The British were well aware of their leverage, and it may be presumed that the promises Woolley made to Absa strongly resembled the British promises to Sharif Hussein of Mecca if not to Djemal Pasha himself.

For all that it would prove catastrophic, the war was a form of liberation for Sarah. It gave her a perfect excuse to leave her stultifying marriage and rush back to Palestine in November 1915. She became openly involved in political activity and resumed her affair with Absa Feinberg, whom the British had returned to Athlit on the *Zaida.* Aaron met Sarah's train at Afullah in north-central Palestine (still the train hub for modern Israel and a prime target for Hezbollah rockets in the most recent war with Lebanon) and urged her to write up her outrage at the Armenian dead and refugees she had witnessed during her journey in a report which could be used for future barter with interested powers – whether British or German or even American was as yet unclear, even to him.

Throughout the winter of 1915, Aaron became increasingly concerned with conditions in Palestine. The British blockade had bitten deep, and on his locust-hunting forays he savagely noted the first signs of famine in an agricultural country where there was no reason to starve. In order to provision his Fourth Army, Djemal Pasha commandeered the lion's share of available foodstuffs. Typhoid fever, dysentery, and malaria, the disease Aaron had almost succeeded in stamping out, were claiming thousands of victims, and otherwise healthy men were entering hospitals where there were few doctors and no medicine, to die of hunger.

The journey he planned was a difficult and a dangerous one, but he had no choice. Wandering by moonlight in the wasted vineyards of Rosh-Pinna where he had gathered his first sprigs of *Triticum diccocoides* in 1906, Aaron mourned what he feared was the death of his dream for Palestine. His fields had been pillaged to feed Djemal Pasha's army, his forests cut down to make ties for the Turkish railroad. Though he found room in his heart to pity the "poor devils" of Turkish conscripts thus exposed to attack from the air, it was the land's desolation that grieved him most.

Leaving Sarah behind was perhaps the most difficult decision he had to make, but she was the only person he trusted to help him, even in his own family. She would remain at Athlit as his chief of operations and his proxy in their chief mission: rousing the *Yishuv* to an anti-Turk insurgency planned to synchronize with an Allied invasion. Absa would be her lieutenant in the north, and Naaman Belkind and Yussuf Lishansky would cover operations in the south, while Aaron went to England to persuade the British to send them arms and money.

In the community of Haifa, six people had already died of hunger before winter set in. "Winter promises to be very hard indeed for the poor people, and nowadays, who isn't poor!" Aaron wrote in his diary. In the beginning of 1916, Djemal attacked the Anglo-Palestine Company, which had become the bank for Jewish settlers and a large part of the Arab population as well, forcing it to liquidate its business in Palestine and to shut down all its branches. With no money and food scarce after the locust plague, the misery of the masses increased day by day. Malaria appeared on the heels of famine, followed by typhus, cholera, and smallpox. The Turkish army pillaged the countryside for supplies and conscripts, and to discourage social unrest through terror. The strategy was effective. Even the hotheads of Hashomer rebuffed Sarah's initial overtures to join the insurgency, and she was forced to recruit among a handful of family connections.

On the roads, Aaron saw those healthy enough to work at hard labor, building a strategic road from Damascus to Jerusalem. Djemal Pasha had ordered that the civil and military authorities' lives would be forfeit if their sections were not completed on deadline. The Kaimakam or mayor, of Nazareth was ordered to complete the stretch from Nazareth to Afullah, a distance of eight miles, in fifteen days. Old men, women, children, and invalids, Arabs and Jews, were driven to work under the whip. The road was finished in forty days, but the Kaimakam kept his head nonetheless. "Doubtless the Pacha laughs about it to himself," wrote an increasingly cynical Aaron, in his usual erratic spelling. "But the trick was played, and the road finished."

Aaron ranted at such shoddy methods of intimidation, but the money being spent impressed him. Though proximity to Djemal Pasha made him lose optimism that a peaceful accommodation with the Turks could be reached, he still saw opportunities.

> It is evident that cruel exactions have been imposed upon the natives, but it also must be acknowledged that gold has flowed rather freely during the building operations . . . Things have changed lately. Last year nothing was done without the Germans who hoarded substantial fortunes while sacrificing themselves to the cause of their dear Ally. This year it looks as if they were being eliminated. One can feel the influence of Djemal Pacha who does not particularly care for them. Alliance does not necessarily imply Love does it?

It was a question Aaron was to ask himself often during the next phase of his career – his alliance with the British. Overhead, he could see their new airplanes, which increasingly harried the Palestinian coast, raining down deadly *flechettes*, or steel arrows, on the Turkish army and heralding a turn in the fortunes of war. British airplane production had ramped up in the first two years of war, erasing the

Germans' early lead. Aaron viewed the planes with foreboding, if not horror, and reserved his sympathies for the road workers who toiled on, blissfully ignorant of a change in the nature of modern warfare.

Aaron, as Ruth Mack wisely observed, could be all things to all men. Throughout the winter of 1915-16 he suppressed his concern about famine and swilled cognac with the German officer corps, who were at ease with his fair hair and *deutschfreundlich* pronunciation. He listened to their misgivings about their Turkish allies. He noted the numbers of Armenian recruits in the Turkish army and how they belied the atrocity stories being circulated by the Germans. Through the same rumor mill, he learned the whereabouts of British spies such as the Boutaggys (a family of Christian Arabs who worked for Lawrence). He referred to Djemal Pasha as his "friend" and "protector," and defended his despotism with the argument that he got the roads built. Since Aaron was increasingly aware that his diaries might be seen by other eyes than his, this passage is a revealing one:

> Personally I approve of him [Djemal Pasha], as I have always contended that roads are the first means of progress which the Government ought to provide for us. And I can but admire the strength of character of our General in Chief. . . In his place I should be a little frightened. It is well and necessary to make our population appreciate the advantages of war – a slight compensation for their many sacrifices. It is certainly a duty to uphold the Government's prestige and awaken new enthusiasms. But I should be rather worried at the thought that Rosch-Pinah is only sixty to seventy miles from the coast "as the crow flies" – and that nowadays our foe has wings and can follow the trail of the crow – a bird of ill omen. What a moral defeat if an enemy plane should appear above our holiday fields when we are so poorly equipped! . . . From a psychological standpoint, I should like to know if he trusts to his lucky star, or if his contempt of the enemy makes him fearless.

On November 25, Aaron traveled to Beirut, where he enviously noted the "pleasant signs" of economic animation. Comparing Lebanon's prosperity with Palestine's misery, he felt the stirrings of inadequacy — and a deep-seated transformation began. He confided to his diary, "It is humiliating for an observing man of science to be thus ignorant of War questions which he has always scorned and which, nevertheless, are today of such overwhelming influence in everybody's life."

Aaron did not enjoy being humiliated. In his mind, science now took a backseat to war, and his scientific accomplishments increasingly became the means to a political end. He was expecting a telegram from Washington and rushed to the American consulate, only to find it closed for Thanksgiving. Aaron's diaries do not specify what was in the mysterious telegram, but he seems to have anticipated a summons to America from the United States Department of Agriculture. The Consul's obtuseness made him indignant, as obtuse people always did, and he responded in his diary with the arrogance that would cost him so much when openly expressed: "If I ever return to America and have luncheon again at the White House, I shall tell President Wilson how well we are represented. It is a disgrace for the States. And I shall have to rub it in."

Aaron planned his escape from Djemal Pasha's clutches via Constantinople, "where it would be useful to see our friend Morgenthau before leaving for the States." Knowing that Morgenthau had brokered a deal for Standard Oil to purchase exploration rights in Palestine shortly after meeting with Aaron in 1913, Aaron stressed to the Consul the necessity of having his photographic records, maps, and geological sketches sent clandestinely from the Beirut Consulate to Morgenthau. Morgenthau had spent the greater part of the term of his ambassadorship from 1913 to 1916 "interpellating" for Standard Oil in the Ottoman Empire, and in interceding on behalf of the Armenians who lived on the contested ground. In this he worked closely with Pastor Johannes Lepsius, the head of the German evangelical movement, even supplying him with official records for his reports, which first brought the "starving Armenians" to Western attention.

Though the German-born Morgenthau was known for his ambiguous stance on Zionism, he spent the next phase of his career trying to negotiate a backdoor sale of Palestine by Turkey to the Jews. "The great neutral," the United States, had continued to hang on to its neutrality and continued to assure Turkey of its friendship. In autumn

THE LOCUST HUNTER *99*

1915, Morgenthau revived hopes of a negotiated peace by proposing that Britain and Germany submit sealed copies of their minimum war aims to President Wilson in Washington. Wilson promised to destroy the correspondence to avoid embarrassment to either side. Once more, efforts to negotiate a peace came to naught over competition for Mesopotamia and Egypt, but Morgenthau did not give up. In May 1916, he was indiscreet enough to make this clear in a highly publicized speech in Cincinnati that elicited heated denials from the Turkish Porte. Aaron's future involvement with Morgenthau would put him, and Sarah, in the crosshairs of some very dangerous enemies.

6.

Felix Krull, Confidence Man

O n June 5, 1916, the Arab revolt lost its godfather. The HMS *Hampshire* was hit by a torpedo off the Orkneys and Field Marshal Kitchener, the minister of war, on a mission to Russia, was drowned. Not everyone mourned his loss. C. P. Scott, editor of the *Manchester Guardian* and a champion of Zionism, uncharitably remarked that "as for the old man [Lord Kitchener], he could not have done better than to have gone down, as he was a great impediment lately."

Upon Kitchener's death, Minister for Munitions David Lloyd George replaced him as war minister, and the focus of the War Office shifted from West to East. A hawk and an annexationist, Lloyd George set his sights on "knocking the props," i.e., Turkey, away from Germany, in an effort to make contact with Russia and Romania overland and thus exposing the Central Powers to invasion from the rear while the main German armies were held in France.

Palestine became the hinge of his strategy – the British were now imitating Germany. In February 1915, realizing that annexing the Suez Canal was for now impossible, German military advisors insisted that a good railway connection with Syria and the Sinai Peninsula was the best way to force Britain to an early peace conference. Field Marshal Colmar von der Goltz urged the speediest possible completion of the Baghdad Railway, which had stalled because of the high costs of tunneling through the Taurus and Amanus mountains, so that Germany could threaten the source of Britain's world dominion, India. Based on the campaigns of Alexander the Great and particularly the Persian Nadir Shah, who had conquered India in 1739 in less than three months with only a hundred thousand men, Goltz concluded the costs would be far lower than maintaining a state of constant preparedness in Germany. Britain would be forced to the conference table if Germany only moved closer to it.

Djavid Bey, the Turkish finance minister, was summoned to Berlin to conclude a formal agreement to advance the Turks a subsidy of forty million marks toward the completion of the railway, which the Turks were expected to match or exceed. Djavid, taking a page from Djemal Pasha's playbook, made brazen demands – i.e., that Turkey would only come up with its share if Germany completed tunneling within six months, a near impossibility. He also entered into independent discussions with Italy, not yet at war with the Central Powers, and with unidentified French bankers, to see who could come up with the best postwar deal. The Turks pressed for the appointment of one of their own to collect revenues, with an eye to nationalizing the line after the war. Six months after Djavid signed the subsidy agreements in Berlin, the progress of the railroad remained at a standstill, largely because the bulk of the labor consisted of Armenians who had been deported or executed at the hands of the Young Turks.

Sir Herbert Samuel developed his idea for a "national homeland for the Jews" in early conversations with Lloyd George and Chaim Weizmann, a research chemist from the University of Manchester and a crony of Churchill's from his early career as Manchester Member of Parliament. Churchill plucked Weizmann from his university laboratory to work for him at the Admiralty when Weizmann discovered acetone, a key component in the long-range shells used to break the deadlock in France. Lloyd George's adoption of the Zionist cause was based on sound military strategy. If Field Marshal von der Goltz was going to narrow his focus and contain his costs by striking at India through the Baghdad Railway, Lloyd George would trump his hand and take the land bridge over which the railway must cross – Palestine.

In July 1916, a month after Kitchener's death, Aaron traveled from Damascus to Constantinople with fellow NILI member Liova Schneersohn (a distant relative of the famous Brooklyn *rebbe* Menachem Schneersohn), who passed as his secretary. He traveled under an alias, using the name of a Sephardic Jew, Hayyim Cohen, and carried an *irade* from Djemal that permitted him to travel anywhere in Europe to advance his scientific work. It would seem odd that Djemal could grant this favor given that Turkey was at war with half of Europe, but Djemal was dealing secretly with Germany, England, and Russia.

The effect of Djemal's duplicity on the struggling minorities of the Ottoman Empire was already catastrophic; perhaps to cover his own tracks, in January 1916 Djemal Pasha had shown his government proof that Russia was arming and paying Armenians to start an uprising and thus declared it justifiable to clear the whole region by genocidal means. Like many a modern tyrant, he not only understood but relished media manipulation, and by 1916 he was already approving the use of propaganda films showing Anzac soldiers raping Turkish women. Though Talaat and Enver both feared and loathed him, they could not afford to eliminate him by their usual means because he had perfected the politics of pan-Islamism. The Committee of Unity and Progress leaders were considered by the great mass of Turkish people to be unbelievers who held power only by force. Djemal Pasha, for all his duplicity, had successfully preached in public the doctrine of the unity of Islam and the necessity of maintaining a strong, independent Muslim power. He convinced his constituents that it was his aim and ambition to win back for all Muslims the ancient glory of the Caliphate, and his co-leaders feared that assassinating him might provoke a popular uprising.

There are many inconsistencies in accounts of Aaron's uneasy relationship with Djemal that reflect Aaron's struggle to make profitable alliances. On the one hand, he grew fearful that the wake of the unpredictable tyrant would swamp all his own plans, and he recorded every useful observation made in Djemal's den in Damascus for later deposit in a leather diplomatic pouch kept buried in the cellar of the experiment station at Athlit. On the other hand, he availed himself of Djemal's confidence to travel freely. Given the tangled alliances of the time, it is even possible that Djemal facilitated Aaron's escape to England so that he could act as his emissary to His Majesty's Government.

Before leaving Damascus on July 15, Aaron made two great discoveries: one, a bottle of Schlitz beer, which he noted in his diary as "the beer that made Milwaukee famous" before drinking it with nostalgic relish; the other, the success of a German colleague in distilling lighting oil out of the bituminous limestone of the Yarmuk Valley. This latter process was expensive but seemed essential, the "salvation" of the

Turkish army. It was not only of strategic but also commercial importance. The man of science now embarking on his second, far more
ambiguous career was also collecting opportunities to develop Palestine after the war.

At the German Embassy in Constantinople, Aaron claimed that he
had information on a new type of oil-rich sesame seed that would be of
vital interest to the fuel-starved Reich. He was granted a visa on this
basis, and also learned that Morgenthau had greatly harmed the position of the Grand Rabbi in Constantinople by those indiscreet remarks
he'd made in Cincinnati about the possible sale of Palestine to the Jews.
He left Schneersohn behind to await instructions and in August traveled on alone on the Balkanzug (the Berlin-Constantinople leg of the
Orient Express) to Berlin, where he was warmly received by Otto Warburg and his sponsors in the German scientific community.

The diaries do not record Aaron's visit to Berlin, and it is not clear
what information Aaron passed on to his German colleagues about sesame breeding, but he did make contact with the American rabbi Judah
Leon Magnes, in Berlin on a relief mission at the time and whom Aaron
had met in 1907. Magnes was suspected to be a German agent by both
the British and the American Department of Justice, which conflated
him with an actual German agent named von Magnus. In fact, Magnes
was a Russian Pole who attracted the interest of the British and American security forces because of his work in organizing mass protest
demonstrations against the Russian pogroms and his adherence to a a
form of radical pacifism that opposed the war but embraced the formation of a Jewish defense regiment in Palestine. A master fund-raiser, he
led efforts to subsidize the American Jewish Joint Distribution Committee, which was intended for the relief of war victims, and of which
Aaron was president in Palestine. Magnes arrived in Europe on behalf
of the committee in 1916 with the full cooperation of the German Foreign Office (obtained through the good offices of the Warburgs) and
both military and civil authorities, to alleviate the sufferings of Polish
Jewry. He was met with suspicion by the emerging Zionist leadership
in Europe and by pro-Ally Jewish notables, who took pains to inform
Russian authorities of his forthright attacks on czarist tyranny. Many,
like Chaim Weizmann, were taking advantage of the chaos of war to

realign the politics of world Jewry, and regarded Magnes's opposition to the dismembering of Turkey as anti-Zionist.

In September, following in the footsteps of the Armenian emissaries sent by Djemal Pasha, Aaron moved on to Copenhagen, a popular place for British agents to pick up fresh passports, thus erasing any traces of having been in Egypt or England. Upon his arrival he received a letter from Alex, who was living in New York with Rivka and promoting his new book, *With the Turks in Palestine,* which, culled from his *Atlantic Monthly* series, dramatized the author's exploits as a resistance fighter. Alex urged Aaron to come to the United States without delay for reasons he did not make clear in his letter but, it may be presumed from Alex's contacts, involved Aaron lending his considerable weight to shift the influential Jews who backed his experiment station off their neutral stance toward the war: "We have already cabled to Lord Eustace Percy of the London Foreign Office. The Washington State Department will do all that is necessary to open the way." Lord Eustace Percy worked closely with Lord Northcliffe, the newspaper magnate chiefly responsible for promoting the war, to spread pro-Entente propaganda in the United States. But Aaron became furious with Alex for publishing a book that not only might expose Sarah to Turkish vengeance, but could undermine his own artfully ambiguous position, and thus put off answering his brother for many days.

Rabbi Magnes joined him a few days after his arrival in Copenhagen. Aaron met with a Danish colleague, who quizzed him gently but persistently on his feelings about British rule in Palestine, a question which he was not inclined to answer. He also met with a German businessman, Leo Minz, whose skills at war profiteering he greatly admired; Aaron helped him to run butter to Germany, which was starving under the British naval blockade, by providing information for Minz's colleague Count Ranzou. Both Aaron's hotel room and his chambermaid were pretty, and he acquired enough Danish to impress the latter. The high holidays passed him by. On October 6 he wrote, "As everybody was at the synagogue for Kol Nidre, I spent the evening alone."

That month, after a long silence, David Fairchild received another cablegram from Aaron. This one, sent from Copenhagen, demanded that U.S. Secretary of Agriculture David Franklin Houston wire the British ambassador with an urgent request for Aaron's presence in America. Secretary Houston was understandably piqued since Aaron's earlier rejection of Admiral Decker remained unexplained; but finally, since Aaron was a valuable "collaborator," he sent a cautiously worded telegram.

Aaron had traded in his cards as a scientist and in return received those of Felix Krull, confidence man (and the hero of the eponymous Thomas Mann novel, who degrades his artistic talents to become a trickster). On October 9, worn out with waiting for permission to travel to the United States, he locked himself in his hotel room and produced a "confession," addressed to Ruth Mack's father, currently president of the Zionist Organization of America. In sixteen far-from-candid pages, he revealed his transformation into a spy — and recanted all of his relations with his German mentors. "The 'turkisation' as applied on the Armenians and the Jews is nothing but a copy of the method of 'prussianisadon' worked out for the Poles in Posnany, etc.," he wrote — worked out, as we have seen, by his sponsors Georg Schweinfurth and Otto Warburg, in conjunction with Bismarck's plans.

> But you should not condemn me. Do not forget, please, that for two years now I could not speak out openly and freely. For two years I had to watch not only my words or my writing but even my thoughts and dreams were under Censure . . . You must forgive me if I am unable to concentrate my thoughts. And then what I have to state is so terrible, can so easily bring about a total break between us, between me and all my former friends, that you must forgive my instinctive hesitation to put it in writing . . . Out with it then. Since the beginning of the War, I have not learned where your sympathies are. Are you pro-Britain, or — excuse me if you feel insulted — pro-German? But you can have no doubt that I am more anti-German than ever, can you? In fact this German War comes, all too soon though, as a complete corraboration [*sic*] of all my

predictions. Did I not see long ago how deep the German poison lay? And did I not *a propos et mal apropos*, always warn my American friends and colleagues even against the poisoned German Science, a thing so many people have recognized now to be right and timely?

Aaron proceeded to recall a conversation with Mack, Fairchild, and two other American scientists in New York in 1912, when he outlined his opinion that Palestine must come under a British protectorate before Germany could open the railroad tunnels it was blasting through the Taurus Mountains. I have not discovered any record of such a conversation in the thousands of documents I have examined. Aaron's letter appears in large part to have been a desperate bid to obtain his passage to the United States, which still enjoyed neutral relations with Turkey. He had, he explained, planned to travel under the protection of Mack's rabbi, Judah Magnes, who hoped that the Young Turks would favor a measure of autonomy for the Jewish settlements in Palestine and vehemently opposed endangering present and future settlement by threatening the Turkish hegemony. Aaron attributed his change of heart to his obtaining knowledge of Turkey's plans to massacre its Jewish citizens while working with Djemal Pasha, an experience which he said confirmed his belief that "Turkey must be entirely torn to pieces" — destroyed like a "nest of wasps because no effort will ever make it into a nest of honeybees." According to his British interrogators, in a report filed later that month, Aaron received this information from Johannes Lepsius, who had it from Morgenthau.

Aaron's association with Morgenthau made him as controversial as the former ambassador himself. Morgenthau was to be recalled from Constantinople in November 1916. His departure was attended by much talk that he had offended the Committee of Unity and Progress by offering to buy Palestine for the Zionists. Apparently Morgenthau's only real transgression was his indiscretion, for considerable correspondence then passed between Abram Elkus, Morgenthau's successor as U.S. ambassador to Constantinople, and Jacob Schiff, head of Kuhn, Loeb, on the subject of concessions on Jewish colonization to be granted by Turkey in exchange for assistance given by Jewish financial circles in America to the Ottoman treasury. Both Talaat, the

Turkish grand vizier, and his finance minister, the Donmeh Jew Djavid Bey, inclined favorably to this idea as communicated in December 1916 to the Berlin Zionist Executive by its man in Constantinople,
Richard Lichtheim.

The idea that American financial brawn might marry with Turkey
through an alliance brokered by one of the leading arbitrageurs of German railway bonds was a source of great alarm to the British Foreign
Office. Russia was slipping out of the Entente because of anticzar-
ist uprisings. France, too, was wavering in her commitment because
of the devastation wrought by the German front. In the corridors of
the Foreign and War Offices in London, the unthinkable became possible: Britain might lose the war. Although exact casualty lists were
never published for fear of giving information to the enemy, by May
1915, she had lost hundreds of thousands of soldiers in the stalemated
trenches of France. A further two hundred thousand dead at Gallipoli
and, a year later, the annihilation of the British garrison in the siege of
Kut-al-Amra, along with twenty-five thousand of their would-be Allied
rescuers, did not play well with an increasingly disaffected public. Britain, drained of young men and almost bankrupt, desperately needed
another ally to win the war. But "the Great Neutral" stubbornly clung
to its neutrality out of distrust for Britain's imperial aims and prewar
domination of oil – and because its prosperous German American citizens were a powerful voting bloc well-represented in the banking
structure.

Throughout 1916, Sir Cecil Spring-Rice, Britain's ambassador to
Washington, whose intemperance in politics was possibly fueled by his
intemperance in the use of alcohol, informed Foreign Secretary Grey
that the United States Congress feared war with England more than
it feared war with Germany. Popular anger at the British blockade's
interference with American commerce had eroded the propaganda
advantage produced in America by Germany's violation of Belgian neutrality in 1914, and British "navalism" was now equated with German
militarism. Spring-Rice complained that "all the enemies of England
have been marshaled against us" in the American voting population
and "the Irish have lent their power of political organization to Jews,
Catholics, and Germans."

Unlike the Germans and the Irish, the Jews were not united in anti-British sentiment, but Jacob Schiff, their recognized leader, was "openly pro-German" according to Spring-Rice, who saw the banking community he represented as agents of German interest. The most powerful German agent in Washington, Spring-Rice noted with bitter disapproval, was "Herr" Paul Warburg, the most influential member of the Federal Reserve and cousin to Aaron's mentor, Professor Otto Warburg of Berlin University:

> The German Ambassador is constantly with him and through him is supposed to exert a great deal of influence over the head of the Treasury . . . The Democratic party . . . was thrown upon the Jewish . . . for financial support and advice. This gives the Jewish community a great influence in Washington, and in addition . . . as they control the majority of the advertisements, their influence is very great. It would be untrue to say that they are altogether on the German side but a very large number of them are and I am assured that some of the principal reasons [*sic*] for this is their dislike and fear of Russia.

Aaron walked both sides of the street. In what appears to be a counterconfession to Victor Jacobson, head of the World Zionist Organization in Copenhagen, Aaron boasted of having succeeded at fooling the British into taking him to London to serve his own goals for Palestine. "To see me," he wrote to Jacobson in French, "one would conclude that I am soft, indolent [*mou*], and jovial. But you know me, at heart, to be spiky [*angular*], hard, and serious. You know also that I know how to want, to want with tenacity and perseverance, to want with all the optimism of our race, and to sometimes transform my will into power." What he wanted, according to this letter, was a Palestine independent of any Great Power. In an obvious bid for the leadership of such a new state, he said he would fight "singlehandedly" to achieve it, by any and all means at his discretion. He would be called unjust and ungrateful, but, unlike Chaim Weizmann, to whom he referred backhandedly, he was prepared to risk everything he had.

Jacobson was a risky choice of confessor. A Russian Jew who had somehow obtained Ottoman nationality, he headed the Berlin Central Zionist Office before the outbreak of the war caused it to split into three entities and to relocate in London and Copenhagen. Along with Otto Warburg and Arthur Hantke, he formed a triumvirate that represented the lawfully constituted governing body of Zionism worldwide, and in this capacity he had regular contact with the German Foreign Office through the august personage of the German undersecretary of state, Arthur Zimmermann. This was the same Zimmermann who, in 1917, sent a secret telegram to Germany's ally, Mexico, proposing that Mexico attack the United States; decoded and dispatched to Washington by Sir William Reginald "Blinker" Hall, Churchill's director of naval intelligence at the Admiralty, it pitched America into the war and became known to history as the Zimmermann Telegram.

On October 10, Aaron, depressed and feverish with apprehension, received a piece of news that hardened his determination to proceed to the United States. He does not reveal it in his diary, but it appears to have been the cablegram he requested Secretary Houston to send while Aaron was still in Constantinople, asking him to come to the United States under the aegis of the Department of Agriculture.

The United States' neutrality toward Turkey was, as yet, intact, and his Turkish citizenship gave Aaron a slim chance of safe passage. Magnes offered to share Aaron's stateroom as a further protection. All that remained to be settled was the issue of a safe conduct from the British consulate that Aaron, as an enemy alien, needed to clear the naval blockade. However, the British consular official denied his request and suggested he leave for Berne with doctored papers, which Aaron, sensing a trap, angrily refused. He was able to arrange a secret meeting with the British ambassador, Sir Ralph Paget — a "lame gentleman" as Aaron described him — who assured him he would not be "annoyed" at Kirkwall, which is in the Orkney Isles of Scotland and is the entry point for the Scapa Flow. At the time, the British nervously anticipated that the German navy would break out of the Baltic Sea via the Scapa Flow and invade England.

Paget contacted the British intelligence station in Berne, Switzerland, which instructed Paget to route Aaron to London on the *Oscar II,* a Danish ship bound for New York. Aaron continued to insist on a written guarantee that he would not be taken prisoner. Paget continued to deny it. The manager of the Scandinavian American Shipping Line, who also did not trust the British, refused him a ticket. Aaron called Sir

Ralph a liar, which seemed to work. Twenty minutes after he hurled his accusation, he received his ticket and a letter from His Majesty's Government assuring Scandinavian American that the Kirkwall authorities had been advised not to detain the *Oscar II.*

Aaron set sail for New York on October 19. He sent news of his arrival in the United States to Ambassador Elkus, who, as Morgenthau's successor in Constantinople, was attempting to complete his negotiations to buy Palestine for the Jews. Aaron's actions suggest that he either was taking part or aspired to take part in this transaction, which would have made Palestine an American satellite, not a British one – and which certainly did not accord with the Admiralty's plans.

In a small and poorly ventilated stateroom, his snoring prevented his shipmates from sleeping. He noted the large number of German women on board, particularly a beauty named Olga Bernhardt with whom he flirted for most of the voyage, with sardonic appreciation: "Being an Ally, Olga honored me with a few confidences which surely she would not have entrusted to me had I been an Englishman."

On October 22, Aaron's boat docked at Kirkwall, where British inspection officers came onboard the ship. There are gaps in Aaron's diaries that obscure what took place next. Apparently after all his vehement protests in Copenhagen, Aaron explained to the commanding officer that he must make him his prisoner. "The trick was played. I was placed under careful guard; the Captain of the ship was informed that my stateroom was full of German stuff, and after taking leave of Magnes, at 4 o'clock I was taken away – a prisoner." Aaron was pleased that the beautiful Mlle. Olga displayed considerable distress. He was taken to the guardhouse of the Orkney Reserve Force, where a certain Sergeant T. H. Bond informed him that he was not a prisoner but that, as his position was "irregular," he would be taken to London. On November 1, David Fairchild and Secretary of Agriculture David Houston learned from their evening papers of the arrest of "famous Turkish spy" by British officers at Kirkwall – and that it was none other than their valued collaborator, Aaron Aaronsohn.

With the connivance of Sir Ralph Paget, Aaron had planned his own arrest as a ruse to protect his family. If the newspapers announced his capture, he reasoned in his diary, Djemal Pasha would be less inclined to retaliate against Sarah and the others, given that Aaron had tricked him into allowing his escape to Europe. But that night in his hotel room, listening to the snoring of Sergeant Bond, "the first time I have ever been under guard," it struck him that the British, for all their protestations to the contrary, had in fact taken him prisoner. Even the lamest official's most superficial reading of his "confession" to Jacobson would certainly have inspired such an action.

Though intelligence historians aver that Britain never turned a single highly placed double agent throughout the course of the Great War, the way in which its Special Intelligence (one of the many predecessors to MI6) handled Aaron Aaronsohn indicates that it regarded him as exactly such a prize. The charade Aaron had conceived with Sir Ralph Paget and intelligence headquarters at Berne would not, in the end, protect his family, but it did temporarily shield his high-level contacts with the Turks — and kept him, temporarily, from attempting to sell Palestine out of the British fold.

At seven thirty the next morning Aaron was taken under escort from the Hotel Albert at Kirkwall and put on the train to Inverness. There was no hotel that night, only a twenty-minute stop to change trains. Aaron arrived at Perth at 5:40 the next morning, was allowed three hours to breakfast and wash up, and then put on the train to London. He arrived at King's Cross Station at 6:40 PM and was taken directly to Scotland Yard, which housed Special Intelligence.

His interrogators were of a flatteringly high level. They included Sir Basil Thomson, head of the criminal investigation department in charge of counterespionage activities during the war; "Blinker" Hall, who was soon to become legendary for breaking the code of the Zimmermann Telegram; Colonel Walter Gribbon, London liaison for the Eastern Mediterranean Special Intelligence Bureau or EMSIB; and Sir Mark Sykes, the "amateur of genius" (according to his biographer) whose unbridled enthusiasms — and the rash and often conflicting promises of territories in which they resulted — were to cause such problems in drawing the boundaries of the Middle East at the war's conclusion.

Sir Basil, a stiff-spined colonialist who led Scotland Yard's transition from a top-hatted league of civilian gentlemen to a military force during a rash of Fenian railway bombings during the 1880s, firmly believed that "if you want to get the truth out of a man, you must have his eyes at a lower level than your own." He consequently reserved a battered leather armchair that had lost one caster and suffered the partial amputation of its other three legs, bringing the seat to within twelve inches of the floor, for what he described in his memoir as the "dreary procession of spies" that passed through his chambers on their way to execution or internment. According to Sir Basil's logic, "In native communities, the chief stands erect when he questions an inferior, and the man cowers on the ground at his feet." He therefore prided himself on spotting the culpable by their tendency to try to raise themselves up by their elbows whenever an embarrassing question was asked of them.

However, it was impossible to embarrass Aaron, or to make him feel inferior to anyone. He spread his bulk comfortably in the low chair and proceeded to lecture Sir Basil and his other interlocutors at length: on Zionism; the potential of a Jewish state; the geography, geology, and culture of Palestine; the Turkish military situation; and the writings of the first-century Roman historian Flavius Josephus, which conveniently corroborated Aaron's own theory that quantities of freshwater lay below the surface of the Sinai Desert, only waiting for pipes to bring it to the surface.

It is safe to say that Sir Basil had never met anyone quite like Aaron Aaronsohn before. He paid the closest attention to the man's disquisition on how he could show the British army where to drill to find enough water for their advance through the Sinai without piping a drop from Cairo. The Beersheba sector – the same route Djemal Pasha had taken in his assault on the Suez Canal – Aaron told his interrogators, was the weakest link in the Turkish defenses, chiefly owing to the fact that the wells in the area had been left untouched. Sir Basil paid even closer attention to Aaron's urgent pleas for the British to launch an invasion of Palestine before the Germans completed blasting the last of their twenty-two railway tunnels through the Taurus Mountains. Aaron warned them that the Germans were on the verge of completing this essential project, and could thereafter rapidly deploy their troops from Constantinople to Palestine and the Suez Canal.

Walter Harold Gribbon, an ambitious career intelligence officer and one of the first British specialists in Middle Eastern affairs, was another rapt member of Aaron's select audience. More than two decades later,

Gribbon would summarize his wartime experience in Palestine with the discreet observation that "intelligence began to be recognized as the indispensable requirement of the plan." "The plan" meant General Edmund Allenby would succeed in capturing Jerusalem in a mere two weeks by mobilizing British troops across the supposedly waterless Sinai by a path unmarked in "even the most comprehensive and up-to-date" British military handbook on the Sinai at that time. (That handbook, the *Military Report on the Sinai Peninsula*, was compiled by T. E. Lawrence, and was the major resource for commanders and staff officers, even though it was not up-to-date on the most recent infrastructure installations, such as the network of roads laid by the Ottomans as part of their military preparations.) It was Aaron, seated on Basil Thomson's stool of penitence, rather than Lawrence, who supplied the correct information out of his observations on Djemal Pasha. After the war, another of Aaron's inquisitors, Director of Military Intelligence Lieutenant-General George Macdonogh, attributed Allenby's capture of Jerusalem, an enormous propaganda victory that turned the war in Britain's favor, to the intelligence provided by Aaron.

Macdonogh did not exaggerate. The primary weakness on the Eastern front was lack of reliable intelligence, and particularly a lack of highly placed contacts within the Turkish administration. Until 1917, the outcome of the war was highly uncertain, and the use of double agents was common to both sides. However, these agents were as a rule low level, ill informed, and for the most part illiterate. The Sinai Bedouin most often employed by the British switched loyalties according to the best paymaster, and the Ottomans would play the switchers to gather information on their adversaries. By the second year of the war, the Ottomans automatically suspected every Arab of being a British double agent, which made those few Jews who were willing to risk spying an increasingly attractive prospect. However, the British could not easily assess how the Jews of Palestine felt toward Britain. American Jews, who supplied the bulk of charitable funds to their coreligionists in the Holy Land, were still largely pro-German, both by language and by ancestry. The Zionist position on the war as enunciated by the Berlin leadership was unequivocally neutral. The majority of the *Yishuv* hoped to avoid the horrors of war by honoring this directive, and deeply resented the exposure that any adventurers might bring.

For his interrogators in London, Aaron had arrived at a most opportune time. Up to that point, the conduct of the war had been schizoid, split between "Easterners" who espoused fighting the war in the Ottoman theatre and "Westerners" who held it could only be won by defeating Germany head-on in the fields of France. Kitchener and Churchill, now commander of the burgeoning Royal Air Force as well as the Royal Navy, had joined the Easterners, led by Lloyd George, whose interest in Zionism was incidental to "knocking away the props" from the Central Powers by knocking Turkey out of the war. As we have seen, his overall strategic intent was to make contact with Russia and Romania through Turkey, thus exposing the Central Powers to invasion from the rear while the main German armies were held in France, but the army opposed this as impracticable.

In December 1916, Lloyd George unseated Asquith. He was finally in a position to implement his view that securing Palestine, the neck of the Baghdad Railway and the overland route to India, presented the only victory that could redeem the appalling casualties in France and justify the war to an increasingly angry public. As the German paper *Die Reichsbote*, monitored by Britain, vindictively but accurately remarked, "England in the possession of Palestine would signify the isolation of Central Europe, the keystone to King Edward's policy of encirclement which England will not give up even when she will soon have to regard the present war as lost."

Within the granite confines of Scotland Yard, Aaron revealed Djemal's plans for a second attack on the Sinai. Aaron had been in a perfect position to observe Djemal's efforts to set up a better communications infrastructure in the Sinai, pave new roads there and in the Negev, install a communication system, drill wells, and establish reservoirs along the planned routes of advance. Most important from the perspective of British strategic planning in the Near East, in 1915 Djemal had built a light rail extension southward from Jerusalem to Beersheba. In 1917, the British would build their own military line to sustain Allenby's advance. After the war, they connected it with Djemal's line. This would become the cynosure of postwar development, connecting the Near East, the Far East, Europe, and Africa through the last link in the railway system begun by Germany and the Turkish government as the Baghdad Railway. The British, who were, as previously described, reluctant investors in this system, would reap its benefits by commandeering its engineering. Thus the war, which wreaked so much havoc, was in their view and that of the Zionists who switched their allegiance from Germany to Britain in this period, the herald of a prosperous new dawn.

Of all of the assembled powers in Sir Basil's office in October 1916, the éminence grise was Sir William Reginald Hall, called "Blinker" because of an incessant facial twitch that his daughter attributed to childhood malnutrition. Hall had attended a military boarding school where the little boys had to fill their empty bellies by stealing turnips from the neighboring farms. The twitch, apparently, was no impediment. The boy grew into a short, handsome man with the pitiless beak and predatory nature of a hawk, whom the American ambassador to London, Walter Page, described to President Wilson as the "one genius the war has produced . . . All other secret service men are amateurs by comparison . . . For Hall can look through you and see the very muscular movements of your immortal soul while talking to you."

Hall's genius had a distinctly sinister cast. He gleefully deployed all the weapons of deception, disinformation, double agents, bribery, and blackmail that we now associate with dirty tricks but that, over eighty years ago, were quite foreign to the conventional officer corps of the Royal Navy. "No man could fill his place," remarked American attache Edward Bell, half in fear, half in admiration. He described Hall as "a perfectly marvelous person but the coldest-hearted proposition that ever was – he'd eat a man's heart and hand it back to him." Hall was known as a ruthless and devious operator. When a British judge gave a light sentence to a German spy on the grounds that he was only passing back to the Germans locations of factories of no particular military importance, Hall took care to identify the judge's home as a factory site in a false report sent back to Germany in the spy's name. The judge's home was subsequently bombed.

Under Hall's tutelage, the Admiralty led the War Office in the production of anti-German, "black" propaganda, which included concocting stories of war atrocities in Belgium. Hall had a very broad mandate from which to operate. MI6, loosely formed in 1912, had little time to build up a spy network abroad by the time the war began. There was as yet no Special Operatives Executive to undertake sabotage in

Germany or to encourage resistance in German-occupied territories; no Double Cross Committee to turn enemy agents and supply false information; no Political Warfare Executive to conduct propaganda. Those gaps in intelligence were filled by Hall's men and Hall's organizations. Records of his experiments are still sealed as a security risk to the British nation, because "many of the methods he employed are still in use today."

One of the many pies in which Hall had his fingers was organizing and running the Arab Bureau in Cairo. The Admiralty had a vested interest in maintaining what was called the "highway" to the Persian oil fields, for oil powered the new, fast battleships favored by First Sea Lord John "Jackie" Arbuthnot Fisher and his predecessor, Sir Winston Churchill, for the Royal Navy. Matters of intelligence related to Palestine, Syria, and Egypt, the buttresses of the highway, were funded by the Admiralty. Thus David Hogarth, who held the honorary title of admiral; T. E. Lawrence; and Mark Sykes, who was to become Aaron's passionate advocate and close friend, were all "in Hall's pocket," as Marjorie Napier, one of Hall's secretaries and a shrewd observer of intelligence circles, put it.

Hall knew immediately that Aaron was too valuable an intelligence asset to let out of his pocket. The Arab Revolt was flagging. The War Office in London, alarmed at the lack of on-the-ground intelligence in Palestine and Syria that had resulted in disastrously inaccurate reports of Turkish troop strength in 1915, needed a permanent liaison officer between NILI and EMSIB, the Eastern Mediterranean Special Intelligence Bureau.

On October 27, 1916, Aaron met again with Mark Sykes, who quizzed him on his "national nuance" toward the Jews. Fat, untidy, kindhearted, and irreverent, Sykes was born a wealthy Roman Catholic Tory baronet. He was elected to the House of Commons in 1911 at the age of thirty-six, and at forty was appointed to the de Bunsen Committee to advise the Cabinet on how to carve up the Ottoman carcass after the war. Despite his fondness for bad puns and for caricaturing his illustrious colleagues in satiric doodles, Sykes controlled the enormously influential interdepartmental de Bunsen Committee by virtue of the fact that he was the only member who had been to most parts of the Turkish Empire and spoke many of its languages. His easygoing charm hid a shrewd political savoir faire. Strict academicians such as David Hogarth cordially detested him as a "bundle of prejudices, intu-itions, half sciences . . . [whose] instincts lay in parody . . . a caricatur-ist rather than artist, even in statesmanship." But Sykes cultivated key players like Cabinet Secretary Maurice Hankey and Blinker Hall. The three joined forces, going behind Churchill's back to try to buy Tur-key out of the war after Britain's disastrous assault on the Dardanelles.

Sykes gave his name to the Sykes-Picot Agreement (Georges Picot was the French envoy to the Arab world) that in March 1916 promised Syria and Mosul to the French but that was later considered an embar-rassment. In October 1915 the British had presented Mosul to the Arabs in another secret agreement between Sir Arthur Henry McMahon and the Grand Sharif Hussein of Mecca by which the Arab lands, includ-ing those which six months later were promised to the French, were to form a pan-Arabic federation, an "independent league of states in alliance with Britain which was also the basis for the Arab Revolt. Sir Henry had left a conveniently vague paper trail behind him, and the exact nature of his promises, known as the Hussein-MacMahon corre-spondence, has been the subject of exhaustive scholarship ever since. Sykes also failed to leave a written record.

These agreements were all made to retain a narrow strategic advan-tage. Britain's chief concern was to win the war, after which one could always negotiate. Even Picot doubted that the Arabs would contrib-ute anything of value to the Allied cause. He told his foreign minis-ter to quickly ratify the preliminary agreement concluded January 3, 1916 – before the British had a chance to become disillusioned with the Arabs and to regret the excessive concessions they had made to the French in order to enlist Hussein's aid.

By 1916, France was close to collapse and needed a strong economic incentive to continue the war. Britain, which did not want any com-mon borders with Russia for fear of invasion, wedged French territo-ries between them with Sykes-Picot. Strategic weakness dictated all of these choices, and drove Britain to make yet another conflicting set of promises, this time to the Jews.

When Mark Sykes traveled to St. Petersburg in early 1916 to nego-tiate the final stages of the Sykes-Picot Agreement with Picot and Russian Foreign Minister Sergei Sazenov, he noted the new power of

Russian Zionism in the Communist movement. Despite his own early paranoia about Jewish world domination (his Cambridge tutor, the classicist E. G. Brown, complained that young Sykes "saw Jews everywhere"), he conveyed to the Foreign Office his impression that worldwide Zionism would be a useful recruit to the Allied cause. He devised a compromise scheme involving an Arab sultanate in Palestine alongside a chartered Zionist company under British protection, giving the Jews a powerful economic compensation for the indignity of being Arab subjects.

Sykes, who had previously supported the Arabs with fervor, now had equally opportunistic reasons for supporting the Jews. He was increasingly aware of Germany's plans to dominate the Middle East, and, perhaps, of the negotiations between French bankers and the Young Turks to complete the Baghdad Railway. He strongly suspected his French allies were playing a double game. If the Entente Powers won, the French would stake their claim to Syria, Palestine, and northern Mesopotamia. If they did not, Sykes feared they would make a deal with their former German partners, with whom they maintained close contact through Swiss intermediaries throughout the war. A Teutonised Turkey would make the French into the "pawn of international financiers of Teutonic bias" like the Rothschilds and the Warburgs, and the Middle East into a Franco-German condominium. Control of Palestine would give Berlin further leverage for exerting pressure on the papacy, the Eastern Orthodox Church, and Zionism. Almost as soon as the Sykes-Picot Agreement was signed, Sykes leaned toward amending it to give the British sole control of Palestine in return for British support of French claims in Syria. A British-Zionist alliance, he reasoned, would provide a way to out-maneuver the French without breaking faith, and at the inevitable peace conference, a useful card to play against any German moves to rally her Jews to buttress her claims.

Upon his return to London, Sykes immediately set about convincing the Jewish leadership — notably Moses Gaster, Chief Rabbi of the wealthy Sephardic community — of the merits of his plan. But Gaster, a secretive and pontifical egotist, struck Sykes as an unconvincing advocate. It was only after Sykes met Aaron Aaronsohn in Sir Basil Thomson's office on October 27, 1916, that he felt he had found the right man to convert himself — and others — to the Zionist cause.

"The more Sykes saw of Aaronsohn," Sykes's biographer wrote, "the more he liked his forthright patriotism . . . and the more Aaronsohn's confidence in Jewish colonization appealed to him. If Rabbi Gaster a few months before had provided Sykes with the grace note of Zionism in Europe, here was Aaronsohn who had actually played the trumpet in Palestine."

That night, Aaron wrote to "Darling Oubi [Rivka] and dear Lel [Alex] "in a characteristic rush of euphoria: "Here — I had the good fortune to meet eager ears and open minds. I have reason to believe that had our friends been better informed sooner, they would have acted in consequence." He asked Alex to obtain a copy of his "confession" from Judge Mack and to ascertain who, among their friends, knew of, and were sympathetic to, NILI's efforts. "It is only after receiving this indispensable information that I shall know exactly in what terms I must couch my official reports, as well as my private letters." In the interest of establishing relations with their "future associates," the British, they must continue to deceive their other friends, as well as the U.S. State Department. "You must have understood by my telegrams that far from stimulating the Department of State and our Washington friends to intervene in my favor, you must calm them and make them accept the version that I was taken away from the boat as the result of untimely zeal on the part of a Kirkwall subaltern, but that although taken to London I was treated with every consideration. They apologized to me and placed at my disposal all available means of transport to the U.S." Perhaps with an uneasy premonition, he closed on an unusually wistful note: "Why are you both in New York? Does this mean a break with Albert and Ana [Mack]? It would be a pity . . . In this hotel I am known only as William Mack."

Aaron was not ordinarily prone to wishful thinking, but his letter could not have been further from the truth. Sykes's fondness for Aaron was a product of the information he provided. Aaron's fertile brain had been joined to the enormous juicing apparatus of the British Foreign Office, which was bent on extracting its full measure. Eager to win his freedom, he outperformed himself. During the weeks he was

ensconced in Sir Basil's office, in addition to everything else, Aaron
provided British military intelligence with reports on top-ranking German and Turkish military personnel, including Generals Liman von
Sanders, von der Goltz, and Kress von Kressenstein, as well as Enver,
Talaat, and Djemal Pasha, whom, Sir Basil's report stated, "informant
claims to know . . . better than any non mohammedan in Syria."

Aaron described his former patron as a shallow, vain, jealous, and
above all unreliable poseur; he appears to have influenced Grey's decision not to repose any faith in Djemal's promised uprising at this time.
He pointed out the cracks in the German-Turkish alliance caused by
the German army's need for more Turkish conscripts, and the conse-
quent Young Turkish intrigues for a separate peace. He reported on a
secret book, circulated privately and written by Johannes Lepsius, in
which Lepsius documented the attempts of the German government
to prevent a renewal of the Armenian massacres or any future massacres of Jews and Christians, and to repudiate all connection with them.

Most important, he wrote a memo on the resources of Palestine
that, widely circulated, became the basis for parliamentary arguments
that the country could sustain large-scale Jewish immigration. One of
the arguments most frequently used by parliamentary skeptics against
the Zionist cause was that it was impossible for Palestine to accommo-
date more than a fraction of the numbers the Zionists claimed could
be settled there. Chief among those skeptics was Lord Curzon, who,
as former viceroy of India, had a strong allegiance to the India Office.
Simla, the capital of the British Raj, was locked in a bitter competition
for funds and attention with Cairo, the center of Near Eastern affairs.
That fall, Aaron convinced Assistant War Secretary William Ormsby-
Gore that the Palestinian wilderness could be made to blossom like
the rose by Jewish skill and industry. His argument was to defeat even
Lord Curzon and to create a firm platform for the Balfour Declaration, Britain's 1917 statement of support for a Jewish homeland in Palestine. Ormsby-Gore incorporated elements of it into his own memo
to the War Cabinet of November 22, 1916, which commenced the Balfour negotiations.

Aaron was not unselfish in maneuvering for the *Yishuv*'s liberation.
He aspired to become the official instrument through which Britannia expressed her Zionist policy. But much though they might admire

him as a man, his interlocutors were reluctant to grant him that power.

Aaron's primary usefulness to the British was as a superspy, not a policy maker. His willingness to go to heroic lengths, to put his own and his family's lives at stake to gain the confidence of those in power rendered him suspect in their calculating eyes. He was too passionate to be a mere careerist, detested compromise, and was incapable of marching to any drumbeat other than his own. In a military or diplomatic setting, he could not be counted on to toe the party line. He was robust and engaging, but was also temperamental, militant, quick to scent an injury or hold a grudge. His astute judgment, coupled with his encyclopedic knowledge of the East, made him an indispensable advisor to Sykes, William Ormsby-Gore, and all others behind Lloyd George's Eastern policy, but ultimately, the authority he craved would go to those more canny aspirants who avoided the messy business of serving on the front lines.

When the British government chose its Zionist mouthpiece, it chose Chaim Weizmann. As evident in his discovery of acetone, Weizmann was a gifted scientist like Aaron, but in every other way he was Aaron's polar opposite. Suavely diplomatic and cold-blooded, although capable of great charm, he fortuitously arrived in England shortly before the first abortive Russian Revolution of 1905, which shook the czarist regime without bringing it down. He was introduced to the Foreign Office by Rabbi Moses Gaster as the man most fit to wear Theodor Herzl's mantle. He had early contacts with Grey's successor, Arthur Balfour, to discuss the future of a Jewish Palestine, and it is clear that the weight given Aaron's memo to the War Office in 1916 made him a serious rival for the leadership of the nascent state.

On November 3, 1916, the Director of Military Intelligence presented the Under-Secretary of Foreign Affairs with his compliments and a copy of Aaron's report, accompanied by a special request that the identity of the informant not be disclosed. He summed up Aaron thus: "The person in question talks most freely and well and is very correct in his statements whenever they could be controlled. Of course we do not know the object of his visit to this country but he might be just as observant of things here as he has been in Turkey and a purveyor of information of the conditions in England, if he was to go."

On the following day, November 4, Sir Cecil Spring-Rice cabled Sir Edward Grey information from Washington about "a certain Aaron Aaronsohn." The information came from a politically ambitious, Manchester-born academic who was Weizmann's natural ally, Professor Richard Gottheil of Columbia University. "He is a most honorable man – head of an American Jewish Experimental Station at Athlit, Palestine. But all his friends here – like Judge Mack – are rabid Germanophiles. He was coming in the tow of Dr. Magnes, and would understandably have been made use of in their propaganda here. I thought it best that you should know this."

Spring-Rice's telegram destroyed any remaining chance that Aaron would be allowed to go on to America. On November 5, Aaron tried to pin EMSIB liaison Walter Gribbon down on the conditions of his proceeding to Egypt, conditions that included clarifying the promises that Leonard Woolley had made Absa Feinberg in Cairo in 1915 – particularly those specifying an independent Palestine in exchange for NILI delivering a Jewish insurgency against the Turks. Gribbon informed Aaron that Woolley had been taken prisoner by the Turks and incarcerated at Kastamouni, with no possibility of contact. Not only was it impossible to verify the promises made to Absa, but the Turks had also sunk the *Zaida,* severing Absa's – and NILI's – only links to the British in Cairo.

Aaron worked at the War Office every day including Sundays, unwilling to accept the payment offered him lest he be obligated to the British. His diary was his only confidant. At night he wandered London's foggy, shuttered streets in search of a meal that did not involved fried sardines or broiled meats, fearful of the zeppelins overhead and mindful of what they meant for the journey ahead of him. On November 5, he presented Gribbon a note for the Foreign. Office – "a short, superficial note, which, however, will be sufficient to begin with." To this day, the Foreign Office says that it has not retained any of Aaron Aaronsohn's papers; nor does the note surface in the considerable collection of Foreign Office papers collected by Israeli scholars at the Aaronsohn Archive in Zichron Ya'akov. However from his diaries, Aaron appears to have presented Gribbon with a reiteration of Woolley's alleged quid pro quo, the reason behind his own long, dangerous, and increasingly discouraging journey to London. Again, no documentation of these promises survives, but since the Foreign Office identified that "inhabitant of Athlit" as a nationalist (one of those "Zionists who regard nationality as of greater importance than religion and for the present confine themselves to endeavoring to obtain freedom for colonization in Palestine"), it may be presumed that they strongly resembled those already made to Mohammed Sharif al-Faruqi, Sharif Hussein of Mecca, and Djemal Pasha himself.

Over the next three weeks, Aaron made more than a dozen attempts to pin Gribbon — and the Foreign Office — down. Each time he was politely fobbed off, and asked for yet another report to prove his bona fides, including some propaganda for Lord Bryce entitled "Pro Armenia." He walked and walked, incognito, avoiding the Jewish Quarter of Whitechapel for fear of an unlucky meeting with another Zionist leader. Another winter loomed, bringing more famine and disease to the people of Palestine. Sykes, he discovered, was the go-between for the War Office and the Foreign Office. He feared he had been led on. It had been two months since he left Berlin, and still he had nothing to show for it. Soon he would be completely penniless.

On November 14, Aaron asked Gribbon to send two telegrams: one to Henrietta Szold, asking for five hundred dollars; the other to M. le Baron Edmond de Rothschild's assistant, requesting the favor of an interview. The following day Gribbon, evidently having heard through channels that the Foreign Office did not want Mr. Aaronsohn free to intrigue with the French, told him he was to leave for Egypt in three days. Aaron agreed, but on the condition that Gribbon meet with him for an hour to settle what he thought was his — and Palestine's — due. For the next several days, Gribbon avoided him, and Aaron deliberately missed his boat. On the seventeenth, he lay in wait outside Gribbon's office and caught him. He explained that "if they wanted our work to yield good results, they must consider it as a contribution — modest, perhaps — but nevertheless a contribution. If we continue to have — on one side — people who risk everything and work with all their heart — and on the other — people who accept everything but promise nothing and remain distrustful — then the whole thing must be dropped."

Gribbon also did some explaining, which Aaron described to his diary. "As for the Foreign Office, they cannot bind themselves in any way. But the fact that I am sent to do what I suggested after having offered my services in the name of a certain group and a certain cause, is sufficient proof that they are disposed – should the case occur – to grant us what we have requested. Under the circumstances, one must draw one's own conclusions and . . . if one does not understand, then as the English say: 'A wink and a nod are the same for a blind mule.'"

Aaron came away from the encounter elated at Gribbon's confidences, which he took as evidence of friendship, but on the eve of his departure reality once more pitched him into gloom:

> I must confess that so far as wasting time is concerned –
> without being able to remedy it in any way – I have certainly
> wasted enough for the past 4 months . . .
>
> I have probably been too frank with them, or else they
> have taken it all for cunningness, but the fact remains that I
> have obtained nothing. They do not give us any "credit" for
> this whole year of suffering and danger. We must go to Egypt
> anew, and start from the beginning, and make good . . . Had
> I been alone, striving towards a personal goal, I should have
> long ago sent them to the devil. But we are not concerned –
> neither are our nerves or our whims. The cause is con-
> cerned and we must lay aside pessimism and begin anew.
> So be it.
>
> Perhaps it is better thus. If we fail, we alone shall suffer.
> But if we succeed, at least we shall not be indebted to
> anyone, and we shall have the right to say that our own
> efforts and merits have overcome all obstacles.

Aaron had made the journey to England believing that he could choose his own allies, but in achieving his goal he had to pay the devil his due. When he put himself in the power of the English, he chose them and, in the pitiless eyes of men like Blinker Hall, that choice was irrevocable. Wandering around the gray streets of London, cold, hungry, and poorly dressed, he had many occasions to regret it.

Aaron's Germanophile friends in America now viewed him as Britannia's lackey and, worse still, a self-serving betrayer of the Zionist cause. Ruth Mack's letters, no doubt at her parents' urging, ceased. The following summer, she married Hermann Blumgart, a medical student at Harvard. Henrietta Szold, now addressing him coolly as "Dear friend," informed Aaron she could no longer supply him with funds for the Jewish Agricultural Experiment Station. Judge Mack debated with Louis Brandeis whether he was a traitor. His patron, Julius Rosenwald, declared he would have nothing further to do with him. The way to America was barred. On November 24, with neither promises nor provisions to take back to Palestine and under the watchful eye of a young Captain Thomas Traill, he was put on the steamship *Karmala* bound for Cairo.

He Who Writes the Dispatches

And there were many other leaders or lonely fighters to whom this self-regardant picture is not fair. It is
still less fair, of course, like all war-stories, to the unnamed rank and file: who miss their share of credit, as
they must do, until they can write the dispatches.

— T.E. Lawrence, *Seven Pillars of Wisdom*

Aaron arrived at Port Said on December 12, 1916. He retained the cover of William Mack, age thirty-five, American merchant on business. His choice of incognito reflected not only his by-now unac-cented English but the thrust of his emotions rather than his will. Pre-disposed as he was to be an American Adam, a primeval giant carving his name on an intransigent wilderness, he could not help looking over his shoulder at the world that had opened its arms to him and that he had now thrown away. Still, Gribbon had promised him an active part-nership with British intelligence in Cairo, and he felt confident he could bend it to his will. Instead, he fell straight into a morass of inter-departmental feuding, a treacherous bog that, even in the frontier days of professional intelligence gathering, ate up precious energy and even lives; the friction and rivalry that dominated all branches of the eastern Mediterranean intelligence forces raised the question whether those involved had the time to deal with the enemy at all.

Before the war, almost no permanent, institutionalized British intelligence agency had existed between Istanbul and Cairo. Informa-tion gathering was left to a small force of internal security agents oper-ating in Egypt and Sudan, to the routine diplomatic communications of forty-five British consulates, and to the ad hoc missions of gentle-men (and gentlewomen) travelers whose often eccentric observations were cycled through the Royal Geographical Society.

Much like the sparse Arabist department of American intelligence almost a century later when war broke out in Iraq, the British Intelligence Department in Cairo in 1914 faced a massive manpower shortage that quickly assumed emergency proportions. The department was forced to handle many matters for which it had not been designed: the collection and evaluation of information on an entire army, the processing of unprecedented quantities of political data, vast censorship duties, and satisfying the voracious demand for maps and guidebooks.

The full weight of imperial overstretch was brought to bear on this small, fragile base, which overnight ballooned into sixteen institutionalized bodies on the major Near Eastern fronts: Egypt, Palestine, the Hedjaz (today's Saudi Arabia), Mesopotamia, Gallipoli, Salonika, and the Mediterranean. Each front had its own expeditionary force, and each expeditionary force had its own military intelligence department, in charge of collecting and evaluating field intelligence, producing overall intelligence assessments, censorship, propaganda, counterintelligence, and counterespionage, as well as handling agents, POWs, and defectors.

In the crucial first two years of war, the result was chaos. Eighteen individuals, scattered among numerous and often rival agencies, departments, and bureaus, advised the direction of British policy in emergency conditions in a part of the world famous for its own tribal cabals. For at least a year, there was no effective war directorate in London to report to, merely twenty-three brawling ministers. Lord Kitchener, who, as the hero of Khartoum, was the popular choice for Field Marshal in August 1914, was still mired in a vendetta against his hereditary enemy Lord Curzon; his enemies complained that he was becoming geriatric to boot. Their standoff over whether Indian or Arabian concerns should predicate the direction of policy persisted throughout the war. India hands feared that the Arab Bureau's main business, delivering the Arab Revolt, would incite jihad among the Muslim extremists in their own bailiwick. Arab hands, at Kitchener's instigation, wished to relocate the center of British colonial influence to the Near East.

The Arab Bureau was born out of this fission when the War Office, confounded by the unexpected resilience of the army of "Johnny Turk," compounded the military crises of Gallipoli and Kut by ordering a comprehensive reorganization in the structure of military intelligence between December 1915 and March 1916. The Directorate of Military Operations in London, which until then incorporated the operations and intelligence functions of the General Staff, split. An independent Directorate of Military Intelligence formed under the command of George Macdonogh. The Egypt Command reorganized and for the first time acquired a general headquarters that reflected its incorporation into the regular military hierarchy. Intelligence, which formerly answered to both civilian and military masters, was handed over to the sole authority of the new GHQ. Its chief officer, Brigadier General Gilbert Clayton, remained Director of Intelligence for both the Egyptian government and the Egypt Command, and his overriding concern was the preservation and consolidation of his authority.

Clayton developed an immediate rivalry with General Archibald. Murray's Mediterranean Expeditionary Force, which took over intelligence responsibilities for the eastern Canal zone and the Sinai in early January 1916. His antagonism took the form of an ongoing battle over communications, thus paralyzing effective troop action. When Lloyd George became prime minister at the end of 1916 and tried to instill some life into the moribund EEF, he noted sarcastically, "In Palestine and Mesopotamia, nothing and nobody could have saved the Turk from complete collapse in 1915 and 1916 except our General Staff."

Kitchener sent Sykes on a hasty tour of the Near Eastern horizon to come up with a solution. Sykes, lamenting that the interdepartmental telegrams alone were a nightmare, "a perfect babel of conflicting suggestions and views, which interweave and intertwine from man to man and place to place in an almost inexplicable tangle," hit on the idea of an "Islamic Bureau" – a clearinghouse that would centralize the dissemination of propaganda and military and political intelligence for the Near Eastern campaign. It was duly authorized in February 1916, with its name changed to the Arab Bureau so as not to ruffle already nervous sensibilities at Simla; its chief mission became that of inciting the Arab Revolt.

In anticipation of this event, an elite group of seven newly created officers shipped out to Cairo on Christmas 1915. They were bivouacked in three rooms at the Savoy Hotel, an orientalist fantasy built in the mid-nineteenth century to shelter curious English ladies flocking to see the wonders of the Nile, where boa constrictors and caged

leopards could be purchased from the verandah, and even the antics of
the Arab Bureau were relatively inconspicuous. Their party included
Aubrey Herbert, a gangly aristocrat with a gift for losing himself in
Islamic disguise, who became the prototype for John Buchan's *Green-
mantle*; Leonard Woolley and Stewart Newcombe, Lawrence's fellow
travelers in the Wilderness of Zin; Ronald Storrs, who became the first
British governor of Jerusalem; London *Times* correspondent Philip
Graves, brother of Robert Graves, Lawrence's first biographer; and
Second Lieutenant Thomas Edward Lawrence, the only one among
them with several years of intelligence experience. Lawrence's men-
tor, D. G. Hogarth, had been working for the Admiralty in Cairo since
February, under the honorary title of lieutenant commander.

Hogarth captured the "gentleman adventurer" nature of the group
in an accomplished bit of amateur verse:

> Clayton stability,
> Symes versatility, Cornwallis is practical, Danay syntactical,
> Mackintosh havers,
> And Fielding palavers,
> McIndoe easy,
> And wordie not breezy:
> Lawrence licentiate to dream and to dare,
> And Yours Very Faithfully, bon a tout faire.

The elite band styled themselves the Intrusives, and set about their
tasks of gathering intelligence, interrogating prisoners, monitoring
internal security in Egypt, and infiltrating enemy territory with agents.
Almost as soon as it was invented, however, the Arab Bureau sank
into the quicksand of bureaucratic infighting. The central intelligence
clearinghouse envisioned by Sykes never materialized, but remained
a section of the Cairo intelligence department at Kitchener's insistence. The Admiralty, the War Office, the Foreign Office, and the India
Office, which had heretofore dominated colonial policy, all sparred for
control, with Kitchener retaining the lion's share until his death in
1916 – hence the singular lack of mourning at his demise. Sykes made
policy only as Kitchener's representative and not as the chief of an
independent agency. Blinker Hall, not a man to pass up an opportunity

for influence, questioned the new agency and could only be placated by having his own factotum, D. G. Hogarth, installed as chief. Hogarth worked directly under Clayton and sided with him and Lord Kitchener in expanding British control of the Arab world, a view opposed by Curzon and the Foreign and Indian Offices.

Under Blinker Hall's aegis, propaganda filled the power vacuum that inevitably followed a lack of clear direction. For the first time, as the war stagnated worldwide and it became more and more necessary to revive it by recruiting new allies, the new weapon of propaganda overtook those of conventional warfare. Lawrence, the "doctrinaire without a doctrine," as Arab Bureau historian Bruce Westrate put it, became its premier exegete – and increasingly important in policy circles. This was extraordinary for a very young man whose greatest contribution was his literary talent – and who admitted that he would have preferred a literary career but lacked the discipline.

Lawrence, as biographer Lawrence James has remarked, was the "historian who found a chance to make history, the intellectual able to use his ideas to control others, and the romantic youth who turned the dreams of his childhood and youth into reality." But Lawrence's dream of the Arabs was, true to his personality, always a divided one. He idealized the nomadic Bedouin who personified his youthful imaginings of medieval warriors, but loathed the deracinated, decadent "town Arabs" whose minds were corrupted by the West. He portrayed himself as a messianic liberator who awakened the Arabs' national identity, but even though he adopted Bedouin costume and custom to play that role, he never considered himself one of them, instead he resented them for depriving him of his English identity. He saw himself as a cipher, a nothing, neither English nor Arab, but with each identity at war with the other. Once Sykes-Picot was signed, he wrote in *Seven Pillars*: "My sense of the falsity of the Arab position [meaning that the British had already, in 1916, agreed to give Syria to the French] has cured me of false ambition while it left me my craving for good repute among men. This craving made me profoundly suspect my truthfulness to myself. Here were the Arabs believing me, Allenby and Clayton trusting me, my bodyguard dying for me: and I began to wonder if all established reputations were based, like mine, on fraud." He considered the Arabs "unstable as water" and therefore utterly dependent on him to achieve their freedom; but he had difficulty acknowledging that such freedom, in accordance with his government's policies, consisted of breaking up Islamic unity in favor of creating a swarm of small, weak, perpetually warring client-states guarded by a jealous Britain. Once this form of freedom was achieved, he could not come up with a coherent justification for replacing Ottoman with Hedjazi rule. Nor could he ever acknowledge that the Arabs would never have followed him to revolt in the desert, or anywhere else for that matter, without the encouragement of large sums of money.

A German report to the Oriental Bureau of the Foreign Office in Wilhelmstrasse describes young Second Lieutenant Lawrence as "not a man for deeds. No soldier, no natural leader of men though he had the capacity when the need arose to weave complicated patterns. A dreamer, a man of fantasy, a secretive scholar." Lawrence, however, had a shrewd enough grasp of realpolitik and a gift for attracting father figures such as Hogarth. When he arrived in Cairo on Christmas 1915, he was nothing more than a backroom cartographer, albeit one with previous intelligence experience. He was not well liked, having a high opinion of his own capabilities initially unshared by his superiors, who sidelined him into low-level tasks. Allenby later regarded him as a gifted charlatan, but the otherwise cynical Hogarth played nursemaid to a cuckoo, pouching his young prodigy packets of milk chocolates at the front, defending him from the attentions of his voracious mother — and nagging him to win a Victoria Cross. This, one of the highest of British military honors, could only be achieved by enduring an extraordinary physical danger as witnessed by other troops. Though Lawrence was neurotically afraid of pain, he was ambitious enough to wedge himself, on the basis of his literary skills, into the important position of writing the dispatches back to London. Soon after his arrival in Cairo, he became editor of the *Arab Bulletin,* which was circulated at the highest levels of British officialdom.

In March 1916, Lawrence of Arabia wrote a position paper which makes clear the Arab Bureau's essentially divisive intent. "If properly handled," he observed, "they [the Arabs] would remain. in a state of political mosaic, a tissue of small jealous principalities incapable of cohesion and yet always ready to combine against an outside force." Much as it belies Lawrence's highly publicized pro-Arabism, fomenting division among the Arabs was seen by his superiors as a cost-effective way to prevent jihad: only one of the many instances in which this policy backfired is the murderous rivalry initiated between Sherif Hussein's followers and the Wahhabist tribesmen of Ibn Saud of Riyadh, who were promised virtually the same reward for delivering an Arab uprising but denied it when London favored Hussein. The embittered Wahhabis created the first of the modern Middle Eastern insurgencies, the Ikhwan, in 1920. Though it proved effective as a means of winning a short-term victory for an overstretched and exhausted army, the spy game, as a German competitor observed, was disruptive by nature and led to a web of irresoluble conflicts that benefited only the spies and other security forces thus kept in permanent employment.

In December, Aaron arrived in Cairo with a competing agenda – in effect, a "Jewish Revolt" in Palestine – which put him on a collision course with the Arab Bureau. It was Aaron's great misfortune that while the Arab Bureau was then in place, no corresponding Jewish Bureau existed to support his aims. In fact, he faced considerable opposition from the London Zionist Organization; he had negligible financial support from the British; and he shouldered a heavy load of personal responsibility, for he had unreservedly committed his associates, including his own family. He had refused offers of monetary payment in lieu of the same kind of deliberately ambiguous promises of independence and territories for nation-building that the British had made to the Arabs. Moreover, Aaron arrived with a preexisting antagonism set up between himself and Lawrence, the officer responsible for the erroneous Turkish troop reports Churchill had used to justify his disastrous invasion of the Gallipoli peninsula, and which Aaron had corrected during his Secret Service interviews in London.

As intelligence agents, Aaron Aaronsohn and T. E. Lawrence were the very antitheses of each other. Lawrence was Aaron's junior by fourteen years; a graduate student on a glorious and irresponsible adventure, who used his literary talent to embellish his reports and sometimes joked that outright fiction was the best way to reconcile conflicting intelligence reports. Though he was capable of acts of great courage, some of his biographers have speculated that his derring-do was a desperate means of compensating for what he felt to be his own inherent weakness – his unmanly fear of pain. Aaron relied on his scientific knowledge as the basis for his intelligence. He was gambling with the lives of his family and the future of his country. He wanted nothing more than to serve in active combat, not only to cement the political promises made him, but also, one suspects, to relieve years of pent-up frustration. During his tenure in Cairo, he petitioned at least four times to be sent to the war front and also supported the petitions of the Russian nationalist Vladimir Jabotinsky to form a Jewish regiment to counter the claims of the Arab Revolt. He was fobbed off each time with the assurance that he was needed more behind the lines. In the global propaganda campaign that overtook the Arab Revolt at the end of the war, there was only room for one hero, and that hero was to be British.

By the time Aaron arrived in Cairo, enthusiasm for the Arab Revolt had already begun to flag in the War Office and Zionism was gaining ground. Now in the enviable position of extracting payment from both the British and Djemal Pasha's Turkish coffers, the Arab chieftains were in no hurry to risk their lives or their political futures without further showers of British gold. Feisal and his father, Sharif Hussein, had moreover withheld important information on the strength of Turkish troop numbers for good reason: if their British allies knew how weak the Turks really were, they would no longer need the Sharif's good offices. The General Staff would only support it now provided there was concrete evidence of tactical and strategic gains. Only the Arab Bureau, which had been put in place to create the "revolt in the desert," still whole-heartedly supported it – and just as wholeheartedly opposed any effort to supplant it

Aaron's first impression of his new client, he confided to his diary, was of "nothing but distrust and reticence, smallness and pettiness." The tight, clubby, Oxford world that bred the intelligence officer corps had no room for outsiders, particularly those who challenged their views. While they could deride most of their Arab informants as what Edward Said would later call the "Other," i.e., slothful, illiterate, hopelessly, even endearingly venal, the European-educated Aaron was uncomfortably like them – with some essential and irritating differences. He was no Old Boy. He had no patience for the cleverness of High Table, for the arch pun or the after-dinner charade. He was unfashionably intent on achieving a result, inimical to any bureaucracy but particularly to the top-heavy and well-padded colonial bureaucracy. He was direct rather than elliptical, vitriolic rather than sarcastic, and prone to vent his impressive temper on colleagues rather than on underlings. He was embarrassingly emotional — he cried when his agents died unnecessarily — and could not be relied on to toe the party line. He was massively self-assured, at times appallingly arrogant; but unlike his brother Alex, an indefatigable self-promoter, he worked for the most part in the shadows. He was totally dedicated to realizing his own goal of an economically independent Palestine and was therefore difficult to appease or manipulate. In short, he was, in the eyes of the Arab Bureau, an altogether dangerous and quite unpleasant mix.

The Arab Bureau's Leonard Woolley, still languishing in a Turkish jail, had, in typical Secret Service fashion, left no notes behind of his contact with Absa Feinberg and the NILI organization. His replacement was a Captain J. M. Smith, who viewed Aaron with deep suspicion. Aaron in turn considered him "always an idiot," an accolade he bestowed on many of his British colleagues.

Smith declined permission for Aaron to travel back to Athlit to patrol the Palestinian coast. Officers from the EMSIB station at Salonika had called in with their misgivings about the pro-German stance of Aaron's supporters, Rabbi Judah Magnes and Henrietta Szold. (In the case of the Hungarian-born Szold, who deeply resented the patronizing attitude of Jacob Schiff et al., this was a profound error.) Aaron was to be detained — indefinitely — at Alexandria, while his bona fides were scrutinized yet again, this time by military intelligence for the Egyptian Expeditionary Force in Cairo.

With no contact from Absa, and fearful that the life of his best agent, whom he called his "Knight without fear and without reproach," might be in danger, Aaron threw one of his stellar tantrums. He threatened to break with the English entirely. Captain Smith's commanding officers, Simpson and Sir Gilbert Clayton, flattered Aaron with the assurance that they would not have sent for him if they distrusted him, and that he was far too precious to them to lose. A day after his confrontation with the English, they cleared him to travel up the Palestinian coast to Athlit on the trawler *Goeland*.

A ferocious storm made it impossible to land, and Captain Smith refused Aaron's demand that he reserve special signals to warn the inhabitants of Athlit of dangers – such as evacuations, massacres, or capture. Aaron tried to convince him of the value of his human capital, but Smith replied coolly, "This does not interest us very much as it has no influence on the military situation." He also refused to allow Aaron to alleviate his most pressing concern by bringing supplies on board the *Goeland* to relieve the famine at home. Two days after the resulting argument, Aaron was once more informed that he was grounded in Alexandria. "I must say this made me furious enough to break up everything," he fulminated to his diary.

> It was bad enough in London to have to wait days and weeks
> pending an order or a mere word. But here, in Alexandria,
> it is a thousand times worse. I do not cease from cursing the
> day we made the unfortunate decision of cooperating with
> our friends. One must have neither nerves nor warm blood
> . . . to be able to work with them. I have decided to wait
> until communications are again established. Then Absa can
> continue with them if he wishes. As for myself, I give it up.
> Regarding administrative activities, the British – to me –
> seem almost beneath the Turks.

A few days later, he wistfully recalled the administrative talents of the Germans – and the America he had left behind:

> We are only within a few days march of Gaza, and with some
> willingness and a little more energy than what our friends
> practise, we could become masters of the whole coast
> within a few days, but we are not prepared, we have no
> precise information, and as for technical details which they
> could secure – they are too lazy to do so. With such meth-
> ods, it is not astounding that the Turkish armies constitute
> a real obstacle and that oceans of blood will flow in vain
> before the Germans are beaten . . . It is heart-rending! It is
> the first time I have seen the English at work and what I
> have seen does not tend to inspire me with respect . . . Not
> only the Germans but neither would the Americans act in

that way.

Aaron found that the "committee-sickness" of the Russian Zionists was nothing compared to the British mania for bureaucracy. Its
arcane and often futile workings reduced him to paroxysms of rage.
While even British intelligence nominated his agents "the Very Reliable" — the equivalent of "Best in Field" — they consistently refused
to trust Aaron with either information or with money, a refusal due in
equal parts to parsimony, a lingering distrust of his German and Turkish contacts, and a growing apprehension that the promises made to
him might come home to roost.

He had little alternative but to move forward on the course he
had chosen. On January 6, 1917, Ruth's father, Judge Mack, wrote to
Judah Magnes with his considered response to Aaron's confession,
after showing it to the other members of the board of the Jewish Agricultural Experiment Station. Julius Rosenwald and Louis Marshall
called Aaron a traitor for taking the king's shilling. Rosenwald felt even
more strongly than Marshall:

> He is absolutely done with the Station, and will not consent
> to another penny going over. . . . both he and Marshall of
> course believe, and I share this view, that it would be
> dangerous under all of the circumstances for the Station as
> an American corporation to pay anything to Aaron. Fur-
> thermore, he cannot for a moment understand why there
> should be the slightest hesitation on Aaron's part in
> permitting his expenses to be paid by those in whose
> service he is now engaged.

Mack, though personally sympathetic, thought that Aaron, by his
independent actions, had endangered not only the official Zionist position of absolute neutrality in the war, but that of the United States government as well, and chastised his "lack of wisdom." Only Brandeis,
who was as loath as Aaron to show his hand, expressed no opinion.

A deep anger, increasing with time and exposure, fueled Aaron's
interactions with those who poisoned his friendships. Barely a month
after his arrival, that was compounded by the dreadful news that Absa
was dead — killed, Aaron was convinced, by the delays engendered by

British mistrust and sloth. In a desperate attempt to restore contact with Cairo after Woolley and the *Zaida* were torpedoed, Absa and Yussuf Lishansky had set out across the Sinai for Egypt. A Bedouin guide betrayed them to a gang of his fellow marauders and rival spies. In the ensuing melee, Absa was fatally shot and Lishansky badly wounded. In spite of his wounds, the former Hashomer agent made his way to Port Said to deliver the news. In the spirit of the propaganda war waged by the Arab Bureau, its members later spread the rumor that Lishansky had shot Absa in the back so that he could have Sarah to himself This story originated with Tzvi Aaronsohn, who was angry that Aaron preferred Sarah over himself to head NILI and was jealous of Yussuf's influence over Sarah.

Ironically, Aaron's definitive clearance had arrived three days before the news of Absa's death, in the person of Norman Bentwich. Bentwich, who came from Foreign Office–approved Jewish students' circles at Oxford that included Leonard Stein (later political secretary of the Jewish Agency for Palestine and author of the definitive history of the Balfour Declaration), historian Philip Guedalla, and Lewis Namier (a Central European émigré who achieved a knighthood and who followed Stein as the Jewish Agency's political secretary). Bentwich was an ardent, sometimes mystical Zionist who, to "prepare the way" for the Jews to reenter Palestine, signed up as a captain in Army intelligence, where his duty was to suggest the names of Jewish friends who could be approached for secret service in neutral countries.

In the beginning of 1917, Bentwich was summoned to Cairo by Major Wyndham Deedes to interview Aaron to second-guess whether the "romantic story" that he had told the War Office in London was true and "how he could give service to us." After only a few hours spent walking along the banks of the Nile, Bentwich was overwhelmed by Aaron's "irresistible eagerness and a convincing knowledge that could move equally statesmen of vision and staff officers of precision." Aaron's own accounts of their talks were not so flattering: "Truthfully speaking, I am afraid Bentwich's mind is too English-like – in other words, that it works slowly." His further impressions of the British were even less favorable, and lead the reader to suspect that if Aaron was ever in favor of a British Mandate in Palestine, it was only for the most pragmatic of reasons.

Aaron continued to fight for money and access to communications. When he was refused more than the barest allowance for his agents, Aaron asked the ineffable Captain Smith "how and why they expect to be served without money or supplies, or any protection for their agents, when the latter – to say nothing of hundreds of others – are risking their lives for them."

That bleak January of 1917, Aaron received a telephone message that a "Captain Core" wanted to see him. He was conducted by clandestine means to room no. 69 at the Savoy in Cairo, to find the Honorable William Ormsby-Gore waiting for him. Ormsby-Gore, who with Mark Sykes and Leopold Amery shaped the course of Lloyd George's Eastern policy, profusely complimented Aaron on the report he had made in London and pressed him to submit information on prominent Jewish personalities. Based in large part on that information, in February Ormsby-Gore wrote an exhaustive review of the Zionist movement that is included with position papers on the Balfour Declaration, concluding that

> the whole influence of Judaism outside Germany will be
> directed [vis-à-vis the war] in accordance with the attitude
> of respective powers regarding the Palestine question . . .
> The slightest hint from the Entente Powers that this
> peaceful penetration would not be opposed, and Zionism,
> as a whole will veer to the Entente side. On the other hand,
> any suggestion that . . . Jewish colonization would be
> resisted . . . would serve to throw the whole weight in
> international Zionism against us.

In March 1917, Ormsby-Gore joined the War Secretariat and built its long-term model for Syria and Palestine based on his immediate experience in Cairo. Aaron indelibly stamped Ormsby-Gore's memoranda with the imprimatur of his ideas, significantly one dated April 1, 1917, which embellished his previous interviews with Sir Basil Thomson et al. by meticulously describing avenues suitable for the invasion of Palestine in terms of landing places, climate conditions, Turkish troop morale, inhabitants' attitudes, and water supplies. Ormsby-Gore's description fascinated Secretary of War Sir Maurice Hankey, who commended it strongly to Sir William Robertson, Chief of the Imperial General Staff, and to Prime Minister Herbert Asquith. It later became the ground plan for General Edmund Allenby's assault on Jerusalem in November of that year.

Aaron's status at the Arab Bureau rose immeasurably, but in proving his worth he multiplied the opportunities for conflict with Lawrence. He was asked to work on the military handbook for South Palestine – and to correct Lawrence's earlier work. He made "slight additions" to Hogarth's description of the geography of Transjordania. He consulted on the printing of a geological map. By late March, he was allowed Access to explore the new, highly restricted technologies of wireless intelligence and photo air reconnaissance, augmenting the air reconnaissance photos with details from his groundwork. His work on a military handbook of Southern Palestine was so highly praised at general headquarters and in the corridors of Whitehall that he was magnanimously granted his own copy. He was consulted – and listened to – on essential matters of troop strategy in the long-range planning to liberate Jerusalem, in particular, which points to drill for water in the desert. He was asked to advise on propaganda, to which he wickedly replied, "As to the moral influence, there should be intelligent propaganda – superior to the bribing of a few rascally Arab chiefs. Jones understood what I meant." Aaron meant Lawrence and his "rascally" Auda Abu Tayi, the brigand chief of the Howeitat tribe of Bedouin and of the Bedouin clanship of northern Arabia. Lawrence had secured Auda's allegiance with a payment of ten thousand pounds sterling, but the bribe, though exorbitant for its day, paid off in frill when Auda and his followers captured the Red Sea port of Aqaba in 1917. That event made Lawrence, who took credit for leading the important victory, attired in his trademark Arab garb, a military hero, much to Aaron's chagrin.

When Aaron was granted the highest honor of writing an entry for the *Arab Bulletin*, Lawrence revenged himself by extensively blue-penciling Aaron's article. The blue-penciled copy is included in Foreign Office files with the papers for the Balfour Declaration. Notwithstanding Aaron's essential contribution to the foundation of the Jewish national homeland, he was kept almost entirely in the dark about its progress.

•◦• •◦• •◦•

On April 9, 1917, Sarah arrived in Port Said on board the *Managem*. Sarah Aaronsohn was the force, both moral and organizational, behind NILI. Only she had the tact to hold the more temperamental members of the group together, the suppleness and the strength of temperament to confront the hostility of the *Yishuv* as well as the Turkish enemy. But the constant struggle was wearing her down. She was pale and anemic, malnourished, and – for the first time – frightened as well.

NILI at its peak comprised twenty-three active members with a web of additional contacts, in auxiliary and administrative posts connected with the Ottoman army and with German military personnel. After Absa's death, Sarah took over as chief of operations at the experiment station. Just as he had, she recruited local agents, gathered information, and turned it over in written form to a courier, who traveled from Cairo on board the *Zaida*'s successor, the *Managem*, as often as Turkish surveillance permitted – about once a month. Absa and Woolley had agreed on a system of visual signals that could be read from the sea so that information drops could be arranged without the danger of actual meetings: a prearranged pattern of open and closed windows or of brightly colored laundry hanging from an outdoor line. This system allowed Sarah and her agents to go about their business without arousing suspicion by a prolonged absence, but was severely limited by errors in reading the signals and by the length of time that necessarily elapsed between communications. This meant that much of the information so painstakingly gathered was already outdated by the time it reached Egypt. Sarah's other great problem was the behavior of NILI's members, many of whom were interrelated and shared secrets indiscriminately, or boasted, like her lover Yussuf Lishansky, of his clandestine activities and the debt of gratitude the community owed him.

Sarah had risked a trip to Cairo to bring news of the "Armenianization" of Jewish Jaffa and Tel Aviv at Djemal Pasha's hands. Two Yemenites, hanged on trees, were all that remained of the city's Jews. Her arrival put Aaron on the horns of a serious dilemma. The plunder of Jaffa confirmed the *Yishuv*'s worst fears about the dangers to which NILI's work exposed it, but that danger paled in comparison to the exposure of his own family, especially Sarah, as head of NILI, if his position with the British in Cairo were to be discovered by the Turks, or if her absence roused suspicions.

Not only did Sarah face the possibility of retaliation from the Turks, she faced the possibility of betrayal from her own people. Envy of the Aaronsohns ran deep in the *Yishuv*. Informing on them now offered a tempting way to settle old scores under the guise of self-protection while getting rid of the most influential citizens of the First Aliyah. The only way for Aaron to "restore prestige" and reassure the *Yishuv*'s leaders that he was working in their interests, he boldly proposed, was for the British to entrust him with the same substantial sums – in gold – that Lawrence was allotted to bribe his rascally Arabs.

Aaron's overseers understood that bribery was in order, but here the British were caught in a trap of their own devising. Both the Vatican and the French were clamoring to get relief funds into Syria, which at that time included Palestine. However, the hardliners at the Foreign Office, headed by the dyspeptic George Kidston, were reluctant to allow any gold past the British naval blockade, where it might fall into the hands of the Turks, and insisted on maintaining an absolute embargo until Syria was liberated by invasion. Changes in leadership and internal brawling at the war directorate had held up plans for an advance since February, and a general who could take over from the ineffectual Archibald Murray had not yet materialized. Meanwhile, the threat of a humanitarian scandal mounted and allowed the enemy a golden opportunity to seize the moral advantage.

The idea of a postwar British protectorate for the Jews of Palestine provided an effective argument against those who would accuse Britain of pursuing the war for purely annexationist reasons. This was not lost on Britain's enemies. Early in 1917, as Russia pulled out of the Entente following the March Revolution and the vast majority of Russians, including Jews, wished no further exposure to the ravages of war, the British Foreign Office received an urgent telegram from MI6 in Berne. Sir Francis Hopwood, chief of the Swiss station, relayed the news that the German envoy to Copenhagen had just asked a prominent Zionist leader whether the Zionists could act as intermediaries between the Central and Allied powers. (The Zionist leader, unnamed in the dispatch, was probably Victor Jacobson, Aaron's confidant in Copenhagen.) This unnamed leader assured the German envoy that they could, provided the German government upheld certain promises of creating a national homeland for the Jews under Turko-German protection.

George Kidston, now Under-Secretary at the Foreign Office, noted with tongue only slightly in cheek that "Zionism is presumably either an association or a newspaper," and that its internal feuds were too arcane for the "mere Gentile" to follow. Kidston, from his Constantinople days, had no great love of Jews. He had, however, a firm understanding of realpolitik, and on April 25 he wrote a characteristically unvarnished memo: "The Jews in Palestine are now suffering in a modified form the same persecution which the Armenians have suffered for so long with the active participation of the Jewish elements in the Committee of Unity and Progress . . . On the ground of sentiment, therefore, there is little to be said for the Jews, but the question of whether we should make an effort in present circumstances to relieve their distress is rather one of high politics." He carefully weighed increasing press coverage of the German government's discomfiture at Djemal Pasha's excesses, and its efforts to blame him personally for Jewish persecutions in Palestine; by adopting such a stance Germany hoped to preserve the "valuable structure of Zionist cultural work, in which the German Empire must have well-founded interests in terms of future and very promising trade relations." The tyrant's arbitrary cruelties presented a unique opportunity to counterweight the well-publicized good behavior of the Germans toward Jews in occupied Poland and the pro-German propaganda that invited American Zionists and their sympathizers to reflect on what Germans were doing to restrain the Turks from working their wicked will on Jews in Palestine.

With discreet alarm, Kidston pointed out that "one British naturalised Jew [probably Sir Ernest "Windsor" Cassel] has already suggested that he should be allowed to approach the German Emperor through neutral channels in order to enlist his sympathy for the suffering Jews of Palestine." Despite his personal antipathies, he recommended that "we should keep the thing as much as possible in our own hands and get all the credit we can for our action." It was essential to eliminate any German intervention, but, he warned, "It would be advisable if possible to institute some machinery to keep control of the transmission of funds" that were being raised in considerable amounts by Russian and American Jewry. That machinery, after some negotiation with the reluctant Sir Reginald Wingate in Cairo, who dreamed wistfully of avoiding entanglements in local feuds, was to be NILI.

Kidston's deliberations were to provide the means by which Aaron could triumph over Lawrence and seize command of the diplomatic cables, but only at the cost of putting Sarah at even greater risk. Two days after she arrived in Cairo, Sir Mark, now Major Sykes, greeted Aaron warmly with the news that the April 6 declaration of war on Germany by the United States had greatly improved the Zionist position in England. Sir Mark, known previously for his anti-Semitic views, took Aaron into his confidence in the most flattering terms, telling him that "since he was talking with a Jewish patriot, he would entrust me with very secret matters — some of which were not even known to the Foreign Office." These products of Sir Mark's fertile brain included buying off Djemal Pasha; the postwar disposition of Syria; and the advantages of creating a postwar buffer state uniting Jewish, Armenian, and Arab interests to circumvent the treaty that Sykes himself had concluded the previous year with Britain's erstwhile ally, France, and which the Foreign Office already considered a failure along with the Arab Revolt.

Above all, they discussed the best means of recruiting American Jews to the Allied cause. Business was booming in the United States, which supplied the Allies with war materiel without suffering invasion, and few wanted to interrupt such a boom by becoming involved in a European conflicts But the United States had made extensive war loans to Britain, which, after Russia pulled out of the Entente in March, were in danger of being lost. The American government now hoped that a dramatic eleventh-hour entry into the war, making the world "safe for democracy," could protect America's investment without losing too many of its troops. It might also serve to even the playing field in the oil race. Shifting public opinion to favor the war presented the chief difficulty, particularly as Wilson had won office on an antiwar platform, and to that end the United States government had just created its own propaganda division, known as the Committee on Public Information. The CPI was designed by Edward Bernays and Walter Lippmann, and became the foundation for the modern science of public relations. It focused its sights on immigrant groups, who were exhorted to prove their loyalty by joining the war effort. Paramount among these groups was the sizeable, wealthy, and influential German American community, led by the very men Aaron's confession to Judge Mack had forced him to abjure. Aaron's contacts with Schiff, Warburg, Mack, et al. would be invaluable, despite their previous falling-out.

Sensing that the tide was turning in his favor — and might even wash him back into the fold — Aaron increased his demands for relief money for the persecuted and famished Jews of Palestine, a comprehensive evacuation scheme, and worldwide publicity for the Jaffa refugees' plight. Sykes offered to forward Aaron's report on the evacuation of Jaffa (the old seaport of Tel Aviv), which was based on Sarah's account and included an eloquent plea for relief funds, directly to the panjandrums at the Foreign Office. After some arguing with Major Deedes on the presentation of the "facts," Sykes wired Sir Ronald Graham, a Foreign Office dignitary sympathetic to Zionism, on April 29 with his usual dubious spelling:

> Aaron Aaronson [*sic*] asks me to inform you that Tel Aviv has been sacked. 10,000 Palestine Jews are now without home or food. Whole of Ysub [*sic*] is threatened with destruction. Jemal [*sic*] has publicly stated Armenian policy will now be applied to Jews . . . Aaron Aaronson and I agree in present crisis Weizman's [*sic*] presence here essential.

On May 8, Assistant War Secretary Ormsby-Gore advised Sykes from London: "I think we ought to use pogroms in Palestine as propaganda. Any spicy tales of atrocity would be eagerly welcomed by the propaganda people here — and Aaron Aaronsohn could send us some lurid stories for the Jewish papers." Aaron was only too happy to oblige. The manufacture of propaganda put him on an equal footing with Lawrence, and with Weizmann as well. It might even be his ticket to the front. Burning to be a hero and thus to prove his credentials to lead his country, he outdid himself.

From her brother, Sarah understood her mission to be to turn on the spigot of relief funds worldwide, "stirring up public conscience" by transmitting the most dramatic accounts of the Turks' Armenian-style persecution of the Jewish community to the world press. Pulling out all the stops of a "great actress," as she described herself she spared no detail – except for the fact that there was no massacre as she reported. Her story of the sack of Jaffa was smuggled out of Cairo in the diplomatic pouch of the Foreign Office and widely disseminated by Reuters, followed by others from the Judaean colonies. Money poured into Zionist headquarters in London, almost fifty thousand pounds accumulating overnight, with the promise of much more to come.

Aaron, unaware for the moment that far greater sums hung in limbo, was happy to receive two thousand pounds and declare it a victory: at least it was the thin end of a wedge into the famine in Palestine. The problem was now how to get the money into the country, since the Turks had embargoed the circulation of gold coin. Sarah regarded this as her personal mission. Not only had she cultivated the most amiable relations with the German and Turkish authorities, even with Djemal Pasha himself, she could never resist the most dangerous assignment. It did not occur to her that she might fail. After a long and painful argument with her brother, Sarah insisted on going back to Palestine, a position that might easily turn into a sacrifice if Djemal Pasha were to discover the source of the excessively unflattering stories now circulating on the world wire.

Despite his well-grounded fears for her safety, Aaron wrote in his diary that night: "How bravely and how calmly she offered herself. . . Her duty called her to where danger existed and I should not try and prevent her from going back."

Lawrence, according to his journal entries, was in Arabia at the time. But all the other young lieutenants flocked to see the flamboyant young heroine taking tea at Groppi's café in Cairo and, according to her proud brother, "admired her exceedingly."

8.

"Our People"

> ... the whole mission was arranged too much m
> an "American way," i.e., a lot of "external trap-
> pings" and a great deal of pomp – and zero inside.
> Our people will sign our Declaration for us.
>
> — Chaim Weizmann

American publicist and political operative Lowell Thomas was later to harrow audiences with gripping accounts of how his hero, Lawrence of Arabia, disguised as an Arab woman, "penetrated hundreds of miles into enemy territory, where he obtained much of the data which finally enabled Field-Marshal Allenby's forces to overwhelm the Turks." In fact, neither Lawrence nor the Sherifian forces known collectively as the Arab front operated in the Palestinian sector before Allenby's November 1917 advance on Jerusalem. However, the bulk of the data for Allenby's advance was, indeed, gathered by a woman – a pale, fragile-looking young Jewish woman with an aureole of chestnut hair like her brother Aaron. In the sense that Sarah Aaronsohn did his work for him, Lowell Thomas was right – Lawrence was indeed a woman.

On her return from Cairo to Palestine in May, Sarah undertook the first of a long series of reconnaissances in the company of Abu Farid and Yussuf Lishansky, who had also returned from Egypt. Their destination was Jerusalem, with a long detour to include Nazareth, the Turkish military headquarters in the north. Dressed demurely in a blue suit and white dressmaker blouse of her own manufacture, she set out in the carriage belonging to the experiment station in full view of her censorious neighbors, ostensibly to shop. From the moment she set out, she recorded everything that could be of use to Military Intelligence in Cairo: troop movements, crop conditions, and the mood of the population. Most important of all, she placed agents, paid in British gold, to track trains. This was NILI's chief source of information about Turkish troop movements; by counting the numbers of troops on trains, Sarah provided Aaron with the essential information that had been lacking in other reports on the defense of the Suez Canal. The gold was essential as well, for while the core group of NILI worked for an ideal, she had to assure the loyalty of lower links as well as that of the *Yishuv*, which, though it loudly condemned NILI, was not above taking Sarah's money to pay for food.

Sarah, like her brother, had direct and at least superficially friendly contact with the enemy and, if the challenging gaze in her photographs is any indication, she clearly enjoyed taking risks. In Jerusalem, she and Yussuf scandalized the citizens of Zichron Ya'akov by staying at Fast's Hotel together. Parading her best Paris-inspired finery, she strolled the lobby. However, Sarah's charms were not directed so much at Yussuf as the young German officers crowding the bar – and at such dignitaries as Meissner Pasha, the Germans' chief railway engineer, and General Liman von Sanders himself.

According to Abu Farid, her Arab driver and bodyguard, Djemal Pasha not only knew her but had a decided fancy for her. Abu Farid was hazy on exactly how and when Sarah encountered Djemal Pasha in Palestine and was often taken to task by Aaron for his tendencies to embroider the truth; but Abu Farid claimed the tyrant, who had already evidenced his taste for Jewish women, held a grand fete in Sarah's honor and offered to build her a palace on the banks of the Nile. "That night," Abu Farid told the *Jerusalem Post* in 1944, "she succeeded in getting details from him about the Turkish plans to invade Egypt, which sent to Aaron in Egypt, proved of great importance in the defense of the Suez Canal area."

Given Djemal Pasha's awareness of Sarah, the smuggling of atrocity stories out of Palestine to Cairo, where they could be disseminated to the Foreign Office and thence to the world press, was the most dangerous assignment Sarah could take on. Despite her bravado, she could not know that she was caught between secret diplomatic machinations both Britain and Germany had set in motion by the time of her return to Palestine.

.·. .·. .·.

As we have seen, from the beginning of the war and even before hostilities commenced, the German Foreign Office had made determined moves to keep world Zionism in Germany's camp by maintaining good relations with the Berlin Zionist Executive. On June 29, 1914, Hans von Wangenheim, the German Ambassador to Constantinople, told Richard Lichtheim, the Zionist representative in the Turkish capital, that should the Jews in Palestine be persecuted, he would do his best to protect them. On August 30, 1914, Arthur Zimmermann – that same Zimmermann whose intercepted telegram proposing Mexico and Japan attack the United States as allies of Germany finally tipped America into the war – became another advocate for the Jews. Zimmermann, who in 1914 was undersecretary for foreign affairs, instructed Wangenheim, who worked closely with then-American Ambassador Henry Morgenthau, "to see to it, if necessary, that the Palestinian Jews, regardless of nationality, remain unmolested." On November 3 he added that "it would be very wise if the Turkish government also tried to win the sympathies of international Jewry, particularly in America, by an accommodating treatment of Zionism."

Germany not only wished to strengthen the German-Jewish leadership within the Zionist movement and reap the maximum propaganda benefits, but also to find a solution to its own refugee problem, as millions of persecuted Russian Jews came under German control during the war and threatened to migrate westward. In the event of victory, Germany wanted to prevail on her Turkish ally to lift all restrictions on immigration and allow all Zionists to move to Palestine, which would then become a national homeland under Turkish suzerainty and the joint protection of the Great Powers. However, the Young Turks disliked foreign interference and remembered the Capitulations with considerable bitterness; Djemal Pasha was particularly touchy on the subject. Germany by this time considered Turkey a highly unreliable ally: some of its leaders, notably Djemal Pasha, had acrimoniously disagreed with the German General Staff about recapturing Baghdad. The German government therefore declined to make more definite commitments to the Zionist cause, though it issued a top-secret document in November 1915 emphasizing that it was "politically advisable to show a friendly attitude toward Zionism and its aims" and instructed its consulate to help the Palestine Jews by all practical means. In Palestine and in German-occupied Eastern Europe, the friendship of large Jewish populations might prove useful in the event of a negotiated peace. Already the combatants were anticipating the Paris peace talks of 1919, which would decide the boundaries of the new Near East, and both Britain and Germany had much at stake in how the redrawing would effect their paramount objective: control of the overland route to India.

The British Foreign Office also hung back from issuing a public declaration supporting Zionist aims, in part because of the promises they had already made to their Arab allies. Nevertheless, the Foreign Office concluded that the Germans were assiduously courting the Zionists and might at any moment publicly identify themselves with the Zionist cause. Early in spring of 1917; spurred by the reports of MI6 in Berne of German overtures to the Berlin Zionists, and by German press reports of all political persuasions pointing out the advantages for Germany and her Turkish ally to be gained from a solid understanding with the Zionists – as well as the disadvantages of allowing Britain to steal the initiative – the British FO lumbered into action. It was a case of the tail wagging the dog. The German press reports were generated in large part by a former General Staff officer who became a military correspondent and could not have appeared without the assent, if not the prompting, of the German government. They were never translated into a public commitment, which would have cost more in terms of Turkish irritation than the Germans were prepared to pay, particularly after the fallout from Morgenthau's 1916 statement that the sale of Palestine to the Jews had been agreed to by the Turks under German pressure.

Germany's greatest incentive for assuring the Zionists of a national homeland evaporated with America's entry into the war, an event in which Jewish public opinion played a leading role. By this time, all combatants were exhausted. Casualties on all sides were in the millions. Britain was nearly bankrupt because of the money she had poured into building up her naval advantage. Germany was near starvation because of Britain's successful blockade of her ports. France, with the highest loss of lives, was virtually depopulated of young men and pursuing clandestine peace negotiations with the Turks. Lloyd George, horrified by the enormous casualties of the still-fruitless battles on the Western front, and squeamish of the political risk they continued to entail, favored a short, sharp military solution on the principle that it would ultimately be the least painful one. "My constant wish [was] to strike the enemy where he was weakest," he wrote in his memoirs – meaning that it was necessary first to deal the Turks a "heavy military blow, and then offer them terms designed to buy them out." And where the enemy was weakest was in Palestine, where Turkish troop numbers proved to be much lower than originally estimated. As frustration at the long-delayed invasion of Palestine mounted on all sides, those who would annex her allied themselves inextricably with Zionism.

Soon-to-be prime minister Lloyd George's terms were much harder than the Turks were willing to accept. Unlike the French, and the Asquith government, Lloyd George's government would not consider a peace with Turkey unless Armenia, Mesopotamia, Palestine, and Syria were detached from the Ottoman Empire. Since these were terms that the Turks would "fight to the death" to avoid conceding, this meant prolonging the war until the main objective, smashing the Baghdad Railway "and all it represented," in the words of Mark Sykes, could be delivered to the British public. The invasion of Palestine would be an indefinitely prolonged occupation thinly disguised as a British protectorate of Zionist interests.

In May, news trickled out through Jewish channels that Britain planned to "give" Palestine to the Jews. The Berlin Zionist Executive redoubled its efforts to convince the German Foreign Office that the time had come for Germany, in her own interests, to define her support for a Jewish Palestine and to advise Turkey to do the same. The Zionist Executive pointed out that not only were Britain and France, both competing for the mastery of Palestine, wooing the Zionists; but the Americans, who were not at war with Turkey, had recently launched a top-secret initiative under Morgenthau and Aaron's close friend Felix Frankfurter, to negotiate a separate peace with the Turkish leadership.

The political maneuvering of the British and German Foreign Offices increased the friction that already existed between German, bourgeois Jews, eastern European Jewish socialists, and, in Palestine itself, between the Jews of the First and Second Aliyahs. By 1917, a considerable divergence had opened up in the leadership of the Zionist organization worldwide. Before the war, the organization headquarters was situated in Berlin, the nearest European capital to Russia, the spiritual center of world Jewry. Its financial center, however, was in London. When the war broke out, headquarters were prudently moved to neutral Copenhagen, but the real center of the organization remained where the money was. From London, Chaim Weizmann, president of the British Zionist Federation, and two other Russian Jews, Nahum Sokolow and Yehiel Tschlenow, directed activities beyond the influence of Berlin. This enabled Weizmann and his friends to operate with almost complete political autonomy, independent of pro-German or neutral elements within the Zionist movement. Weizmann lost no opportunity to stick close to court and accrue power. Weizmann's natural constituency was the Russian and Eastern European Jews who stood to gain much in wealth and power in a postwar Palestine and were by now a force to be reckoned with in British labor politics. It would not be to his advantage if the Berlin Executive were to retain its authority after the war.

The official position of the World Zionist Organization as directed by the Berlin Executive was one of absolute neutrality, to protect Jews from combatant hostilities and create a new foundation, free of European rivalries, for Zionism after the war. But the London Executive took a different stance.

The British government was already indebted to Weizmann for the discovery of acetone. To attribute the signing of the Balfour Declaration to this obligation, as some Jewish journalists did, may have been no exaggeration – in 1915 and 1916, hawks like the newspaper magnate Lord Northcliffe blamed Gallipoli and the war of attrition along the Maginot Line on the dearth of high-explosive, long-range shells. Northcliffe effected Kitchener's downfall, the resignation of Admiralty leader Lord Jackie Fisher, and, eventually, the reorganization of the Asquith government through his incessant harping on this one point When Churchill replaced Fisher as head of the Admiralty, he brought Weizmann into the Admiralty, as its director of laboratories.

In the spring of 1917, greatly alarmed that Germany's renewed promises of a Jewish national homeland would cause America's powerful German-Jewish community to defect, the British Foreign Office launched an untested new weapon. It was literary, not technological – a global propaganda campaign designed to transfer the loyalty of the world's Jews, who were the hinge vote in America and in Eastern Europe, from Germany to Britain. The launching mechanism was the communications network of the Zionist Organization of Great Britain, hooked up to Jewish population centers all over the world and tightly controlled by Weizmann. In the words of a lengthy report by William Ormsby-Gore:

> In April 1917, the London Bureau definitely determined to work for a Jewish Palestine under British auspices. It established close connections with the British Government and endeavored to secure a declaration by the latter approving its aims. Its policy, therefore, was in the first place to popularise the idea amongst all Zionist organisations and Jews generally throughout the world; secondly, to prepare to execute reliefwork in Palestine as soon as military operations should make this possible, so as to secure a definite position in that country; and thirdly, to give publicity to all news which would undermine the position of Turkey with the Jew and subsequently of Germans and Austrians also. In short, it endeavored to win world Jewry, not only to the Zionist cause, but also to the side of the Entente.

The communications machinery of the Secret Service was placed at the disposal of the London Zionist Bureau, which took full advantage for telegraphic messages and correspondence all over the world. (The unlucky official in charge of the pouch, aptly named Alfred Read, complained frequently and bitterly about Weizmann's verbosity.) In return, the Foreign Office approved communications "when necessary" and combed all responses for its own information. Weizmann, for his part, launched a letter-writing campaign calculated to shift President Wilson's close confidant, Louis Brandeis, off his Berlin-inspired stance favoring United States neutrality with Turkey and into the stance of Sir Mark Sykes. This attempt to counterbalance the Sykes-Picot Agreement became known as the Arab-Armenian-Zionist entente:

> These three nations (Arabia, Armenia, and a Jewish Palestine) will form a powerful barrier which would prevent

the spread of German might all over the world. That is why
I think a Jewish Palestine must become a war-aim for
America, in exactly the same way as Alsace-Lorraine or an
independent Poland.

When the United States declared war on Germany, its relations
with Turkey remained cordial. Though forced to sever diplomatic relations with Washington, the Turkish Porte avoided German pressure
to declare war on the United States and maintained informal contact
through the Spanish Embassy. Wilson, perhaps with an eye toward
catching up with Britain in the oil race by securing Turkey's allegiance,
blamed German militarism for the war, expressing the belief that if the
peoples of Turkey, Austria-Hungary, and Bulgaria were offered some
desirable proposition for achieving their independence, they might opt
out of the war. This would isolate Germany, thus achieving, in Wilson's
words a "bloodless victory."

Aaron's memo on Britain's attack plan for Palestine, included in
the papers for the Balfour Declaration, is dated April 2, 1917, four
days before the United States declared war. The inclusion makes clear
that the campaign for a Jewish national homeland under British protection was fought on two fronts – in London, where Weizmann duly
popularized the notion of a British mandate, and in Palestine, where
NILI delivered the intelligence necessary to secure a British military
victory. Clearly Aaron and Sarah were the heroes of the second front.
However, Weizmann's proximity to the gods of the Foreign Office gave
him greater access to their internal divisions, which he was able to turn
to his own advantage.

The Balfour Declaration, named for a November 2, 1917, letter, sent
by Arthur Balfour to Lord Walter Rothschild, the patriarch of English
Jewry, was ironically named. Arthur Balfour was in fact the hinge in
an ongoing power struggle between Lloyd George and the soon-to-be
deposed prime minister, Herbert Asquith. Balfour had hedged his bets
between Lloyd George's annexationists and Asquith's "Turkophile"
proponents of a "soft peace" until American troops could cover the
British flank in France. While in the United States on May 14, 1917,
to rally pro-war sentiment, Balfour agreed with President Woodrow
Wilson's version of the soft peace, i.e., that the Allies should make

concessions to Austria and Turkey if they broke with Germany. Two days later, U.S. Secretary of State Robert Lansing had the first of several meetings with Henry Morgenthau, recently returned to the life of a private businessman, on the premise that Turkey might welcome a separate peace if it could be relieved of the fear of the *Goeben* and the *Breslau*, the two German battleships that still lay at anchor in front of Constantinople with their guns now trained on the city to ensure Turkey's loyalty. Morgenthau proposed to use his Turkish contacts to enter the Dardanelles and destroy the warships. He was also prepared to use "judicious bribery," in the U.S. State Department's words, to buy Djemal Pasha out of the Young Turk triumvirate. On May 24, Lansing informed Balfour that Morgenthau was willing to go to Switzerland to contact Talaat, Enver, and Djemal Pasha through two former Turkish cabinet ministers in residence there. Balfour responded: "If matters took a positive form, the results might be of enormous advantage."

The genesis of the Morgenthau mission has been obscured to this day. U.S. State Department special agent William Yale maintained that it originated with Morgenthau. Morgenthau insisted to the end of his life that he was pledged to secrecy regarding its origins. Isaiah Friedman, author of *The Question of Palestine*, one of the definitive histories of the period, identified it as a State Department move that had Wilson's full approval, even though both the State Department and Wilson denied any knowledge at the time. But according to Sir Mark Sykes, the Morgenthau mission was conceived in the British Foreign Office by Asquith's supporters, including Sir Louis Mallet, former ambassador to Constantinople; Undersecretary for Foreign Affairs Lord Robert Cecil (later to win the Nobel Peace Prize); and one of the highest-ranking members of the War Cabinet, Lord Alfred Milner. By pushing separate peace negotiations with Turkey, the Foreign Office, wrote the enraged Sir Mark, "has been carefully destroying everything" he had accomplished in the past two years with Sykes-Picot, the Arab Bureau, and his new hobbyhorse, the Zionist cause. "Luckily," he commented, "Zionism held good and the plots to bring Morgenthau over and negotiate a separate peace with Turkey . . . were foiled."

The prospect of a soft peace with Turkey, though it preserved the official Zionist vision of Jewish autonomy in Palestine under the protection of the Great Powers, was not good news to the leader of the

London office of the World Zionist Organization. The London Zionists did not want the Turks granted any guarantee of territorial integrity that would deprive the Jews of a homeland, and Weizmann formed a natural alliance with the Foreign Office annexationists.

On May 23, 1917, Aaron received "sensational news" in Cairo that Weizmann had just published a speech saying Palestine would be given to the Jews. Weizmann's announcement was premature. The British were still playing their cards close to their chest, waiting to see what the Germans would do, and Aaron waited in vain to see an official press report. Having learned through Sykes that Weizmann led the London movement to secure the Balfour Declaration, Aaron gave him his full support.

That month in London the attitude of the War Cabinet toward Turkey underwent a remarkable change. General Jan Smuts, the hero of the Boer War who was at that time being pressed by the War Cabinet to take over the Near East command, expressed very decided views on the strategic importance of Palestine to the British Empire. Lloyd George concluded, based in large part on Aaron's memo of April 2, that Palestine could now be used to knock Turkey out of the war. Smuts, however, declined to forfeit his hero's status; he felt the Palestinian campaign was destined to fail because Czar Nicholas II's forced abdication in March 1917 and Russia's subsequent abandonment of the war under Alexander Kerensky and the Provisional Government made the Eastern flank too vulnerable to German invasion from the north. On June 5, the British Cabinet found a replacement in General Edmund Allenby, whose two previous commands in France had ended in massacres. Given a last chance to redeem his military career, he accepted command of the Egyptian Expeditionary Force. He set sail for Cairo two weeks before Morgenthau did, with stern instructions from Lloyd George that "the Cabinet expected Jerusalem before Christmas."

With so many interesting developments in London, Weizmann gave a cool response to Sykes's urgent request for his presence in Cairo: "Dr. Weizmann enquires whether in view of existing military situation in Palestine it would not be better for him to postpone his departure to Egypt for a month or six weeks and to continue his propaganda work in Europe and America. He feels that to come out now may prove a waste of time but, if you still press for his immediate services, would be glad to know what use you will be able to make of them."

Sykes wrote back to Weizmann's employers at the Admiralty with considerable irritation: "W. should come out as soon as possible if we are ever going on, no matter what the date of our proposed advance. He should be told to drop propaganda if we are going to stop where we are for good, as latter can only add to the sufferings of his people who are already beginning to be punished . . . It is the opinion of Aaronson that W. should come out, however if W. sees fit to appoint Aaronson to act in his place I have no doubt the latter would be ready to do so."

Neither Aaron nor Weizmann was willing to cede power, as both aspired to be the first leader of the new Zionist order. On June 14, having found out about the Morgenthau mission from Louis Brandeis, who had met several times with Balfour in May, Weizmann called in at the Foreign Office and told Sir Ronald Graham: "I am expecting to see Mr. Morgenthau employed in some intrigue for a separate peace with Turkey and believe he is coming to Europe for this purpose. If so, the whole thing is a German move." Sounding as if he had been reading John Buchan late at night, he said Morgenthau was acting on behalf of an "international ring of Jewish financiers . . . violently hostile to both Great Britain and to Zionism." Weizmann had already informed Britain's ambassador to Washington, Sir Cecil Spring-Rice, who fired off a long cable to the Foreign Office in a state of high agitation at the "Germanophile" tendencies of Morgenthau and his chief fundraisers, Jacob Schiff and Paul Warburg. Spring-Rice followed up two days later with persuasions that the former American ambassador was a German agent attempting to extricate the Reich from impending military collapse. These communications – and their results – are particularly interesting in light of United States State Department documents revealing that the German Socialist Party was at that time moving the Reichstag in the direction of making peace; Germany in fact had allowed Vladimir Ilyich Lenin to cross the border into Russia to pull her out of the war altogether.

Since the Foreign Office was plagued by a high degree of uncertainty about Zionist loyalties, accompanied by a high degree of uncertainty as to exactly what a Zionist was, British annexationists seized the high ground. Lancelot Oliphant, a relative of Laurence Oliphant who had railway interests of his own, opined that Morgenthau was "in it to play a part qua Jew," i.e., for money's sake. Crude though this assertion was, it was not ungrounded, given Morgenthau's previous relationship with Standard Oil; the Turks' need to secure finances to complete the Baghdad Railway; and the international railway interests of Jacob Schiff's company, Kuhn, Loeb, which had allies in both the French and German camps. A faction of the war-weary French, led by former finance minister Joseph Caillaux, were pursuing their own secret negotiations to entice Turkey out of the war by bankrolling the completion of the Baghdad Railway. Weizmann's Buchanism may have also referred to the fact that the Rothschilds had houses in both Paris and Frankfurt and – much to the ire of Lloyd George's ally Lord Northcliffe, who called it a "dirty German-Jewish international attempt to bully us into advocating neutrality" – had pressured the *Times* to remain neutral in the early stages of the war. Since securing the petroleum resources of the Ottoman Empire and smashing the Baghdad Railway were by this time Britain's main war objectives, it was only natural for the Foreign Office annexationists to impute their own motivations to others.

The Morgenthau mission had a second prong, of which Balfour was well aware. After Asquith's downfall, Lloyd George, perhaps in order to neutralize the powerful faction of Turkophile elements remaining in the Foreign and War offices – i.e., Tyrrel, Cecil, and Milner – appropriated Asquith's peace initiative and tailored it to his own ends. Lloyd George deputized mild-mannered Aubrey Herbert of the Arab Bureau to use his talent for disguise to travel incognito to Switzerland, with the aim of meeting secretly with Turkish leaders. Balfour, evidently fearful that the two secret missions might stumble on each other, informed Secretary of State Lansing that Egypt might be a more suitable rendezvous for Morgenthau because Switzerland was "full of enemy agents."

On June 16, Weizmann again called on the Foreign Office, this time to protest the Herbert mission. The recipient of his calling card, William Ormsby-Gore, wrote a secret and confidential report to his brother-in-law, Robert Cecil:

> On arriving at office I found Mr. Malcolm [of the Armenian Committee] and Dr. Weizmann, a Zionist leader, waiting to

see me . . . Both Mr. Malcolm and Dr. Weizmann were very much excited and very angry . . . Dr. Weizmann thought the sending of Mr. Aubrey Herbert who was notoriously pro-Turk, anti-Armenian, and anti-Zionist, was a gross betrayal and quite incompatible with the encouragement he had received from responsible ministers of this country . . . Both stated they would do all they could to oppose Mr. Aubrey Herbert and his designs, and that they intended to make as much trouble as possible.

According to Weizmann's account of events, Balfour then asked him to intercept Morgenthau on his way to Egypt to talk him out of his mission. No documentation of this secret meeting exists, either in Israel or in England, but in Weizmann's account in *Trial and Error,* he initiated it. Weizmann said Balfour asked him indulgently whether he had spies in the Foreign Office who had informed him of the Herbert and Morgenthau initiatives. It is possible that the Berlin Zionist Executive had a hand in conceiving one or both peace initiatives, as that organization had participated in meetings between the German Foreign Office and Turkish leaders, including Djemal Pasha, who, by a remarkable coincidence, traveled to Berlin and Berne at the same time. Weizmann was in a position to inform the British government of the confidential internal dealings of the World Zionist Organization and of the German government. On June 17, the day after Weizmann's second skirmish at the Foreign Office, Balfour approved a preliminary first draft of what would become known as the Balfour Declaration, a coincidence that, even more than Weizmann's acetone deal strongly resembled a quid pro quo.

Morgenthau has been treated as an egotist, an amateur, and something of a buffoon, but had his mission succeeded, it might have ended the war in 197 and saved hundreds of thousands of lives. Not even William Yale, special agent of the State Department and American military observer with the British forces in Palestine in 1917, could learn what had happened that made it fail. Like the limbs of a dismembered corpse, the reasons are scattered in different boxes at the Public

Record Office. At the heart of the matter are the propaganda stories supplied by Aaron and Sarah Aaronsohn in April and May of 1917 at William Ormsby-Gore's and Mark Sykes's urging.

Morgenthau's official cover for his not-so-secret diplomatic exercise was to evaluate the Jewish dilemma in Palestine, based on Aaron's and Sarah's reports on the evacuation of Jaffa. Their pleas, given the highest possible publicity by the Foreign Office propaganda machine in America had succeeded beyond their wildest imaginings.

On June 21, the day Morgenthau, his wife, and Felix Frankfurter departed New York for Cairo on the SS *Buenos Aires*, which flew the neutral Spanish flag, the *New York Times* revealed that the Joint Distribution Committee headed by Jacob Schiff, Felix Warburg, and Louis Marshall had voted Morgenthau "unlimited funds" for the relief of the persecuted Jews in Palestine. Morgenthau carried with him four hundred thousand dollars in gold, only half of the amount that had already been raised specifically for Palestinian relief, with the contributors' promise of as much as was needed "if the committee were able to reach Jews in the stricken lands." Spring-Rice's attache noted the promise of unlimited funds with discreet alarm to Balfour on June 26; it far exceeded the relief requirements of the Palestinian Jews and might, if allowed to be fulfilled, be used by the Turks to complete the Baghdad Railway in time to bring down a German invasion from the north.

Before departing for Cadiz, Morgenthau advised canceling the American Jewish Congress scheduled for that September, fearing it would pass resolutions denouncing the Turks for committing atrocities and thus jeopardize his plans for a separate peace. Wilson backed him. Following an interview with the president, Rabbi Stephen Wise issued a statement that a temporary postponement of the American Jewish Congress might be necessary "because of the urgency at the time of the public business."

Back in Cairo, Aaron was still wrangling over small change. "They are afraid we might receive too much money," he noted bitterly in his diary. "I reminded them of the fact that, outside of the immediate relief, we had to accumulate funds here, to be used as soon as there is an advance towards Gaza." Despite their liberal use of the diplomatic cables, the British military authorities maintained a tight embargo on all gold going into the country. "I am inclined to think that, under present conditions, nothing would be gained by attempting to resuscitate this form of relief, which would probably be of little use to the persons it is intended to help," Egyptian High Commissioner Sir Reginald Wingate wired Balfour. As funds accumulated, so did concern in Foreign Office circles that they might be accused of soliciting under false pretenses. The Colonial Office inquired pointedly regarding "the use made of the message about the ill-treatment of the Jews for purposes of propaganda." To avert scandal, the Foreign Office telegraphed Wingate at the Residency in Cairo that six thousand pounds were being held "at the disposal of the Special Committee," i.e., Aaron, but could only be drawn on through Weizmann, as head of the British Zionist Executive. On May 28, the Foreign Office fielded another request, to remit "considerable sums" of money from Russia for the destitute of Jaffa. Weizmann requested permission from the Foreign Office to dispatch the money through Holland rather than going through a special committee controlled by Aaron.

In the midst of the conflict that raged around them, the two rival scientist-kings declared their own, private war. At issue was nothing less than the future leadership of Palestine, dictated, as always, by who dispensed *Halukah,* the alms on which the majority of Jews in the country depended. But the amount of *Halukah* had been magnified into a global economic force by Aaron's telegrams and the Reuters wires. What was now accumulating in relief coffers was seed money for the development of Palestine. Morgenthau, who chaired the fund-raising arm of the Joint Distribution Committee in America, had announced a goal of $10 million for Jewish war victims worldwide. Whoever controlled Palestine's share of that money would control the country's economic future. When Brandeis cautiously approved a British protectorate in Palestine in April 1917, opinion among Rosenwald et al. finally swung back in favor of Aaron's great gamble. If he were to make contact with Morgenthau and advise him on dispensing the money, it would finally put him on an equal footing with Weizmann.

In June 1917, with the Morgenthau mission well under way, in a groundswell reaction to what they correctly perceived as a propaganda offensive, the consuls of neutral countries such as Denmark and Sweden flatly contradicted Sarah's massacre reports. U.S. Ambassador Abram Elkus in Berne transmitted a message from Dr. Arthur

Ruppin, considered one of the most knowledgeable sources in Palestine, denying any massacres or cruelties, though confirming the evacuation of Jaffa. The Swedish government decided not to intervene. The Swedish legation deflated the reports still further, reporting that the Turkish government had forbidden the expulsion of Jews from Palestine – though nobody would vouch for Djemal Pasha's cooperation. Aaron, called on to defend himself, hotly accused Ruppin of succumbing to Turkish and German pressures. But on June 25, a report in the *New York Times*, obtained by interviewing a member of the Turkish General Staff in Berlin, not only denied the news of massacres but confirmed that Djemal Pasha was inviting the Spanish, Austrian, and German consuls to visit any place in the land – and that German Foreign Minister Zimmermann had also obtained permission for three prominent German Zionists to make their own tour of inspection. Aaron, informed of these overtures, remarked with grim satisfaction, "All this proves we did well to make a big fuss."

Before the Morgenthau delegation could reach its destination, it was sunk by a storm of transatlantic cables. Based on the narrative contained in Foreign Office records of Turkey during World War I, a solution to the mystery of what happened to the mission presents itself. Weizmann's action in heading it off saved the British Foreign Office a serious, if not fatal embarrassment, not only in its global propaganda campaign but, as we shall see in its bargaining position at the Paris Peace Conference.

On June 25, U.S. Secretary of State Robert Lansing cabled U.S. Ambassador Walter Page in London, advising him that Morgenthau was due to arrive at Cadiz on July 1, and that it was "most important" that Balfour consent to have Weizmann meet him there. Since Balfour had already agreed that Weizmann should abort the Morgenthau mission, this seems, as Special Agent Yale succinctly remarked, "naïve." It is more than naïve in light of the fact that according to Sir Mark Sykes, the "Foreign Office pro-Turk gang" was behind both the Morgenthau and Herbert missions: Sir Mark himself was unaware that Lloyd George, never a man to neglect an option, had his own hand in encouraging Herbert's mission. On June 26, Ambassador Spring-Rice sent Balfour press clips on the "unlimited funds" accompanying Morgenthau. This gave rise to speculations at the Foreign Office that

Morgenthau might seek to negotiate concessions for Jewish immigration and colonization in Palestine in return for providing assistance to the Ottoman treasury through Jewish financial circles in America, an idea discussed in earlier correspondence between Jacob Schiff and Morgenthau's successor in Constantinople, Abram Elkus.

On June 27, Balfour cabled Ambassador Spring-Rice in Washington that the British High Commissioner in Egypt, Sir Reginald Wingate, would fully facilitate Morgenthau in communicating "any peace offers which the Turks were disposed to make." But on the same day, Balfour received word from his ambassador in Rome that the Vatican had made its own inquiries about the Jaffa deportations that had been publicized by Sarah, Aaron, and the British Foreign Office, to see if it could use its influence at Constantinople to stop further abuse. It had received responses from the ambassadors of Germany, Austria, Spain, and Holland that the "persecutions, massacres, destructions of villages, pillagings of houses and hangings of the Jewish people are nonexistent." By July 7, the legation flatly labeled tales of massacres as untrue. Aaron, in Cairo, confided to his diary that he had suffered a "cold roast" at the hands of his erstwhile admirers and was forced to defend his information, which he did by denying he had ever mentioned the word "massacre." This much at least is true: the embellishment was added by Reuters, a news agency pioneered by another railroad tycoon, Baron Julian de Reuter. Nonetheless, the Spanish ambassador to Washington proudly took credit for ameliorating the crisis in the name of his government, Spain having become Turkey's representative in the United States in the absence of formal diplomatic relations: "As a result of the representations made by the Spanish Government to the Sublime Porte," he cabled back to Madrid, "the Turkish Government has ordered the Military Authorities to permit the return to their homes of the Jews who had been expelled from Syria and Palestine." The military authorities so ordered were Djemal Pasha and company, and Djemal was not a man to enjoy taking orders particularly from a foreign power.

On June 28, the straitlaced General Wingate, who trusted Aaron and considered him an honorable man, cabled Balfour from Cairo in some distress regarding his own responsibility in transmitting Aaron's appeal for funds. On July 2, Wingate wired Balfour again, more urgently, with dire misgivings that Morgenthau's anticipated arrival in

Egypt might unravel the very tangled web woven by the Foreign Office, and even jeopardize General Allenby's attack on Jerusalem and thus the last chance for the British government to justify the war:

> The undesirable complications of such a situation, in view of our openly declared Arab policy, are sufficiently obvious. A practical danger from a military point of view seems to be that Mr. Aaronsohn and his friends have an organization for obtaining military information from Syria. Morgenthau is sure to get in touch with "A" [code for NILI] and will very probably utilize this organization in order to communicate with his friends in Turkey. If it is impossible to put a stop to Morgenthau's project altogether, I suggest Switzerland would be an equally suitable field from his point of view and a far less embarrassing one from ours.

On July 4, Wingate wired yet again, this time extremely alarmed at the state of his "irritated and sensitive" star asset:

> Our relations with Aaronsohn are somewhat difficult . . . Money is coming in as a result of telegrams sent in Aaronsohn's name while Sir Mark Sykes was here . . . Military Authorities deprecate remittance through any but authorized channel viz. Dutch agency, which method Aaronsohn considers unsatisfactory . . . He considers our attitude in general as little helpful and he may confidently be expected to approach Morgenthau in hope of getting assistance from him. I gather, moreover, that he suspects us of having no very distinct policy with regard to Jewish question, and we have so little information on the subject that it is impossible to take any definite line with him.

The Foreign Office noted this fiasco with its usual gift for understatement: "The difficulty is that we encouraged the despatch of an appeal for relief of the Jews in Palestine, and that it will not be easy to explain to Mr. Morgenthau, if and when he arrives in Egypt, why we circulated an appeal for funds when it was all along impossible for those funds to be sent to Palestine . . . the question is one of some delicacy and I feel that we owe it to Sir R. Wingate ourselves to suggest how he is to get out of the difficulty, vis a vis of [*sic*] Mr. Morgenthau ''

On the same day that Wingate's third telegram reached the Foreign Office, Weizmann, in the company of a fellow Zionist, a Colonel Weil, who for many years operated the French tobacco monopoly in Turkey, intercepted Morgenthau and Frankfurter at Gibraltar after being smuggled into Spain on muleback through an obscure pass in the Pyrenees. The British commander of the ancient fortress announced a banquet in Morgenthau's honor, at which Weizmann and Weil were also guests. After dinner, the commander and his staff withdrew, leaving the four Jews alone to debate in German, the only language they shared. Weizmann communicated his view that Her Majesty's Government would not consider a peace with Turkey unless it was satisfied that Armenia, Mesopotamia, Syria, and Palestine were to be detached from the Ottoman Empire. Despite Morgenthau's detailed exposition on Turkey's bankrupt and divided state, Weizmann, by his own account, successfully explained to him that any attempt to make a separate peace was foolish and would result in a dismal personal failure for Morgenthau.

Morgenthau, in Weizmann's telling, crumbled without a struggle for no other reason than Weizmann's superior perspicacity. This seems particularly odd given the backing with which Morgenthau had come over. Wilson was heavily invested in brokering a peace, so Weizmann in essence called the president of the United States a fool. Morgenthau's own attitude toward Zionism was ambivalent at best, and the opposition of the London Zionists therefore less than terrifying. But the argument that Morgenthau was afraid of being made to feel personally ridiculous is compelling. The repudiations of wholesale massacre of Palestinian Jews hit the newswires four days after Morgenthau's departure for Cádiz. If Weizmann informed him that his cover story could be proved to have been manufactured, that would indeed have given him good reason to reflect.

Upon receiving Morgenthau's report, Secretary of State Lansing, perhaps concerned that Blinker Hall might be intercepting his communications as well as Germany's, cabled back an abrupt about-face:

> Department surprised and disturbed . . . as text of state-
> ment set out in cable seems to indicate a belief that you
> have been authorized to enter into negotiations looking
> into a separate peace with Turkey. Department desires to
> remind you that your final instructions were to deal solely-
> with condition of Jews in Palestine . . . The President
> requests that you and Frankfurter proceed to Cairo to carry
> out announced purpose of mission, and that under no
> circumstances should you confer, discuss or carry messages
> on any subject relating to the international situation in
> Turkey or bearing upon a separate peace.

Morgenthau disobeyed the president's instructions and did not proceed to Cairo, where Aaron was being carefully sequestered from any
news of him. For over a week he failed to notify the White House of his
whereabouts. Special Agent William Yale wondered at his abrupt lapse,
but Morgenthau's reluctance to go to Cairo is easily explained if Weizmann cast Aaron's information into disrepute.

Weizmann derided Morgenthau, his mission, and his American
sponsors to his close friend, the radical Zionist scholar Ahad Ha'am:
"The whole mission was arranged too much in an 'American way,' i.e.
a lot of 'external trappings' and a great deal of pomp — and zero inside.
Our people will sign our Declaration for us."

On July 8, Morgenthau and Frankfurter sent the State Department a long and confusing telegram in which they stated they were
convinced that because of a greater feeling of confidence in Constantinople due to a recent Turkish victory over the British forces at Baghdad, the time was not yet ripe to enter into negotiations, and that it was
therefore useless for them to proceed to Egypt. Despite his telegram,
Morgenthau never forgave Weizmann for denying him his place in
history, and though he duly collected the pretty ribbons of the French
Legion of Honor for himself and Mrs. Morgenthau, his family later
accused Frankfurter of being a Zionist mole.

Weizmann discovered much that was of interest at Gibraltar, particularly the fact that the war-weary French were prepared to enter into
peace negotiations far more favorable to the Turks than any the British

could offer. He duly conveyed this information to London, and unofficially dispatched Colonel Weil to Switzerland., where Aubrey Herbert of the Arab Bureau was engaged in the second prong of the Foreign Office's secret peace initiative.

Like Morgenthau, Herbert had instructions to explore the terms needed to open the Straits and destroy the *Goeben* and the *Breslau*. The Morgenthau mission was intended to be a means for the British government to get in touch with Talaat and Djemal Pasha to secure their consent to a submarine assault. But, perhaps because his instructions came from Lloyd George, Herbert's mission resembled a "knockout blow" more than a peace initiative: the opening of the Straits was intended to signal the Turkish army to revolt against the pro-German Enver and to lead to Enver's assassination. Like Morgenthau, however, Herbert was given no real negotiating powers.

Herbert's contacts in Switzerland represented an influential anti-Enver, anti-German group interested in forming an alternate government without overturning the existing government for the sake of Allies who might partition Turkey. They saw no objection to recognizing the semiautonomous provinces of Armenia, Arabia, Mesopotamia, Syria, and Palestine, and in fact welcomed the idea of Turkey being ringed by friendly Muslim states; but they would not tolerate them being parceled out to Allies. This was exactly Djemal Pasha's position in his previous negotiations with Foreign Secretary Edward Grey, and Herbert reported back that the would-be sultan would support the endeavor.

The Foreign Office opined that the Turks would consider it a sign of British weakness to open up channels of communication without a significant British military victory. Herbert, who was given no precise instructions other than to carry a diplomatic bag, was left dangling after he conveyed the information that the opposition party would welcome Britain's help in unseating Enver's government but wanted guarantees that Turkey would not be partitioned. On July 28, he left Switzerland by train for Paris for an inter-Allies conference. Sykes, who was also in Paris, sent a memo to the Foreign Office the following day:

> Our main object should be to smash the Berlin-Baghdad
> Railway and all that it meant. A soft peace with Turkey

would leave Germany the dominant power in the Near East. If Turkey were to liberalise her policy toward her subject peoples and grant both the Arabs autonomy and the Jews a measure of autonomy, if French financiers formed alliances with German ones and Pan-Islamism became a Turco-German pawn, Britain's position in India would be subject to perpetual harassment.

The State Department's agent William Yale, who had declined an invitation from Morgenthau to accompany him on his mission the day before he left New York, now requested an intelligence posting in Egypt. The British military attaché at Berne had interviewed him in April and had found his acute observations of interest. He was forthwith attached to General Allenby as a military observer, "a special agent of the Department of State, sent to Egypt to keep the United States Government informed of the events of importance occurring east of Suez."

Yale would no doubt have been keenly interested in Egyptian High Commissioner Wingate's confidential correspondence over the next ten days. "My dear Graham," he wrote Sir Ronald Graham, a Foreign Office official who, during his lengthy service in Egypt, was the first British official to discuss the formation of a Jewish regiment with Vladimir Jabotinsky and who now, possibly more than any other official, urged his government to commit to public support of Zionism:

> I was particularly glad of the news in your telegram of July 9th, that Mr. Morgenthau had been dissuaded from visiting Egypt for the present. Meanwhile my position in regard to Aaronsohn and his companions is still somewhat obscure though I was grateful for your private telegram of July 18th saying that general assurances of support to Zionist organization [*sic*] had been given by Mr. Balfour and Mr. Lloyd George – and I hope you will shortly send me something even more definite after the matter has been considered by the Cabinet. I gather however . . . that the matter is by no means decided and that you wish me to keep Mr. Aaronsohn satisfied without telling him anything very definite. This has been done, though it would of course be

convenient to both him and to myself to know rather more clearly how we stand.

Aaron was more satisfied with the attentions of General Edmund Allenby, who had finally arrived in Cairo. Known more or less affectionately by his subordinates as the Bull for his forceful temper and an obsession with discipline that once caused him to berate a dead man for not obeying orders, he greeted Aaron "exceedingly well," according to Aaron's diary — and thoroughly picked his brains. Aaron's ebullient spirits rose like yeast in hot sun, as they always did when granted an audience by someone powerful enough to implement his plans. After responding in expert detail to Allenby's pointed questions, he launched into his pet solutions for Palestine's agricultural problems, unaware that High Commissioner Wingate had already briefed the general to indulge his temperamental asset on this point above all others.

Allenby had already absorbed Aaron's strategic advice to William Ormsby-Gore and added its main points to his own plan for a "lightning victory" that would shift the emphasis of attack away from Gaza, attack the weaker eastern Turkish line at Beersheba, then roll up the enemy defenses from the east. The success of the plan depended on the intelligence ability to deceive the Turks into believing that the attack would come, as before, from Gaza, and on the military ability to supply the troops with water in the long desert stretch between Beersheba and Gaza. Allenby bolstered Aaron's perennial hope of being sent to active duty at the front and put him to work.

Aaron spent long days in the heat of July wandering along the edge of the Sinai showing Anzac engineers the best water sources along the proposed route to Palestine. It was most likely during the period 1905 to 1908, when Aaron was exploring for Sultan Abdul Hamid, that he mapped the Way of the Wells. It was the same route described in the Book of Joshua and the Book of Numbers, followed by the host of Israel from Kadesh to Hormah in the thirteenth century BC and heavily traveled by Bronze Age traders (who called it the Ways of Horus) long before the Exodus. But the ancient route of springs, wells, and water holes was not sufficient for the scale of Allenby's operation, which included large numbers of camels and horses. Aaron advised drawing water from the plain with spring drills and filters, and taking large supplies of pipe to supply Jerusalem with water once the city was liberated.

Happy at seeing at least one of his grand plans take physical form at last, Aaron, for the moment, forgot about Sarah. At Qantara, on the Sweet Water Canal that still supplies Port Said with freshwater from the Nile, a filtering plant was built to purify six hundred thousand gallons of water a day. Reservoirs were constructed to store the purified water, and a pipeline built to carry it to El Arish, situated on an important water source, the Brook of Egypt. Anzac troops, who thrived on hot sun and copious alcohol, built a broad-gauge railway to accompany it. Truck convoys carried water from pipeline to railhead, where camel convoys with small metal tanks then carried the water forward as the Anzacs continued building both lines a system used throughout the advance.

To supply its cavalry horses, which could not survive long without water, the army advanced to Khan Yunis, Deir el Balah, and Shellal, in what is today the Gaza Strip. These towns and the surrounding villages held water supplies in deep wells, well known to Aaron, that could be tapped by Allied troops. The British then spent the next months preparing the advance from this point relying heavily on NILI's intelligence.

That intelligence was becoming more and more dangerous to obtain. On June 25, as news of the falsified atrocity reports circulated through the world press and diplomatic circles, Tzvi Aaronsohn was summoned to the committee building of the *moshava* (farming cooperative) of Zichron Ya'akov and threatened with banishment of his entire family for their "undesirable" work. Aaron's father, Ephraim Fischel Aaronsohn, was understandably frightened for his children and backed Tzvi in his threats to send Sarah and Yussuf Lishansky away on the next ship. Sarah wrote Aaron bravely, "My opinion is that there is no need to get agitated by every deed and rumor . . . Our people here, especially the family . . . are quickly alarmed by any minor thing and think that, for example, if a Jew says this or that we must stop all activity and literally bury ourselves alive . . . I say, there is talk, there will always be talk, and the work will continue." She went about her work, facing the growing threat of betrayal from within her own community—which now accused her of an adulterous affair with Lishansky. (This much was true: Lishansky was married, with two children, and he and Sarah were quite open about their relationship.)

Hashomer, which depended on noninterference from the Turks and unquestioning obedience from the *Yishuv* to protect the community, decided that NILI must be destroyed. A message was sent from the Hashomer headquarters in the mountain fastnesses above Nazareth to the political committee of the workers' movement in Jaffa, demanding that NILI be dispersed and its active members brought inland under guard and forbidden to appear in any settlement near the coast. If they refused to comply, the directive ordered, "terror must be used against them."

Aaron, preoccupied with his own concerns, paid little attention to Sarah's letters. He was by this time deep in another squabble with Weizmann. The Foreign Office, aware that Aaron's good offices were essential to Allenby's attack, apologetically informed Weizmann that relief monies could only be handled through the special committee in Cairo, controlled by Aaron. Weizmann then petitioned Cairo through official channels to insert his own man, the vintner Ze'ev Gluskin, into the committee. Aaron, who loathed all committees, protested in the strongest terms, described in Foreign Office correspondence as "violent, not to say hysterical." In his diaries he called Gluskin an "imbecile." The Foreign Office, ever suspicious of Aaron's volatile temperament and independent nature, moved its support more solidly behind Weizmann.

On July 21, Aaron had his first news that Morgenthau was due to arrive in Cairo. He was kept unaware that the Morgenthau mission had officially terminated on July 23. Commissioner Wingate had carefully sequestered him and also withheld a telegram from Weizmann requesting that Aaron be appointed secretary to a new committee for assisting Entente interests in Palestine and, coincidentally, receiving, controlling, and distributing relief funds. Wingate feared that informing Aaron of this news "would only lead him to believe that we were more pledged to support his cause than I have reason to suppose we are as yet and be likely to give rise to inconvenience locally."

Aaron inquired into the Morgenthau mission on July 25, when

he was asked to describe its members; and again on July 27, when he "insisted on the interest there would be in having the American Mission come." For Sarah's sake, he reminded Wyndham Deedes, now in charge of the political section of military intelligence, of the urgent need for more gold in Palestine. On August 1, General Clayton, director of intelligence for the Egypt Command, wired Mark Sykes to tell him Aaron was "surprised at the silence" of people he had telegraphed in America, and wanted to communicate directly with Frankfurter and Morgenthau. Ignorant of the fact that four hundred thousand dollars in gold, more than enough to alleviate Palestine's sufferings, had just passed him by, Aaron continued to humiliate himself over two thousand pounds.

Sarah's plight deepened through the summer as her brother locked horns with Weizmann, and Allenby's lightning strike creaked into gear. At a time when Lawrence was spending hundreds of thousands of pounds per month to feed his Bedouins (who increased their demands when they saw the money was forthcoming), NILI received some three to four hundred pounds a month to cover an intelligence network that extended from Gaza to Damascus.

Lawrence's relationship with Feisal and the Arab forces, tribal or regular, depended on money. They would not fight without it. Sharif Hussein received a monthly allowance of £125,000 – an immense sum at the time but one that, because of his constant demands, was raised to £200,000 in May 1917 – paid from Foreign Office funds in sovereigns delivered from the Egyptian treasury. From mid-1916 to August 1917, he received a total of £2.2 million. His son Feisal received a monthly sum of £75,000 raised to £80,000 in 1918. The Hedjaz Arabs were so rapacious that in July 1918 Allenby had to have £400,000 in gold shipped posthaste from the British mint in Melbourne, Australia, to avoid an Arab cease-fire. In addition to functioning as Feisal's military advisor and go-between with Allenby, Lawrence also functioned as direct paymaster to the tribal sheikhs of Syria and the desert area east of the Jordan, for whom he was allocated £200,000 in Foreign Office gold in addition to the outlays for Hussein and Feisal. He was given an additional Secret Service allowance of £200 a month, and when even this proved insufficient, a further £20,000. Between August 1917 and January 1918, he distributed £320,000 to the Syrians and to the sheikhs whose lands lay close to the Hedjaz railway between Dera'a and Ma'an in return for their attacks on the railway and future allegiance to Feisal. But Lawrence could never acknowledge that he led an army of mercenaries, partly in deference to Allied propaganda that the Arab uprising was a popular movement that embodied the historic aspirations of all Arab peoples; and partly, one suspects, because, like many an actor before and since, he had come to believe his own PR.

Finally alarmed by the desperate tone of Sarah's letters, Aaron repeatedly petitioned for the funds she needed. His nemesis, Captain Smith, coldly informed him that his agents were spending too much money and not producing enough. George Kidston prohibited sending any more because the money would "help enemy subjects."

By late summer, Aaron was blind with rage. Anxiety at Sarah's plight, combined with frustration over Wingate's inability to communicate to him any news about the progress of the Balfour Declaration and the delay in General Allenby's attack, caused Aaron to explode over Weizmann's pettiness: "His attitude . . . has shown plainly that there could be no ambiguity. He does not want to work with us." On August 11 he was finally given Weizmann's telegram, but refused his offer of compromise by accepting a sinecure on the aid committee. Both Deedes and Sarah, frightened at last, urged Aaron to capitulate, but he told Deedes to "send the money through neutral channels if you wish to practise charity. We are in politics and I wish to know on what principles the money is furnished."

On August 14, Wingate wired London in considerable alarm:

> Unless he can obtain some proof of confidence from Zionist organization Aaronsohn will refuse to cooperate and will destroy organization he has constructed . . . Matter is urgent as Aaronsohn has experienced difficulties with his people in Palestine. They doubt whether he is really working in their interests . . . Unless Aaronsohn feels he is being treated with confidence he will not proceed. Further if he does proceed he ought to be in a position to give Delegates evidence of both Zionist support and of general approval of His Majesty's Government.

A week later, Wingate authorized Aaron to travel to London to facilitate communication with Weizmann, but also, one suspects, to get him out of the way. Aubrey Herbert, back from Switzerland and reinstalled at the Residency in Cairo, noted: "Now H.E. [His Excellency, High Commissioner Wingate] . . . gathered that H.M.G. had given their approval to the Zionist cause and that if that was so it was his duty to see that no split or division of opinion [among Jews] should occur." That same day, Wingate wired Arthur Balfour directly:

> An additional reason for not alienating [Aaronsohn] is that
> the military authorities attach such importance to retaining
> the use of the organization which he has created in Palestine.
> He is in a position to destroy this organization, and there is
> little doubt that, in his present frame of mind, he will be
> tempted to do so unless some concession is made to his
> views. How far his differences with the Zionists in England
> are due to questions of principle and how far to wounded
> sensibilities I am not able to say.

Djemal Pasha was now in Berlin, meeting with members of the Berlin Zionist Executive in a *pourparler* arranged by the German Foreign Office. The Berlin Executive restated the Zionist official position of neutrality: "In our capacity as the supreme governing body of the Zionist Movement we can give a most positive assurance that our adherents throughout the world never were, and are not now, willing to put the Zionist Movement at the service of any one Power or group of Powers."

A few days later, members of the Russian and Berlin Zionist Executives, including Otto Warburg and Victor Jacobson, met in Copenhagen and agreed that to counter the overtures of the Entente toward the Jews, an equal and parallel effort must be made to enlist the support of the Central Powers — both by direct approaches to their governments and by propaganda modeled on that of the British Palestine Committee. The Berlin Zionist Executive took a particularly rosy view of the Morgenthau mission as evidence of the extraordinarily favorable attitude of the American government toward Germany and Turkey in encouraging Zionism. Yechiel Tschlenow, one of the Russian Zionist Executive members, worked closely with Weizmann.

In a series of conversations guided by the German Foreign Office, Djemal Pasha met with Richard Lichtheim and Arthur Hantke of the Berlin Zionist Executive and told them that the existing Jewish population of Palestine would be treated fairly, but that no further Jewish immigration would be allowed. The Turkish government, Djemal stated, wanted no new nationality questions nor was it prepared to get into trouble with the Palestinian Arab majority who opposed Zionism. He concluded by hedging that some future Turkish government might take a different view, or that he himself might change his mind, but effectively vetoed any public pronouncement in favor of the Zionists.

These discouraging interviews took place at the end of August 1917. A few weeks later, the Berlin Zionists found themselves in a still worse position when the Turks stumbled upon NILI. The discovery of what, from the Turkish perspective, was an act of Jewish treachery immensely benefited both Chaim Weizmann's objectives and those of the British Foreign Office, for it torpedoed any German competition to the Balfour Declaration. In the words of contemporary historian Leonard Stein: "At a time when the Turks were in no mood to show indulgence to the Zionists, and when Turco-German relations were by no means cordial, it is no wonder that the Germans, tempted as they may have been by its advantages, shrank from committing themselves to a pro-Zionist declaration."

9.

The Sacrifice

On September 21, 1917, Sarah tried to contact her brother in Cairo. A courier had arrived that morning with news of Naaman Belkind's torture and hanging. Naaman, Absa's cousin, was a deeply repressed and, by all accounts, childlike man who had long nurtured a grudge against Yussuf Lishansky over Absa's disappearance. Sarah and Aaron, for fear of revealing the true nature of Absa's missions behind British lines, had withheld any explanation of his death to his own family, and the rumors of Absa's murder in the desert at Yussuf's hands, spread by Tzvi Aaronsohn, proliferated in the void. Naaman had been deeply attached to his cousin and was jealous, as many NILI men were, of Yussuf's closeness to Sarah. That August, he insisted on carrying out his own mission. Against Sarah's orders, he set out across the Sinai accompanied only by a Bedouin guide to make his way to Egypt and tell Aaron the full history of Yussuf's misdeeds. In the desert, he fell ill. His guide took him to a Bedouin encampment for help, but instead the sheikh seized him, accused him of espionage, and, despite his protests that he was only going to visit his great friend, Ali Fuad Bey, commander of the Twenty-fifth Turkish Division, handed him over to the authorities at Beersheba. The Turkish military officials gave a banquet in his honor and plied him with alcohol and hashish. Deep in his cups, Naaman suggested that Ali Fuad defect to the British. The Turks then handed him over to the German general Kress von Kressenstein. Despite the Germans' previous commitment to safeguarding the Jews in Palestine, Kressenstein ordered Naaman tortured and then hanged.

Sarah felt certain Naaman had revealed her role in NILI before he died. Sensing the net closing around her, she finally wanted to escape. She wrote to her "Rabbi Aaron" in Cairo:

> If the establishment decides to rise up and oppose us, they
> can certainly stop our work. And if people don't want to, or
> cannot understand its value, why should we go out of our
> way? If people are afraid to risk themselves, can we really
> force them to? And if, god forbid, with all our caution, we
> still fail, it will not be only ten or twenty heads that will roll.
> No, the entire *Yishuv* will be tried and the revenge will be
> terrible and people will point to us and say "Look what your
> work has led to!" . . . Is it worthwhile continuing to endan-
> ger ourselves and to continue until we shall be caught? Or
> is there a chance of stopping at least until their fury has
> passed us over?

Aaron missed her letter by a day, having departed Cairo for London
and his long-anticipated confrontation with Weizmann. In his place,
the British sent their spy ship, the *Managem*, to Athlit. Its captain
carried with him a shipment of gold to free Naaman Belkind, by now
dead, and instructions to evacuate all NILI members. The nights were
moonless. Captain Weldon thought it safe to attempt a mass evacuation, with a second intelligence boat to be mobilized from Famagusta,
on Cyprus, under the direction of Alex Aaronsohn, who at Aaron's
request replaced his older brother in Cairo.

Sarah gave up her place on the first boat to her brother Shmuel and
his family. Her cherished Yussuf was wracked with the chills and fevers
of malaria, and Sarah decided to wait with him until the second boat,
scheduled to arrive on the last moonless night, September 25. Alex's
boat failed to arrive at the appointed time.

In an undated and censored telegram, the only record of which is a
typed transcript in the Beit Aaronsohn Archive, Alex informed Aaron
of the reasons for the delay: the Palestinian coast was closely guarded
by the Turks, and the British navy was "quite opposed to practica-
bility" of a rescue by sea. Alex cheered his brother with the suggestion that Allenby's advance was about to begin, and "no stone will be
left unturned to bring assistance to those to whom we are so much
indebted." However, Allenby's march from Suez to Jerusalem did not
begin until late November due to the virulence of the malaria sea-
son at Gaza. The unpleasant suspicion arises that the British military

authorities refrained from rescuing Sarah for other reasons, such as to sabotage the Berlin Zionists' efforts to achieve a German Balfour Declaration. What was most at stake throughout 1917 – and what the annexationists in the British government feared most – was a Turko-German version of the Balfour Declaration, which would rally Jewish opinion throughout the world behind the Central Powers and strengthen their diplomatic position. The inevitable peace conference that would divide the spoils of war had already, in many diplomatic minds, superseded the war itself. A reformed Turkey would deprive the Allies of plausible justification for the dismemberment of the Ottoman Empire. It was not forgotten that a large number of Jews shared Morgenthau's notion of Jewish autonomy in Palestine under Turkish sovereignty and might present it as a negotiating position at the peace conference. Germany and Turkey had much to lose if news of their brutal treatment of Jewish nationals like Naaman got out.

One reason to believe this suspicion is Alex's rapid and undeserved promotion after failing to rescue his sister. Unlike Aaron, who was denied the opportunity to serve at the front because he was an Ottoman subject, Alex (also an Ottoman subject) received a captain's commission and a Distinguished Service Order on the basis of a military career that included charges of desertion. British military authorities, as we have seen, wished to retain control of NILI. Aaron and Sarah, the two most defiant members, were the closest of allies. To this day, surviving members of the family hold Alex and his insatiable self-aggrandizement responsible for Sarah's death.

The military authorities in Cairo may have been motivated by the desire not to tip off the Turks and bring more troops into the area. However, both High Commissioner Sir Reginald Wingate and Director of Military Intelligence Gilbert Clayton were well aware through their daily correspondence with the Foreign Office of the flurry of high-level diplomacy now surrounding the Balfour Declaration.

On September 25, the day she had expected Alex to arrive on the second boat, Sarah, now approaching despair, put Yussuf in a carriage and drove him to Zichron Ya'akov for the harvest feast of Sukkoth. Two days later, Djemal Pasha's troops in Palestine – now under the German general Erich von Falkenhayn's command – closed in on NILI. The timing was extraordinary. Aaron had just departed for England and

Djemal Pasha for Berlin. His pressing invitation from Kaiser Wilhelm turned out to be a thinly veiled subterfuge to replace his command with that of Falkenhayn, who was also Commander of the Imperial General Staff. The two generals had quarreled sharply over the handling of the combined Turko-German force assembled for the recapture of Baghdad.

The accepted tale of NILI's discovery, recounted by Alex Aaronsohn, is a romantic one: a carrier pigeon, used by the spy group to relay messages to Cairo, came down at Caesarea and was discovered by a Muslim official feeding birds in his garden. The pigeon was sent under special sentry to Constantinople, and the Turks then apprehended Naaman Belkind and tortured him into further disclosures. As we have seen, this was not quite the case, but the discovery was opportune to more than one party. It is possible that Djemal, already nettled at the widespread news reports of Turkish atrocities in Palestine that had cost him much European prestige, learned of his former protégé and confidant Aaron Aaronsohn's contribution to Allenby's invasion strategy through a leak in the Zionist organization during his visit to Berlin. Von Falkenhayn might have learned of Djemal Pasha's backdoor dealings with the British and determined to root out his means of communication. Sarah's arrest and subsequent ill-treatment certainly marks a significant and puzzling change in the official German attitude toward protecting Jews in Palestine.

On October 1, Aaron arrived in London for his destined appointment with Weizmann after spending ten days in Paris, where he met with the Good Old Gentleman, Edmond de Rothschild. The dates of his sojourn suggest that he flew; during the course of the war the RAF operated a Cairo-Paris-London route using their brand-new Handley Pages. He also met with the ubiquitous William Yale, en route to Cairo to observe Allenby's campaign for the U.S. State Department, and passed him a letter for Alex that would contribute greatly to his own undoing. Aaron had written it in Hebrew, seemingly unaware that Yale would immediately have it translated. In it he outlined a conversation with Mark Sykes, in which Sykes had revealed the depth of enmity within the Zionist organization and told Aaron that his letter to Weizmann (about the divisions among Jews in Palestine) was like a thorn in Weizmann's eye. Sykes had begged him to make peace. "I told him I was not going to London to quarrel," Aaron wrote with ill-timed arrogance, "only to tell them their mistakes and to show them the way to do things properly. If they accept, well and good, if not I will go my own way." Unfortunately, he also advised Alex in the letter to "get as pally as you can" with Yale so as to mine him for information. This gaucherie greatly irked the State Department intelligence officer, and he promptly circulated a secondhand opinion that Aaron had stolen his scientific research, much to the detriment of Aaron's standing among his American friends.

There is no mention of Aaron's meeting with Weizmann in London in Weizmann's otherwise exhaustive memoirs and correspondence. A letter from Aaron to Norman Bentwich, sent shortly before Aaron's departure from Cairo, suggests its probable tone and content: "Do you still ignore that Morgenthau and his companions have been back in New York for several weeks, nearly a month? The above named gentlemen [Sokolow and Weizmann] seem to have succeeded in mismanaging this bit of work also. We shall know more about this on my return [to London] in October, I presume."

On October 2, Balfour received a confidential wire from Heron Goodhart, British consul at Berne, regarding a recent meeting in Berlin between Djemal Pasha, Foreign Minister Richard von Kuhlmann, and a leading Zionist, in which "certain promises" were made to the Jews in order to guarantee their cooperation in a new war loan. This in itself is odd. Kühlmann, who took over from Arthur Zimmermann following his resignation in August, was not only cool to the idea of encouraging a German Balfour Declaration, but shortly after his appointment had declared that Germany was not in a position to agree to plans that would rob her capricious ally, Turkey, of a province. Nonetheless, Goodhart warned, "From the above, it would seem that the German Government are making an attempt to counteract the effect of the British effort to liberate Palestine."

That same day, as Sarah took part in a wedding celebrated amid the harvest festival in the streets of Zichron Ya'akov, Turkish troops under the command of Hassan Bey, the Khaimakam of Haifa and one of Djemal Pasha's more notorious villains, entered the village and immediately arrested Sarah, Ephraim Fischel, and Tzvi Aaronsohn. Hassan Bey demanded that Yussuf Lishansky be given up as well, but Lishansky had disappeared into the fields where Sarah had already sent the young men of Zichron and hidden money for Yussuf.

Hassan Bey commenced his own festivities by torturing her father and brother for an entire day in Sarah's presence. She refused to give up her lover. The next day the Khaimakam, still smarting from European censure of Turkish atrocities, called a meeting of the village elders and informed them that unless they gave up NILI, he would do to the village exactly what the Aaronsohns said he had done to the Jews of Jaffa. Then he applied his skills to Sarah, with perhaps an extra fillip from her former admirer, Djemal Pasha.

British reports of Sarah's torments, dutifully pouched from Cairo to London, are unusually tight-lipped: The "gentlemen" of the Secret Service, having exposed her to the danger, were squeamish about the consequences. Two decades later, Ladislas Farago, an agent who aspired to be a writer of thrillers, dug up the details with prurient relish: her torturers pulled out her luxuriant red-gold hair by the roots, extracted her teeth and fingernails, seared her deft palms with irons, subjected her to the bastinado (a punishment still used today, in which the soles of the feet are beaten until they swell and burst), made her dance on red-hot bricks, and inserted freshly boiled, scalding eggs into the most sensitive areas of her body. They flayed the skin from her legs and torso and, mercifully, beat her unconscious. "Doubtless," wrote one of her diffident admirers in the security forces, "they attempted to assault her femininity as well."

All this was done to Sarah in the presence of her male relatives, her childhood sweetheart Reuven Schwartz, and her brothers' friends. She was paraded before her fellow villagers, some of whom rejoiced obscenely at seeing the proud Sarah brought low; four hags danced in the streets of Zichron Ya'akov like the witch hunters of Arthur Miller's *The Crucible*.

On October 4, in London, Edwin Montagu, buttressed by Lord Curzon, again staved off an irrevocable decision on the Balfour Declaration. Balfour retorted for the benefit of the War Office that "the German

Government were making great efforts to capture the sympathy of the Zionist Movement." In fact, the rumors of these efforts were more press plants by the German Foreign Office, desperately trying to retain the loyalty of the world's Jews in the face of rumors of the impending Balfour Declaration. But the false pearls of propaganda were by now real enough to inspire action. Impassioned editorials appeared in Lord Northchffe's London *Times*. The British Foreign Office and even the U.S. Embassy in London exerted pressure on President Wilson – who hung back from approving the declaration because his closest advisor, Colonel Edward House, distrusted Britain's annexationist agenda.

Sarah endured her torture for four days. According to legend, the Jewish Joan of Arc stridently defied her interrogators, forcing even the Khaimakam to admit she was better than a hundred men. The actress in her managed one last great performance. "Your end is nigh," she shouted magnificently through her pain. "You will fall into the pit I have dug for you!" On October 5, after seeing seven of her agents tortured in front of her and fearful that the Kaimakam would carry out his promise to destroy the village, Sarah asked permission to go to the bathroom and change her bloodsoaked clothes. Inexplicably, it was granted her. She went to the bathroom, and while a Turkish soldier stood guard outside, pulled a pistol from its hiding place behind a secret panel. After writing a lengthy letter of instruction and inspiration for the bereft families of NILI that blamed her betrayal on her envious fellow-villagers, she shot herself in the mouth.

Or so the legends say.

On October 6, Weizmann wired Alex Aaronsohn in Cairo: "We are doing our utmost to secure a Jewish Palestine under British auspices. Your heroic sufferings are greatest incentive our difficult work." The purpose of the telegram, Weizmann said, was to "strengthen NILI's position in the face of opposition from many Palestinian Jewish leaders who feared reprisals from the Turks."

Dr. Hillel Yoffe, leader of the *Yishuv* opposition to the Aaronsohns, was called in to attend the dying Sarah. How like a feverish dream it must have seemed to her, to have her brother's enemy minister to her final agonies. Yoffe found her lying unconscious on the floor of the bathroom with blood running out of her mouth. He gave her a caffeine injection to help her regain consciousness. He wrote in his diary: "She recognized me and pleaded, 'For God's sake, let me die! I beg you, kill me. I can't suffer any longer . . .' She cursed the military commander, the civil authority, the police officers, and most of all Osman Bey who had tortured her. When I wanted to rinse her mouth, she wouldn't let me."

At the London headquarters of the World Zionist Organization, the Balfour Declaration was given a final hearing by both Zionists and anti-Zionists on October 7. The beleaguered Foreign Office was flooded by resolutions from three hundred Zionist organizations all over the world. That day, Dr. Yoffe reported from his deathwatch: "Sarah's temperature has gone up but her pains are slightly weaker. She is completely lucid. Her right leg has improved slightly (especially the movement of the big toe) but her left leg and arm are completely paralysed. She keeps begging for an end to be put to her life."

On October 8 he wrote: "Sarah's condition is worse . . . At 3 AM she expressed the fear that she might lose her mind."

On October 9, the text of the proposed Balfour Declaration was sent to Sir Herbert Samuel, and he approved the policy he had initiated three years earlier. Also on that day, Dr. Yoffe wrote: "Sarah's pulse has weakened considerably despite injections of camphor and caffeine. She asked to say goodbye to her father . . . and to all the friends who come to her room. She asked them for the last time to look after her old father and pleaded once more that he be released . . . At 8:30 she gave up her soul without having revealed a thing to the Turks."

Ephraim Fischel was released later that month through an amnesty resulting from the secret Turkish peace negotiations, which continued after Aubrey Herbert left Berne until the Balfour Declaration was signed. On October 25, the Russian Zionist Executive leader Yechiel Tschlenow, arriving in London from Copenhagen, brought news of

Sarah's arrest and torture to Weizmann, who "suppressed" it from
Sarah's brother and commanding officer, Aaron. Aaron's services were
needed elsewhere; moreover, Weizmann could not have been eager
to have him rush back to Palestine, where he might not only disrupt
Allenby's advance but attract undesirable attention to himself from
the ranks of newsmen massing to mark the forthcoming capture of
Jerusalem.

On November 2 the Balfour Declaration was announced to peals
of celebration at the Royal Opera House in London. The following
week, the Bolsheviks took power in Russia away from the neutral Provisional Government. A meeting held at the Foreign Office immediately following the Balfour signing decided that the Russian Zionists
Tschlenow, Nahum Sokolow, and Vladimir Jabotinsky should proceed
to Russia at the same time that Aaron Aaronsohn would proceed to
America, all to promote an Armenian-Arab-Zionist entente, which
was Sykes's attempt to neutralize the effects of his secret agreement
with Georges Picot.

On November 13, Colonel French and Sir Ronald Graham of the
Foreign Office sent Weizmann a copy of a report received from Rotter-
dam with the odd request that he take no steps to publish it through the
World Zionist Organization before consulting them. The report was of
Sarah's death, and the diplomats' coldblooded assessment of its propa-
ganda value is far more chilling than any gruesome eyewitness details.

> I should be glad if you would have published through
> Reuter's Agency the following statement which is authen-
> tic, laying stress on the fact that it is received from Alexan-
> dria. Please do not mention Holland as being the source of
> the information . . .
>
> Begins: — It has been reported by refugees that owing to
> the great pressure the Allies are putting on the Sinai front
> the Turks are committing atrocities on the Jewish colonists
> in Palestine. The particular Turkish officials who are
> already well known as having participated in the massacre
> of the Armenians brought accusations against the Jews for
> espionage and treason and fomented strife between

non-Jewish population and Jews. With the aid of the Turkish officials several Islamic [*sic*] communities were pillaged, particularly the community of Sicaron Jacob [meaning Zichron Ya'akov], terrible atrocities were committed on the helpless people, both men, women, and children.

So as to extort confessions many men and women, together with some American subjects [*sic*] were stripped and chastised in public, some so severely as to cause death. Some men and women were taken away and nothing more is known of them . . . The Refugees beg most earnestly that reports from neutral Consuls in Palestine should be immediately asked for so as to avoid the possibility of the Turks denying these atrocities and solicit interference on behalf of the Jews of Palestine.

French noted with his customary scrupulosity:

Dear Sir Ronald . . . I am doubtful 1) about the desirability of saying that it comes from Alexandria, and 2) as to whether the publication is opportune at all. I gather that the report is probably true, and the pretext of the severities, that the Jews have been obtaining information for us. Anti-Zionists have I believe, prophesied that this would happen if Zionism were granted, and it seems possible that they may make capital out of the story.

By what appears to be an extraordinary coincidence, at the same time the propaganda obscuring Sarah's torture and death was percolating through the rarefied air of the Foreign Office, Lawrence recorded an entry in his campaign diary that became the most celebrated incident of his 1922 war memoir *Seven Pillars of Wisdom*. On November 20, 1917, he slipped into Dera'a, just over the Syrian border of the Galilee, disguised as an Arab in order to sabotage this strategically vital junction of the famous Damascus-to-Medina Hedjaz railway. Questioned and arrested by a Turkish sentry, he wrote, he explained that his white skin and blue eyes were due to his being a Circassian conscript. But Lawrence, his later biographers have pointed out, spoke little or no Circassian, and his boyish features and unique blue eyes were already famous in the Arab world as those of Aurens, his Arab nickname. That night, according to his account, Lawrence suffered an ordeal strongly resembling that suffered by Sarah Aaronsohn, in the course of which, he wrote, "the citadel of my integrity had been irrevocably lost." He was ushered into the presence of the governor, Nahi Bey, a sadistic tyrant who, when Lawrence rejected his advances, ordered him stripped, raped, and whipped to within an inch of his life. But here their ordeals differ in the most significant way: Lawrence, as he lay in a warm stupor allegedly savoring his degradation and pain, was directed to a secret door by a friendly Kurdish guard, given clean clothes, and allowed to tiptoe to freedom. Sarah Aaronsohn died from the horror of her injuries. It would be remarkable if the same military authorities were to capture two master spies within the same month, kill one, and release the other. Lawrence's later biographers have dismissed the Dera'a incident as fabrication, based on its unlikelihood, on Lawrence's well-documented tendency to embroider the truth, and based on his confessions to Captain Walter Stirling and Colonel Richard Meinertzhagen, who upon seeing Lawrence naked in his bath, noticed that the only weals on his back appeared to be recent and self-inflicted. From other war diaries and the logbook of the Royal Field Artillery, on the two nights that he was supposedly in Dera'a, it seems Lawrence was actually on reconnaissance in the Wadi Yutm with Colonel Pierce Joyce of the Arab Bureau.

Aaron was allowed to leave London for America on November 17, still ignorant of his sister's death. He was elated over news from Sykes that Balfour had credited him with Allenby's progress. The night before he left, he attempted to argue Israel Zangwill out of fomenting anti-Arab feeling. (Zangwill was later to propose a scheme to run the Arabs out of Palestine and into Iraq, a position propagandists conflated with Aaron's views.) Aaron was, however, fuming over another slight from Weizmann, who made sure he was "personally accredited" to Brandeis but forbidden to speak to the press.

Aaron arrived in New York on November 26. The next day, Reuters published the report received from Rotterdam with text supplied by Weizmann. All mention of "Sicaron Jacob" was expunged. The location of the atrocities was changed to Jaffa, where it was said all the leading men of the community were hanged in the presence of their

families for espionage and treason. The Foreign Office forwarded
Aaron his brother Shmuel's announcement of Sarah's and his father's
deaths (the latter a mistake). Aaron received the cable on December
1, and for six days returned none of Weizmann's anxious inquiries. His
diary entry, submerged amid detail of the formation of the Palestine
Commission, is curiously nuanced, as if he had, with Sarah's death,
lost his compass between propaganda and reality: "The sacrifice is
accomplished. I knew that we still had to face the greatest misfortune.
But it is one thing to fear it and another to know all hope is lost . . . Poor
father, poor Sarati . . . Her loss is the most cruel."

The diaries then fall silent. On December 6, Weizmann fulsomely
announced to the French Zionist Executive that "Mr. Aaronsohn
arrived safely in America and Mr. Brandeis seems to be very pleased
that we have sent him there," but he did not contact Aaron directly
until January 4, 1918, and then only with the curt and redundant message, "Regret to tell you news received from Egypt that your father and
Sarah both dead. Others are all right."

General Allenby made good on his promise to Lloyd George and
delivered Jerusalem well ahead of Christmas. He captured the city on
December 9 and entered it two days later, with Lawrence at his side.
Lawrence, newly promoted to major, described his triumph as a hol-
low one and attributed his disenchantment to the posttraumatic stress
of the incident at Dera'a. According to his close friend and biographer,
Robert Graves, he took mischievous delight in seeding his memoirs
with half truths rather than with outright lies. If there was no incident
at Dera'a, if in fact he pilfered details from the reports of Sarah's awful
death to enhance his chances of winning the Victoria Cross, and moreover knew that Aaron had mapped Allenby's route to victory, his tone
of self-mockery is easily understandable.

Though Allenby gave Aaron posthumous credit for the "lightning
strike" that made military history, at that time Allenby's invasion
made Lawrence world famous, while Aaron sank into the muck of
obscurity. On December 11, John Buchan, director of information for
the Foreign Office in London, received a request from New York for "a
line on Mr. Aaron Aaronsohn from Richard Gottheil, a friendly Jew."
Looking for work, Aaron had approached the Foreign Office's New
York propaganda office, recently established to rouse America into

complete support of the Allied cause. Buchan, who was already par-
laying his considerable writing talent into a political career, replied
that he knew Aaron through his work in Egypt and would be happy to
have him work for him in the New York bureau. Buchan's gratitude
was entirely candid. Most Foreign Office nabobs disdained propaganda
work as "undignified"; much of it indeed consisted of counterpropa-
ganda to American canards that British officers were effete snobs and
British enlisted men rowdy drunks all too eager to corrupt American
innocents abroad. Though Buchan balked at making his peers in London open their dining clubs to young Yank officers, he enabled the publication of a series of newspaper articles demonstrating the strength of
the temperance movement in Britain to Baptist America.

In the silence of Aaron's diaries, we can only speculate as to why he
approached the propaganda office for work. It was a way of speaking
to the press without speaking directly to the press, and thus a means of
outwitting Weizmann and his constraints. It was also a means of keeping himself occupied in the catastrophic depression that undoubtedly followed his sister's death. Members of the family today say that
his bursts of volcanic energy alternated with bouts of "the black dog,"
the fits of depression that also plagued Winston Churchill. The knowledge that he was responsible for putting Sarah in such an awful position would have been a burden almost impossible to bear.

On December 12, Buchan received a second letter of inquiry, this
one from Professor Lowell Thomas. Thomas, a small man with a black,
clipped, Vaselined mustache, was an odd combination of academic,
journalist, and mountebank, a practitioner of the new science of public relations who was traveling in Europe "at the head of a Mission
authorized by the United States Government to gather data for a series
of patriotic travelogues to help arouse the country" to unquestioning
support of the Allies. In fact, Thomas's mission was sponsored by a private group of Chicago businessmen who were part of the Committee
on Public Information, the unofficial propaganda department of the
United States government.

Thomas's sponsors also included Lord Curzon, Lawrence's first
benefactor, who now headed the Society for Anglo-American Friendship, newly formed to cement the ties between two English-speaking
cultures that had been poised to go to war against each other before

Germany presented an alternative. When Thomas received word of the capture of Jerusalem, he wanted to proceed there immediately with his photographer. Backed by letters from the United States Secretaries of War, Navy, and State, he requested an unprecedented favor: the right to film battles as they occurred. Colonel W. L. Fisher of the War Office, to whom Buchan forwarded Thomas's request, responded indulgently to the American's vulgar request: "Creel and the Secretary of War are very anxious that these gentlemen should meet with success . . . I do think it is important that we should put our case through as many channels as possible. Some will fail and some will succeed, and as the project has the blessing of the Administration I think it would be wise to give them some really good interviews. Let them go to really interesting places and show us in a good light as compared with the French."

Accordingly, Thomas was introduced to Sir Ronald Storrs, shortly to become the first British governor of Jerusalem. Storrs in turn introduced Thomas to the newly minted Colonel T. E. Lawrence, describing the highly photogenic young man with the astonishing blue eyes and sunburnt skin and dazzling white *chatta* as the "uncrowned king of Arabia." Thomas proceeded to film an unprecedented spectacle that today might be labeled a docudrama but was actually more like a companion piece to Rudolph Valentino's *The Sheik*. It was called *With Allenby in Palestine and Lawrence in Arabia* (shortened to *With Lawrence in Arabia* when Thomas published it as a book), and earned Lawrence, who professed to be embarrassed by it, an iconic status similar to Valentino's. A sixty-piece orchestra and a troop of scantily clad nautch dancers, not to mention Thomas's thrilling narration, accompanied real footage of Lawrence leading his Bedouins to the rescue of an unnamed Arab city. The *Manchester Guardian* called it "history without dogma, filled with adventure and beauty." "Housemaids and Boy Scouts love it," Lawrence remarked.

Aaron's new role was not quite so glorious. Buchan's New York office was designed to feed "news" items produced by the British Foreign Office to the *New York Times*, which the FO pronounced "much read by the prosperous Jewish classes." The Foreign Office intended that the Yiddish press should extract and publish the pieces. Gerald Butler, a young Cambridge don who was the Foreign Office liaison in New York, took special pains to, as he said, "perfect our machinery" through the Jewish branch of the FO's Department of Information, established to "conduct propaganda among Jews in all parts of the world, giving it the specific tone required by the Jewish temperament."

The Department was a full-service industry. According to its Foreign Office brief, it supplied news by cable to Jewish and other newspapers circulating in Jewish centers, maintaining a Jewish press agency to supply all Jewish papers with a weekly London newsletter; producing and distributing pamphlets and articles; replying to articles and comments "where necessary" in the general press; and producing and distributing films of Zionist interest, Yiddish plays, picture postcards, and illustrated lectures. Material was produced in England but distributed in the United States under the names of Zionist organizations.

One of the first items widely circulated through this machinery was a cable and accompanying news item received through the British ambassador at Petrograd. The cable, from the Russian Zionist Organization, read: "Jewish History sympathy assistance rendered by British Government in regeneration Jewish nation never eradicated." The news item, submitted for distribution through the "ordinary channels," was a graphic description of the "barbaric cruelty" suffered by old men, women, and children confined in "Austrian Concentration Camps for Jewish War Refugees" — which, according to the report, included hard labor on starvation rations for the men and forced nudity for the women.

Twenty years later, a young Austrian corporal named Adolph Hitler attributed Britain's victory in the first World War to her "amazing skill and really brilliant calculation" at manufacturing propaganda. In his autobiography, *Mein Kampf*, he wrote, with grudging admiration, "I, myself, learned enormously from this enemy war propaganda" — and, in words eerily reminiscent of Walter Lippmann's *Manufacturing Consent*:

> The art of propaganda lies in understanding the emotional ideas of the great masses and finding, through a psychologically correct form, the way to the attention and thence to the heart of the broad masses . . . English propagandists understood all this most brilliantly — and acted accordingly. They made no half statements that might have given rise to

doubts . . . Their brilliant knowledge of the primitive
sentiments of the broad masses is shown by their atrocity
propaganda, which was adapted to this condition. As
ruthless as it was brilliant, it created the conditions for
moral steadfastness at the front, even in the face of the
greatest actual defeats, and just as strikingly it pilloried the
German enemy as the sole guilty party for the outbreak of
the War: the rabid, impudent bias and persistence with
which this lie was expressed took into account the emotional, always extreme, attitude of the great masses and for
this reason was believed.

Aaron did not make an entry in his diary until March 10, 1918. When
he picked up his pen again, he wrote "it was out of the question" to
keep his diary so long as he was in the company of Felix Frankfurter,
Brandeis's amanuensis and "Zionist mole." Aaron may have been
heavily censored, resentful of his gag order, or simply on his guard.
He may also, under the deep waters of his depression, have been gathering information, and meditating on what to do next.

America was not at war with Turkey, and Wilson disapproved of any
participation in Zionist activities in Palestine that might be construed
as aiming at Turkey's dismemberment. American policy, particularly
in military circles, strongly opposed a British trusteeship and shied
away from assuming the responsibility directly. This difficulty might
have resolved itself had America declared war on Turkey. In sending
Aaron to America, Weizmann had hoped to bring this about, possibly
by bringing the full force of Aaron's powers of persuasion to bear on
Brandeis. In Aaron's highly charged state, this force would have been
considerable, but Brandeis, after three months, refused to budge.

Aaron grimly maintained his own grip on aid money, provoking a
treacherous response from the head of the Anglo Palestine Bank, who
wrote Ronald Storrs a politely venomous letter in which he dismissed
NILI and its sacrifices as "frivolous"; denied Aaron's contribution to
the Balfour Declaration; declared that the antagonism between Aaron,
"official political Zionism," and the emerging Jewish Labour Party
made it impossible for the general population of Palestine to accept the
special committee's leadership; and accused Aaron, in his "unlimited

ambition " of trying to starve them into submission. In January, Aaron also received his first letter from Alex on the subject of Sarah's death, beginning with excuses and ending with a brazen request to send copies of Alex's book from America.

In March, the old, ebullient Aaron resurfaced briefly. He was in motion, on his way home, where as part of the newly formed Zionist Commission for Palestine, he would be in a position to address his real passion, the economic development of his country. And in March, he and Ruth Mack resumed contact.

Judge Mack was one of the first people to whom Aaron wrote after Sarah's death. His letter is taken up with the machinations of Zionist politics and betrays nothing of his feelings. In fact, he never mentions Sarah. On March 3, Ruth broke their long silence after hearing the "news," now almost six months old, from Alex. She had married the year before. At the same time that she wrote Aaron a decorous letter of consolation, she also told him how much she hoped he would have to come back to America. She wrote him again a week later, and then again in a fortnight. She was hurt and puzzled at his lack of response: "Good-night. Please write. I have had only the cable for my birthday and the card from France. Of course if you are too busy, don't think of bothering but just if there's time. Ever so much love to you. Ruth."

Aaron had no room left in his heart for romance. The black depression that had always wrestled with his exuberant love of life was crowding out all other feelings. On March 21, in Cairo, he finally learned in full the wrenching details of Sarah's death. "If I should seek revenge on all the cowards and scoundrels," he wrote in his diary that day, as if eager for it to be read, "there would be hardly half a dozen people with whom I could shake hands."

Then, in Palestine, he received another major blow. Despite his discipline, despite his enormous sacrifice, he was once again odd man out, attached to the Zionist Commission for Palestine, where his talents and energies could be made use of, but not officially acknowledged. This was partly the doing of the Foreign Office in London, which, outrageously, had opposed his participation due to his services to British intelligence. In part, it was his own doing, or undoing.

The Zionist Commission for Palestine was headed by Weizmann and consisted of three loyal Russian and four British Zionists, with one representative Frenchman, Sylvain Levi. Aaron was attached to the commission as its agricultural expert. Its stated function was to reconstruct the prewar standard of living by supplying aid and repatriation, to survey and plan the country's "permanent economic development," and "to create harmonious relationships with neighbors." Its unofficial purpose was to inspire the flow of $100 million in development funds from America, the Hundred Million Dollar Fund originally pledged by Schiff and his financial colleagues.

Alex was also in Palestine, but Aaron avoided him. "You know I am not much of a boaster," wrote Alex to Aaron like a parody of himself, "but I can say in all sincerity never in all my life have I done better work, have I been nobler and stronger than during these dark months when – while despised and hated by everybody I fought for these very people without their ever knowing."

Too briefly, Aaron returned to science. He was finally given the opportunity to lift the famine in Palestine. He threw himself into surveying the vast stretches of fertile, untouched soil around Beersheba to increase food production rapidly for both soldiers and civilians. He produced an exhaustive study that became the basis for future agriculture, but then mired himself in politics again, worrying the old question of the flow of aid money like a dog with a bone. Those who contradicted him, including several leading businessmen, he indiscriminately labeled "filthy climber," "intriguer," and "blackguard."

Initially, he professed the warmest admiration for Weizmann, fanned, as always, by the promise of support. "He proved to be a friend with who I have every reason to be satisfied . . . Once more, America is my strength." But their old rivalry soon resurfaced. "It is realized that the question of agricultural production is just as important as the question of the productions of ammunitions," Aaron noted sardonically in his diary.

In mid-April, Aaron's black mood overcame him. Traveling through the Palestinian countryside, he was overwhelmed with guilty memories of Sarah and Absalom Feinberg. "Absa, Absa, where are you?" he wrote in his diary. "Sarati!" His wracking depression was mixed with a good deal of jealousy. Aaron was not accustomed to playing second fiddle. Though he tried his best to defer to Weizmann, his temper, always volatile, erupted. Leon Simon, a British civil servant and fellow commission member who would usurp Aaron's place in developing postwar Palestine, noted in his diary on April 28: "Aaronson [*sic*] has broken out at last," demanding to be fully recognized as a commission member and hinting at "dark intrigues, of which he said we would hear later." The dark intrigues, which are very sketchily documented, concerned the misappropriation of development money.

Stormy scenes developed between Aaron and Weizmann. On June 23, Weizmann wrote his "darling child," his wife, Vera, with whom Aaron was on good flirting terms: "Aaronsohn has left us and doesn't want to work with us any longer. I don't know why. He didn't quarrel with any of us, on the contrary, he parted from us with the utmost friendliness, but for some reasons (I don't know what) he doesn't want to work with us any longer. He didn't become attached to anybody here. He can't stand anybody and nobody can stand him! I don't know what impelled him but really I'm not very upset."

Aaron knew instinctively when he was being manipulated and did not respond well, in the depths of depression even less so. In his reports back to the U.S. State Department, William Yale, also attached to the commission as an observer, described a man he once admired spinning out of control. At a meeting to mediate sharply escalating disputes between Zionists and Syrians, who accused the former of clannishness and exclusionary practices in land dealings in Palestine, he noted disapprovingly that the only discordant note was struck by Aaron's "impulsiveness and vehement denials of accusations that he felt were unjust . . . Mr. Aaronsohn's knowledge of the conditions in Palestine, his familiarity with the agricultural and commercial possibilities of Palestine, his acquaintance with the people and politics of the country can be of great service to the Zionist Commission; but it is to be regretted that his aggressive and self-assertive character is such to stir up bitterness and antagonism among the Arabs . . . It is to be hoped that Dr. Weizmann will keep Mr. Aaronsohn in the background in all of the dealings of the Commission with the Arabs."

Since Aaron's last conversation with William Yale (who was sounding out his allegiances on behalf of the American State Department) and his most recent one with William Ormsby-Gare both revolved around his advocacy of equal rights for Arabs, this appalling irony is only understandable in light of his precarious emotional state. Aaron's own diary is silent on the subject. In fact, it cuts off at April 6 and does not resume until November 24. The April 6 entry reads: ". . . [CENSORED] is now to be a cheap national hero. Poor Absa!" Did Aaron mean Lawrence was the one to be so meretriciously exalted?

In May 1918, England was changed forever by the blowback of the global propaganda campaign, as former prime minister Herbert Asquith plotted his political resurrection. Asquith, as a leading Liberal, favored Wilson's ideal, "peace without victory," i.e., without forcing Germany to pay onerous reparations, which he believed would lead inevitably to another war. In retrospect, Asquith was right, but his convictions put him in the crosshairs of the "hardfaced men," largely Conservatives who had already made considerable fortunes out of the war and stood to make even larger ones out of the peace.

Asquith's plans were shattered by a widely publicized sexual smear campaign that named the Asquiths among forty-seven thousand British public figures inscribed in a so-called Black Book in Berlin as having been sexually corrupted by German agents. The German agents must have been both very busy and very selective, for their targets also included Aubrey Herbert, a shy man not noted for depravity and very happily married, and many other leading pacifists. A few years later, the smear campaign was to have curious repercussions in the strangely familiar affair of Jack Bilbo, a German panderer who wrote a series of infamous letters about his sadomasochistic flogging sessions with T. E. Lawrence at a homosexual club in London.

Newspaper magnate Lord Northcliffe, credited by many contemporary observers and by most historians as the author of the downfall of Asquith's government, publicly distanced himself from the "horrible business," but propaganda was – and is – an excellent cover for commercial interests that would not in themselves be considered legitimate cause for war. Though Margot Asquith considered the smear campaign the dirty work of Lloyd George and Lord Beaverbrook, another one of Northcliffe's connections is of even greater significance, particularly in terms of the mysterious origins and continuation of the war. In the summer of 1909, Northcliffe was introduced to Lloyd George in the tearoom of the House of Commons by Henry Dalziel, distant cousin to Davison Dalziel, the news lord who had taken over the Orient Express. In 1917 Henry Dalziel, who also had an interest in newspapers, bought the influential *Pall Mall Gazette* from Davison Dalziel, and in 1918 Henry Dalziel, now Liberal member of Parliament for Kirkcaldy and leader of Lloyd George's business friends, bought the *Daily Chronicle* to silence its attacks on the prime minister. Both Dalziels were awarded peerages for their wartime services, Davison in 1921 and Henry in 1927. The Dalziel name was to be very prominent in the postwar development of the Baghdad Railway, as the Constantinople-Basra link was incorporated into the Orient Express, a development considered so important by the politicians of the day as to be included in the treaty terms of the Paris Peace Conference. This, of course, would have been impossible if Germany had not been subject to onerous war reparations, which were heavily promoted in his newspapers, as we shall see in chapter 10, by Lord Northcliffe.

Asquith urged Lloyd George to send him as a British delegate to the Paris Peace Conference. Lloyd George wouldn't hear of it unless Asquith took a position in his new government and thus came under his thumb. Asquith refused, and thus suffered an ignominious loss in the general elections, known as the Khaki Election because Lloyd George forced elections immediately after the armistice so that his own position of delivering the knockout blow to Germany would be strengthened by the passions of chauvinism and Germanophobia.

In late July, Aaron left Cairo for London along with Ormsby-Gore. On August 5, he wrote Alex from Turin, and on August 18, from London, after stopping briefly at Paris, where he met once again with Edmond de Rothschild. With a new, uncharacteristic malice, he noted *Le Patron*'s disenchantment with Weizmann, who had announced intentions of breaking up the Jewish Colonization Association, and moreover had antagonized Edmond's son James. The British Foreign Office was particularly sensitive about good relations with French Jews because Francophile Syrians were endeavoring to prove that Palestine was an integral part of Syria and that the postwar settlement should involve the creation of a French-controlled Greater Syria stretching from the old Egyptian frontier to Alexandretta. Aaron also met up with the genius of twentieth-century public relations, "our friend Walter

[Lippmann], camouflaged as a Captain," with whom he enjoyed a close working relationship.

By November 25, Aaron was back in the United States, where he attended a luncheon given by the editor of the American *Nation*, a Progressive magazine with a long tradition of pacifism that employed the talents of both Lippmann and Felix Frankfurter. Aaron subsequently wrote a three-page report to Chaim Weizmann at the World Zionist Organization. The luncheon had honored the Protestant missionary Dr. Barton and his sponsor, Henry Morgenthau, and Aaron outlined Barton's plan: to federate all the oppressed nationalities of the Near East except for the Jews under a nominal Turkish suzerainty backed by British protection. However, the United States would occupy Syria and Palestine in a military and police administration similar to the Philippines, and would mediate in the event of future discord between Britain and France. In order to prepare for this scheme – which bore a linear resemblance to the many Morgenthau had already attempted to broker, the important difference being that the United States would serve an occupying role – the former ambassador proposed to President Wilson that he authorize a so-called smelling expedition, a missionary effort to investigate the interests of oppressed nationalities. This, Aaron dryly noted in his report, was a "striking parallelism" to previous American attempts to use humanitarian missions as a cover for commercial oil exploitation. "I have so far no facts to substantiate the suspicion that the so-called humanitarian aims of Dr. Barton and his group and the aims of Admiral Chester spring from the same source," he reported to Weizmann. "Nevertheless, a certain amount of suspicion is not out of place." The big-business interests behind Barton and Morgenthau included the Rockefellers (Standard Oil); the Morgans (J.P. Morgan Bank); the Steel Trust Company; and Charles Crane, a plumbing magnate with a special interest in water development – stimulated, no doubt, by the prospect of vast and lucrative pipeline projects.

Though Aaron's report was straightforward, informative, and generally disapproving, George Kidston added an ominous note back at the Foreign Office in London, to which Weizmann had wired a copy: "Mr. Aaronsohn's statement on the 'Barton-Morgenthau Case' is enclosed. I do not know what the 'case' is, but it is curious to see our suspicion of some sort of collaboration between these forces confirmed by Dr. Weizmann."

On the day of Aaron's death, the Foreign Office would send an emergency telegraph to Henry Alsberg, another World Zionist Organization delegate to the Paris Peace Conference, requesting a second copy of this report.

10.

Icarus Falls from the Sky

> There are people in the world who want to destroy every-
> thing. They have the fever of destruction. Even when they pre-
> tend they are building, it is only in order to destroy. When they
> put up a new building, they quietly knock down two old ones.
> They build cities so that they can destroy the countryside. They
> destroy space with telephones and time with airplanes. Human-
> ity is now dedicated to the task of universal destruction.
>
> — Jean Giraudoux, *The Madwoman of Chaillot*

It is no accident that surrealism, the revolutionary art form that took a universal language of dreams as its credo, was born in the spring of 1919 in a small hotel on the Place du Panthéon in Paris. André Breton and Philippe Soupault, its inventors, were among the many artists on the fringes of the Paris Peace Conference, where the need for a universal language was glaringly apparent. The turmoil, time pressure, and intellectual dishonesty, reflected back immedi-ately in the clicking shutters of an hysterical press, made surrealists of its youngest and most intelligent diplomats. Jean Giraudoux, then a young diplomat attached to the French delegation, was inspired to write his best-known play, *The Madwoman of Chaillot,* about four eccentric *grandes dames* of the Belle Epoque who rid Paris of a global conglomerate plotting to blow up the City of Lights for the sake of its mythical oil. Another supremely articulate junior diplomat, Harold Nicolson, relieved his frustration at being ignored by his superiors by keeping company with Jean Cocteau, André Gide, and Paul Adam. He described the febrile atmosphere as a "riot in a parrot-house," as world leaders raced to draw new boundaries across Europe and the for-mer Ottoman Empire, police competing nationalisms, feed the starv-ing millions of Central Europe, and create a new international alliance that would make another Great War impossible. All roads led to Paris, where the postwar world order was now being shaped, and speed was the essence of the new age. "The difficulty of all good peacemaking is time-pressure," lamented young Nicolson, who tore his hair out at the carelessness with which the Big Four (David Lloyd George, Georges Clemenceau, Woodrow Wilson, and Italian premier Vittorio Emanuele Orlando) assigned away the happiness of millions: "Hurry entails overwork and overwork entails imprecision." The machine-gun rattle of a million typewriters, the incessant shrilling of a million telephones, the drone of the newly invented airplane, and a Babel of interpreters reduced the largest of events to a blur. In that blur, mistakes were made that would haunt the world for another century. The grand chivalric search for a League of self-determining Nations that would replace the old structure of European alliances overrode the more pragmatic search for equitable reparations, and set the stage for the next world war. The new world order itself became a framework for the old alliances to reassert themselves. As the imperial powers of the nineteenth century rushed to establish mandates in the twentieth, the very notion of self-determination propounded by the pious Wilson made Orlando weep with laughter.

Giraudoux, who wrote *Madwoman* in 1939, replayed tragedy as farce and put the Big Four in corsets. His four madwomen set straight the problems of mankind in the course of an afternoon by locking the perpetrators of destruction in the sewers of Paris and throwing away the key. The Paris Peace Conference dragged on for months. It was perhaps not inappropriate that the leaders who had just sent the flower of their nations' manhood to their deaths should risk their own necks in hastily remodeled war planes like the De Havilland 4, which shuttled them back and forth from London to Paris. Those necks were on the political chopping block, as angry crowds demonstrated against the "Dawdlers of Paris" and their seeming inability to let the vital work of reconstruction begin in Europe and the Middle East. Through it all, Aaron moved like a man in a nightmare, with enough stones in his pockets to shatter the Hall of Mirrors at Versailles.

The delay arose largely from Britain's insistence, in collusion with France, on continuing its naval blockade of Germany long past the armistice, to bludgeon Germany into accepting war reparations terms guaranteed to strap her into penury for the next six decades. Hundreds of thousands were to die of cold and starvation in Germany alone while the interminable treaty was thrashed out, a treaty that many observers found more punitive than the war itself.

Reparations were particularly ticklish where America, and America's president, was concerned. Wilson's foreign policy as well as his *amour-propre* rested on his invincible sense of his own moral rectitude. America's president insisted that the peace settlements should not lead to future wars. The Fourteen Points that he presented as the basis for a comprehensive peace agreement stipulated that there would be no economic vendettas, no unjust claims, and thus no punitive reparations paid by the losers to the winners. The legacy of the Franco-Prussian War, the huge cash forfeit paid out by France to Germany, along with its provinces of Alsace and Lorraine, must finally be laid to rest. Germany had signed the armistice ending the war on the understanding that she would only be responsible for damage done by unlawful acts of war, i.e., aggressive acts against civilians, not for the costs of the war itself.

As winter wore into spring, it was by no means certain that Germany would sign the peace treaty. Under the terms of the armistice, she had already given up all the territory conquered since 1914, as well as most of East Prussia and Alsace-Lorraine. Allied troops occupied the Rhineland, and Germany handed over its submarines, Big Berthas, mortars, airplanes, and machine-guns, along with five thousand railway wagons, at the express request of the French commander in chief, Ferdinand Foch — who had demanded that the German surrender take place in restaurant car no. 2419 on the Orient Express. However, Germany itself was never occupied. The Allies did not enter Berlin in triumph, as the Germans had entered Paris in 1871. The German command structure, along with hundreds of thousands of trained men, remained strong while the Allies rapidly demobilized due to war fatigue, tax protests, and widespread labor unrest at home. On January 15, Field Marshal Sir Douglas Haig, Commander in Chief of the British Expeditionary Force in Europe, told Winston Churchill, now Secretary of State for War and Air, that the existing British army was "rapidly disappearing," and that unless an army of occupation was created, the Germans and the Turks "would be in a position to negotiate another kind of peace" — perhaps one with the United States in power instead of Britain.

With only thirty-nine divisions left in Europe, the British maintained their punitive naval blockade as their chief form of leverage against Germany. This quickly became a world-class embarrassment for the skittish Wilson and his insistence on making the world "safe for democracy." American Food Commissioner Herbert Hoover, the savior of starving Belgium, sent a three-man team to Germany shortly after the armistice to verify the German National Health Office description of a nation on the brink of mass starvation; Northcliffe's newspapers referred to the Germans' appalling plight as "Hun Food Snivel." Hoover's team reported back that most Germans were suffering from chronic malnutrition – in northern Germany alone eight hundred adults were dying of starvation every day. He insisted that the blockade be lifted to allow 250,000 tons of American foodstuffs to reach European harbors. The Allies accused Hoover of dumping America's pork and dairy surpluses on Europe, and rejected Germany's offer to pay for food out of her remaining gold stores, making it impossible to deliver "one pat of butter or one peck of wheat" to Germany until it surrendered its merchant fleet (inconveniently left out of the armistice agreements) and any gold still left in the vaults of the German exchequer.

Even the British occupation army in the Rhineland rebelled against such brutality to their former enemy. General Sir Herbert Plumer, commander of the occupation army, cabled the War Office that his soldiers could not stand the sight of wasted German children, bloated with edema, pawing through the garbage in British camps. Because prewar Europe had been a highly sensitive, interdependent economic network, which would not be re-created until the European Union, broad swathes of the continent suffered along with Germany. In Prague, the death rate for children under fourteen was 40 percent. Russia, which had lost most of its railroad transport and was unable to replace it with German manufacture, was in desperate straits as well. A plague of lice-borne typhus swept out of Russia and into Germany in 1918, battening on the weakened population. Lice flourish in the absence of soap, and the starving had consumed any fats that might have been used to manufacture it. The typhus outbreak was accompanied by an even more deadly killer, the influenza pandemic, which decimated the world in that year and the next.

"Men," John Maynard Keynes, another young Bloomsbury aesthete who attended the conference as chief advisor to the British Treasury, elegantly remarked, "will not always die quietly. For starvation, which brings to some lethargy and helpless despair, drives other temperaments to the nervous instability of hysteria and to a mad despair. And these in their distress may overturn the remnants of organisation, and submerge civilisation itself in their attempts to satisfy desperately the overwhelming needs of the individual."

On January 10, a pitched battle erupted in Berlin's streets between the Spartacists, backed by Vladimir Lenin with gold and food and orders to turn Germany into a Soviet satellite, and thousands of disgruntled, demobilized veterans known as the Freikorps, recruited to restore order by General Wilhelm Groener. The Freikorps attacked its fellow citizens with flamethrowers, machine guns, hand grenades, mortars, and artillery, leaving an estimated one thousand dead. The Spartacist leaders, Karl Liebknecht and the Polish-born Jewess Rosa Luxemburg, were clubbed to death with rifle butts on their way to prison. That same spring in a Munich beer hall, a rising young star of the National Socialist German Workers Party, Adolf Hitler, gave his first hoarse, spittle-flecked tirade against the Jews to a grimly approving crowd. As the spreading economic chaos threatened to engulf all of Europe, Hitler found in the Freikorps a ready-made constituency.

For two more months, while the Big Four unbuttoned their waistcoats at Paris dinner tables and tasted the pleasures of scandalous theater and the somewhat tamer amateur productions of their diplomat colleagues (including one by Sir Robert "Bob" Vansittart, Lawrence's cousin and Oxford nemesis), tens of thousands of men, women, and children died of starvation in Germany and Austria. Nicolson, Keynes, and the other aesthetes recruited to the conference found the juxtaposition of urbane levity and social decay not only surreal but revolting. It was a very long way from the "humane peace" Woodrow Wilson had promised. To Aaron, it must have evoked painful memories of the blockade in Palestine, of the British stranglehold on gold and food, and of his sister's pleas for both.

Wilson, at the outset of the Paris Peace Conference, held unparalleled power. A devastated Europe depended on America for everything, even its food supplies. "Never before had a philosopher held

such weapons wherewith to bind to him the princes of this world,"
said John Maynard Keynes. But Wilson's insistence on a missionary
vision of a League of Nations led him to ignore the unpleasant fact that
prior to the United States entering the war in 1917, the Allied powers
had secretly promised Italy the territories inhabited by Greeks, Slavs,
Albanians, and Germans; had promised to Romania frontiers that
would place Hungarians under Romanian rule; and had promised to
France areas claimed by the Arabs as the heart and center of their new
independent Arab federation, i.e., Damascus. In the ensuing melee,
the issue of what would happen to Syria became linked to the issue of
reparations.

Lloyd George adroitly stage-managed his Middle East strategy by
directing Wilson's anti-imperialist indignation against the claims
presented by Italy and France, and distracting him from scrutinizing
British-occupied areas such as Mesopotamia and Egypt, which Lloyd
George conveniently excluded from the Big Four's agenda. The Persian
Gulf emirates, Saudi Arabia, and Persia itself were already excluded by
private treaties and alliances, which left Syria the only contested area
in the Middle East negotiations. This one issue produced "a triangu-
lar situation of great embarrassment" between Wilson, Lloyd George,
and Clemenceau.

"What is interesting," said the always perceptive Harold Nicolson,

> ... is that the Arab Question involved Mr. Lloyd George, M.
> Clemenceau and President Wilson in three different but
> extremely unpleasant predicaments. Mr. Lloyd George did
> not see why we, having conquered Syria, should hand it
> over, with increased frontiers and in violation of our
> implicit promises to the Arabs. M. Clemenceau did not
> know how he would be able to still the clamour of the
> French Colonial Party without causing a breach with Great
> Britain. And President Wilson, who was informed . . . that
> the Syrians did not in any sense desire even a French
> "mandate," was much exercised how to reconcile this
> disinclination on their part with, on the one hand, the
> doctrine of self-determination, and, on the other hand, the
> undoubted fact that France and Great Britain had pledged

themselves by treaty to a solution by which that doctrine
would be flagrantly violated.

Britain's friendship with France was new compared to their centuries-old colonial rivalries and European wars. Moreover, because
of her higher troop level in the Near East, Britain felt entitled to play
the leading imperial role. Curzon, the head of the Eastern Committee, and his military advisors did not want a strong French presence in
the southern Mediterranean, close to the Suez Canal, where it would
be easy for her erstwhile ally to muscle in on increasingly vital oil supplies from Mosul and from Persia. "I am seriously afraid," the former
viceroy of India said as early as 1918, "that the great Power from which
we have most to fear in the future is France."

The Paris Peace Conference afforded an excellent opportunity to
renege on the Sykes-Picot Agreement, which Britain had regretted
almost immediately upon signing. According to Sykes-Picot, much of
the Syrian coast, i.e., today's Lebanon, would belong to France. While
Britain would control the sources of oil in central Mesopotamia and
Basra, the gateway to the Persian oil fields, France would control the
access of transport to Europe.

The British wanted the French out of Southern Lebanon. They
wanted control of Haifa and her access to Europe's Mediterranean
ports. France wanted more oil. She already had Algeria and Tunisia,
and was angling for Morocco. She wanted Damascus, the political
nerve center of the Arab world. She wanted a Greater Syria stretching
from Mosul to the Sinai. It was too late for the French to retake Egypt,
but Lebanon, the Syrian hinterland, and Palestine would give her a lock
on the Mediterranean. Backed by *Le Patron,* Edmond de Rothschild,
Palestine's chief prewar benefactor, France therefore opposed a British
trusteeship and wanted an autonomous Jewish entity attached to her
own Greater Syria. Moreover, she insisted that the Sykes-Picot Agreement of 1916, by which Britain and France had already fixed the border
between Palestine and Lebanon south of the Litani River, be upheld.

The controversy smoldered during January and February, during which months Aaron smoldered also. His energies were ill-used,
siphoned off into political discussions about ethnic majorities that
were not his strong suit. Emir Feisal, inseparable from his translator,

Colonel Lawrence, who attended dressed in flowing white Arab robes with a solid gold ceremonial dagger tucked into his sash, was granted an audience before the Council of Ten, consisting of Lloyd George, Clemenceau, Orlando, Wilson, two Japanese representatives, and assorted advisors. By the end of March, when struggles intensified, the council was reduced to the British, French, American, and Italian leaders and became known as the Council of Four. According to Robert Lansing, Wilson's foreign minister, all were entranced by the "perfume of frankincense" when Feisal spoke. The Lawrence of Arabia vogue was in full throttle, fueled by Lowell Thomas's overheated travelogue, now a hugely popular entertainment.

On October 3, 1918, the emir, accompanied by Lawrence and only fifteen hundred Arab cavalry, had galloped into Damascus (whose status was not defined in previous Middle East agreements) and hoisted the Arab standard. "This was an extremely awkward thing," Nicolson remarked. Although Allenby accurately informed the conferees that he had allowed Feisal to occupy and administer the city after he himself captured it, the British maintained that Feisal played a substantial role in liberating Syria and had thus earned the right to rule and to reject French advisors if he chose. The British were endeavoring to slash their way out of the tangled web they had woven; the Turks, no slouches at propaganda, had seized the opportunity afforded by the Bolsheviks' publication of Sykes-Picot to distribute its details to their Arab tributaries. Forced by King Hussein's complaints that Sykes-Picot contradicted the promises they had made to him, the British clarified their position in June 1918 by stating that those areas that had been independently Arab before the war and those liberated by the Arabs would gain independence, while those areas liberated by the Allies or still in Turkish possession would be drawn into one of the Allies' sphere of influence. Hence Feisal's rough ride into Damascus was a premature attempt, as his companion Lawrence blithely put it, to "biff the French out of Syria."

Britain obviously designed this tactic to appeal to Wilson, who was included in the Ottoman negotiations because Britain did not want the responsibility of policing all the new, self-determining nations she was busy creating out of the Ottoman minorities. The problem was Feisal's attitude toward the Jews, who had supported Wilson in his presidential campaign.

At the peace conference, Lawrence held out the vision of a throne in an independent Syria to Feisal, and downplayed the promises the British had made to the French and to the Jews. The British wanted Feisal to agree that Palestine was not part of Syria and to sign an agreement with Chaim Weizmann recognizing the Zionist presence there. Feisal needed British support and signed in January 1919. Weizmann, who also needed to shore up British support for Zionism in Palestine, which was wavering in the face of escalating violence over land distribution between Arabs and Jews, accommodated Feisal on the southern and eastern boundaries of Palestine. This further betrayal – not to mention the sight of Weizmann whispering with the young upstart Lawrence, now fully entrenched in his celebrity role – blistered Aaron's already raw sensibilities.

The French, in order to discredit Feisal, produced Syrian leaders of their own, who claimed that Syrians were not Arabs and deserved a country of their own under French tutelage. The rumblings of French-backed Arab unrest began that January, and Mark Sykes, who was angling for the governorship of Syria, flew to Cairo to quell them. Lloyd George, mindful that Clemenceau had conceded Palestine and Mosul to him at the end of 1918 to guarantee Britain's cooperation with France in negotiating against Germany, checkmated Clemenceau by linking this cooperation with the Syrian issue. Clemenceau, known as the Tiger because of his lethal record as a duelist, was caught between the rock of his French Colonial Party and the hard place of the reparations. He offered to fight a duel with Lloyd George, who wisely declined, but this connection would have fatal repercussions for Aaron Aaronsohn.

On February 3, Aaron embarked on his last great venture. At ten AM Colonel Walter Gribbon fetched him from his chamber at the Hotel Majestic to help design the north and northeast frontier of Palestine. These boundaries were the cynosure of all he had fought for. In Aaron's view, water would make the new Palestine economically independent. Such independence was the first and most important step toward nationhood, but it could not be taken without providing for transborder water development.

To capture Lloyd George's imagination, Aaron adopted the formula "the Jordan and its affluents [*sic*]." But, where Lloyd George saw biblical freshets, Aaron saw the region's water mains. Taking the Litani River in Lebanon as its northern border, his formula for drawing the boundaries included all of the headwaters of the Jordan. "In Palestine, like in any other country of arid and semi-arid character . . . the whole economic life directly depend[s] on the available water supply," he wrote in his painstaking, if less than perfect, English. "It is, therefore, of vital importance not only to secure all water resources already feeding the country, but also to insure the possession of whatever can conserve and increase these water – and eventually power – resources." He scientifically defined his north and northeastern boundaries by the Litani River and by tracing the extension of Mt. Hermon in the ante-Lebanon mountain range and its water basins. Mt. Hermon – "Palestine's real Father of Waters," with its everlasting snows and perennial feeder springs – was essential and "cannot be severed from it without striking at the very roots of its economic life." It desperately needed reforestation and other work to fully function as a national reservoir, and Aaron declared that "no one else but the Jew may be expected and trusted to work these miracles." Given Aaron's hyperbolic style, this may have referred to the resources afforded by the Hundred Million Dollar Fund and his own expertise. The Litani River, a focus of fighting in today's Lebanon, was "of vital importance to Northern Palestine both as a supply of water and power," and Aaron suggested that an international agreement be forged to utilize it for both the development of Northern Palestine and Lebanon.

Sir Henry Wilson, Commander of the Imperial General Staff and Lloyd George's military advisor, approved Aaron's plan immediately, but for very different reasons than those Aaron had in mind. Aaron's network of water sources reached as far as the oasis of Damascus, and whoever controlled Syria's water mains would control Syria. Aaron was assured by Colonel Gribbon, in charge of Ottoman affairs at the War Office and DMI Lieutenant-General George Macdonogh's assistant at the peace conference, that "my British friends would defend my

North and Northeastern frontier, but did not want to displease Feisal in giving us satisfaction so far as the East and South were concerned." Aaron's proprietary sense of his boundaries was a sign of trouble. He latched on to ideas like a pit bull, and with the sense that each day, more of his original vision was being stolen from him, along with the meaning of Sarah's brief existence; "his" boundary assumed life-or-death proportions.

On February 14, Woodrow Wilson left Paris to shore up his faltering support at home; the British took advantage of his absence to float several schemes that would leave France with nothing near what she had been promised under Sykes-Picot. Two days later, Mark Sykes arrived in Paris, having just returned from a disastrous Cairo excursion, in which he failed to stop the swell of Arab unrest with threats to withdraw British support. At the Hotel Lotti, Sykes succumbed to influenza. "A big loss!" lamented Aaron, who was now excluded from the Star Chamber of Zionist meetings. Moreover, his painstaking draft of the north and northeastern boundaries of Palestine, supported by "scientific arguments of which no one had previously thought," had been mangled in the rudest possible way by financial experts who, he complained bitterly, couldn't tell a thalweg from a watershed. The Russian Zionist leadership had assumed its own mandate and refused his request for funds. "Matters have reached a point that is absolutely unbearable," he confided to his diary. "It is impossible to keep up one's self-respect under such conditions." He begged Weizmann to allow him to resign. "I was sick and tired of remaining in the false position of a mistress who is loved in the privacy of one's room – but not recognized before the world." He presented Weizmann with an ultimatum that he doesn't describe but that probably involved being legitimatized with a befitting official position in the postwar reconstruction effort. Weizmann tried to get him to advise a Zionist conference in London, but Aaron refused.

Aaron's diaries cut off midsentence on February 19, 1919, with a curious notation: "Interrupted." His entries for the three months preceding the end of his life remain missing, even after repeated requests for information from the Foreign Office, the Ministry of Defence, the Central Zionist Archives, and the Aaronsohn Archive at Zichron Ya'akov, Israel. Members of the family believe they were destroyed by Alex Aaronsohn at the request of the British military, and a series of letters between Alex and General Allenby in the early 1930s suggests they are right. The following reconstructs his last three months, using his own, scanty correspondence, official documents, and the diaries and correspondence of others.

Felix Frankfurter arrived in Paris March 1 and inveigled Aaron into staying on to work on the boundaries. Frankfurter remained sanguine that the British Mandate in Palestine was fait accompli. Frankfurter was Brandeis's factotum, and Brandeis, a carefully balanced thinker who maintained a good deal of distance from Weizmann and his ideology, was interested above all in Palestine's economic development. Aaron was therefore of the greatest importance to him.

"A word as to Aaron," Frankfurter wrote Brandeis with the kindness of a man who unlike Aaron benefited from a mentor.

> In regard to him all kinds of irrelevancies and personal clashes have made people forget his indispensable — no other word is accurate — need to us. His defects are as plain as a barn door but they too are easily dealt with if he is harnessed to work under effective conditions as thus far he has not been. Not only have we no other expert in regard to a thousand and one technical Palestinian matters, including the central question of the boundaries, but he is a great expert in the eyes of those English and Americans who, in the last analysis, will determine the issues. He is persona gratissima to everybody who matters for us in the American and English delegations. Instead of utilising him to the full as a scientist all these weeks he has been allowed to fritter away his spirit and energy in futile bickerings and disorganisations. I think now there is an end to all this.

Frankfurter's optimism was premature. Old European rivalries reignited over Turkey, which, along with reparations, was the great spoils of the war and almost impossible to negotiate because of all the secret treaties and conflicting promises made during its course. Bolshevism was only one reason why Russia wasn't invited to the peace conference: Sykes-Picot was in itself an attempt to renegotiate the first secret treaty, the Constantinople Agreement of March 1915, which gave Russia parts of eastern Anatolia, Constantinople, and the Bosphorus Straits.

In November 1917, the Earl of Drogheda had clearly enunciated what would become Britain's position in Paris, and fully justified Prime Minister Orlando's mirth at the notion of self-determination:

> There is also the future danger which would be entailed by allowing Turkey to emerge from the war still, relatively speaking, a strong State, and with (in spite of her recent defeats) an enhanced military prestige. There is no doubt that in present circumstances the Turks would insist on the Sultan retaining the Caliphate, with all the prestige that attaches to it in the Moslem world. Pan-Islamic intrigues, so far from being checked, would be redoubled, and we might have great trouble to face. Present gain, in fact, might mean far greater future loss.

When Turkey concluded an armistice with Britain on October 31, 1918, Djemal Pasha, Enver, Talaat, and the other wartime leaders of the Committee of Union and Progress (CUP) immediately fled the country on a German submarine bound for Odessa to avoid prosecution for their crimes against Armenians. (Talaat and Djemal Pasha died in 1921 and 1922 respectively, both at the hands of Armenian assassins. Enver was killed in 1922, fighting the Red army at the head of a Turkic guerilla band near the Afghan border.) A competition arose to fill the ensuing power vacuum between Sultan Mehmet VI, who inherited the Caliphate upon his brother's death in July 1918; the Liberal opposition, who had pledged a separate peace to Aubrey Herbert; what was left of the CUP; and representatives of the Allied powers, who tried to influence Ottoman politics but soon began fighting among themselves. Mehmet, destined to be the last Ottoman sultan, actively pursued appeasing the Allies, especially Britain, to get a more favorable peace treaty. Unfortunately, though he was by no means a nationalist, what mattered most to him was what mattered most to the British: the preservation of Constantinople as the seat of the Caliphate and of his own authority over the Muslim population of the Middle East.

At the same time that he begrudged France her Greater Syria, Lloyd George wished to see Turkey lose all her Arab territories – Syria, Mesopotamia, Palestine, and Arabia – and America assume mandates for the privilege of policing Armenia and Constantinople. However, the United States, never having declared war on Turkey, did not share Britain's appetite for carving it up and moreover had a strong economic incentive not to. Oil was reemerging as a source of tension between Britain and the United States, along with a potential new arms race. The Admiralty, having gotten rid of the Russian menace, did not want to see a strong America at the eastern end of the Mediterranean, particularly when the oil for its ships was at stake.

Like most difficult decisions at the peace conference, Turkey's disposition was tabled until May, when, because the German negotiations would also be on the table, Britain would have the most leverage over France. As in 1916, with Turkish suzerainty left dangling, the fate of a Zionist Palestine could not be decided, and Britain could not behave as its trustee without justifying accusations that she was landgrabbing. Woodrow Wilson publicly vowed support for a Zionist Palestine but was subject to other pressures imposed by the matter of self-determination – notably the wishes of the Arab peoples and those opposed to dismembering Turkey. Weizmann petitioned Brandeis to come to Paris to shore up Wilson and issued a strongly worded directive to the Zionist ranks: "It is absolutely essential at this most momentous stage of our work that there exists complete unity in all sections of the Jewish population and, above all, the strongest discipline, as otherwise the result of our laborious and patient activities will be seriously endangered." In January 1919, he followed General Gilbert Clayton's suggestion to recall Vladimir Jabotinsky from the Zionist Commission because of his "radical opinions": the founder of the Jewish regiment had reported pessimistically on the British military situation in Palestine and alleged discrimination against the Jewish population there.

Weizmann cleverly played on the fears of Clayton, Wickham Steed, and others, that if the Jews were "disappointed" over Palestine there would be "too much bitterness produced in the new world," and they would be "driven" into anarchy and Bolshevism. It was not taken as an idle threat. Lloyd George was called home to deal with violent labor riots in Newcastle in February – the well-organized Eastern European

Jews in London's East End constituted another large and potentially disruptive bloc of workers. The Irish capitalized on the general disorder with fresh demands for their own self-determination. In India, an ascetic Hindu named Mohandas Gandhi was igniting rampaging mobs with his nonviolent protest movement, *Satyagraha* (fidelity to truth).

Weizmann's skillful deployment of carrot and stick resulted in more boundary concessions. On January 31, he jubilantly wrote his "Verochka": "The English are apparently now prepared to go much further than ever before and are prepared to agree to the whole of Transjordan up to the Hedjaz road . . . I . . . think that the northern boundary should be as far south of Syria as is compatible with the water-supply."

On March 9, fresh fighting broke out in Egypt over the question of Egyptian autonomy, fighting so severe that the British suddenly faced losing control of the country altogether. The March riots forced Britain to retrench. Arab nationalist disturbances increased in Palestine, due, Balfour and Clayton were convinced, to aggressive behavior by Zionists and their leaders. By early April, Weizmann was once more promising that "the power and influence of the entire Zionist Organization will be directed to the avoidance of everything in utterance or act which would justify a misunderstanding of our purposes."

As the peace conference ground into April, world events cast a dim light on the prospect of making the world safe for democracy within the framework of the fragile Anglo-American "special relationship." In Amritsar, the sacred city of the Sikhs, an angry mob that had just attacked two local banks knocked an Englishwoman off her bicycle and beat her senseless, offering a pretext for British troops to open fire on a peaceful crowd of six thousand pilgrims, leaving four hundred dead and fifteen hundred wounded. In Ireland, said the *New Statesman,* one of England's most respected liberal journals, Britannia ruled by "bayonet and machine-gun."

Wilson returned to Paris in mid-March greatly weakened by a rebellious Republican Congress that did not want to support Europe financially; in addition to opposition from the Senate, he had confronted a tumultuous demonstration of Irish Americans demanding independence for Ireland. Lloyd George promptly picked the same fight Britain had picked with Germany before the war. Eager to avoid an arms race with America that would cripple his cash-strapped nation, the British prime minister attacked Wilson's attempt to strengthen the Monroe Doctrine in the convenant for the League of Nations; however, he suggested he might change his mind if the American president agreed to abandon his navy's shipbuilding program, which would soon make the U.S. fleet the equal of the British navy. Lloyd George and Clemenceau proceeded to take turns mugging Wilson over control of the Saar; the disposition of the mandates over Germany's and Turkey's former colonies; and, most important, the punitive reparations that South African general Jan Smuts had persuaded Wilson to ratify, in the form of pension payments. This face-saving ploy doubled the number Wilson had been prepared to accept, allowing him to pacify Congress and facilitate repayment of America's $8.7 billion in war loans.

Wilson's constitution, sapped by the loss of his control and the spectacle of his Fourteen Points being blown to shreds by Lord Northcliffe's unrelenting anti-German propaganda, gave way. On April 3, he fell ill with what his physician, Rear Admiral Dr. Cary Grayson, diagnosed as influenza but Herbert Hoover believed was a stroke. Cynical diplomats chalked it up to evasion. Although the president recovered three days later, he handed over many negotiations to Colonel Edward House, who had never favored dismembering Turkey.

Falling back on self-determination, in April Wilson appointed a commission to determine the popular will — the King-Crane Commission, led by Charles Crane of the "Smelling Expedition," which subsequently got lost in the dust of other diplomatic efforts. Aaron, originally considered for the commission's Syrian flank, considered it a frivolous appointment and turned it down: "I should probably feel much honoured that the high-minded Zionist leaders have deigned remember my existence. I daresay, though, it is a bit late in the day . . . Will you please then inform your mandataries [*sic*] that I duly appreciate their feelings and shall spare them therefore, the unpleasantness of my company."

Turkey and reparations, the two most difficult items on the table, hit the agenda at the same time, in late April and early May. Both the British and the French governments were afraid of being overthrown if the reparations figures turned out to be too small. Lord Northcliffe, who was heavily crossinvested in shipping as well as railways, led the

British hue and cry for "full indemnity from Germany and ton for ton" restitution for British shipping losses. Lloyd George and Clemenceau urgently needed to justify the high human cost of an unpopular war and to restore their bankrupt treasuries by shifting the burden of payment for their war loans away from their taxpayers onto German shoulders. The horrors of war had made their constituents unwilling or unable to work, Keynes wrote, and the desire for vengeance made them greedy. Nothing less than Germany's merchant marine fleet, her coal, her steel, her railroads, and all her stores of gold would satisfy them. The conservative papers, stirring the pot of atrocity stories, all cried for the largest figures: as Lloyd George moved into conciliatory mode, Lord Northcliffe – whom Lloyd George had pointedly not invited to the Paris Peace Conference – accused even the prime minister of being under the sway of pro-German forces.

In the first week of May 1919, a German financial delegation composed of private bankers was called to Versailles to review the treaty terms. It was headed by Max Warburg, a distant cousin of Otto's and brother of Paul, and by his legal counsel, Carl Melchior, an M. M. Warburg and Company partner. Both Jews were sensitive to the rancorous atmosphere attendant on the peace process. Warburg in particular feared an anti-Semitic backlash if the Entente terms proved too harsh, and tried to convince the German government to send its Finance Ministry officials instead; but the government insisted that he and his colleagues had more foreign stature and negotiating skills, and the Allies would thus be more sympathetic to them. Perhaps the German government thought it could appeal to the Jewish American vote – by a neat irony throughout the war, the Warburg banking network had managed to remit money through Germany to Palestine despite the British blockade.

Otto Warburg, Aaron's mentor and a leader of the Berlin Zionist Executive, was called on by Lord Alfred Milner to write an opinion as to what should constitute the northern boundaries of Palestine. Warburg supported Aaron's original assessment. He also wrote an opinion on German private-capital investment; since Palestine was not a German colony, its investors hoped to maintain their commercial interests there.

Max Warburg believed that Germany would be fully restored in a postwar world. He was staggered by the actual reparation figures when they were previewed in the newspapers in April and warned no German delegation would sign such a document in the face of mounting unrest at home. With faith in President Wilson's idealism, he approached Colonel House through Thomas Lamont, an American member of the Reparation Committee and a partner at J. P. Morgan. Warburg was intent on meeting with Wilson to lay the groundwork for a reasonable settlement. Wilson ducked a face-to-face encounter and ignored a memo in which Max railed against the British naval blockade and demanded a neutral arbitration court to decide the outstanding questions of war guilt and reparations. By virtue of his illness or the political quagmire into which his rigid principles had led him, Wilson appeared to be having second thoughts about everything, including Zionism. Several times in May, Felix Frankfurter sought the president's reassurance of his support.

On May 1, Aaron's British employers dashed the last of his hopes of the payment he had sought all along for his services: the hope of a broad economic base for the new country that would lift the fortunes of both Arab and Jew. The Political Section of the British Delegation to the Peace Conference rejected his northern boundary out of hand, despite the Military Section's promises of support. The Political Section felt that "so far as the irrigation of Palestine is concerned the headwaters of the Jordan in the Banias area . . . should be quite sufficient without the necessity of taking into account Mr. A's extreme projects." Aaron, with the backing of the Military Section, drew his line considerably further north above the mouth of the Litani to include a strategic stretch of that river, the entirety of Mt. Hermon, the basin of the Upper Jordan, as well as the vital train junction of Dera'a. His "extreme project" was to lift the water of the Litani over the narrow divide into the Jordan basin, thus increasing the volume of water available for irrigation and, coincidentally, hydroelectric power. Aaron saw a unified, up-to-date water-management system as the key to success in the region, one that would help the Lebanese realize the agricultural potential of the Bekaa Valley as well as carry water to the Negev Desert. He also undoubtedly saw himself as the only person to manage this great project, so dear to Brandeis's heart and certain to attract funding. The British Political Section, on the other hand, objected that the Syrian and Lebanese governments would never consent to Aaron's "maximum demand"; even more important, they claimed, his map would include within the boundaries of Palestine a strong, well-organized Arab nationalist, Muslim population.

Because the diaries are missing, Aaron's response to this final disappointment can only be surmised. However, by now he knew that Britain had other reasons for turning down his boundaries. Earlier, on April 27, Robert Szold, Henrietta's brother and head of the new Zionist Relief and Construction Department in Jerusalem, had cabled Frankfurter: "If a Commission comes now it will receive unfavorable and hostile reports from everyone and every argument will be set up to show the impossibility of carrying out our scheme, that the land cannot bear it and the population will not tolerate it." In a "Secret and Confidential" memo, Szold accused Britain of "rampant old-time imperialism," using Palestine as a beachhead to grab all of Syria to the north; of encouraging Arab activity at the expense of the Jews, if not actively stirring up agitation against them; and, in effect, of trying to back out of the Balfour Declaration. He implored Frankfurter to persuade Wilson to issue a statement protecting the Jewish national homeland, and, if it was not guaranteed in the peace treaty, to implement an American mandate in Palestine.

Palestine was in fact on the brink of anarchy, impelled by the April publication of Egyptian press reports that President Wilson and the Allied nations had concurred that the foundations of an independent Jewish state should be laid in Palestine. The source of the reports was a March 4 meeting in Washington between Wilson and a Jewish delegation headed by Judge Julian Mack, in which the president, according to his officials, had been noncommittal. It was unclear how the news had been leaked, but the result appeared to be the fulfillment of Aaron's bleak predictions that the premature founding of a Jewish state would lead to civil war.

In Paris on May 7, in the Château Trianon, Count Ulrich von Brockdorff-Rantzau and five fellow German delegates were led to the "table of the accused," situated next to a window filled with flowering cherry trees, a mocking promise of spring. Brockdorff-Rantzau, the Kaiser's first cousin, turned pale and trembled with nerves and exhaustion as Clemenceau informed him that there would be no face-to-face negotiations on the peace. One of the few senior foreign service members who had defied the German military leaders Erich Ludendorff and Paul von Hindenburg in calling for an early peace, Brockdorff-Rantzau refused to accept the war-guilt clause. He was given fifteen days to accept the treaty terms, or the Allies, who had lifted the blockade to commence negotiations, would resume it.

On May 8, Alex Aaronsohn again exercised his appetite for drama – in a way that, this time, helped sign his brother's death warrant. He cabled Aaron and Felix Frankfurter from Palestine that the British had betrayed them yet again: "I deplore to have to state that the British have lost all power and prestige here. The Arabs dictate to the British Administration . . . Never has she shown herself more weak and unfair than here in Palestine!" Implicit in his "secret" cable, inevitably read by the censor, was the threat that the millions of Jews remaining in Russia, Poland, and the Ukraine would unite in despair at the stillbirth of Palestine. "And if it be true that a dozen Jews have made Bolshevism which destroyed Russia and is threatening the world, what is going to happen when desperate millions are going to organize the most destructive power the world has ever known?"

On May 9, Britain's Political Section disdained Aaron's northeastern boundary because it would increase the Muslim population of Palestine. The Political Section included, however, its own demand to include the same water-rich territory in a new southern Syrian state also to be under British mandate. That same day, British troops opened fire on a political rally in Dublin. The rule of terror was now out in the open, and the life of one man, valuable though Aaron might be, was political small change.

Two days later, Aaron was on the diplomatic shuttle plane to London. There is no record of why he went there or what his movements were over the course of his four-day stay. However, Weizmann was already in London with the other official Palestinian Jewish delegates to the peace conference, having called a special meeting with William Ormsby-Gore, David Hogarth, and Arnold J. Toynbee, the soon-to-be-famous historian who was then, along with Harold Nicolson, a young advisor on boundaries. Colonel Walter Gribbon, Aaron's handler, was to represent the War Office. The purpose of the meeting was for the Zionist delegates to "negotiate" the aims and scope of the Inter-Allied

Syrian Commission, which was to become part of the King-Crane Commission, with the Foreign Office. Commander Hogarth thought the King-Crane mission – to determine who the majority of peoples of the soon-to-be-former Ottoman territories wished to hold their mandates, a "dishonest enterprise," ripe for mischief. President Wilson had told Charles Crane that the United States remained committed to the Balfour Declaration but that his commission had to "go through the motions" as far as Palestine was concerned. "Of course, the whole commission is a sham," wrote Frankfurter, because the Turkish peace settlement had not been concluded and would revert to the League of Nations "on a totally different basis" than that contemplated by the commission.

Weizmann's letters are uncharacteristically silent on exactly what the Zionists negotiated – they contain a six-day gap when the meeting took place. Palestine was left out of King-Crane's eventual itinerary. Aaron's diaries from the same dates are believed destroyed. It is not unreasonable to assume that Aaron arrived in London fresh from his stunning disappointment in Paris in an extremely heated if not hysterical state, barged into the meeting, and presented Weizmann with a final version of his long-debated ultimatum, including a demand that the Foreign Office honor its promises regarding his boundaries. If he did not get his way, it would be fully within his range of behavior to threaten to smash the Balfour Declaration, just as in 1917 he had threatened to smash NILI, and effect an American mandate in its place. He had, by now, nothing to lose – a dangerous position in which to put a man like Aaron. He had a direct line to President Wilson through Felix Frankfurter, Louis Brandeis, and even the unorthodox Henry Morgenthau. Furthermore, according to his 1917 interview with the U.S. State Department's William Yale, he not only personally opposed the immediate foundation of a Jewish state in Palestine, but would fight against it with his highly placed contacts in the United States. William Ormsby-Gore, assistant war secretary, would have been highly susceptible to this form of blackmail, having encouraged Aaron's propaganda activities in the first place; David Hogarth, Lawrence's mentor, was no great lover of Aaron or of a Jewish Palestine; and Toynbee (who worked with Lord James Bryce) was only too aware of where an investigation into wartime propaganda might lead.

The platform of reparations, intended to punish Germany so severely that it would never start another war, stood on two shaky legs: that Germany had started the war by invading neutral Belgium, and that German troops had behaved atrociously toward civilians. The first was never firmly established and to this day remains a subject of debate. Keynes and others were convinced that the war began six weeks before the invasion of Belgium with the assassination of Archduke Ferdinand at Sarajevo, an event in which Germany had no part. The prime piece of evidence used by a harried young staffer named John Foster Dulles in establishing Germany's war guilt was then-Ambassador Morgenthau's account of a July 5, 1914, meeting between the Kaiser and his chief advisors at a hotel in Potsdam seven days after the Sarajevo assassinations. At that meeting, Morgenthau had alleged that the emperor of all the Germans announced his readiness for war; this was later debunked as fiction in 1926 by Sidney Fay, the authoritative historian of the war's origins.

Fay attributed the "legend of the Potsdam Council" to a garrulous waiter and to the ambitious Count von Wangenheim, German ambassador to Turkey. Why Morgenthau, an anti-Zionist suspected of being a German agent intimately connected to the German-Jewish banking industry, and who had always enjoyed the most cordial relations with the German Embassy staff in Constantinople, would repeat such a serious canard remains a mystery — unless it served his own purpose of many years and in many forms: to pursue friendly, potentially commercial relations with Turkey. Morgenthau, like Aaron, was on the fringes of the conference in Paris. He had never lost sight of his ideal of a unified Turkey friendly to United States interests, and reconstituted it under the mantra of self-determination as a "federation of all oppressed minorities under a nominal Turkish suzerainty." Embittered by the way he felt he had been betrayed over his aborted peace mission in 1917, he had become increasingly vocal in his opposition to Zionism. Despite his by now unmitigated anti-Zionism, and with a reputation as a loose cannon, Morgenthau attended the peace conference even though he had failed to be elected as a delegate, as a minister without a portfolio.

The second charge which endangered Britain's reparations claims, that German troops had committed atrocities on civilians, was supported by the kind of propaganda stories that Aaron had a hand in writing at the instigation of William Ormsby-Gore. That knowledge alone made Aaron, in his "irritated and sensitive" state, as the Egyptian High Commissioner Sir Reginald Wingate put it, a dangerous man at the peace conference. Aaron had even more explosive information on Ambassador Morgenthau's aborted mission: that British officials had kept almost $1 million raised by German-American Jews from reaching their starving, civilian coreligionists in Palestine was preeminently newsworthy – not to mention the fact that a beautiful young woman, a true Jewish heroine, who had provided the British army with its chief source of intelligence in Palestine, had died as a result. With increasingly close scrutiny of the blockade by Liberals like Herbert Asquith, who with his ambitious wife, Margot, lunched and plotted in Paris, waiting in the wings to pounce on Lloyd George's every mistake, the publication of such news might compromise not only Britain's moral stance in the Balfour Declaration but in the all-consuming question of reparations as well.

All three Britons, Ormsby-Gore, Hogarth, and Toynbee, must have blanched at the thought of how such a presentation might affect the righteous American president and his support of reparations, not to mention the still-kicking idea of an integral Turkey. As we have seen, on the last day of Aaron's life, Henry Alsberg, one of the Zionist delegates, received an urgent request from the Foreign Office for Aaron's November 1918 report on the "Barton-Morgenthau Case" and the future of Turkey and Asia Minor as envisaged by Morgenthau and the American Board of Commissioners for Foreign Missions.

On May 15, Aaron left for Paris, apparently having made some headway in London, carrying "documents of vital interest to the Paris Peace Conference" – his boundary maps. Tsilla Feinberg, Absa's sister, lunched with Aaron in London before his flight and begged him not to get on the plane. Weizmann, according to Aaronsohn family members, was supposed to fly back with him but, at the last minute, decided not to. Weizmann's letters corroborate the fact that he cancelled in such haste that he left his cigarettes on the plane.

Israeli historians, perhaps seeking to romanticize their lost leader, have attributed Aaron's own haste to a pressing birthday engagement with a mysterious female, but it is unlikely that Aaron, in his highly agitated state, would have had much time for social niceties. In fact, there was no time to waste. England's labor problems had produced a transport strike and there were no boats that day. Frankfurter was in Paris, Warburg was in Paris, and, to the best of Aaron's knowledge, so was Henry Morgenthau — though he had in fact been called unexpectedly to Poland by Washington to intercede in behalf of its Jews. "Le Patron" Edmond de Rothschild, who had no great fondness for Weizmann and upheld the French government's position on annexing Palestine to Syria, was also in Paris. The Ottoman carcass was on the butcher block, much to the distress of Harold Nicolson, who observed the levity with which "these irresponsible men," Lloyd George, Clemenceau, Italian foreign minister Sidney Sonnino, and Wilson, were slicing up the Middle East "as though dividing a cake." And on May 17, Germany's delegation was scheduled to respond to the treaty terms, a position that gave Aaron his greatest leverage.

There are many irregularities in the Kenley-Paris flight manifest for May 15, 1919. Aaron is listed as "Herr Aaronsohn," even though he carried a British passport and is described as a British national in the documents of the Paris Peace Conference. The pages of the flight records for that day are badly stained with what appears to be either water or smoke and, in one instance, are overwritten, but it is clear that an unusual number of unscheduled flights took off, with military personnel as passengers. Despite what was later reported as an intense fog, two scheduled flights carrying a Captain Chadwick and a Lieutenant Vance preceded Aaron's. The two RAF officers left Kenley at 0030 and arrived in Paris at 0515, then left Paris at 0955 and arrived at Kenley at 1640, apparently staying in the air for almost twelve hours in Aaron's flight path. Another scheduled flight carrying a Lieutenant Briggs left Paris for Kenley at 1210, in time to intercept Aaron's flight. There is no time of arrival recorded for Briggs, who is logged in as having arrived from Paris at Kenley three days later. In what appears to have been an unscheduled flight, a Lieutenant Fitzgerald-Eager left Kenley for Marquise, the RAF base near Boulogne, at 1200 but did not record a time of arrival. The only other takeoff, which has a question mark next to it in the records for that day, was Aaron's.

Aaron's plane was cleared for takeoff at 1340. The two-seater mail plane carried Aaron and his military pilot, Captain Elgie Jefferson. According to the flight manifests, Jefferson was not one of the regular pilots on the London-Paris run and had only flown it once before, with T. E. Lawrence as his passenger.

Elgie Jefferson was only twenty-three. The last descendant of a proud family of Manx landowners, and his curmudgeonly father's pride and joy, he had enlisted in the King's Liverpools in 1914, a Boy Scout leader straight out of a school still known for its brand of muscular Christianity. He developed a reputation as a daredevil pilot in France, where he was decorated with the Mons Star after being shot down. He was also attached to the French army and received the Croix de guerre. Recovering from his war wounds, he was tapped by the Air Ministry as the RAF was forming and, only weeks before, had established a record time of seventy-five minutes to Paris with Colonel Lawrence, an airplane buff, in tow. He was recently married. Two weeks after his death, an article by him on the subject of his war adventures appeared in the school paper of his alma mater, King William's College, where his father had been an Old Boy before him. "Those stirring days are over, alas!" the young man lamented. "Still, we did have a good time!"

A plague of bad weather had further ravaged Europe that spring. The Channel was stormy. There was dense fog as well, a chronic problem at Kenley, where the fog descended so quickly and so heavily that at night it was sometimes impossible even to walk down the long hill leading from the train station to the aerodrome. Only days before, a plane carrying the Conservative Leader of the House of Commons, Andrew Bonar Law, had been denied clearance under the same conditions.

In 1919, aeronautics was still in its infancy. Under the aegis of Winston Churchill, military awareness of the airplane had emerged during the war, and a handful of small established companies like De Havilland, which was to become the British equivalent of Boeing, threw themselves into turning out hundreds of new flying machines that, though nowhere near the scale of World War II production, far outstripped their previous capacity. To meet the pressures of military demand, they subcontracted components to companies with no experience in aviation. Wings, fuselage, and tailplane were made by one company; engines by another; instruments and wheels by yet another. The final product was cobbled together at makeshift aerodromes like that at Kenley, a village golf course appropriated by the Royal Flying Corps in 1917. The assembly-line process had its perils: over half of all airplane crashes in World War I were caused by mechanical failure. After the war, the remaining planes were converted to VIP status by slapping on coats of silver paint and installing such luxuries as cocktail cabinets and, astonishingly, wireless telephones.

Aaron's plane came from one of seven hangars crammed with aircraft standing on their tails to save space. The only runway was the slick grass of the common. Several fatalities involving a DH-4 had already occurred. With demobilization under way, the aerodrome had run short on personnel. It was guarded by Boer War veterans, men in their late middle age who were easily bribed by anyone lacking a midnight pass. Local boys from the neighboring villages seized the opportunity to plunder airplane parts for their farm machinery. The commanding officer, Air Vice-Marshal R. P. Willock, was reprimanded sharply by inspector Sir John Salmond for running one of the worst stations Salmond had ever seen, a criticism with which Willock heartily concurred.

Undoubtedly, the realization that there was little satisfaction for him in the ordinary comforts of human life added to the urgency of Aaron's swift return. The British had betrayed him. Weizmann had betrayed him. The Turks had sacked his library and taken all his precious research to Damascus. It would take him years to reconstruct it. Worst of all, Sarah was gone and he was responsible.

As they left the tiny grass landing circle and headed due east for the Channel, Aaron could see beneath him the vast arterial railway system of the empire pumping its way out of the heart of London. Already the newspapers were blaring that the great railroad undertakings commenced in the decades before the war — in the reign of Napoleon III, to be exact, when the idea of a Channel Tunnel connecting England with the continent of Europe first emerged — would now be completed. Charing Cross Station would be transferred to the south of the Thames and expanded to make it the leading terminus in Europe.

The construction of the Channel Tunnel would commence, on an even grander scale than had hitherto been contemplated. Most important of all, a new transcontinental highway would be opened from Charing Cross to Baghdad, and thence to India. "This, one of the greatest of all inter-Allied post-war Reconstruction reforms," announced the *London Daily Chronicle,* "would promote the common interests of the Allied nations in Europe and the East and forever destroy the German dream of Oriental conquest." Never before had a tourist conveyance enjoyed such political significance — the Big Four at Versailles had ordered an Orient Express route reopened. The first postwar Grand Express had departed Paris for Constantinople exactly one month before, avoiding the defeated lands of Germany and Austria.

Davison Dalziel had done very well out of the war, having just acquired all the track of the Constantinople-Basra system previously owned by Germany. All German government property, including railways, had to be surrendered without payment, while at the same time the Germans remained liable for any debt incurred for the purchase or construction of said property, or for the general development of Germany's colonies. At the cost of, conservatively estimated, ten million dead and twenty million wounded, the coveted, much-fought-over "historic highway" that had brought the Aaronsohns to Palestine a generation earlier was now in the hands of the British — at a knockdown price.

In the 1st century, Boulogne-sur-Mer furnished the base for the Roman invasion of Britain. Today it is a smaller, tattier version of Brighton, and all that remains of the original Roman harbor is a steep row of stone fishermen's houses preserved by the tourism council. On the afternoon of May 15, 1919, those living in the dank cottages would have had a splendid view of what the local paper, *La France du Nord,* reported the next day as "one of the strangest accidents in aviation history."

According to the newspaper reports, at about three thirty PM, just as it was about to cross over the French coastline, Aaron's plane capsized in Boulogne harbor. The flotilla of fishing boats returning from the day's catch spied a small plane floating, driven by the wind, in the deep water at the harbor mouth and identified it as one belonging to the new London-Paris service. Some bales, wrapped in oilcloth, floated close to the plane. The fishermen rallied their ramshackle vessels but arrived too late to save the two "unfortunate pilots," one of whom had already disappeared. The other, apparently succumbing to powerful currents, went under before their eyes. Their bodies were not recovered. However, the master of fishing boat no. 328, Captain Henri Ramet, who later testified in a British court of inquiry, was able to rescue the bulky parcels that bobbed lightly on the surface of the treacherous water. He respectfully deposited the parcels, mailbags carrying documents "of considerable interest to the Paris Peace Conference," with the marine registry. Later that evening, they were picked up by an official car and transported to Marquise, the RAP camp near Boulogne, where they were subsequently taken on to Paris — along with the pilot of a second plane.

Both *La France du Nord* and *Le Télégramme* noted the most unusual feature of this most unusual accident: "By a singular coincidence, not one airplane but two fell into the sea at almost the same time. The passengers of the first plane were drowned."

The second plane appeared to be chasing the first. Shmuel Katz, an Israeli historian and former Likud Knesset member, speculates that its pilot shot Elgie Jefferson in the heart, thus causing the plane to crash. *Le France du Nord* made a brief, frustrated attempt to get at the facts. Giving up, it stated politely: "It was a unique incident, the exact details of which will never be known."

The day after Aaron's death, Wilson renewed his support for Palestine. Two days later, Weizmann and Frankfurter thanked Feisal profusely for renewing his efforts to reconcile Arabs and Jews. Weizmann wrote Julius Simon, "You can take it that the British Mandate for Palestine is decided." In the next breath he expressed his deep sense of loss at the "terrible disaster with Aaronsohn," and, in the breath after that, asked Simon to send him five hundred Viafidis Egyptian cigarettes to replace those lost on Aaron's plane. Five days later, the London *Times* carried a May 18 dispatch from its Paris correspondent that described the death of the one man who, according to William Bullitt, might have engineered a workable solution to the dilemma of Palestine's boundaries, as that of "the best type of outdoor Jew." It was followed by tributes from the *Jewish Chronicle* and the Zionist Office in London. All, however, were based on a carefully prepared statement by the British Foreign Office. All neglected to mention the remarkable fact that two planes, not one, came down in Boulogne harbor that Thursday. According to these reports, Aaron's plane was lost in fog over the Channel. By an amazing coincidence, the news of his death was also lost, in a fog of Northcliffe-generated publicity for the first transatlantic flight ever attempted – in which the two pilots, believed lost off the coast of Newfoundland, were miraculously recovered mid-ocean by a Danish ship.

Yet another remarkable coincidence raises the bizarre possibility that the Paris Peace Conference, with all its entanglements, nudged Aaron into a last alliance – with his youthful nemesis, Lawrence. At the very least, it raises the suspicion that the Admiralty was using its airplanes for something other than travel. Lawrence and Aaron were closer in their views than is commonly believed. Although Lawrence had been disturbed by Aaronsohn's hopes that, in time, the Jews would secure all land rights from Gaza to Haifa, he predicted future conflict on the same premise: the unwillingness of certain Jewish communities to employ Arab labor. He shared Aaron's dim view of the Polish-Russian-Jewish leadership and felt that a "broadminded, liberal type of Jew" of exactly Aaron's description was needed to win Arab confidence. He also believed that the wave of Eastern European Jewish immigration enabled by the Balfour Declaration would act as a catalyst for anti-British Arab nationalism. On April 7, Lawrence suffered a devastating emotional blow when his father fell victim to the Spanish influenza produced by the war. It is perhaps sentimental to believe that this blow drove him to a rapprochement with Aaron, but unpredictability was Lawrence's trademark as well as Aaron's. Most important, Lawrence, like Aaron, was bitterly disappointed by his government's failure to keep its promises, albeit to the Arabs, at the Paris Peace Conference, and threatened to destroy his own work. "Men prayed me that I set our work, the inviolate house, as a memory of you," he wrote to the mysterious S.A., "but for fit monument I shattered it."

On May 3, Lawrence abruptly left Paris for Cairo, traveling on a Handley Page bomber. "His" Arabs, the Hedjazi Arabs led by the Hashemite King Hussein and his son Feisal, were caught in the cogs of the India-Foreign Office rivalry. The India Office, throughout the war, had backed the Wahhabi zealots of King Ibn Saud of Riyadh, members of a Muslim fundamentalist sect Lawrence once compared to Cromwell's Roundheads. The Foreign Office had backed the Hashemite dynasty. Now the Wahhabists were threatening an insurrection, and Lawrence aspired to squelch it at the head of Hashemite tank troops.

Fortunately, as far as the India Office was concerned, Lawrence did not arrive in Cairo until mid-June. On May 17, only two days after Aaron's fatal accident, his aircraft struck a tree near Rome. There is no RAF account of this accident, and it is unclear why his departure for Cairo was delayed. Lawrence escaped with a concussion and two broken ribs, but both his pilots were killed. When Lawrence recovered from his injuries after a few days, he pressed on to Cairo, but was forced into following a roundabout route by a series of mechanical hitches that also forced him into the company of the India Office's man, the persuasive Harry St. John Philby. By the time they arrived in Cairo together, Ibn Saud, to whom the India Office had offered a generous annuity, had called off his Roundheads. The delay of the plane enabled Britain to escape an armed clash with the creator of modern-day Saudi Arabia. Such was the distrust engendered of the flying abilities of British military craft that the bodyguard of Prince Faisal ibn Abdal Aziz in Paris threatened to kill himself if his young charge took to the air accompanied by a British intelligence officer; thus, drily noted the intelligence officer in charge, the princeling "lived to rule at home in Riyadh."

In response to a request for information on Aaron's fatal plane crash from this author, the head of the Royal Air Force Historical Branch forwarded "extracts" held in the files of the Public Record Office and the Royal Air Force. They are handwritten, barely legible in places, and altered by conservators. According to these extracts, the fishing boat captain Henri Ramet saw Aaron's plane fall into the sea as the engine exploded but found no trace of either occupant. The engine, according to the official inquiry in the Beit Aaronsohn Archive, had been checked the night before and found free of problems. They make no mention of the "documents of considerable interest to the Paris Peace Conference" other than that they were used to identify the plane as that flown by Captain Jefferson on that day. Nor do they mention the second plane.

On May 26, the "unrecognisable" body of a British officer washed ashore near La Panne, seventy-five miles to the north. It was identified only by the papers found on it as that of Captain Jefferson, and, say the RAF reports, buried in Dunkirk Town Cemetery without delay. That same day, by another amazing coincidence, Hawker and MacKenzie, the two would-be transatlantic pilots sponsored by Lord Northcliffe, entered London in triumph to claim their ten-thousand-pound reward.

Aaron's body was never found.

II.

Inconvenient Heroes

> Genre will become stronger than truth. Genre will become truth.
> — Jeanine Basinger, *The World War II Combat Film: Anatomy of a Genre*

Aaron Aaronsohn, T.E. Lawrence, and Sarah Aaronsohn were larger-than-life personalities, their foibles and talents invaluable in wartime, but highly inconvenient in peacetime. As the propaganda campaign gave way to a postwar literary boom in war memoirs, "more or less bad," as historian Desmond Stewart justifiably remarked, and the film adaptations thereof, various attempts to prune the inconvenient heroes into exploitable form came to resemble an inept murderer's attempts to conceal a body: the more it is covered, the more it rises to view.

Alex Aaronsohn was among the first to cash in on his celebrated siblings, both literally and literarily. Beginning in July 1919 and ending only shortly before his death in 1948, the enterprising Alex entered into a voluminous correspondence with the British War Office to obtain the official records of his brother's death so as to collect his life insurance. He was unable to do so because the War Office never supplied a valid death certificate. The same, apparently, was true of Elgie Jefferson, whose family, by November 1919, still had not received notification from the War Office that their son was dead.

Jefferson's father, known to his neighbors as a fierce old gentleman with a fondness for litigation, which he sometimes won, sued to recover his son's body, with no success. He died the following year, of a broken heart, it is said, and the Jefferson line died out. The family mausoleum in the quiet churchyard of Malew on the Isle of Man is inscribed "Also in loving memory of Capt. Elgie B. B. Jefferson (Temporary Major) son of the above who was lost off the Belgian coast in fog while flying with Peace dispatches and mails of the Paris Peace Conference, May 1919."

This is peculiar in light of the fact that on May 26, 1919 — the same day that the body presumed to be Jefferson's washed ashore near La Panne – General Edmund Allenby in Cairo received instructions from the War Office to notify Aaron's family of his demise and of the War Office's very deep regret that "no trace has been found of either Aaron Aaronsohn or the pilot." Most bizarre of all, although Jefferson's burial is officially recorded on the Debt of Honour Register maintained by the Commonwealth War Graves Commission, there is no corresponding grave in Dunkirk Town Cemetery.

Aaron's insurance company, La Baloise of Switzerland, was not satisfied with the War Department Court of Inquiry report on his death, which contradicts both itself and the account given by the witness, Captain Henri Ramet of the fishing trawler *Notre Dame de Boulogne*, to the local newspapers that same day. Baloise had requested "absolute evidence" of Aaron's death "in the event that Mr. Aaronsohn should have been found not to have been killed," and later declined to pay the insurance.

Aaron had at least one true and constant mourner. Ruth Mack, in the second year of medical school at Tufts after having been turned down by Harvard because of her sex, wrote Rivka in August: "Haven't written because I couldn't. I've tried so many times. And Now I shall have to keep down my real thoughts; or this letter will also be unfinished . . . Oh, it's impossible to write . . . There is only one person to whom I want to write or talk, and that is Aaron."

Rivka never forgave Ruth for breaking with Aaron after his confession to Judge Mack in 1916, and would not answer her letters. In November 1920, Ruth tried Alex: "My dear Lel . . . You can't think how much it hurts me to be cut off from you: for two reasons: [*sic*] first because I care about you all; and secondly, because you are the only links left me with Aaron. I can't bear to lose the only real connection that remains of him."

Alex was busy with other matters. Apparently unsuccessful in his attempt to bring suit against Baloise (which requested that he pay the policy premiums), he capitalized on his brother's name to found his own homegrown fascist party, the Sons of Benjamin, in 1922. Alex, said his great-nephew Ran, today professor of geography at Hebrew University in Jerusalem, "used political ideas as horses to his chariot and turned them whichever way he chose." Out of high dudgeon, at a labor strike, Alex founded the Sons of Benjamin in partnership with Itamar Ben-Avi, son of the Hebrew language crusader Eliezar Ben-Yehuda and editor of the right-leaning Palestine *Daily Mail*. Mussolini had not yet come to power in Italy, and fascism meant little more than street-fighting against "Reds and Bolshies" at the time; however, this outlook dovetailed neatly with the existing antagonism between the colonists of the First and Second Aliyahs in Palestine. The breakdown of the old imperial order after World War I left a vacuum waiting to be filled. In Palestine, as in Britain, Germany, and Italy, there were those who aspired to create new empires even before the ink on the peace accords was dry. Alex, who had always adored and exploited his older brother in equal measure, now co-opted his ideas, tailoring them to enhance his new political status.

The Zionist left was well organized and led by experienced politicians like Weizmann, but the right still lacked a charismatic figure. Aaron Aaronsohn and Absalom Feinberg, the most likely candidates, were both dead. Vladimir Jabotinsky, the Russian journalist and ardent nationalist who founded Palestine's Revisionist party and its youth movement Betar in 1925, lacked a political base among the native sons of the First Aliyah. The dashing, imperious Alex, who developed a taste for dressing up for public events à la Lawrence, in gold circlet and Bedouin robes, was the perfect poster boy.

Jabotinsky assimilated many of Aaron's ideas, taking as his foundation stone the territorial integrity of Eretz Israel, the Land of Israel, which he described by Aaron's maximum boundary of 1919. The only surviving facsimile of Aaron's prewar maps is in Jabotinsky's atlas, a work of political geography published in 1926 that surveys different areas of the world in terms of their ability to absorb large numbers of immigrants. The former Likud representative Shmuel Katz, who has written his own biography of Aaron, speculates that the British had him killed because they didn't want him making common cause with Jabotinsky. Given their widely divergent views on Arabs, such an alliance was unlikely. Aaron drew up his boundaries for strictly economic reasons and believed that a working partnership between Jews and Arabs firmly grounded in equal rights was essential for the success of the future state; he even wanted to absorb the politically well-organized Arabs of Rasheyya within the new boundaries. Until such time as Jews and Arabs were acclimatized to such close relations, he believed Jewish immigration should be strictly limited and that Jewish sovereignty would be politically dangerous. Jabotinsky also believed in the legitimacy of Arab claims but took an opposite tack: precisely because the Arabs' claims were legitimate, it was they who were politically dangerous and must be separated from the Jewish population by an "iron wall" of Jewish military force until such time as they accepted the settlers' presence. Jabotinsky used the biblical constructs of Judaea and Samaria, the ancient terms for the West Bank, to ideologically justify the Jewish claim that these lands belonged inalienably to Eretz Israel and to the large numbers of Eastern European pogrom victims who would resettle there. He implacably opposed Palestinian self-determination or Jordanian sovereignty and further believed that Zionism and European colonialism would make permanent common cause against all the Arabs in the eastern Mediterranean. His credo was adopted by the Likud Party later in the century. Although Likud admired Aaron as a hero, it overlooked his more assimilationist approach.

Many Palestinians like the Aaronsohns already felt dispossessed by the "Reds and Bolshies" of the Second Aliyah who had swamped them in superior numbers and political strength. As soon as the Ottoman colonial order broke down, two more combustible elements were added to the simmering broth of resentments between those who aspired to be squires and those who aspired to be communards. One was the division of labor. The other was the division of land.

Douglas Valder Duff, British police commissioner of Jerusalem from 1923 to 1928 and a colleague of Alex Aaronsohn's in his continuing capacity as British intelligence officer in Palestine long after the war was over, described the Aaronsohns as "what might be called rigid Conservatives in our British sense" — private entrepreneurs who were strenuously opposed to Communism in every form. Duff, himself a "rigid Conservative" and a prolific author in the "Boy's Own" vein, was one of the first to promote the legend of Sarah as the Jewish Joan of Arc. In his capacity as a law-enforcement officer, he directed his barbs at Aaron's enemy, David Ben-Gurion, head of the socialist Poale Zion, who justified the tenet that Jewish colonists could employ only Jewish labor with the logic that this was the only way the Jews could avoid the charge of enslaving the Arabs. Duff pointed out that "it is here that the rub comes, [*sic*] the Arab does not understand this, and only sees himself excluded from work on the land which he has been accustomed to look upon as his own." In consequence, Duff saw little hope of peace between Arabs and the new colonists, the Jews, who were tenant farmers fearful of eviction if they went against the judgment of the collective, resisted the temptation of cheap labor, and hired their coreligionists instead.

Alex did not prove to be the stuff of legend. His political career was tarnished by sordid squabbles over real estate and the taint of thuggery. He traveled surrounded by a retinue of well-armed young toughs whom he maintained with abundant funds, supplied, his fellow villagers whispered, by the British. Another financial sponsor was the spiritualistically inclined widow of American soap magnate Joseph Fels, who became enamored of the dashing young officer. In 1924, with Mary Fels' bankroll, Alex undertook the purchase of lands for the private farmers' lobby of the Sons of Benjamin, which had fought to obtain land and other benefits from a Zionist leadership favoring collective agriculture. According to one of the few village witnesses still living, he then secretly registered the land in a relative's name and divvied it up among a few cronies, including his sister, Rivka. When the swindle was made public, Alex resigned the leadership of the Sons of Benjamin and sailed for New York and Mary Fels' palatial apartment on the fourteenth floor of the Ansonia Hotel. Poor Mary tried her best to make him over into the Jewish Krishnamurti with the help of séances and other spiritual activities, but he fell further into disrepute, earning a reputation as a debauchee, from which he only emerged sporadically to peddle "true stories" of his siblings' exploits under the nom de plume Simple Soldier.

In 1924, Rivka finally wrote Ruth Mack — with a favor to ask. Ruth, upon graduating from medical school, had gone to Vienna to study psychoanalysis with Sigmund Freud while her husband, Herrmann, completed a fellowship in London. The marriage broke up in 1924 and Ruth stayed in Vienna, becoming widely recognized as one of Freud's most talented disciples, intimately associated with his family. Rivka wanted her to cure Tzvi Aaronsohn of the epilepsy she insisted he had acquired as a result of his tortures at the hands of the Turks. Ruth, obviously offended at Rivka's long silence and her complaints to Ruth's parents of Ruth's "rancor," sadly replied: "I can understand your not writing. I've stopped writing letters, too. They are so useless." There was no real cure for epilepsy, Ruth told Rivka, and her letters stopped.

On one of his sporadic forays in search of literary glory – and shortly after his ignominious departure from Palestine – Alex Aaronsohn appeared in London and, encountering Raymond Savage in a barber shop, pressed him to represent a book on the activities of NILI. Savage, who had been General Allenby's adjutant in Jerusalem and was starting up a literary agency, had cornered the market in war memoirs and represented both Allenby and T. E. Lawrence. According to Lawrence's younger brother, Professor A. W. Lawrence – who as Lawrence's literary executor burnished his legend just as Alex burnished Aaron's – Savage persuaded Allenby to write an introduction to improve the book's chances of commercial success, apparently under the mistaken impression that Alex was his brother Aaron. This tale is doubly dubious since Allenby worked closely with Aaron and wrote a moving tribute to his deceased friend and colleague in 1919: "The death of Aaron Aaronsohn has deprived me of a valued friend and of a Staff Officer impossible to replace. He was mainly responsible for the formation of my Field Intelligence behind Turkish lines ... A keen Zionist and Palestinian, he extended towards his non-Jewish neighbors a broadminded sympathy which was of material assistance to the Administration in Palestine. I owe much to his wise counsels, his moderation and his prudence." Savage appears to have played along with one of Alex's habitual efforts to hitch his brother to his own chariot, if only to encourage him to keep his distance from the Lawrence franchise.

Nothing came of this venture, but Alex made one more sad and desperate approach to Allenby. In 1933, after a further series of financial disgraces, he wrote Viscount Allenby a letter apparently triggered by reports of a Lawrence film in the making. His letter combines adulation with delicate hints of blackmail, in one breath proposing Allenby for the Nobel Prize and in the next revealing that Alex had gathered up all of his late brother's diaries, including the fateful last two months, to publish his own book on NILI. (Aaron, apparently mindful of the historic record, kept several of his diaries on carbon paper.) Allenby expressed a keen interest in Alex's "enclosures," though it is unclear from the correspondence whether the diaries were actually delivered to him. The viscount abruptly refused to see Alex in Jerusalem, and that ended their correspondence. The proposed book was never published and, according to family members, Alex destroyed the diaries.

The younger Aaronsohn died of an embolism in Nice, just as Palestine obtained its independence in 1948. His obituary reads as if describing Aaron: "All who knew him cherish the memory of his magnetic dynamism, his unchanging good humor, and his profound sympathy for all that is human." Ruth Mack, after fleeing Vienna when the Nazis entered it, and after the breakup of her second marriage, died of cancer in New York in 1946, at the age of forty-eight.

In the mid-1930s, Alexander Korda, the legendary Anglo-Hungarian film mogul who moonlighted for British intelligence, purchased the film rights to *Revolt in the Desert*, Lawrence's abridged version of *Seven Pillars of Wisdom*. With storm clouds gathering over Europe and with Winston Churchill's encouragement, Korda planned to film an idealized vision of Lawrence's career that would inspire the British people to rally to the new war effort. Lawrence objected to the film on the grounds that it would cause him "inconvenience," and Korda dropped the project until Lawrence's death, five months after their initial discussions. Although Lawrence failed to explain the exact nature of the inconvenience, the secretive hero shrank from any examination of his personal life, particularly of his love life, which filmmakers found equally if not more compelling than his historic role.

To S. A.

I loved you, so I drew these tides of men into my hands
And wrote my will across the sky in stars
To earn you freedom, the seven-pillared worthy house,
That your eyes might be shining for me
When we came.

Death seemed my servant on the road, till we were near
    And saw you waiting:
When you smiled, and in sorrowful envy he outran me
    And took you apart:
          Into his quietness.

Love, the ay-weary, groped to your body, our brief wage
    Ours for the moment
Before earth's soft hand explored your shape, and the blind
    Worms grew fat upon
          Your substance.

By now, the identity of the real S.A. of the highly erotic dedicatory poem that opens *Seven Pillars* has become, like that of the W.H. of Shakespeare's sonnets, one of the great literary mysteries of the twentieth century. Generations of biographers have tried, and failed, to know the enigmatic Lawrence by the one great love that dominated his life. Scholarly assumptions, originating in hints from the military and encouraged by A. W. Lawrence, range from a homosexual Arab youth named Sheikh Ahmed, to an "imaginary person of neutral sex," but the honorific *Sheikh* is incongruous to the poem's sexual heat, nor does it fit the poem's striking resemblance to Romeo's speech to his entombed Juliet.

Ah, dear Juliet,
Why art thou yet so fair? Shall I believe
That unsubstantial Death is amorous,
And that the lean abhorred monster keeps
Thee here in dark to be his paramour?
For fear of that I still will stay with thee
And never from this pallet of dim night
Depart again.
Here, here will I remain
With worms that are thy chambermaids. Oh, here
Will I set up my everlasting rest
And shake the yoke of inauspicious stars
From this world-wearied flesh.

Lawrence had a particular devotion to Shakespeare and once admired him in a letter: "There was a man who hid behind his works, with great pains and consistency. Ergo he had something to hide, some privy reason for hiding. He being a most excellent fellow, I hope he hides successfully."

In 1936, a year after Lawrence's death, a group of Hollywood fringe intellectuals were discussing the future of Palestine over drinks at a hotel in Santa Barbara. Arab-Zionist rioting had just reached new heights of viciousness, escalating from the beating of two Arab shoe-shine boys by pedestrians in Tel Aviv to sniper attacks on Jewish motorists and retaliatory bombs in Arab coffeehouses. However, the group – which included a professor and his sixteen-year-old daughter, and a soi-disant screenwriter named Ladislas Farago – was more inter-ested in Lawrence's love life. Farago, whose name, according to Web-ster's, means medley or hodgepodge (as in "farrago of nonsense"), was an adventurer of vaguely Hungarian extraction who had migrated West to shake the golden boughs of Hollywood and was also on the payroll of several European intelligence agencies.

Inevitably, the conversation turned to the identity of the real S.A. The Hollywoodites were keenly aware of Korda's film and his quest for a love interest on which to hang the elusive hero. According to Farago, the sixteen-year-old advanced her theory that S.A. was in reality Sarah Aaronsohn, a "flamehaired Jewess" whose wartime exploits equaled Lawrence's own. She reasoned that the two must have met in North-ern Palestine when Lawrence was researching his Oxford dissertation. Why wouldn't the war hero have fallen in love with the Jewish Joan of Arc? asked the teenager, whereupon Farago, who also moonlighted as a journalist, jumped out of his chair, telephoned "interested parties in England," and was forthwith given carte blanche to take the party of four to Palestine to verify the story. There, said Farago, he obtained a sworn affidavit from Sarah's sister, Rivka, that the flamehaired Jewess and the golden warrior had never met. This satisfied the "interested parties in England," and the matter of Sarah Aaronsohn and T.E. Law-rence was officially laid to rest.

As unlikely as this story may seem, it has passed more or less unquestioned for more than half a century as proof that Lawrence and Sarah Aaronsohn never could have, never would have, known each other. But MI6 historian Stephen Dorril recently identified Ladislas Farago — who became a successful writer of spy thrillers — as a dupe responsible for "boobytrapping the historical record with an extraordinary number of hoaxes, forgeries, unanswered propaganda ploys and assorted dirty tricks."

On the eve of Palestine's independence, around the time of Alex Aaronsohn's death, another British intelligence officer, Somerset de Chair, interviewed A.W. Lawrence on the subject of Lawrence's connection to the Aaronsohns. The interview provides a context for Farago's farrago.

De Chair's interest had been piqued by the young daughter of Ernest Altounyan, the bisexual poet, physician, and close personal friend of Lawrence since his Oxford days, who had nursed a deep infatuation for Lawrence. Altounyan's daughter told de Chair that Lawrence had been in love with Sarah Aaronsohn, and that Altounyan, who had served as medical officer to the Arab Legion of Sir John Glubb, "Glubb Pasha," at Palmyra, had visited Sarah in Tel Aviv. Altounyan corroborated de Chair's story and, with some trepidation, referred him to A. W. Lawrence. Professor Lawrence impressed de Chair with the evasiveness of his answers — despite the lengthy memorandum the professor had surprisingly prepared on the subject of the Aaronsohns, reserving his more scurrilous remarks for his own brother's rival:

> Aaron Aaronsohn was one of those water people, what do
> you call them, hydrographer is that the word, and was
> employed by the Turks to find water for them in the Sinai
> desert. He went down there and managed to fall off his camel
> and break his collarbone, whereupon he asked to be sent to a
> specialist in Berlin, and there managed to persuade the
> authorities in Berlin that he was a good person to send over
> to America. On the way to America the ship was stopped by a
> British warship and Aaron Aaronsohn was found in his cabin
> completely surrounded by subversive literature which was
> almost piled up to the ceiling . . . And he was then sent out by
> us to the Middle East to find water on the other side. He had
> all of the plans of his surveys with him in an aeroplane just
> after the war which crashed in Calais harbour and the French

police sat on the quay and watched him drown . . . Anyway,
that was the end of Aaron Aaronsohn.

According to Professor Lawrence, in 1937, "two Jews called Oppenheimer went to an American publisher called Green-berger [*sic*]" with
the story that Lawrence had been in love with Sarah Aaronsohn, and
that a mysterious ride he made to Damascus in June 1917 was to visit
her. The Oppenheimers produced a synopsis of the story, which "in
course of business" was sent to Raymond Savage, Lawrence's literary
agent. Savage, who had procured Allenby's foreword for Alex's book on
NILI, looked up Alex's original synopsis and found it identical except
for the addition of Sarah's story. According to this report, "Green-
berger," the publisher, was interested enough to send two emissaries
to Palestine to "get all the evidence" from Rivka Aaronsohn, who still
lived at the family residence in Zichron Ya'akov. Rivka, with Alex, had
kept the family records, and said she had "all the diaries and letters"
to support it. However, she did not produce them.

The younger Lawrence, who was by this time his brother's literary executor, said he had discussed the matter of Lawrence's relationship with Sarah Aaronsohn with Moshe Shertok (also known as Moshe
Sharett), then David Ben-Gurion's political secretary for the Jewish
Agency. Shertok had said, "Rivka was quite capable of forging letters
and diaries and [he] was surprised she had not done so." In fact, the
"sworn statement" Farago had obtained from Rivka read: "The story
that my sister, Sarah Aaronsohn, ever had a romance with the late Col.
T. E. Lawrence of Arabia, much less married him, is entirely untrue.
In fact, my sister never even met Col. T. E. Lawrence at all." The statement was deposited with Raymond Savage, who happened to be de
Chair's literary agent as well that of Lawrence and Allenby. Professor Lawrence requested that de Chair not write anything on the subject, a request de Chair honored until 1968. In the Lawrence archive at
Oxford, bequeathed by A. W. Lawrence, de Chair's twelve-page memo
has been cut down to two innocuous pages. Fortunately, a duplicate
of the original document exists in the archives of the Imperial War
Museum in London.

Why Professor Lawrence would have discussed the matter with
such a high-ranking political figure as Shertok, who became the first

foreign minister of Israel, reflects the fissure the ever-inconvenient Aaronsohns came to represent in the emerging nation. After World War I, the Zionist left pilloried the family and NILI as irresponsible adventurers, while the Zionist right glorified them as martyrs, responsible for steering Britain toward the Balfour Declaration. Shertok, and Shertok's bosses, came from the left. Ben-Gurion in particular carried a longstanding grudge dating back to the Hashomer days. They had a vested interest in keeping Sarah and Aaron Aaronsohn buried as deeply as possible, particularly on the eve of independence, when the idea of a liaison between a heroine of the Jewish resistance and a notorious Arabist would not play well in Petach Tikvah. Weizmann, shortly to become Israel's first president, also had a vested interest in burying the history of Aaron's contributions, even his achievements as a scientist. Weizmann's wife, Vera, went so far as to appropriate the NILI motto for the epigraph of her autobiography without acknowledging its members and their lost and broken lives.

Korda's ambition to make a Lawrence epic was serious business, a matter of intense parliamentary interest. Film scholars estimate that by the middle of the 1930s, some eighteen million Britons, largely members of the working classes, went to the cinema at least once a week. This caused none other than John Buchan, now a member of Parliament, to remark in the House of Commons in 1932: "Whether we are interested in the film or not we cannot deny its enormous public importance. It is the most powerful engine of propaganda and advertisement on the globe today. It appeals to every class. It has enormous influence on the education of youth. It is an amazing platform for the dissemination of ideas, good and bad."

Lord Northcliffe, the progenitor of the propaganda war, had died barking mad in 1922, convinced that the Germans had poisoned him, but the British Board of Film Censors, set up on the eve of war in 1912, already had a clear policy on political subjects – to effectively prevent any discussion of them on film. The censorship rules prohibited the disparaging of public figures and national institutions; criticism or ridicule of the armed forces, police, monarchy, government, and church; "controversial politics"; and "stories or scenes which are calculated and possibly intended to stir up social ferment and unrest." The story of Lawrence's connection with Sarah Aaronsohn, widely publicized by journalists at the time, was both controversial politics and a potential source of unrest. There was considerable public ill-feeling about the revolt of Mandate Palestine, stemming from the increasingly murderous attacks on British soldiers by Jewish resistance groups such as the Stern Gang and Hashomer's successor, the Irgun. The idea of a movie dramatizing a liaison between an English war hero and a notorious Jewish insurgent would, equally, not play well in Newcastle.

To guard against any political contretemps, Korda engaged Lieutenant Colonel W. F. Stirling, a recipient of the Distinguished Service Order and Military Cross, who had served as governor of Jaffa between 1920 and 1923, as technical and military advisor. Colonel Stirling's chief function was to approach the Colonial and Foreign Offices. In exchange for technical support, he offered them script approval on such delicate matters as showing the Turkish forces in retreat. Stirling was the officer to whom Lawrence confessed that he had fabricated the famous scene of his rape at Dera'a and remained as advisor on the film throughout its many incarnations under Korda.

Korda conducted a five-year campaign to make the film of *Revolt in the Desert* against the strong objections of the Foreign Office, on the grounds that such a film would compromise the British government's diplomatic relations with the Turks, who on the eve of World War II were considered important allies. Korda's ordeal is the subject of a classic case study in political film censorship by scholars Jeffrey Richards and Jeffrey Hulbert. Under the pretext of not offending the Turks, the Foreign Office launched a campaign of attrition against the making of the film, using the British Board of Film Censors and informal contacts by Robert Vansittart, Lawrence's cousin and permanent undersecretary at the Foreign Office. (In what appears to have resulted in a mutually satisfactory relationship, Korda ended up with a knighthood, and Sir Robert, an aspiring playwright, was hired to write screenplays on imperial subjects.)

Diplomatic relations with the Turks appear to have been among the least of Korda's headaches, however. Palestine erupted in 1936 following Arab and Jewish campaigns to drive out the British, making film production impossible. As if that weren't enough, shortly before Lawrence's death, Korda's uncooperative hero had pursued yet another forbidden romance — with British fascism.

The Lawrence film finally made in 1962 by David Lean begins with the famous scene of a lone motorcyclist roaring along a dozy English country lane, smiling enigmatically as his 1935 Brough picks up reckless speed. His electric blue eyes intent on some inner demon, he sees two boys on bicycles too late and ends his journey in a ditch, his golden head brought low into the dust and the tumult inside it stilled forever. However, the real backstory for that scene is far more dramatic than mere psychosexuality, tempting though that might have been as a means of illuminating the many dark corners in the Lawrence legend. Entirely omitted from Lean's film is that far from seeking refuge from his sexual conflicts in random flight on his motorcycle, Lawrence was actually returning home from a highly specific errand at Bovington Camp post office, near his cottage at Cloud's Hill in Dorset. He had just wired his acolyte Henry Williamson, an ardent supporter of Sir Oswald Mosley's British Union of Fascists, inviting him to Cloud's Hill to discuss whether Lawrence should go to Germany to try to negotiate a separate peace with Hitler.

This incident had a precedent in one that had once infuriated Winston Churchill. In February 1922, an increasingly disillusioned and despairing Lawrence gave up his job as special advisor on the Middle East under Churchill, who was then Lloyd George's new choice as Colonial Secretary, and retired from public life. Lawrence petitioned Hugh Trenchard, Chief of Air Staff, to enter the RAF as a lowly airman under an assumed name without Churchill's knowledge. Churchill, when duly informed vetoed the idea. In July, Lawrence was approached and offered his own brigade by representatives of the Irish Free State, who were aware of his affinity for rebel leader Michael Collins (assassinated one month later by his own followers near Cork). Lawrence slyly informed Churchill, who choked on the idea of the Hero of the Hedjaz serving in the Irish Republican Army, and quickly smuggled him into the RAF under the name and rank of Private Shaw.

Lawrence's desire to enter the RAF as a lowly enlisted man, however, may not have been entirely his own. During or before 1922, Lawrence took part in flagellation bouts in Chelsea emceed by a German pimp, Jack Bilbo. In an odd echo of the smear campaign that brought down Asquith's government, Bilbo, who also styled himself Bluebeard, attempted to blackmail Lawrence by revealing that he was considering selling his memoirs to a German magazine. Lawrence tried to have him deported by the Home Secretary, who had no such powers. Though the Metropolitan Police have no file on him, Bilbo was somehow persuaded to depart England for Germany, where, in 1932, he once more announced his intention to publish. This time Lawrence approached his cousin at the Foreign Office, Sir Robert Vansittart, a man famed for the violence of his prejudices (*Vansittartism* has passed into English usage as a term for extreme hostility to all things German). Vansittart, who hated homosexuals as much as he hated Germans, agreed to contact the British Embassy in Berlin to exert pressure to ban Bilbo's book. Nothing more was heard from Bluebeard, but Lawrence had by now handed Vansittart and others a heavy rod with which to beat him.

One of the others may have been the still-powerful Curzon, who became Lawrence's enemy when, during the protracted boundary negotiations that took place during his tenure, Lawrence attacked him in private and in public as "of course the enemy," the most bloodthirsty of the "old men," whose backstage maneuvers to preserve their own power paralyzed British Middle Eastern policy immediately after the war and made fresh conflicts inevitable. Lawrence threw his support to Winston Churchill, who gave him a position in the Colonial Office, and opened the way for Churchill to snatch the glittering prize of overseeing the Middle East from the former viceroy of India, thus ushering in the decline of Curzon's career. Foremost among those leading Conservatives who opposed fascism was Curzon's secretary, Lord Robert Vansittart. Biographer Desmond Stewart suggests that Curzon and Vansittart used confidential information on Lawrence's sadomasochistic sexuality, compiled through government channels, to blackball him from advancement under Churchill; they also arranged to bankroll the then-penniless national hero on the condition that he join up as an ordinary enlisted man and submit to corporal punishment.

The brutal treatment Lawrence endured following his fall from grace in the early 1920s suggests the kind of brutal hazing undergone by public schoolboys in Vansittart's cradle, Eton, to prepare them to submit to a life in the Civil Service. From 1922 to 1934, Lawrence submitted to beatings by a series of men whom he paid to honor a set formula. According to one of them, John Bruce, Lawrence engaged him in 1922 at the age of seventeen after an interview in a flat owned by

Lawrence's fellow Arab Bureau officer Francis Kodd. (Rodd, son of the British ambassador to Egypt, had visited Lawrence in the hospital after his near-fatal plane crash on his Saudi adventure. In March 1922, he left his Foreign Office job suddenly and without permission to join an expedition to the French Sahara. He died Lord Kennell of Rodd in 1978.) Lawrence told John Bruce he had fallen into debt and dishonored his family by a series of trangressions that could only be expiated through abject submission to a penitential regime devised by "the Old Man." This seems to have been another kinsman, Fetherstonhaugh "Hugh" Frampton, who had refused to stand as Lawrence's guarantor when he fell deeply into debt following his resignation from the Colonial Office. Until 1934, Bruce beat Lawrence regularly, in strict accordance to a list of indictments, drawn up by Lawrence but reflecting Frampton's reasons for refusing him, and which included insolence to the King and involvement with "the damn Jews." Only if Lawrence agreed to this regime of corporal punishment would Frampton take care of his debts (the cottage Lawrence was living in when he died indeed belonged to Frampton). The beatings were administered to Lawrence's naked buttocks in the presence of an "uncle," identified only as R., beatings so severe that a third party was required to ensure they did not become fatal. The ritual of the whippings included a "Circassian thong" of the type Lawrence said was used on him at Dera'a, and otherwise echoed his fictitious account of that strange evening, which by now had affected his life more deeply than had it been real.

In wiring Henry Williamson on the day of his death in 1935, the former hero may have leapt, like an aging star faced with diminishing and demeaning offers, at one more chance to play a role on the world stage. Having launched his own attack against the "hardfaced old men" of the British Foreign Office in 1922, Mosley's very similar attack might have appealed to him. A reading of Lawrence's last book, *The Mint,* suggests he had become a pacifist. If he still suffered from guilt over Sarah Aaronsohn's death, or over his assumption of her brother's laurels, acting as the agent of appeasement not only would have provided a spectacular and this time very public means of penance, but would scotch any efforts to explore his life in film.

Lawrence's reemergence into public life came at a critical moment in British history. Mussolini had not yet invaded Abyssinia (later

Ethiopia), and many in the British establishment still held the view that Fascism could be used as a bulwark against Soviet Russia. Desmond Stewart has remarked that Lawrence's being in the military, subject to his superiors' orders, had solved the problem of keeping a hero under control in public; but when he left the RAF in early 1935 he regained his freedom to publish his opinions or join a party, which must have alarmed those who feared the talismanic value of his name. If allied with that of Mosley, whose anarchic star was rising in an England in the throes of calamitous social and economic decay, it would be alarming indeed. Mosley believed that Germany and Russia would win the coming war, hence his mission to achieve a separate peace with Hitler while the British Empire was still intact. In this he was by no means isolated. The British establishment in 1935 consisted of a Conservative Party evenly split between those who opposed the Fascist powers (foremost among them Vansittart) and those who wished to appease them. Records released in 1981 reveal that from 1933 Benito Mussolini supported the British Union of Fascists with cash payments totaling some sixty thousand pounds sterling. Apparently, the Italian dictator hoped to keep Britain neutral. But in 1935, Mussolini invaded the fertile, oil-producing plains of Abyssinia, an event that convulsed the Conservatives.

Lawrence's death in 1935 came shortly after he left the RAF and one month after Abyssinia was invaded. A week before his fatal accident, Lawrence was asked by a journalist if he planned to become dictator of Britain. His answer deepens the lingering mystery surrounding his death, thought not to have been an accident by historian Stewart and others. "Every now and then," Lawrence biographer and military historian Basil Liddell Hart noted, his subject was fond of hinting that he "might come back to do something bigger than before." He would compare himself to Count Belisarius (hero of a novel by another one of Lawrence's friends, his biographer, the poet Robert Graves) who, pushed into obscurity by Emperor Justinian I in 548 AD, returned to defend his nation when the need arose. Immediately after Lawrence's death, officials searched his cottage at Cloud's Hill and presumably removed any documents compromising Britain's security, while detectives kept vigil against press invasions and stories circulated about mysterious fires set ablaze by sinister agents of foreign chancellories to destroy his books and papers.

Vansittart's fingerprints are all over the Foreign Office's success-ful move to squelch subsequent efforts to glorify the dead hero in film. Korda disposed of his rights to two film companies, New World and Paramount, but retained a strong interest in the Lawrence material. On June 26, 1939, he solicited Vansittart for a Foreign Office opin-ion, "as naturally we wish to avoid any risk of conflict after the pic-ture is made and after a vast sum of money has been expended on the making of the film." Korda volunteered to make a Lawrence of Arabia movie that would skim over Lawrence's adventures in Arabia against the Turks to concentrate on his contributions to the Royal Air Force. Vansittart graciously replied: "The new arrangement of the film . . . is, from our point, most satisfactory, and we are particularly glad to note that the emphasis of the story is to be shifted from Lawrence's exploits in Arabia to his subsequent career in the Royal Air Force. It seems unlikely that the film, as you describe it, will contain anything at which the Turks can take offense."

As both men well knew, the film was dead. Nothing more was heard of it until after Vansittart's death in 1958, when Anthony Nutting (for-mer minister of state for foreign affairs under Anthony Eden, of Suez fame) published his official biography on which the David Lean film is based. Lean got the green light shortly thereafter, and the long-planned screen version of *Revolt in the Desert* finally made it to the screen in 1962, rechristened *Lawrence of Arabia* – and with a fashion-ably gay hero in place of any embarrassing political backstory.

Lawrence's close friend and biographer, Robert Graves, insisted Lawrence was heterosexual in a letter protesting the film. "The sug-gestion that he was a homosexual is almost indecent. The truth seems to be that he was flogged into impotence at Dera'a and thus unable to consummate his heterosexual love for S.A."

Graves ghostwrote the poem "To S.A." and further assisted Law-rence in toning down its more personal references. He later changed his tune to accord with the official view that "S was a person and A was a place." This view was actually a request made by Stewart New-combe, who as a member of the Arab Bureau knew both Aaronsohns well, in an undated letter to Ronald Storrs. However, in Foreign Office dispatches, the head of NILI was often referred to as "the inhabitant of Athlit." S. (of) A. could just as easily mean Sarah of Athlit as Sarah

Aaronsohn – Sarah, not Aaron, was the operational head of NILI in Palestine. Graves expanded his explanation to declare, even later, that S.A. stood for Son Altesse, a chivalric nickname for Lawrence's Arabic instructor, a Miss Farida el Aki, who vigorously denied being the real S.A. while she still had the breath to do so. Graves, who accused literary agent Raymond Savage of "cashing in on the [Lawrence] racket," may have compromised his own value as an historian by aspiring to write a Lawrence screenplay. In two pieces written for the American magazine market that refuted the homosexual element in David Lean's film *Lawrence of Arabia*, he contradicts himself several times, first saying that S.A. was patterned on a character in an historical novel about the Crusades, then that she was a real person who was caught behind Turkish lines in World War I. Lawrence, according to this last account, had visited her in Damascus during the war – the famous mystery ride of June 1917 in *Seven Pillars* – but asked Graves to "slur over" the incident in his 1927 biography, *Lawrence and the Arabs*. Lawrence specifically asked him to say nothing of what he might have heard from Graves's brother, Phillip, who worked with both Lawrence and the Aaronsohns in the Arab Bureau. To honor this request, Graves said he destroyed a letter from S.A. to Lawrence, which had fallen into his hands in 1927 when he was writing the book.

Nutting dismisses Sarah Aaronsohn as a "romantic legend" who died in a Turkish prison in March (rather than October) 1917, eight months before the Turks supposedly captured and tortured Lawrence at Dera'a.

> This evidence equally disposes of the story that Lawrence was in love with a Jewish lady, called Sarah Aaronsohn – a British secret agent living behind the Turkish lines at the time of the Arab revolt. According to this piece of fantasy, having been flogged into impotence at Dera'a, Lawrence renounced his love and this was the cause of his tragedy. From this it is concluded that the love poem entitled *To S.A.*, which serves as a dedication of the *Seven Pillars of Wisdom*, was written by Lawrence for Sarah Aaronsohn. But this romantic legend unfortunately does not stand up. Apart from Lawrence's vow of abstinence, official enquiries have revealed that the two never met and never could have met.

Nutting was acquainted with Graves and was obviously acquainted with Graves's letter because he lifted a phrase from it, "flogged into impotence at Dera'a," but he never mentions Graves. Instead, he denies the substance of Graves's letter, that Lawrence was never a homosexual and that he and the female S.A. had a passionate, though unconsummated, relationship. He also ignores the substantial evidence in Somerset de Chair's lengthy 1946 memo, which would have been readily available to him along with other Foreign Office files. Instead, Nutting coyly hints at a form of suppressed homosexuality created by the shock of Lawrence discovering his illegitimacy, in tandem with a British public school experience never described, which together created the "horror of physical contact with any other human being" that Lawrence described in *Seven Pillars of Wisdom*. Nor does Nutting betray any acquaintance with Lawrence's own denial of the Dera'a incident, recorded by his friend Walter Stirling in 1928. The "official enquiries" he cites are those of Ladislas Farago.

Douglas Valder Duff, who described himself as a soldier of fortune who took up the pen to atone for the "unworthiness of some of the courses I have followed," knew Lawrence, as well as what was left of the Aaronsohn family. He and Lawrence retired to the same Dorset township. Like Lawrence, Duff left the services with considerable bitterness toward his employers, whom he felt had betrayed his principles. According to a letter he published in the British *New Statesman*, January 5, 1957, "T. E. Lawrence a few weeks before he was killed, told me that we had both dedicated a book to Sarah Aaronsohn and asked me if I had known her when she was still alive." The former policeman dedicated his own memoir, *Palestine Unveiled*, to Sarah Aaronsohn, "the martyr maid who died for Palestine and a world unworthy of her sacrifice." In the same letter, he revealed that he had acquired some significant Aaronsohn documents. However, all of Duff's papers disappeared after his own death in 1978, and the national registry of archives shows no trace of them. To Duff, who admired Alex Aaronsohn, the official silence on the subject of the Aaronsohns was easy to explain: "Because Alexander did not agree with the official Zionist policy of the era, the Aaronsohns were kept obscure."

When, after the war, Zionist opinion divided over the Aaronsohns, what was left of the Aaronsohns divided among themselves. In 1936,

Ephraim Fischel Aaronsohn died at home in Zichron Ya'akov, faith-
fully attended by Alex and Rivka. His last will and testament, much to
the chagrin of Shmuel and Tzvi, left everything to the two junior members of the family, including all records of NILI and of their heroic (and
eminently filmworthy) siblings. By the 1950s, when the campaign for
a Lawrence film once more heated up, Rivka was the only Aaronsohn
left in Zichron Ya'akov, alone in the dim house with its echoes of gran-
deur. The house became an official archive after 1967, when the Six-
Day War rehabilitated the memory of Aaron Aaronsohn and his vision
of Greater Israel. During Rivka's tenure as keeper of the family flame,
however, much that was of value to the historical record disappeared
from the archive.

In 1959, with Rivka's full support, a transplanted Englishwoman
living in Palestine wrote a highly romanticized version of the Aaronsohn saga, using novelistic techniques to fill in the gaps in the record.
Though it appears to have been written to capitalize on the publication of Nutting's *Lawrence of Arabia* and the imminent production of
the film, the book, titled *The NILI Spies*, was the first serious attempt
to resurrect the Aaronsohns. The author, Anita Engle, whose only previous writings were on the subject of ancient glass, quoted Douglas
Valder Duff and Abu Farid, only to draw the same conclusion reached
by Anthony Nutting: that there never was, never could have been a
relationship between Sarah Aaronsohn and Lawrence, "except that no
story about the Middle East during World War I would amount to a row
of beans unless Lawrence could be dragged into it somehow"

More than twenty years after his own investigations, Somerset de
Chair wrote an irritated letter to the London *Times* on the subject of
a series of articles by the newspaper's special Insight team journalists
Phillip Knightley and Colin Simpson, which in 1969 became their book
The Secret Lives of Lawrence of Arabia. The articles exonerated Lawrence of the charge of homosexuality and painted him as capable of loving women such as George Bernard Shaw's wife, Charlotte, from the
lofty haven of a chivalric ideal, *le chevalier sans peur et sans reproche*.
They brought up the subject of Sarah Aaronsohn as a candidate for the
real S. A., but dismissed the possibility on the basis of the NILI files
held at the Aaronsohn family archive in Zichron Ya'akov, "which show
that though Lawrence was in touch with her they never met."

De Chair was aggrieved that two upstart journalists had stolen a march on him in print. "As usual, I seem to have been doing the right thing at the wrong time, but, as I have kept silence out of respect for Professor Lawrence's wishes for so long, perhaps he will allow me to make some comments." He reasoned that if he were to write a love poem to Elizabeth Taylor he would not title it "To M.T." (Miss Taylor) or even "To M.B." (Mrs. Burton), and he asked: "Where, if there was no connection between Lawrence and Sarah Aaronsohn, does all the smoke come from? Why is her name suggested at all?"

If the Foreign Office opted to present a homosexual Lawrence to the moviegoing public in preference to his less palatable political flirtations, the plaintive de Chair may be right after all. Lawrence was an immensely complicated human being who, for all his perverse ambition, also possessed a quixotic sense of integrity that led him to rebel against all that ambition might have brought him. In that sense, it is not only the poem "To S.A." that pays belated and backhanded tribute to the brave young woman who gave her life for Allenby's advance, but its accompanying acknowledgment to "the other leaders and lonely fighters" as well. The men of the Arab Bureau were advised of the details of her torments. Undoubtedly the hypersensitive Lawrence was haunted by the thought of Sarah's magnificent body shattered and violated. The similarities in the punishment Lawrence later endured at the hands of R., "the Old Man," to both his fictional torment at Dera'a and the very real torment Sarah endured at the hands of the Turks suggest that the Etonians were punishing Lawrence for being a liar – making him suffer a fate like that which he had misrepresented, and that, since he concurred in their bad opinion of him, he cooperated. Perhaps the real meaning of the Dera'a fiction is that Lawrence would have preferred to take Sarah's fate upon himself. Whether he loved her in the flesh is almost beside the point. One does not have to be that much of a romantic to imagine that Lawrence paid tribute to Sarah's animal courage in a form that embodied another great fantasy, of a simple human happiness that he could never have.

12.

Aaronsohn's Road Map

> There was a merchant of Baghdad who sent his servant to the
> market to buy provisions and in a little while the servant came,
> white and trembling, and said, Master, just now when I was in
> the market-place I was jostled by a woman in the crowd and
> when I turned I saw it was Death that jostled me. She looked at
> me and made a threatening gesture; now, lend me your horse
> and I will ride away from this city and avoid my fate. I will go to
> Samarra and there Death will not find me. The merchant lent
> him his horse and the servant mounted it, and he dug his spurs
> in its flanks, and as fast as the horse could gallop he went. Then
> the merchant went down to the market-place and he saw me
> standing in the crowd and he came to me and said, Why did you
> make a threatening gesture to my servant when you saw him
> this morning? That was not a threatening gesture, I said, it was
> only a start of surprise. I was astonished to see him in Bagh-
> dad, for I had an appointment with him tonight in Samarra.
>
> — W. Somerset Maugham, "Death Speaks"

If great nations, to paraphrase Zola, are built on great crimes, then modern Israel rests uneasily on Aaron and Sarah Aaronsohn's bones. From the day of his death in May 1919 to the time of this writing, first the British Mandate of Palestine, then Israel, France, and Syria have failed to reach an agreement over Aaron's northern boundary. Even the most comprehensive Middle East peace agreement to be yet achieved, the 1995 Israeli-Palestinian Interim Agreement on the West Bank and Gaza Strip — also known as Oslo II — foundered over sixty-six square kilometers in the Golan Heights because a final agreement could not be reached until permanent borders were decided.

As the political geographer J. Prescott has remarked, "the most common cause of boundary disputes can be found in the history of the boundary" — in other words, that dispute is caused by the boundary evolving despite unresolved claims. Aaron accurately foresaw that water would always be a primary source of conflict with Syria for Palestine unless it could be neutralized early on by the relatively simple means of engineering. He would have been horrified to learn that the lack of political will to achieve an essentially pragmatic solution would eventually embroil the entire Middle East.

Conflict and water, in the Middle East, are intimately related, but to address the problem, the chicken must first be separated from the egg, a task policy makers and their scholarly advisors have been slow to tackle. Understanding all of the ramifications of water issues in a region that has little water winds back into the paths of nationalism, even mysticism. From the prehistory of the desert Arabs, who fought continually over grazing rights and wells in lands where water and pasture were desperately scarce, to today's complex engineering projects and riparian disputes, water is God, the source of life as well as the source of conflict. Before Islam, the Bedouin worshipped wells and springs; Arab lore has it that the Dome of the Rock in Jerusalem, over which many peace talks have broken up, is built over the source of all waters.

On a less poetic level, a close examination of historical documents reveals that water has driven conflict between Israel and Syria since the Paris Peace Conference of 1919, which terminated with neither a peace treaty with Turkey nor a final delineation of Palestine's northern boundary. It was generally agreed that Britain should receive the mandate for Palestine, and France for Syria and Lebanon; but the Syrian-Palestine border remained undecided, largely due to dissension between Britain and France over the development parameters of their new acquisitions. On September 19, 1919, Chaim Weizmann, seeking to expand the northern boundary as suggested by the British Political Section at the peace conference, laid siege to Winston Churchill with a last memo written by Aaron Aaronsohn, whose primary concern was the economic development of the new country. Weizmann wrote: "I should like to say that in the discussions and negotiations with the French Government now in progress with regard to the northern frontier, from the point of view of Palestine the deciding factor is the question of water supplies. I have much pleasure in enclosing a memorandum on that subject in which this subject is dealt with very thoroughly and, in my opinion, convincingly." When Churchill proved difficult to convince, Weizmann invoked as consultants Sir Louis Dane and Sir John Benton, who had worked together on a large irrigation project in India's Punjab and whose plans to dam the Litani River in what was now French Lebanon made "the extreme projects of Mr. A[aronsohn]" look mild by comparison. On January 28, 1920, Benton, fresh from India, suggested that if it proved impossible to secure for Palestine northern boundaries that included the whole of the Bekaa Valley, which was at that time Syria's breadbasket along with the Galilee, then an attempt should be made to construct and maintain a dam for water collection outside Palestine. (This plan, which ran parallel to a short-lived scheme to establish a British mandate in southern Syria, was realized by a Russian Zionist, Pinchas Rutenberg, in 1926, but destroyed by the Jordanians during the War of Independence.)

The French staked their own claim to the Jordan headwaters and insisted that the Litani was needed for development in Lebanon, while the snows of Mt. Hermon, also coveted by the Zionists, provided water for Damascus. They espoused a Greater Lebanon under French control, which would include the Bekaa Valley, the *vitayet* (district) of Beirut that reached down into Northern Palestine, and the Galilee. Their Greater Syria would comprise today's Syria, Jordan, Iraq, and Israel. They adamantly opposed all British overtures by reminding the British of the obligations incurred by their wartime alliance.

The Hashemite Emir Feisal, who, along with T. E. Lawrence, had become a British idol of the Near Eastern campaign, and to whom young nationalist Arabs looked as the best means of foiling Zionist aspirations, agreed with the French that Greater Syria should be under single rule but disagreed on who the ruler might be. The French did not want a British straw man in charge. The British, who were eager to conclude an all-embracing Middle East agreement that would calm an increasingly unruly Arab population, ultimately concluded that their alliance with the French was a higher priority than their wartime liaison with Feisal.

In September 1919, Prime Minister David Lloyd George and General Edmund Allenby, commander of Britain's Egyptian Expeditionary Force, proposed redrawing the northern boundary far south of the water resources delineated by Aaron, extracting in return a promise that France would forget about Greater Syria. A fortnight later,

Allenby evacuated his troops from Northern Galilee, leaving all the water resources and the Jewish settlements in French hands. Without British protection, the settlements of Metullah, Kfar Giladi, Tel Hai, and others became prey for Arab marauders, and have remained flash points ever since. Although even Jabotinsky advised him to abandon the northern settlements because they were indefensible, David Ben-Gurion, in the process of metamorphosing Hashomer into a regular militia, insisted on hanging on.

On March 1, 1920, Tel Hai fell, with the loss of the Jewish Regiment hero Joseph Trumpeldor. Two days later the Jews evacuated Metullah and Kfar Giladi. On March 7, Feisal, out of patience with Great Power politics, proclaimed himself king of Greater Syria, which in his lexicon incorporated Lebanon, Transjordan, and "Southern Syria," meaning Palestine. Riots, incited by one of Feisal's followers, Hajj Amin al-Husayni (later infamous for negotiating with Hitler), erupted among Palestinian Arabs at the feast of Nebi Musa, otherwise known as the Prophet Moses, a particularly volatile holiday because it shared dates with Passover. Chaim Weizmann left immediately for San Remo, Italy, where on April 25 the British and French split Syria into two parts, north (Syria) and south (Palestine and Iraq), with France taking Syria and Britain the rest. Feisal rejected this division and the French booted him out of Syria. He subsequently became the first modern ruler of Iraq.

On June 21, 1920, the French proposed a compromise that retained all Jewish settlements within the existing boundaries of Palestine, but it allocated to Syria almost all of the water resources Aaron had required for Jewish economic development. In the agreement, finalized by the French and British governments in March 1923, the entire Litani and the Jordan headwaters of the Ayoun and Hasbani rivers would originate in Lebanon before flowing into Palestine. The Banias springs would originate and flow for one hundred meters in Syria, then into Palestine: only the Dan springs remained entirely in Palestine. Despite strenuous opposition by Weizmann and his colleagues, this plan was confirmed in March 1923 and ensured conflict for years to come.

.•. .•. .•.

Water resources were the single most important factor affecting population growth in Mandate Palestine, where the British administration determined how many inhabitants the land could absorb according to the volume of water (today, the Palestinians' right of return is similarly, if tacitly, linked). Scarcity of water was sufficient cause to limit immigration, a colonial administrative response to internal security problems, as the Arabs met the threat of European or Yemenite Jews flooding into Palestine with exponentially increased resistance. In 1878, Palestine had 340,000 inhabitants; in 1915, 722,000 — including Arabs attracted by the promise of new regional prosperity. The "full economic development of Palestine" included plans to increase the Jewish population by four million, which alarmed British military authorities charged with keeping the peace as it involved large-scale expropriation of Arab lands, particularly that of the large landowners or effendi. Weizmann termed this "compulsory" expropriation, "a right which is given to railway companies in this country, a right which is carried out in all advanced countries under a democratic rule . . . We don't desire to turn out Mahomed in order to put in Mr. Cohen as a large landowner, but we desire to break up the badly managed large estates and to transform them into Homesteads for the small farmer."

In the late British Mandate period of the 1930s, the Jewish population ballooned with refugees from Nazi Germany, to the satisfaction of some Zionists who believed the population explosion would help realize the country's potential. Sensing that partition was imminent because of increasing tension between Jews and Arabs, the Jewish Agency developed an intensive settlement program in Northern Galilee where Tel Hai, Metullah, and Kfar Giladi had fallen, building fifty-five farm communities between 1936 and 1939 to reinforce the projected boundaries — and to guarantee the inclusion of what Jordan headwaters were left from the mandate period. It was clear to the Zionists that the Galilee region with the Jordan headwaters, the coastal zone with its major population centers, and the Negev Desert were the minimum three areas necessary to absorb the coming "ingathering of exiles" into a viable Jewish state, but the building of these communities provided fresh opportunities for conflict with Syria.

The Zionists were advised by Walter Clay Lowdermilk, assistant chief of the U.S. Soil Conservation Service, who advocated a plan of regional water management. The plan, to develop irrigation on both sides of the Jordan and to build a canal from the Mediterranean to the Dead Sea to generate hydroelectric power and replace the diverted freshwater, bore a strong similarity to Aaron's, though it was supposedly based on the Tennessee Valley Authority. Any partition, Lowdermilk wrote, "seems bound to disrupt the country's economic frame, and wreck the chances of large-scale development." In 1944, Mekorot, the national water company, proposed moving the mandated northern boundary upstream on the Jordan to where the river meets the Hasbani, Dan, and Banias headwaters; eastward along Lake Huleh to allow for a conduit; and upstream along the Yarmuk, taking an eighty-square-kilometer swathe of Transjordan to develop a series of water impoundments. These plans also involved lifting Litani water into the Jordan watershed, exactly as Aaron had proposed only days before his death. Though the plans were not implemented at the time, they remained on a strategic wishlist.

By 1947, a Britannia eviscerated by another world war could no longer maintain her grip on empire. A spasm of decolonization shook the globe and supplanted the doctrine of self-determination, just as the United Nations had replaced Wilson's League in October 1945. On February 2, 1947, Britain turned Palestine over to the UN, and, in May 1948, the last British troops departed the new state of Israel. In the ensuing War of Independence against Jordan, Egypt, Iraq, Syria, Lebanon, and Saudi Arabia, Israel lost the three tiny areas it considered most necessary for water development: Givat Banias, its access to the Banias springs; the town of El Hama, including a small trangular area adjacent linking the Yarmuk to Lake Tiberias; and another patch of Lake Huleh, the Daughters of Jacob Bridge there having been targeted by Israeli planners as the site of the first major Israeli water reclamation project. Syria, which occupied the territory, agreed to withdraw from everything except El Hama and Givat Banias – provided that the remainder were turned into a demilitarized zone (DMZ) whose sovereignty would be negotiated in the future. That future has turned out to be the present day.

The Jordan headwaters became Solomon's baby. The Hasbani River now rose in Lebanon, with the Wazzani, its major spring, situated only a few kilometers north of Israel's border. The Banias flowed for five kilometers into Syrian territory before crossing into Israel. As before, only the Dan still rose and remained in Israeli territory. The confluence of the three, the Jordan, flowed along the Israeli-Syrian border, often through the DMZ, until it reached Lake Tiberias, Israel's major source of freshwater, which was now — the most important difference — ten meters inside Israel. The Yarmuk rose in Syria, then became the Syria-Jordan border until it joined the Jordan. South of Lake Tiberias, the Jordan first formed the Israel-Syria border, then the Israel-Jordan border below its Yarmuk junction, finally flowing wholly into Jordanian territory and the Dead Sea one quarter in Israel and three quarters in Jordan.

In the early 1950s, both Syria and Israel announced competing water-development plans. When, in 1951, Jordan announced plans to tap the Yarmuk, Israel began draining the Huleh swamps, which lay within the DMZ. A series of border skirmishes escalated over the summer of 1951 to July 1953, when Israel began building the intake of the giant National Water Carrier that would transfer water out of the Jordan basin all the way south to the Negev Desert, at Daughters of Jacob Bridge. Syria opened fire on the construction site and protested to the United Nations. John Foster Dulles, who in 1919 wrote the sketchily researched German war guilt memo that became one of the underlying causes of World War II, had by this time risen to become the U.S. Secretary of State who chased the Arabists out of the State Department. He visited the region, now flooded with German Jewish refugees, and wrote yet another memo, dated June 1, 1953 — a queasy echo of the "gentile Zionism" that had prompted Britain to make the long-forgotten land of Palestine a focal point of World War I: "The Near East possesses great strategic importance as the bridge between Europe, Asia and Africa . . . This area contains important resources vital to our welfare . . . Surely we cannot ignore the fate of the peoples who first received and then passed on to us the great spiritual truths from which our own society derives its inner strength."

President Eisenhower, backed by the UN, tried unsuccessfully to mediate a comprehensive settlement of the Jordan river system. In

a tactic that Aaron would have heartily approved, Eisenhower's special envoy, Eric Johnston, kept the politicians out of his meetings
and, using technical personnel only, came up with an engineering
plan that would produce the maximum amount of water, to be divided
equitably among the four nations. The Johnston plan was the closest
all four states have come to cooperating over water or any other issue,
but when it was made public in 1954, politicians opposed it and it was
never ratified.

Conflict broke out anew in the early 1960s as Israel completed its
National Water Carrier and began pumping water from Lake Tiberias.
These waters flowed from the Jordan's sources in the Golan Heights
and allowed Israel to irrigate the increasingly populous coastal plain
and the Negev Desert, which indeed blossomed like the rose – with
settlements. But Israel's diversion threatened the waters of Syria, Lebanon, and Jordan. President Nasser of Egypt called the First Arab Sum-
mit in 1964 to come up with a counterstrategy. The result was a plan
to divert the Jordan headwaters from reaching Israel. In 1965, Israeli
tanks and bombers attacked the diversion works in Syria, setting off
a chain of border violence that led Israel to bomb two storage dams
in Syrian territory in April 1967 – which caused Egypt to attack two
months later in support of its pan-Arab ally. Although Egypt's aggressive action has been popularly attributed with bringing on the war, the
deeper and long-building cause was water. Historian Michael Oren,
known for his authoritative account of the Six-Day War, says that
in 1967 land and water were inextricably linked in the Israeli mind;
Israel's attempts to assert sovereignty over the DMZ were really to
stop Syria from diverting the Jordan. "Without control over the water
sources we cannot realize the Zionist dream," Prime Minister Levi
Eshkol told his government at the time. "Water is the basis for Jewish
existence in the Land of Israel." And in his memoir, *Warrior*, Ariel Sharon, then a young colonel in the Israeli Army, acknowledged: "People
generally regard June 5, 1967, as the day the Six Day War began. That
is the official date. But in reality the Six Day War started two and a half
years earlier, on the day Israel decided to act against the diversion of
the Jordan."

The post-1967 boundaries were determined by an unsigned cease-
fire agreement that gave Israel the essence of Aaron's northern

boundary: all of the Jordan headwaters except a section of the Hasbani River plus a dominant position overlooking the Yarmuk that
made diverting the headwaters impossible. Israel's occupation of the
West Bank gave it effective hegemony over the lower Jordan as well.
Only the Lebanon boundary remained as it was in 1923. Moshe Dayan,
defense minister in 1967 and a notorious hawk, remarked, "Israel had
achieved provisionally satisfying frontiers, with the exception of those
with Lebanon." A little political genealogy is in order here. David Ben-
Gurion, who became Israel's first prime minister, suggested in 1941
that the Litani River should be Israel's northern border, and he and
Moshe Dayan advocated Israeli occupation of Southern Lebanon and
the Litani. In 1948, the Israeli Army occupied Lebanon up to the Litani elbow but then pulled back to the 1923 British Mandate border in
the hope that peace with Lebanon's Christian leaders would enable
joint Lebanese-Israeli water development to get under way without
territorial annexation. That this peace proved elusive led to Israel's
invasions of Lebanon in 1979 and 1982, under the command of Ariel
Sharon. The Litani was, once again, a major strategic objective in the
2006 Israeli invasion of Lebanon, by a coalition government in which
Shimon Peres, who began his political life as Ben-Gurion's aide, was
a partner.

With the final – or what seemed to be the final – recovery of the
northern end of Aaron's maximum boundary in 1967, his memory, and
that of NILI, came due for rehabilitation. Absa Feinberg's bones were,
miraculously, rediscovered under the date palm in Sinai where his Bedouin betrayer had buried him. They were officially carbon-dated and
reinterred with full military honors on Mount Scopus in Jerusalem.
Sarah Aaronsohn, the Jewish Joan of Arc, was also duly enshrined in
the elementary school curriculum and as the heroine of several children's books and plays. Only the full figure of Aaron remained shadowy
and indistinct, as perhaps befitted a man of so many allegiances. Felix
Frankfurter attempted a surprisingly incoherent biography in 1937
but, after raising the ominous portent of the "bloodstained hand" that
ended Aaron's life, never completed it. Despite Aaron's heroic stature, to fully explore his life would rattle many skeletons, both Right
and Left. The centerpiece of his political philosophy, the necessity of
a foundation of egalitarian economic cooperation between Arab and

Jew, also remained conspicuously absent from the doctrine of Greater, or Eretz, Israel, which, in the worldview of the Likud Party, became synonymous with his maximum boundary.

Not surprisingly, the recovery of that boundary was soon in question. The ongoing territorial dispute between Israel and Syria hinges on United Nations Resolution 242, which mandated in 1967 that in exchange for peace Israel must give back all land acquired by conquest from its Arab neighbors in 1967. The dispute is over to which boundaries Israel would withdraw: the international boundary between the French and British mandates (1923); the Armistice Line resulting from the War of Independence (1949); or the boundary as it stood on the eve of the Six-Day War, June 4, 1967. While Syria insists on the June 4, 1967, demarcation, Israel argues for boundaries based on the 1923 international division between the French and British mandates – the essential difference being the three tiny but strategically vital demilitarized zones that control access to the Banias River and to Lake Tiberias, or the Sea of Galilee.

In 1977, Likud, which conflated Aaron's ideas with those of Jabotinsky's Iron Wall of military force and biblical claims to Judaea and Samaria, won by a landslide. It was a ballot-box revolution in Israel's traditionally Labor-dominated politics, driven by voter anger at losses suffered in the Yom Kippur War of 1973, at the downturn in U.S.-Israeli relations during the Carter administration, and at United Nations Resolution 242. The resolution calling for the return of all territories conquered by Israel in 1967 guided the 1978-79 Camp David Accords for a comprehensive Middle Eastern peace. Carter's government used water as a lubricant for peace and offered to fund a large portion of construction costs if Jordan could reach an understanding on water allocations with Syria and Israel. However, in the hands of the Likud government, water was used as a weapon instead. Menachem Begin, the former Irgun commander who became a Likud prime minister, was a disciple of Jabotinsky, as were his foreign minister, Moshe Dayan; his defense minister, Ezer Weizmann (nephew of Chaim); and his minister for agriculture, Ariel Sharon.

Sharon, who was a water hawk, developed what became known as the "big plan" for using Israel's military power to establish political hegemony in the Middle East: first, to destroy the PLO's military infrastructure in Lebanon; second, to install a friendly Maronite government that would sign a peace treaty to restore Israel's pre-statehood interest in the Litani and allow joint Lebanese-Israeli water development to begin along the lines suggested by Aaron in 1919; and third, to destroy or weaken Syria's presence in Lebanon. War in Lebanon, he reasoned, would transform the entire Middle East, breaking the backbone of Palestinian nationalism and facilitating the absorption of the West Bank into Greater Israel. Hundreds of thousands of Palestinians would flee Lebanon and the West Bank to Jordan and ultimately create a Palestinian state on the East Bank, thereby ending international pressure on Israel to withdraw from the West Bank.

Assistant Secretary of State Philip Habib, a Lebanese-American who later succeeded in brokering a cease-fire between Israel and the PLO that resulted in the PLO's evacuation to Tunisia, spent three years trying to forge an agreement. In 1979 the talks broke down. Syria dammed the Yarmuk's upper tributaries and Israel continued to draw water from the lower river, leaving Jordan with no option but to curtail water use in agriculture and in urban areas. Sharon became defense minister in Begin's cabinet. In 1979 and 1982, he launched his invasions of Lebanon, in which the Litani River was the primary strategic objective. After extensively bombing the Bekaa and Beirut, where Israel inflicted the most severe damage on the large Palestinian population, it turned over portions of Southern Lebanon to the South Lebanon Army to create a "security zone" that conveniently controlled the Upper Jordan. When Israel captured the Qirawn Dam, she confiscated all hydrographic charts and technical documents related to the Litani and its installations. Border tensions and accusations of water theft proliferated. "Lebanon in the 1980s was the hapless arena for the collision between the dominant and expanded Israel which Begin was determined to build and the rival regional order with which Asad tried to stop him," remarked Hafez al-Assad's British biographer, Patrick Seale. "In shorthand terms, 'Greater Israel' went to war against 'Greater Syria,' both controversial concepts of uncertain definition but which certainly ruled each other out."

Sharon's "big plan" backfired badly – almost as badly as the 2006 invasion of Lebanon that appears to have been inspired by it. Unlike the administration of George W. Bush in 2006, President Ronald Reagan and his advisors grasped the ultimate agenda of Sharon's big plan and summarily rejected it. Alexander Haig was forced to resign from the Reagan cabinet for tacitly approving the Israeli invasion and was replaced by George Schultz, a board director at Bechtel who became known for his view that Syria was intractable to diplomacy. Sharon lost what was left of the goodwill of the United States by allowing Phalangists to massacre hundreds of men, women, and children in the Palestinian shantytowns of Sabra and Shatila. In February 1983, he was removed from his post as minister of defense, a cut he never forgot. Three months later, Israel and Lebanon signed an agreement recognizing the international border but preserving the "security zone" – this time under the control of a United Nations Interim Force – to prevent the use of one country's territory for terrorist activity against the other. The agreement, however, was contingent on Syria withdrawing its forces from Lebanon, which Syria failed to do. Instead, it regained control over Beirut and its highway to Damascus, while the Shi'a of South Lebanon, who had originally welcomed Israel's advance because of tensions with the Palestinians, spawned a new militant group called Hezbollah, which, with Iranian and Syrian support, dedicated itself to driving Israel's soldiers out of Lebanon.

The failed invasion cost Israel 660 dead, exacerbated its economic difficulties, and tarnished its image abroad. For the rest of the decade it languished in a political limbo, polarized between the Labor coalition of Shimon Peres, who maneuvered to find peaceful solutions to the Arab-Israeli conflict, and the Likud cabinet of Yitzhak Shamir. Diplomats like Schultz and James Baker, who were spearheading the Reagan administration's efforts to revive the peace process, despaired at Israel's apparent decision-making paralysis. When the Intifada began in a traffic accident in the Gaza Strip in 1987, diplomatic pressure ratcheted up. Baker may have cost his boss the Jewish vote when he insisted in an address to the all-powerful American Israel Public Affairs Committee, familiarly known as AIPAC, that Israel lay aside its vision of Greater Israel and exchange the occupied territories for peace.

.•. .•. .•.

The most right-wing government in Israel's history took office two months before Saddam Hussein invaded Kuwait in August 1990. Ten days into the crisis, the Iraqi leader ingeniously linked the Gulf and Arab-Israeli conflicts to the suggestion that Iraq might withdraw from Kuwait if Israel withdrew from all occupied Arab territory and Syria withdrew from Lebanon. Since Iraq and Syria had made common cause against Turkey earlier that year in a serious water dispute, presumably Hussein felt confident he could deliver. The administration of George H. W. Bush dismissed his offer as a cheap propaganda ploy. Sharon, then Housing Minister in Shamir's cabinet, called loudly for military action against Iraq, and Richard Cheney, then secretary of defense, issued a statement in Israel's name – a bizarre move for a U.S. secretary of defense – saying the country might retaliate with "nonconventional" weapons if Iraq used chemical weapons against it.

The 1990 Gulf War; the collapse of Syria's ally, the Soviet Union; and George H. W. Bush's threat to withdraw $10 billion in aid to Israel brought about the first public, face-to-face peace talks between Arabs and Israelis in Madrid, in October 1991. Three years later, Israel and Jordan signed a peace treaty ending more than four decades of strife, with the all-important caveat that "water issues along their entire boundary [of the Yarmuk and Jordan rivers] must be dealt with in their totality," meaning a final border agreement with Syria. This proved easier said than done, as Syrian and Israeli leaders once more failed to reach agreement over the Golan Heights, and Palestinian delegates broke ranks with Syria in an effort to reach their own accord.

In October 1994, Israel tried a sweeping solution to the problem by suggesting, at an economic conference in Casablanca, that the entire map of the Middle East be redrawn along the lines of water development. Israel was promoting a "Common Market for the Middle East" similar to the European Union, but the Arab nations, concerned that Israel planned to replace physical occupation with economic occupation, would have none of it. Not only did they not mention any form of cooperation with Israel in their position papers, but they even excluded it from their maps. Their fears were grounded in widespread rumors that Israeli engineers were studying Lake Tana in the Ethiopian Highlands, the source of the Blue Nile. Like Turkey's downstream neighbors, Syria and Iraq, Egypt justifiably feared Israel was trying to control it through the seemingly benign medium of water engineering.

In 1995, Oslo II was signed to great fanfare in Washington DC. This seems odd in light of the breakdown of the Casablanca Conference, but the Clinton administration was as fond of the doctrine of preemptive peace as the second Bush administration would be fond of the doctrine of preemptive war. Despite the backslapping, a final agreement had to be postponed to the final stages of the talks, when the permanent borders would be decided. By the time of this writing, that decision had not been made.

According to *The Missing Peace*, the narrative of Dennis Ross, President Clinton's chief administrator during the Oslo process, Israel's proposal balanced security against water needs. It divided Syria into four security zones, put limits on the whole range of Syrian armaments and where Syrian forces could be stationed within Syria's own boundaries, stipulated constraints on how the Golan Heights could be developed so as not to affect the water feeding the Sea of Galilee, and linked Israeli withdrawal from the Golan to a timetable of normal relations. Syrian president Hafez al-Asad's counterproposal to such maximal demands, unsurprisingly, limited the size of the security zones and constraints on Syrian forces to a minimum; stipulated that full diplomatic ties with Israel would not be resumed until it reached peace agreements with Jordan and Lebanon; and, finally, conditioned the Israeli withdrawal to the borders that stood on the eve of the Six-Day War, June 4, 1967. This broke the deal. According to Ross, Yitzhak Rabin, Israel's peacemaker, "exploded," and rejected any deal on the basis that full withdrawal, in his view, had always meant to the 1923 international border. The difference between the two lines was the sixty-odd square kilometers of the DMZ and their vital implications for both the Banias springs and Lake Tiberias. Rabin, Ross said, feared a Syrian presence on the lake would give the Syrians a claim to its water. According to riparian law, such sovereignty would also give Syria a share in whatever was pumped out of it into Israel's National Water Carrier, i.e., Israel's freshwater supply all the way from the Galilee to the Negev Desert.

Israelis protest that Syria is a water-rich state, pumping more from the Euphrates and Orontes rivers alone than is available to Israel from all of its natural sources. Syria, on the other hand, has protested that it depends on the Euphrates for 85 percent of its total renewable water supply. That source has been threatened since the 1980s by the ambitious dam projects of Syria's neighbor and longstanding enemy, Turkey, where the Euphrates waters rise, and by several years of biblical drought. Both Israel and Syria face skyrocketing increases in the demand for water, brought about by years of rapid population growth.

Negotiators between the two countries tend to downplay the importance of water — possibly because, being finite, it is so very difficult to negotiate. However, Ross has pointed out that Syria and Israel's inability to come to terms over the Golan Heights also made it impossible to reach an agreement on a peaceful Israeli withdrawal from Syria's satellite, Lebanon, which would have made Hezbollah less of a force. The impasse strengthened Hezbollah's hand and, by implication, kept the Palestinian pot boiling in Israel as well.

Rabin's assassination that year brought the peacemaking process to a halt, and Israel's negotiations with Syria did not resume until 2000, after Ehud Barak, a Labor general who ran in Rabin's image, took over as prime minister of Israel from Likud leader Benjamin Netanyahu. Discussions resumed with a colloquy over maps — as strange as it may seem, the June 4 boundary, so hotly disputed, did not exist on any map. According to Shimon Peres, "it was a concept, not a map"; conceivably, Peres meant the concept of Greater Israel delineated in Aaronsohn's 1919 maps. Israeli sources tend to date the disputed boundary as of June 5, 1967, the day after the invasion. Using a map of the 1948 armistice lines between Israel and Syria, generals from both sides tried to define the border according to where their forces were actually deployed on June 4, 1967. Since both sides were using this tactic to buttress their bargaining positions, the inevitable argument broke out once more, with Israel at one point laying claim to the rich agricultural lands east of the Jordan River and the northernmost part of the lake — exceeding even the 1923 line. Ronald Lauder, the cosmetics scion and diplomat-businessman in the mold of Henry Morgenthau, who also happened to be a close friend of Benjamin Netanyahu, sent President Clinton an eight-point paper he claimed included final

points agreed on by both sides, which only sowed confusion. Ultimately, the bargain came down to Israel offering Syria sovereignty over
what Ross called "more than 100%" of the land of the Golan Heights
but retaining the shoreline of the Sea of Galilee. Asad, now terminally
ill with cancer and preoccupied with his legacy, walked away, saying
"he could not last in power for a day" if he were to agree to what Barak
was asking.

On November 5, 2000, as the casualty count from weeks of violence between Palestinian civilians and Israeli troops in the West Bank
mounted to the scale of a small war, a full-page ad appeared in the *New
York Times*. While the *Times* news coverage linked the demise of the
decade-long peace process to rancor over possession of the holy places
of Jerusalem, the ad's implication was that water resources were to
blame. Its banner read, "The day the water disappeared in Israel,"
and it warned that Israel's water will run out in 2015, perhaps even
sooner. (Syria claims the same about its own water supply.) "Farmers,
the land developers of the Zionist dream, are suffering water-cuts of
up to 50%," it proclaimed. "Healthy wells are often defended by strong
fists and shotguns." Placed by the Jewish National Fund under Lauder's
direction, the ad goes on to state that Israel is running a fifty-three-bil-
lion-gallon water deficit, made imminently more perilous by the sali-
nization of Lake Tiberias.

Lauder's view of farmers in the Golan Heights was heavily romanticized and out of date, but he was right about the water running out.
The kibbutz dream has consumed itself. The Lake Huleh aquifers and
Lake Tiberias have been heavily salinized because of Soviet-style heavy
irrigation by farmer-settlers since 1948. In the 1980s, the exhausted
ground collapsed into the aquifers essential to the whole ecosystem;
with the aquifers drained, both farming and the region died. In the
mid-eighties, dust storms appeared, and leachates filtered down to
Lake Tiberias. Jordan River diversions for the National Water Carrier have diminished the river's flow to one-eighth what it was in 1953.
As a result, both Lake Tiberias and the Dead Sea are dropping at an
accelerated rate, affecting tourism, mineral production, the microcli-
mate – and the water supplies of Syria and Jordan.

True to Lord Curzon's pessimistic vision, Israel's open immigration policy has resulted in demographics beyond the limits of its

available water to support. It has been overexploiting its water for over a decade, drawing down its aquifers beyond replenishment rates by about 15 percent. The coastal aquifers, especially in the politically critical Gaza area in which almost 1.4 million Palestinians have been penned, are strenuously overpumped, with seawater intrusions an increasingly serious problems. To the Palestinians, water is the most obvious symbol of their economic oppression: many of the fights in the Occupied Territories have started over the fresh green lawns, irrigated flower beds, and sparkling swimming pools of the Jewish settlers, while nearby Palestinian villages are denied drilling rights and have running water, polluted by sewage, only one day every few weeks. The Palestinians complain that even if the Oslo Accords had been followed to the letter, they would have given Israeli water authorities a lock on water resources. The intractability of politicians has thus created a series of boxes from which it is now almost impossible to escape.

This has led full circle to one of modern history's most stunning ironies. In 1996, as the Oslo Accords bogged down over these three tiny land areas, two American companies, Halliburton and Bechtel, handed Turkey the means by which to resurrect the Ottoman Empire – by exporting its abundant water to its parched neighbors to the south – in the form of a massive, five-thousand-mile water carrier known as the Peace Pipeline. Too expensive for any one government to undertake, the proposed pipeline mingled public and private, national and international investments in much the same way as the Baghdad Railway.

The timing of the Peace Pipeline was extraordinary, to say the least. In 1987, the year the Intifada first broke out, Joyce Starr, director of Near East studies for the Center for Strategic and International Studies (CSIS), a conservative Washington-based think tank known for its network on Capitol Hill, pointed out in a controversial study that water will be worth more than oil going into the twenty-first century, particularly in the oil regions where it is scarce. In geopolitical terms, this translates into an emerging water crisis that "could sunder already fragile ties among regional states and lead to unprecedented upheaval within the area."

Not so coincidentally, in 1986, Turkey, which had endured serious problems with its downstream neighbors, Syria and Iraq, since
implementing its grandly ambitious dam and reservoir program, had
announced plans for the relationship-building Peace Pipeline – plans
that were actually conceived by CSIS. In a 1988 interview, Starr said
the five-thousand-mile engineering feat was the most innovative proposal for peace in the Middle East to date: "It is within the realms of
possibility; it is a serious scheme which is well-intended."

Perhaps. The idea of working around Syria's and Israel's seeming
intractability with a universal delivery system is an ingenious and in
many ways a noble one, but requires the highest degree of diplomatic
sensitivity because of the irritated sensibilities of the countries it must
pass though. The proposed pipeline crossed the boundaries of eight
countries, some highly antagonistic to Turkey. Notable among these
were Syria and Iraq – whose borders would have to be plowed under,
just as Serbia's were in World War I, for the vast scheme to work. Oil-
pipeline politics also have played a large role, but in the sense that to
avoid further confrontation between Israel and Syria over the headwaters of the Jordan, the United States circumnavigated its way into what
is now a far more lethal confrontation in the Middle East, it has truly
scheduled an appointment in Samarra. Stephen Pelletiere, the CIA's
senior Iraq analyst during the 1980s, said in a *New York Times* opinion piece that completing the Peace Pipeline was America's underlying war objective in the 2003 invasion of Iraq. When I visited Israel in
2005, one of Aaron Aaronsohn's surviving relatives in Israel pointed
out to me with tongue not quite in cheek that I should have titled my
book *Aaronsohn's Road Map*.

The involvement of Halliburton, the parent company of Brown &
Root, did not bode well for its success but instead recalled the darkest
element of the Baghdad Railway, the role played by commercial interests and their media relations in bringing about and sustaining not only
a prolonged and ghastly war, but a fractured and unsustainable peace.

Halliburton was in fact founded in 1919, just after the First World
War ended and the former Ottoman Empire was being sliced up like a
rich cake by the Great Powers, by a Texan named Erle Halliburton, who
invented a way to fortify oil wells with cement. The mature company
discovered the benefits of government patronage during the Vietnam

War, when its support for President Lyndon Johnson won it several military contracts. Joyce Starr is a former Foreign Service officer whose home base, CSIS, has been called a "parking-lot for former government bigshots," meaning hardcore Reaganites waiting it out between administrations, and a "conservative propaganda machine." It grew out of the Georgetown School of Foreign Service but was severed from the university in 1987 when Starr wrote her report on the Peace Pipeline, partly because the university was disturbed by large contributions from some of the nation's biggest defense contractors and partly over questions of scholarship. Richard Cheney, then Republican senator from Wyoming, was on the advisory board of CSIS at the time and became a senior vice president at Halliburton. Brown & Root, a subsidiary of Kellogg Brown & Root, "one of the world's largest diversified energy services," which was acquired by Halliburton in 1962, was approached by the Turkish government to do the feasibility study for the Peace Pipeline in 1986. CSIS lobbied the United States government in 1987.

The chief funders of CSIS included Richard Scaife, Justin Dart, and Exxon. CSIS has been dominated through the years by members with strong ties to government and industry. These include Sam Nunn, longtime chairman of the powerful Senate Committee on Armed Services, who served as its chairman and CEO; Henry Kissinger; Zbigniew Brzezinski; Carla Hills; and Brent Scowcroft, who have all served as board members. The group focused on national security and "advancing the global interests of the U.S.," with an emphasis on crisis management in other countries. In 1989 it solicited the first Bush administration to promote the integration of international economic policy with domestic and other foreign policies such as security.

Turkey, even more than Israel, is at least potentially our most valuable ally in the Middle East. It contains the entire region's water mains, the Tigris and Euphrates rivers, in which imperial power has been vested for millennia. Together with the main North African water system of the White and the Blue Nile, the Tigris-Euphrates system formed the two main arteries of the Ottoman Empire and of the Arab Empire that preceded it. Because Turkey sits upstream from some of America's more troublesome opponents, Iraq and Syria, it controls their water supply.

Turkey suffers from chronic balance of payments and inflationary problems, and went through a prolonged period of foreign currency shortage in the 1970s and 1980s. In 1980, a military coup toppled Prime Minister Suleiman Demirel, a hydraulic engineer and dam builder. The ambitious Turgut Özal, a self-made manager from the private sector, well connected in big-business circles, who headed economic reform under Demirel, took power as prime minister when the coup ended in elections in 1982. Özal staked his government on rescuing Turkey's economy by reining in spiraling energy costs with hydroelectricity. Building on projects initiated by Demirel, Özal planned a massive system of dams and reservoirs surrounding the headwaters of the Tigris and Euphrates, a scheme even grander in vision than Nasser's monument to Egyptian nationalism, the Aswan Dam.

Dam projects have long been favored by the governments of developing countries, at least in part because they have been darlings of the World Bank and therefore magnets for funding. In the 1970s, emerging markets came into investment vogue and Özal's pet project was designed to be the biggest water management program in the Middle East. Known as the Southeast Anatolia Project, or GAP (for Guneydogu Anadolu Projesi), it was originally conceived by Kemal Atatürk, founder of the modern state and its first democratic leader, who saw in the 1930s that the way to reinvent the Ottoman reach was to harness and sell its abundant hydropower. Today the biggest dam in the network, one of the five biggest dams in the world, bears the name of Atatürk.

Özal, who was part Kurd, originally conceived the huge project as a means of bringing jobs and foreign investment to his impoverished and politically unstable home constituency, the eastern Anatolian plains between Diyarbakir, Urfa, and Mardin. GAP was intended to transform this blighted area by filling deserts with reservoirs, canals, and fresh crops, revolutionizing agriculture and creating three million jobs for the Kurdish villagers who made the area their stronghold. These villagers had provided a recruiting ground for the separatist Kurdish Workers Party, or PKK, when it was founded by Ankara University student Abdullah Öcalan in 1978. However, many of the militants had been radicalized by mass displacement during previous land reform in the 1970s. Fearing further dislocation, they entrenched themselves in the mountains in northeastern Turkey where the Tigris and Euphrates rise, and – instead of being properly grateful for Özal's opportunity – threatened to blow up the projected dam installations, eventually creating hundreds of million-dollar losses in delays.

As the delays increased, costs metastasized. The Turkish government announced its intention to fund basic infrastructure but periodically ran out of money. Accusations of corruption proliferated, and led to increasing unpopularity for the government of Özal, who had been forced out of office by financial scandals during the military regime that followed Demirel's ouster. When construction began on the first of the dams in 1981, both Iraq and Syria protested that it would eventually deprive them of up to one-third of their water, a claim that was privately admitted to be true by some Turkish engineers. The World Bank grew wary of advancing loans, skeptical at first of the project's overall potential as the most economical way to meet Turkey's energy needs, and then of its political risk. As the protests got hotter, Syria backed them by providing support and shelter for the PKK.

In 1987, after Turkey announced the Peace Pipeline and shook hands with Brown & Root, Turkey and Syria reached an accord based on Turkey's promise to maintain a steady flow of the Euphrates in exchange for Syria's promise to quell the PKK. Turkey, however, quickly became dissatisfied with Syria's compliance. In 1988, a team of executives from Brown & Root toured eight Middle Eastern capitals with Turkish officials in tow to canvass financial support but were met with considerable skepticism. In the first week of October 1989, Özal threatened that unless Syria ended its support for the PKK, Ankara would consider shutting off the Euphrates: the Atatürk Dam was near completion and Turkey was in a position to cut water flow without damaging the dam or compromising its own hydroelectric supply. By 1990, the World Bank and other organizations were putting pressure on the Turkish government to put more of its own capital into the projects, and declined to advance more money until there was agreement between Turkey and its neighbors. The United States, considered the single greatest influence on the World Bank, was the next most likely port of call; however, not one without its quid pro quos.

Four years after striking up a strategic relationship with Brown & Root, Turkey played a little-known role in the first Gulf War when it shut off water from the Euphrates River for a month. This ostensibly took place to fill the Atatürk Dam, but also to bring Iraq to heel. The story went largely unreported on this side of the Atlantic, possibly because it would tarnish the Top Gunmanship of the United States military to be so backed by a dastardly act against thousands of hapless civilians. I heard much of it while traveling in Turkey, albeit in guarded tones – turning off Iraq's tap is considered a war crime. Skeptics regarded the Peace Pipeline as a disguise for an illegal means to bring Iraq under control; and the Peace Pipeline itself as a public relations exercise to cloak a naked power grab. Özal's generals, always the decisive factor in Turkish politics, protested that he was overstepping the normally ceremonial role of the presidency to curry favor with the United States and abrogating the cautious foreign policy principles laid down by Atatürk, who had experienced firsthand the disaster wrought by Turkey allying herself with foreign powers. Turkey's implicit threat regarding its control of the water supply went no further and in fact backfired badly by deepening Syrian hostility toward Turkey and drawing Syria and Iraq closer together.

Özal died of a heart attack in 1993, but not before putting the Peace Pipeline on the table at the Oslo discussions. Between 1993 and 1996, to the accompaniment of loud criticism by Arab nations, Turkey and Israel signed a series of agreements furthering joint military and economic cooperation based in large part on their advantageous positions as upstream riparians. Shimon Peres, today an integral part of Israeli prime minister Ehud Olmert's coalition, was a key player. "The cooperation between two powerful upstream countries for increasing water supply and achieving an efficient water demand management in their own countries and more crucially, in the region offers a mere means to break today's deadlock," wrote a Turkish research associate at the University of Texas at Austin, in a position paper on the relationship of the Peace Pipeline to the Oslo impasse that brushed aside the question of political consensus. There was one glitch in the argument: if Israel were to honor UN Resolution 242 and hand back the Golan Heights, she would no longer be the upstream riparian, or might have to share that status with Syria.

Syria's hostility toward Turkey deepened. It once more sheltered the PKK and provoked chronic instability in southeast Turkey. This erupted into a not-so-minor war in the mid-1990s that killed at least thirty thousand people. In 1998, Ankara threatened full-scale war against Syria if it did not close the PKK training camps within its borders and extradite the PKK leader, Abdullah Öcalan. Syria grudgingly complied but tensions over the Euphrates erupted again in summer 1999, when severe drought gripped the country and Turkey started construction on its fourth large dam on the Euphrates.

In 1996, when Syria's relationship with Turkey seemed shattered beyond repair, a position paper spearheaded by neocon stalwarts Richard Perle and Douglas Feith in conjunction with an Israeli think tank circulated in Jerusalem and Washington. The paper, titled "A Clean Break: A New Strategy for Securing the Realm," focused on Israel allying itself with Turkey and Jordan to "contain, destabilize, and roll-back some of its most dangerous threats," meaning, specifically, that Israel seize "the strategic initiative along its northern borders by engaging Hizballah [*sic*], Syria, and Iran, as the principal agents of aggression in Lebanon." In discussing a quest for "peace for peace" reflecting "continuity of values with Western and Jewish tradition," the paper, which coincided with the inauguration of the government of Benjamin Netanyahu, proposed the most radical redrawing of the Middle East map. It advocated, among other things, that Israel focus on the removal of Saddam Hussein from power as a means of foiling Syria's regional ambitions; that it form a "natural axis" between itself, Jordan, central Iraq, and Turkey that would "squeeze and detach Syria from the Saudi Peninsula"; and liberate itself from a "stalled and shackled" Labor economy by developing itself as a missile shield for United States interests, thus removing the threat of blackmail that "even a weak and distant army could pose to either state." "Not only would such cooperation on missile defense counter a tangible threat to Israel's survival, but it would broaden Israel's base of support among many in the United States Congress who may know little about Israel but care very much about missile defense."

One way to control both Syria and Iraq was through the Peace Pipeline. With Öcalan safely jailed and the PKK in retreat, Turkey moved ahead in the new century with projects that had stalled over years of conflict. It announced plans to expand tenfold the area in Turkey under irrigation along the Euphrates by 2010, which would reduce the flow of water from that river into Syria by as much as 50 percent and contaminate the rest with pesticides and fertilizers. It also announced plans to extend GAP to the Tigris headwaters, building a dam at Ilisu, a Kurdish area forty miles north of the Syrian border, which would further reduce the Tigris flow into Syria and Iraq by as much as one-third despite projections that populations were expected to double their 1998 levels in all three nations, thus certainly accelerating conflict over water resources.

According to Stephen Pelletiere, the CIA analyst who said that completing the Peace Pipeline was America's underlying war objective when it invaded Iraq in early 2003, "No progress has been made on [the Peace Pipeline] largely because of Iraqi intransigence." In a *New York Times* op-ed shortly after the invasion began, he criticized the second Bush administration for pretending to go to war on the grounds that Saddam Hussein committed human rights atrocities against the Kurds of Halabja. "With Iraq in American hands . . . America could alter the destiny of the Middle East in a way that probably could not be challenged for decades — not solely by controlling Iraq's oil, but by controlling its water."

Pelletiere remarked that even if America didn't occupy the country, once Saddam Hussein was driven from power, "many lucrative opportunities would open up for American companies." As a former CIA employee, Pelletiere could not name Kellogg Brown & Root, Halliburton, and Bechtel, the companies that would profit the most. His article, however, pointed out that the Kurds of Halabja, who provided the administration of George W. Bush with its pretext to go to war against Iraq in 2003, were gassed in 1988 not by the Iraqis but by the Iranians, who were attempting to take the dam at Darbandikhan. This dam is Iraq's biggest river control project and part of an impressive system built before the first Gulf War to shield The Land between the Rivers from Turkey's upstream water depredations.

That America could "alter the destiny of the Middle East . . . not solely by controlling Iraq's oil, but by controlling its water," was, and is, a suggestion fraught with sinister possibilities. Controlling Iraq's water is a game plan for controlling Iraq's behavior, and thus ensuring the continuity of the supply of oil. If Iraq's and Syria's – or Jordan's, or Saudi Arabia's, or for that matter, even Israel's – behavior fails to please the upstream riparian and its ally, i.e., Turkey and the United States, the tap can be shut off, just as Turkey threatened to do to Iraq and Syria in the late 1980s and in 1990. What a stunning new way to fight a war on the cheap, with no boots on the ground or messy casualties to report. That it also happens to be a war crime was apparently a minor obstacle to those eager to obtain control. Arab nations clearly viewed it as a naked imperialistic grab and loudly announced their preference for desalinized water, which though considerably more expensive can be easily and independently delivered via state-of-the-art technology developed in the Gulf states.

The Baghdad Railway, which brought the first Zionists to Palestine, began with peaceful intentions and ended in World War I. It was so integral to the imperial war plans that Ferdinand Foch, commander of the French army, ordered the German surrender to take place in restaurant car #2419 of the Orient Express. Hitler, who never forgave or forgot, ordered Foch's successor to surrender in the same car and then, when it became apparent that his forces were losing, ordered that #2419 be blown up so that Germany could not be humiliated again. The politics of the Peace Pipeline are uncomfortably reminiscent of those of the Baghdad Railway – including the fear that a conduit, constructed in peacetime for commercial purposes, could overnight be put to hostile use; and that complex international financing could create thorny issues of ownership and control as the project nears completion, not to mention the invasion of sovereignty. If Syria's boundaries were to be plowed through along with Iraq's to make way for the pipeline, no one should be surprised if its displaced and disgruntled nationalists take aim, just as Gavrilo Princip did at Sarajevo on June 28, 1914 – thus becoming the man who started World War I. The eastern pipeline's proximity to the main Gulf oil pipeline invokes hair-raising sabotage scenarios. Since Turkey's domestic politics hinge on a delicate balance between a traditionally secular military and an increasingly Islamist population, it is not difficult to foresee a point where its strategic goals might differ from those of its Western partners. Israel has already voiced considerable concern at such a close partnership with a Muslim nation. If foreign forces were stationed to provide security, yet another opportunity for conflict would present itself. It is not difficult to foresee a full-scale regional war over the Peace Pipeline that would draw in the twenty-first-century Great Powers, perhaps pitting the United States against a newly invigorated Russia coming to aid its old ally, Syria, as Cold War tensions reignite

Ironically, first the 2003 invasion of Iraq by the United States, and then Israel's 2006 invasion of Lebanon, initially caused Turkey and Syria to mend their fences. The cooperative effort was perhaps given an extra push by the disclosure of Operation Clean Break, which was posted on the Internet and reported in the *Washington Report on Middle East Affairs*. According to Dr. Imad Moustapha, Syria's ambassador to the United States, Turkey and Syria initially settled their water issues amicably and opened up a new era of free-flowing trade relations and border agreements as well. However, the context for Ambassador Moustapha's comments was Hafez al-Assad's answer to Dennis Ross in 1995, when the American negotiator asked him what kind of a relationship Assad envisioned with Israel after a peace agreement. Dissatisfied with Assad's first answer, "One of peace," Ross then asked him which relationship with a neighbor state the relationship he sought with Israel might resemble. "Turkey," Assad replied, evoking a history of rapid shifts characterized by hostility and rivalry.

Two weeks before Israel's attack on Lebanon in July 2006, I received a terse letter from Prime Minister Ehud Olmert's office in Jerusalem. It was a response to a protracted series of inquiries I had made regarding the northern boundary, dating back to the summer before Ariel Sharon's January 2006 stroke, when the then-prime minister and aged warrior made a tectonic shift away from his Greater Israel policy. The reason, Sharon said in a *Jerusalem Post* interview, was that people were not immigrating in sufficient numbers to justify it – because of the continuous and seemingly intractable conflict aroused by Israel's aggressive territorial ambitions.

I had asked the office of Sharon, who had once publicly acknowledged his debt to Aaron Aaronsohn, what the official position was on the northern boundary in light of Aaronsohn's ideas. In the ensuing months, Sharon was silenced by his stroke so I never received his answer. Olmert, however, considers himself Sharon's disciple and is, moreover, a descendant of Israel's Herut aristocracy, which traces its political lineage back to Jabotinsky. I now addressed my inquiries to him. Olmert's diaspora affairs advisor acknowledged receipt of my inquiry by the new prime minister and regretted that "any plans he may consider regarding Lebanon and Syria cannot be divulged."

What followed was Israel's invasion of Lebanon, which destroyed the country's infrastructure, caused over one thousand deaths, displaced more than a million people, and did even more damage to Israel's image abroad and at home than Sharon's most brutal incursion in 1982. As in 1982, much of the invasion had to do with securing the Litani River, and with the complaints of Israeli hard liners that farmers in poverty-stricken Shi'a South Lebanon were diverting water from the Hasbani. The source of the complaint, a four-inch pipe, bore no comparison to the immense National Water Carrier system, but the hard-liners nonetheless threatened to start another water war over it. Avigdor Lieberman, an ultraconservative Knesset member who led the complaints before he became foreign minister in the administration of Binyamin Netanyahu, also advocates bombing Egypt's Aswan Dam for no intelligible reason — Egypt and Israel have been at peace since 1974.

According to Dr. Moustapha, the invasion opened up a new, if limited, opportunity for peace. In addition to knocking the main prop out from under Operation Clean Break by drawing Turkey and Syria closer together, he told me in 2006 in the hushed salon of the Syrian Embassy, decorated in the gracious style of a Damascus mansion, with white brocade sofas and inlaid tables and heavy, rich drapes, "The war in Lebanon has proved to the Israelis that they cannot continue to depend on military superiority to preserve their settlements. The only way to secure the northern boundary with Syria is to sign a peace agreement."

But after the invasion, and even in its devastating aftermath, Olmert categorically refused to give back the Golan Heights. Syrian officials stated, with equal vehemence, that there will be no comprehensive peace in the Middle East until the Golan is returned, and emphasized the point by insisting that Lebanon should not reach any accord with Israel until Israel withdraws from the Heights.

Despite the evidence from the past that competing claims to the sweet waters of the Galilee — and the development plans they might nurture on both sides of the border — have proved nonnegotiable, in the now-former Syrian ambassador's view, water is incidental to the ideological differences between the two nations. "Once a peace treaty is signed, these [water] issues will disappear," he said. The ambassador's seeming complacency was tempered at the time by reports that Syria, alarmed by Turkey's progress in developing the Euphrates, was mobilizing its water resources and proceeding to dam the Yarmuk River just as it did at the onset of the 1967 war — thereby considerably reducing the flow to Israel and Jordan.

Sadly, Dr. Moustapha is technically correct. If geopolitical differences could be set aside — if in fact the clock could be turned back to May 14, 1919 — if equitable, transborder freshwater development along the lines that Aaron Aaronsohn or Eric Johnston had envisioned could be delivered to the Middle East, the lives of its badly battered people could be considerably improved. Such a tangible good might even induce them to begin to trust each other. Today, the task is made easier by the fact that new, energy-efficient and cost-effective methods of laser desalinization — in which Israel excels — could give all Middle Eastern nations with seacoasts an independent means of augmenting their fresh-water supplies. Although the United States and Israel have, for now, lost any credibility as honest brokers, midwifing a Middle East water fair trade agreement is surely a mission for a United Nations or World Bank in need of reinvention — or even for extra-governmental billionaire philanthropists like Bill Gates, George Soros, and Warren Buffett, who has already invested in northern Israel. If all the countries who are currently involved in feeding the Middle East arms race could be persuaded to divert their exorbitant military budgets for even one year to the task of delivering water technology, what a difference it might make. But the ideological issues, as Hafez al-Assad biographer Patrick Seale remarked at the time, were still emotionally defined by Greater Israel versus Greater Syria — or, geographically, defined by sovereignty over a one-hundred-meter strip off the shoreline of the Sea of Galilee.

Time is short, and politicians slow to get out of the way. In the eyes of radicals on both sides, the most expedient solution might be, like Iraq, to get rid of Syria altogether. According to *Al-Zarqawi: The Second Generation of Al-Qaeda*, a biography of the militant leader who was killed in Iraq by American troops in 2006 written by a radical Jordanian journalist, Fouad Hussein, Al-Qaeda is following a twenty-year plan in which the third stage, which was expected to last from 2007 to 2010, focused on destabilizing the secular regimes of Syria and Turkey. The removal of Bashir al-Assad's government, a longtime goal of jihadis still seething over his father's savage repression of the Muslim Brotherhood in 1982, would allow Syria to be infiltrated by Al-Qaeda, putting it, finally, on Israel's doorstep. In that sense, if their politicians could have only seen it, not only Syria and Turkey, but Syria and Israel might have made the most expedient of bedfellows.

As soon as a cease-fire was declared in Lebanon, a heated public debate broke out in Israel on the advisability of engaging Syria directly in talks. Instead, Ehud Olmert, desperate to shore up his shaky coalition after the catastrophically ill-judged invasion and. the subsequent calls for his resignation, took in Avigdor Lieberman's far-right Israel Beteinu party and gave Lieberman, a forty-eight-year-old Soviet immigrant who favors annexing Jewish settlements in the West Bank and transferring most Arab citizens of Israel to a future Palestinian state, the position of deputy prime minister responsible for "strategic threats" against Israel.

Despite Olmert's continued public denials of any intention to give up the Golan trophy, in January 2007 the Israeli newspaper Ha'aretz revealed that two years of back-channel negotiations had resulted in the outlines of a possible peace deal between Israel and Syria that would return the Golan to Syrian sovereignty but conserve Israel's water. These seemingly incompatible goals would be reconciled by maintaining the Golan as a demilitarized national park that would not only symbolize peace but, hopefully, promote tourism, trade relations, and foreign investment. According to Ha'aretz, the deal was the brainchild of Alon Liel, a former ambassador and director-general (briefly) of the Israeli foreign ministry, who took matters into his own hands when Sharon's government rebuffed an attempt by Syria to re-establish formal negotiations and joined forces with Ibrahim Suleiman, a Washington-based. Syrian-American businessman active in the official peace talks between Israel and Syria from 1992 to 2000. An unnamed Swiss diplomat mediated their discussions, and U.S. Vice President Dick Cheney was informed of their progress.

In April 2007, after presenting their plan before the Knesset's Foreign Affairs and Defense Committee, Liel and Suleiman told reporters there remained only "very minor things that could be fixed in two or three sessions" — and that a peace could materialize in six months if Syrian and Israeli officials could only sit down and iron out their differences. However, the remaining differences were not minor ones. Although the plan was a creative way around the deal-breaking strip of Lake Tiberias shoreline, its published details did not include any mention of water-sharing or development. Moreover, in addition to giving up its strategic interests in Lebanon, what Olmert wanted before even entering into official talks was for Syria to cut its ties to Iran, Hezbollah, and Hamas. His preconditions were viewed by many as too steep a price to pay for what amounted to a symbolic peace. As the distinguished commentator on Syrian affairs Patrick Seale remarked, it was like asking Israel to cut its ties to the United States. The Tehran-Damascus-Hezbollah axis is seen by its members as their main instrument to contain U.S.-Israeli aggression. From that perspective, such a peace (particularly one informed by Dick Cheney) might very well conceal an ironfisted effort to detach Syria from the rest of the axis and open up the "Shi'ite Crescent" running from Iran into Iraq, Syria, and Lebanon to Israeli and U.S. influence.

At the time that this book first went to press in 2007, no further agreement had been reached, and none was anticipated until both Olmert and George W Bush left office (in 2008 and 2009 respectively). Ironically in the light of subsequent developments, observers such as Michael Oren argued that any agreement forged between Syria and Israel over the strongly-voiced objections of the Bush White House could trigger a significant conflict between Israel and its main supporter, the United States. In spite of, or perhaps because of, the White House's official stance, a string of highly-placed members of Congress visited Damascus, along with UN Secretary General Ban Ki-moon and European Union foreign policy chief Javier Solana, leading to speculation that it was only a matter of time before Syria came out of diplomatic purdah. But the heightened stakes in turn led to now-familiar indications that the prospect of peace itself could turn into a *casus belli.* According to the Israeli press, a top Syrian official at the time warned that Damascus would liberate the Golan by force if Israel rejected Syria's peace proposal. President Bashar Assad suggested that Israel's refusals to enter official peace talks without preconditions could lead directly to war. Analysts predicted with increasing pessimism that any minor incident between Israel and Syria could quickly spiral out of control because of the likelihood that Israel's leadership would react with hair-trigger force after its debacle in Lebanon. Given the build-up of military arsenals throughout the Middle East, it was conjectured, such an event could easily escalate into confrontation with Iran: thereafter it is not difficult to imagine, as Barbara Tuchman described the beginning of World War I, the red edges of war spreading over another half of the world.

It must have seemed almost opportune when Syria was split by civil war in 2011 and Assad himself was penned into vastly reduced territory, not by Israel or indeed any easily identifiable power but a highly mobile, aggressive army of irregulars who called themselves The Islamic State of Iraq and the Levant, and who took it upon themselves to break up Iraq and Syria as if directed by Operation Clean Break. By an eerie coincidence ISIL — which originated as Jama'at al-Tawhid wal-Jihad in 1999, participated in the Iraqi insurgency after pledging allegiance to al-Qaeda in 2004, and then entered Syria shortly after the 2011 civil war began to take advantage of the country's fractured state — seemed to be acting on the 1916 advice of T.E. Lawrence to the British Foreign Office that, in order to "properly handle" the Arabs, they must be kept in a state of political mosaic, a "tissue of small jealous principalities, incapable of cohesion and yet always ready to combine against an outside force." Curiously, the 2015 London trial of a Swedish man accused of terrorism in Syria collapsed after it became clear that British intelligence had been arming the same rebel groups the defendant was charged with supporting. The prosecution was forced to abandon its case, apparently to avoid embarrassing the intelligence services. More curiously still, ISIL (now generally known as ISIS) tacticians appear to have made an extensive study of the Peace Pipeline and have targeted rivers, canals, dams, sewage, and desalinization plants on the premise that whoever controls increasingly scarce water supplies in the semi-arid region — where the longest and most severe drought in fifty years is considered a factor in Syria's political destabilization — will control the outcome of the conflicts in both Syria and Iraq.

By July 2014, the Sunni Islamic rebels controlled most of the key upper reaches of the Tigris and Euphrates, the lifelines for all of Iraq and much of Syria, and tightened their grip on water installations to cut off supply to the largely Shia south. Both ISIS and Syrian government forces are said to have cut off the water supply to Aleppo to bring it under control, causing panic and chaos in a city of almost three million people. Experts who say that water is already being used as an instrument of war by all sides, including Turkey, also say water is even more tactically important than oil because of the sanitation and health crises that deprivation causes.

Water is also, in the wrong hands, a weapon of mass destruction. In Iraq, the massive five-mile-long Haditha Dam, whose security was one of the first objectives of the American troops invading Iraq in 2003, has once more become a flashpoint, as has the giant Mosul Dam that supplies much of Kurdistan and its fierce peshmerga fighters, who are on the front lines resisting ISIS. If ISIS succeeds in capturing the dam at Haditha, it could paralyze the entire country by opening the lock gates that control the flow of water, flooding the countryside with billions of gallons of water and cutting off all electrical power to Baghdad.

It is therefore a somewhat jarring turn of history's kaleidoscope, of the "countless colored fragments" of the records left behind by the actors in past events, past lives, and past worlds that inform our notion of the continuum on which we travel, that almost a century after Aaron Aaronsohn's death world leaders at last appear to be paying at least some serious lip service to his ideas. In what appears to be an effort to pull back from the brink of utter disaster in the Middle East – in the aftermath of not only the 2003 invasion of Iraq but the 2006 invasion of Lebanon, the 2012 invasion of Gaza, and the ongoing Syrian civil war – the British House of Lords, the House of Commons, the Oxford Union, the European Parliament, the League of Arab States, the World Bank, the World Economic Forum, and the United Nations have all finally agreed: water-sharing and intra-state water cooperation are probably the best means for resolving conflicts, in not only the Levant but India, Pakistan, Afghanistan, China, Nepal, Bangladesh, Egypt, and Sudan. What captured the attention of these august constituencies (aside from the mounting devastation wrought by conventional diplomacy and its failures) was a series of studies produced from 2002 onwards by an India-based think tank, Strategic Foresight Group, which advertises itself as the first government advisory body to identify water insecurity as central to the 2002 crisis in India-Pakistani relations that spurred the Group's creation. They are further motivated by the political mobilization of the environmental movement and the climate change debate, which foresees a 25 to 30 percent reduction in river flow worldwide in the next thirty years, just as population and food demand skyrockets and creates endless possibilities for resource wars.

In 2008 SFG, which advises twenty governments, released a study identifying twenty trends that would impact global security and global economies in the next twenty years. In 2009 it focused its attention exclusively on water. In 2010, the group inspired Switzerland to launch an international "Blue Peace Initiative" on water security in the Middle East, which held its first annual High Level Forum in 2013. But the real driver for all of this high-minded activity was ISIS's incursion into Iraq and Syria and its targeting of water resources, which appeared to bring SFG's more dire prophecies perilously close to fruition.

If ISIS – and/or the Kurds, who wish to establish an independent state in the northern part of Syria – succeed in splitting Syria into three or more autonomous entities, the stage is set for violent water wars for many generations to come ,which will make child's play out of those who contributed to the formation of the Jewish state.

In 2012, just as Syria descended into chaos, HRH Prince Hassan bin Talal of Jordan, chairman of the United Nations Secretary-General's advisory board on water and sanitation and leader of the Blue Peace initiative, introduced a toolkit for building "innovative legal and diplomatic instruments" to create broader peace frameworks out of resolving water disputes. The key to peace, according to bin Talal's partner, the Strategic Foresight Group, is its own "water cooperation quotient," a theoretical construct that uses ten parameters of economic, environmental, institutional, legal, political, and technical factors to score both legal and operational cooperation between countries that share a water body. Based on evidence from 205 shared river basins and 148 countries throughout the world, a study produced by SFG concludes that, "Any two countries engaged in active water cooperation do not go to war for any reason whatsoever, including land, religion, economy or terrorism."

Jordan's own long experience in riparian cooperation should somewhat temper Prince Hassan and SFG's claims. Although it is true that the so-called semi-annual Picnic Table Talks on equitable allocations of the Jordan and Yarmuk Rivers between Israeli and Jordanian water officials went on regularly for some forty years since the early 1950s, the two nations did go to war during that period, notably the Six-Day War in 1967, the War of Attrition between 1967 and 1970, and the 1973 Yom Kippur War. Though their relations have been largely peaceful since the 1980s, Jordan's scant water resources (it is considered the fourth-poorest nation in the world in water terms) have been stretched to the breaking point—first by successive waves of Palestinians fleeing the *nakba* (literally the "catastrophe" of their 1948 eviction from Israel) then the sixteen-year Lebanese civil war, and, more recently, by floods of Syrians fleeing the brutalities of civil war and ISIS. While it is understandable that Jordan should be among the first to try to turn water sharing into a "structured process to create regional mechanisms for cooperation" specifically by engaging political leaders from rival riparian countries and enabling them to negotiate trade-offs between water and other public goods, Jordan should also be the first to remember that lack of political will prevented the original watershed-wide sharing plan developed by President Eisenhower's special envoy, Eric Johnston, from ever being fully implemented.

It is comforting to imagine, with Strategic Foresight's founder and executive director Ilmas Futehally, that "If the international community mobilizes political will mobilize behind the new architecture of water and peace, the alternative grim scenario of water wars can still be averted before the world crosses the tipping point." But the on-the-ground reality is that the architecture of water and peace is hardly new, the problem is now a global one with many more moving parts, and the tipping point, as *Middle East*'s Beirut correspondent Marwa Oswan remarks, is "momentarily." In Osman's view, "manageable trans-boundary solutions" can only be secured by ultimately putting all basins and strategic dams under the watchful eye of "trustworthy people".

Who those trustworthy people might be — "government forces or UN people" — is ultimately left to the reader's imagination, but a broad hint is provided in a 2014 *New York Times* editorial in which a Wall Street investment banker advocated for Israel's antagonists, including Iran, to see its water technology as a solution to their problems. It is indeed a charming notion that Eros might yet triumph over Thanatos in the tortured psyche of the Middle East, but under the far-right government that recently took power in Israel, unlikely to occur. At the most recent Herzliya conference (Israel's annual strategic gathering of generals, ministers, and ex-Mossad chiefs), a senior official was heard to remark that Israel's strategic position had never been so good, thanks to the fragmentation caused by the wars in Iraq and Syria and the Islamic State jihadis, the neutralization of Assad's chemical weapons, the collapse of Libya and the imminent collapse of Yemen, the Egyptian military's crushing of the Muslim Brotherhood and its own squeeze on Hamas in the Gaza Strip. Jordan, the progenitor of the grand plan for saving the Middle East through water cooperation, it should be noted, has come through the Arab Spring with its monarchy intact and maintains discreet but intimate security relations with the Jewish state.

Walking through graveyards is a favored way of communing with the past, and as I wandered through the ordered crosses at Dunkirk, whose ranks give no hint today of the chaos that produced them, I thought of how Aaron might look upon the "evolution" of his hard-fought boundaries. Though some may disagree, I believe he would be appalled at what has been done at least partly in his name. What he had wanted, with all the strength of his enormous will, was an independent Palestine, free from both *Halukah* and from enmeshments with Great Powers, a Palestine that would make not only itself but its neighbors fruitful. He observed long ago that the young country would have no economic future without a working marriage between Arab and Jew — not out of any ideological sentiment, but because it made sense. Despite his temperament, shrewd and pragmatic common sense drove his tremendous appetite for risk and summed him up as a human being. If he were alive today, he no doubt would be making a whole new host of enemies by kicking down the doors of the Knesset and shouting that any deal on the Golan that did not include a region-wide water plan was nonsense. He would ally himself with the international environmental movement, if only to avoid the pitfalls of Great Power politics, and brandish the latest studies by former generals who conclude that global warming makes future wars over scant resources inevitable, particularly in areas of the world where conflicts already exist. In a voice hoarse with repetition and with a gloomy relish in the accuracy of his own predictions, he would have pointed out that Israel's 1994 peace with Jordan still depends on solving Jordan and Yarmuk water issues "in their totality." He would shout for talks with Syria to commence without preconditions and without delay, for Jordan and perhaps even Turkey to be included down the line in building a platform for cooperation on water throughout the Middle East, for Israel to put an end to Great Power meddling once and for all by turning toward neighbors instead of walling itself away from them — the only way, he would say, to avoid the death of the dream for which he had sacrificed so much. But to even think of implementing that plan by destroying two countries, by deploying an unpredictable army of pseudo-medieval mafiosi in the name of religion to shatter the lives of hundreds of thousands of men, women and children, to wreak a level of destruction that is perhaps irreversible — I believe he would have regarded that as a grotesque travesty of the freedom he and his sister fought for.

What Aaron confided to his diary almost a century ago — "If we fail, we alone shall suffer" — is no longer true. The stakes are far higher than they were in his lifetime. If Israel fails, the world will suffer. But if by some miracle Israel were to become, not a bullying, profiteering water colonialist but a trustworthy component of an international will for good, her inconvenient hero's deepest dream might at last be realized: "We shall not be indebted to anyone, and we shall have the right to say that our own efforts have overcome all obstacles."

Acknowledgments

It should not come as a surprise that in attempting a history of the controversial Aaronsohns, I have encountered more obstacles than the norm. To those who were kind enough to guide me at least part of the way, I owe my heartfelt thanks: to Peter Mangold of St. Antony's College, Oxford, and to Peter Hennessy of King's College, London, for introducing me to the intricacies of the Public Record Office; to Sebastian Cox of the Royal Air Force Historical Branch, for spending an afternoon of his valuable time going over the records of Aaron Aaronsohn's long-ago death with me; to Ran, Tamar, and Aaron Aaronsohn Jr., for their memories; to Esther Efrati, director of the Beit Aaronsohn Archive in Zichron Ya'akov, Israel, for her invaluable patience and cooperation over several weeks of difficult research; to the director of the Central Zionist Archive, Jerusalem, for telling me I had the right map; to the skillful and dedicated archivists and librarians, too numerous to name, of the P.R.O., the Bodleian Library, the Imperial War Museum, the British Library, the Library of Congress, Yale University Library, Columbia University Library, UCLA Library, UC – Berkeley Library, and NYU Library; to Ora Cummings, for her translation skills and guidance around Israel; to Peter Rutenberg, for his German expertise; to Shmuel Katz, for allowing me to read his English-language manuscript of "The Aaronsohn Saga" and for his company; to Shaul Katz, Yigal Sheffy, and Moshe Feldman, for their knowledge; to Genevieve Panoz, Marie-Paul Frederick, and Michel Du Bois, conservators, for a very informative and entertaining walk through Dunkirk Town Cemetery; and to Victor Winstone, for the inspiration of his book *The Illicit Adventure*. To Dr. Imad Moustapha, Syrian ambassador to the United States, I owe many thanks for his time and his insight. I must also thank Dr. Hicham Hamdan, Lebanon's ambassador to Argentina. To Peter and Teresa Marinker, I owe friendship and unstinting hospitality: Most of all, I owe my agent, Julia Lord, and my editors, Tim Bent, Andrea Schulz, and Stacia Decker, the chance to make it happen. And to Ali Amir-Ebrahimi, who has seen me through a lot of dark nights, I owe my love and the hope that some day, our people will once more live in peace.

Select Bibliography on Source Notes

The main sources of information in this book are official correspondence and other records of the British Foreign Office, War Office, Cabinet, and Air Ministry held at the Public Record Office in London; contemporary news accounts; and Aaron Aaronsohn's diaries and other personal papers held at Beit Aaronsohn in Zichron Ya'akov, Israel. Interviews with surviving family members are identified in the text. Included below are other reading sources that inform each chapter.

CHAPTER I: THE JEW IN THE BATHCHAIR

For a fictionalized account of Turko-Jewish conspiracy theories, see John Buchan's *The Thirty-Nine Steps*, from which the chapter epigraph is taken.

Aaronsohn, Ran, *Baron Rothschild and the Colonies: The beginnings of Jewish colonization in Eretz Israel* (trans.), Yad Yitshak Ben-Tsevi, 1990.

Barsley, Michael, *The Orient Express: The Story of the World's Most Fabulous Train*, Stein and Day, 1967.

Dominian, Leon, *Frontiers of Language and Nationality in Europe*, Henry Holt, 1917.

Ferguson, Niall, *The House of Rothschild: The World's Banker 1849–1999*, Penguin, 2000.

Friedman, Isaiah, *Germany, Turkey and Zionism 1897–1918*, Oxford University Press, 1977.

Friedman, Isaiah, *The Question of Palestine 1914–1918: British-Jewish-Arab relations*, Routledge & Kegan Paul, 1973.

Herzl, Theodor, *Diaries of Theodor Herzl*, ed. Lowenthal, Gollancz, 1958.

Levin, Alexandra Lee, "Aaron Aaronsohn," *Hadassah Magazine*, March 1970.

Manuel, Frank E., *The Realities of American-Palestine Relations*, Public Affairs Press, 1949.

Oppenheimer, H. R. *Reliquiae Aaronsohnianae*, Imprimerie Jent, Geneva, 1931.

Oppenheimer, H. R., *Florula Transiordanica*, Imprimerie Jent, Geneva, 1931.

Oppenheimer, H. R., *Florula Cisiordanica*, Imprimerie Jent, Geneva, 1931.

Stern, Fritz, *Gold and Iron: Bismarck Bleichroder and the Building of the German Empire*, Penguin, 1977.

The travel diaries of Aaron Aaronsohn's explorations in Palestine and Syria, 1904–1911. In French.

Yergin, Daniel, *The Prize: The Epic Quest for Oil, Money & Power*, Simon and Schuster, 1992.

Zurcher, Erik Jah, *Turkey: A Modern History*, I. B. Tauris, 2001.

CHAPTER 2: THE SPIES OF MOSES

Aaronsohn, Aaron, *Agricultural and Botanical Explorations in Palestine*, U.S. Department of Agriculture Bureau of Plant Industry, Bulletin no. 180, 1910.

Barsley, *The Orient Express*.

Dominian, *Frontiers of Language and Nationality in Europe*.

Ferguson, *The House of Rothschild*.

Gribbon, Walter, *Agents of Empire: Anglo-Zionist Intelligence Operations 1915–1919*, Brassey, 1995.

Katz, Shaul, "On the Wings of the Brittle Rachis: Aaron Aaronsohn from the rediscovery of wild wheat (Urweizen) to his vision for the progress of mankind," *Israel Journal of Plant Sciences*, vol. 49, 2001.

Katz, Shmuel, *The Aaronsohn Saga* (published in Hebrew), Tel Aviv, Ministry of Defense Publishing House, 2000.

Manuel, *The Realities of American-Palestine Relations*.

Ma'oz, Moshe, ed., *Studies on Palestine in the Ottoman Period*, Magnes Press, 1975.

Oppenheimer.

Palestine Exploration Fund, *Thirty Years' Work in the Holy Land*, A. P. Watt and Son, 1895.

Sheffy, Yigal, *British Military Intelligence in the Palestine Campaign 1914–1918*, Frank Cass, 1997.

Shilony, Zvi, *The Jewish National Fund and Settlement in Eretz Israel, 1903–1914*, (trans.) Yad Yitshak Ben-Tsevi, 1990.

Stern, *Gold and Iron*.

Teveth, Shabtai, *Ben-Gurion and the Palestinian Arabs: From Peace to War*, Shocken, Jerusalem, 1985.

Valder Duff, Douglas, *Palestine Unveiled,* Blache and Sons, Ltd. Glasgow, 1938.

Winstone, H. V. F., *The Illicit Adventure: The Story of Political and Military Intelligence in the Middle East from 1898 to 1926*, Jonathan Cape, 1982.

Yale, William, interview with Aaron Aaronsohn, July 197, 2/11/12, William Yale Papers, Yale University.

Yergin, *The Prize*.

CZA ZI/629, Sheinkin to Wolffsohn, May 8, 1905; PRO FO 608/98/9516 and 858.

CHAPTER 3: FLYING THE ZIONIST KITE IN AMERICA

Aaronsohn, Aaron, travel diaries.

Adler, Cyrus, *Jacob H. Schiff: His Life and Letters*, vol. 2, Books for Libraries, 1972.

Barsley, *The Orient Express*.

Bentwich, Norman, *For Zion's Sake*, Jewish Publication Society of America, 1954.

Birmingham, Stephen, *Our Crowd: The Great Jewish Families of New York*, Harper & Row, 1967.

Chernow, Ron, *The Warburgs: The Twentieth-Century Odyssey of a Remarkable Jewish Family*, Random House, 1993.

Fairchild, David, *The World Was My Garden: Travels of a Plant Explorer*, Charles Scribner's Sons, 1939.

Friedman, Isaiah, *The Question of Palestine*.

Howe, Irving, *World of Our Fathers*, Harcourt Brace Jovanovich, 1976.

Los Angeles Herald Examiner, Dec. 8, 1912.

Henrietta Szold letters and diaries, Schlesinger Library, Radcliffe College. Diaries, March 25–April 6, 1910. Undated letter from Aaron Aaronsohn to Henrietta Szold. Bertha Szold Levin to Henrietta Szold, March 20, 1909.

PRO FO 115/2615, McCormick to Osborne, March 31, 1917. PRO FO 608/98/8858 and 9516.

U.S. State Department Petroleum Files 867.6363; 6363/1. Requa, M. *Petroleum Resources of the United States*, U.S. Government Printing Office, March 9, 1916.

CHAPTER 4: MINUET

Aldington, Richard, *Lawrence of Arabia: A Biographical Enquiry*, Collins, 1955.

Bentwich, Norman, *My 77 Years: An Account of My Life and Times*, Jewish Publication Society of America, 1961.

Engle, Anita, *The NILI Spies*, Frank Cass, 1959.

Daniels, Josephus, *The Wilson Era*, vol. 2 1910–1917, University of North Carolina Press, 1944.

Fairchild, David, "The Dramatic Careers of Two Plantsmen," *Journal of Heredity*, vol. 10, no. 6, June 1919.

James, Lawrence, *The Golden Warrior: The Life and Legend of Lawrence of Arabia*, Weidenfeld and Nicolson, 1990.

Halkin, Hillel, *A Strange Death*, Public Affairs, 2005.

Katz, *The Aaronsohn Saga*.

Lawrence, T. E., *Seven Pillars of Wisdom*, Doubleday, 1926.

Lawrence, T. E., *Crusader Castles*, Michael Haag Ltd., 1986.

Lawrence, T. E., *The Wilderness of Zin*, Jonathan Cape, 1936.

Mandel, Neville J., "Ottoman Policy and Practise: 1881-1908," in *The Arabs and Zionism before World War I*, Berkeley, University of California Press, 1976.

Manuel, *The Realities of American-Palestine Relations*.

Meinertzhagen, Richard, *Middle East Diary*, 1917-1956, Cresset, 1959.

Morgenthau, Henry III, *Mostly Morgenthaus: A Family History*, Ticknor and Fields, New York, 1991.

Munroe, Elizabeth, *Times Literary Supplement*, Oct. 2, 1968.

Nutting, Anthony, *Lawrence of Arabia: The Man and the Motive*, Hollis and Coster, 1961.

Oppenheimer, *Reliquiae Aaronsohnianae*.

Richards, Vivyan, *Portrait of T. E. Lawrence of the Seven Pillars of Wisdom*, 1936.

Segev, Tom, *One Palestine, Complete: Arabs and Jews under the British Mandate*, Metropolitan, 2000.

Stewart, Desmond, *T. E. Lawrence*, Hamish Hamilton, 1977.

Teveth, *Ben-Gurion and the Palestinian Arabs*.

Winstone, *The Illicit Adventure*.

De Chair, Somerset, undated memo, 6/389/D, Knightley-Simpson research files for *The Secret Lives of Lawrence of Arabia*, Imperial War Museum, London. U.S. State Department 867.6363/3. Ruth Mack to Aaron Aaronsohn, Feb. 7, 1914, Beit Aaronsohn; narrative in Ruth Mack correspondence; Beit Aaronsohn, Zichron Ya'akov. Yoffe correspondence, Beit Aaronsohn. Douglas Valder Duff to the Editors, *New Statesman* and *Nation*, Jan. 5, 1952. London Mercury, #188. Forster, E. M., "The Mint," *Listener*, Feb. 17, 1955.

CHAPTER 5: THE LOCUST HUNTER

Buchan, John, *A History of the Great War*, vol. 3.

Churchill, Sir Winston, *The World Crisis*, vol. 1, 1911-1914, Scribner's, 1928.

Djemal, Mohammed Achmed (Djemal Pasha), *Memories of a Turkish Statesman 1913-1919*, Arno Press 1973.

Engle, *The NILI Spies*.

Fairchild, David, *The World Was My Garden*.

Frankfurter, Felix, unpublished biography of Aaron Aaronsohn (fragmentary), Frankfurter Papers, Library of Congress, Washington.

Friedman, *The Question of Palestine 1914–1918*.

Fromkin, David, *A Peace To End All Peace: The Fall of the Ottoman Empire and the Creation of the Modern Middle East*, Avon, 1989.

Lowry, Heath, *The Story Behind Ambassador Morgenthau's Story*, Isis Press, Istanbul, 1990.

Morgenthau, Henry Sr., *Ambassador Morgenthau's Story*, Doubleday, Page & Co., 1918.

Stein, Leonard, *The Balfour Declaration*, Simon and Schuster, 1926.

Tuchman, Barbara, *The Guns of August*, Dell, 1963.

Weber, Eugene, *Eagles on the Crescent: Germany, Austria, and the Diplomacy of the Turkish Alliance*, 1914-1917, Cornell University Press, 1970.

Abu Farid interview, *Jerusalem Post*, 1944, Jabotinsky Institute, Tel Aviv.

Aaronsohn, Alex, "Saifna Ahmar, Ya Sultan!," *Atlantic Monthly*, July 1916.

Aaron Aaronsohn Diaries, Nov. 23-25, 1915, Belt Aaronsohn.

Samuel, Herbert, *Memoirs*, London, 1945; Samuel papers St. Antony's College, Oxford.

PRO FO 371/54620, Mallet to Grey, Sept. 30, 1914; PRO FO 371/3057/ 104018, F.O. to Spring-Rice, Tels. 1591 and 2012; PRO FO 383/ 222/599, #209164, George Kidston, British Embassy staff, Constantinople; PRO FO 371/2671/35433; PRO FO 371/2489/69757, "Copenhagen Miscellaneous," May 29, 1915; PRO FO/371/2492/20074, Dec. 29, 1915; PRO FO 371/2492/3123 #201112, Grey to Buchanan, Dec. 29, 1915 and Nicolson to Grey, #20112, Dec. 29, 1915; CAB 37/123/43, Jan. 1915; CAB 42/2/5, War Council Meeting, 3/10/1915; CAB 42/2/14; CAB 37/139.

U.S. State Department 867.00/758, Oman to Secretary of Navy Houston, April 6, 1915; State Dept. Petroleum Files 867.6363-867.6363.1; 867.00/799, Morgenthau to Secretary of State, Dec. 1, 1915.

CHAPTER 6: FELIX KRULL, CONFIDENCE MAN

Aaron Aaronsohn diaries, Jan. 13, July 14, Aug. 15, Oct.-Nov. 1916, Beit Aaronsohn.

Adelson, Roger, *Mark Sykes: Portrait of an Amateur*, Cape, 1975.

Beesly, Patrick, *Room 40: British Naval Intelligence 1914–1918*, Hamish Hamilton, 1982.

Bentwich, *For Zion's Sake*.

Childers, Erskine, *The Riddle of the Sands: A Record of Secret Service*, Oxford University Press, 1995.

Epstein, Jonathan A., paper delivered to New York Military Affairs Symposium, Dec. 1, 2001.

Fleming, Thomas, *The Illusion of Victory: America in World War I*, Basic Books, 2003.

Friedman, *Germany, Turkey, Zionism.*

Fromkin, *A Peace to End All Peace.*

Gardner, Brian, *Allenby*, Cassell, 1965.

Gribbon, *Agents of Empire.*

Sheffy, *British Military Intelligence in the Palestine Campaign.*

Thomson, Sir Basil, "Memoirs" (published in *English Life*); *The Story of Scotland Yard*, Literary Guild, 1936.

PRO FO 115/2011, Aug. 2,1916; PRO FO 371/2783/221220, WO. to F.O., "Reports of an Inhabitant of Athlit," dated 3, 9, 16, 23 and 30 November 1916; PRO FO/371/2559/3516, Spring-Rice to Primrose, 1 April 1916; PRO FO/371/2835/18095, Spring-Rice to Cecil; PRO FO 371/2559/35166; FO 371/2783/221220; FO 371/3053, Gustav von Doebbeler in "Die Reichsbote"; FO 371/3057/104218, Sykes memo of July 29, 1917; FO 371/3044/1173; FO882/25; FO 371/3049/41142; FO 115/2001; CAB 37/123/58; CAB 37/124/59 "American Opinion."

Aaron Aaronsohn to Victor Jacobson, Oct. 30, 1916, Beit Aaronsohn; Aaron to Rivka and Alex Aaronsohn, Oct 28, 1916; Aaron Aaronsohn to Judge Julian Mack, Oct 9, 1916, Beit Aaronsohn; also Henrietta Szold Archive Jewish Historical Museum, Baltimore.

CHAPTER 7: HE WHO WRITES THE DISPATCHES

Bentwich, *My 77 Years.*

Fromkin, *A Peace to End All Peace.*

Gribbon, *Agents of Empire.*

Halkin, *A Strange Death.*

James, *The Golden Warrior.*

Mack, John E., *A Prince of Our Disorder: The Life of T. E. Lawrence*, Little, Brown, 1976.

Sheffy, *British Military Intelligence in the Palestine Campaign.*

Thomas, Lowell, *With Lawrence in Arabia*, Hutchinson, 1925.

T. E. Lawrence exhibit, Imperial War Museum, Dec. 2005.

Weizmann, Chaim Letters, vol. 8, no. 432, to Sir Ronald Graham, 6/13/1917.

Westrate, Bruce, *The Arab Bureau: British Policy in the Middle East, 1916–1920*, Pennsylvania State University Press, 1990.

Winstone, *The Illicit Adventure.*

Aaron Aaronsohn diaries, Dec. 1916–July 1917, Beit Aaronsohn. "Aaron Aaronsohn," *Arab Bulletin*, April 21, 1917; "Present Economic and Political Conditions in Palestine" by Aaron Aaronsohn, cf. FO 882/14; also CAB 21/15, memorandum by William Ormsby-Gore, 1 April 1917; Gore to Hankey, 4 April; Hankey to Gore, Robertson, 10 April 1917.

Mack to Magnes, Jan. 6, 1917, Beit Aaronsohn. Sarah to Aaron Aaronsohn, Aug. 23, 1917, Belt Aaronsohn. Edmund Allenby letter of testimonial, July 14, 1919, Belt Aaronsohn; Sir George MacDonough, speech at Royal Artillery Institution, Woolwich, Dec. 4, 1921, reported by *New York World*, Beit Aaronsohn. Sarah to Aaron Aaronsohn, June 25, 1917, Belt Aaronsohn. Abu Farid, *Jerusalem Post* interview, Jabotinsky Institute, Tel Aviv.

FO 371/3062; FO 371/3053/ 93349, *Franlfurter Zeitung* reprinted in *Times* of London, May 8, 1917; FO 800/25; FO 800/210.

Somerset de Chair memo, undated, Knightley-Simpson Archive, 6/389/D, Imperial War Museum.

Hogarth-Lawrence correspondence, Middle East Centre, St. Antony's College, Oxford. Sledmere (Mark Sykes) Papers, Ormsby-Gore to Sykes, 8 May 1917, private and confidential. Middle East Centre, St. Antony's College, Oxford. *The Arab Bulletin*, 1915–1918, Bobst Library, New York University.

CHAPTER 8: "OUR PEOPLE"

Cobbing, Felicity, *Allenby's campaign*, unpublished paper for the Palestine Exploration Fund, 2002.

Engle, *The NILI Spies*.

Friedman, *The Question of Palestine*.

Lloyd George, David, *War Memoirs*, vol. 4.

Manuel, *The Realities of American-Palestine Relations*.

Morgenthau, Henry Sr., *Ambassador Morgenthau's Story*.

Morgenthau, Henry III, *Mostly Morgenthaus*.

Pound, Reginald, and Harmsworth, Geoffrey, *Northcliffe*, Cassell, 1959.

Seymour, Charles, Ed., *Intimate Papers of Colonel Edward House*, New York, 1926.

Stein, *The Balfour Declaration*.

Weber, *Eagles on the Crescent*.

Weizmann, Letters, vol. 8, #466, to Brandeis, Jan. 14, 1917; Aug. 1, 1917.

Weizmann, Chaim, *Trial and Error: The Autobiography of Chaim Weizmann*, Harper & Bros., 1949.

Yale, William, *Ambassador Henry Morgenthau's Special Mission of 1917*, World Policy, 1949.

Yale to Leland Harrison, State Dept., letter of Oct. 24, 1917, William Yale AEU, Yale University.

Aaron Aaronsohn diaries, May–August 1917. Sarah to Aaron Aaronsohn, June 25 and Sept. 21, 1917, Beit Aaronsohn.

F.R.U.S. Supplement 1, May 16, 1917; Supp. 2, April 11-17, also July 14, 1917; State Dept. File 763.7215815; 763.72/6662.

PRO K692/126711; K692/126709 K692/126711-12; FO 371/3087/251272; FO 371/471, Secret and Confidential Report, Communications of the Zionist Organisation in 1917 by William Ormsby-Gore, Oct. 9, 1917; FO 371/3057/104218, FO 371/5057/11707,117850; FO 371/3053/ 72699/399, Tune 25, 1917; FO 371/3053/95472, May 14, 1917; FO 371/ 3053/117744; FO 371/3053/84173, 174977, 59349, 59351; FO 371/ 3055/127504; FO 371/3057/130633; FO 371/3057/87895; FO 371/ 3057/27172; FO 371/3044/1173; FO 371/3083/156401.

Central Zionist Archives, Z4/305/1.

Sledmere Papers, #55, note by Ormsby-Gore, Secret and Confidential, June 12, 1917; #69, Sykes to Clayton, July 22, 1917; #70, Sykes to Clayton, July 22, 1917.

New York Times, June 21, 1917.

NOTE: The German correspondent in question was Major Franz Karl von Endres, who had served under Goltz in Turkey before writing for the *Muncher Neueste Nachrichten*.

CHAPTER 9: THE SACRIFICE

Farago, Ladislas, *Palestine at the Crossroads*, Putnam, 1937.

FitzHerbert, Margaret, *The Man Who Was Greenmantle*, John Murray, 1983.

Friedman, *The Question of Palestine*.

Katz, English translation of Dr. Hillel Yoffe's diary, in *The Aaronsohn Saga*.

Lawrence, A. W., ed., *T. E. Lawrence by His Friends*, Cape, 1937.

Lawrence, *Seven Pillars of Wisdom*.

Lloyd George, *War Memoirs*, vol. 2, Little, Brown & Co., 1933-1937.

Meinertzhagen, *Middle East Diary*.

Pound and Harmsworth, *Northcliffe*.

Ross, Stephen, Asquith, Lane, 1976.

Scheersohn, Menachem, "From Tyranny to Freedom: A True Story of the Terrible Sufferings of the Jews Endured [*sic*] at the Hands of the Turkish Government during the Great War: My Arrests, Adventures and Exiting [*sic*]

Incidents and Escape from the Turks," unpublished (and unpunctuated), Beit Aaronsohn, Israel.

Stein, *The Balfour Declaration*.

Weldon, L. B., *Hard Lying: Eastern Mediterranean, 1914–1919*, London, Herbert Jenkins, 1925.

Weizmann, Letters, vol. 8, #515; vol. 49 and ff; #118, #218.

FO 371/3058/193040; FO 371/3058/174095; PRO/K692/180051, 180052; FO 371/3053/193643; FO 371/3055/90899, Nov. 11–13 1917; FO 371/3057/235703; FO 371/3057/236789, telegram, Lowell Thomas to John Buchan, Dec. 13, 1917, 176998/N/51, telegram Dec. 13, 1917; FO 371/3057/34/N/51, Dec. 21, 1917 and enclosure, Buchan to Butler, Dec. 22, 1917; FO 371/3394/84173, Weizmann to Brandeis, 14/01/1918, Brandeis to Weizmann 08/04/1918, also #16946, 27/01/1918; FO 371/3394/11053#14189; WO 95/4415, RFA Motor Section; ADM 53/44609.

Lowell Thomas Archive, Marist College, New York.

Aaron Aaronsohn diaries, Nov. 1917–March 1918, Beit Aaronsohn.

Agricultural Survey by Aaron Aaronsohn, March 1918, Beit Aaronsohn.

Leon Simon diary (unpublished), April 28, 1918, C.Z.A. Z4/16017.

William Ormsby-Gore, "Report on the Existing Political Conditions in Palestine and Contiguous Areas by the Political Officer in Charge of the Zionist Commission," August, 1918, C.Z.A.

Interview, Aaron Aaronsohn Jr., Aug. 30, 2005.

Knightley-Simpson Archive, 90-2.

Secret and Personal, Maj. J. Wood to Alex Aaronsohn, Sept 26, 1918, Beit Aaronsohn; Alex to Aaron Aaronsohn, Oct 3, Beit Aaronsohn; Aaron Aaronsohn to Norman Bentwich, Sept. 7, 1917; Aaron Aaronsohn to Judge Mack, Jan. 5, 1918; Alex to Aaron Aaronsohn, Jan. 18, 1918; Ruth Mack to Aaron Aaronsohn, April 7, 1918; Alex to Aaron, 24/03/1918; Aaron to Alex, Aug. 18 and Aug. 31, 1918.

Weizmann Papers, Rehovoth, Box 146 and Box 20, Folio 71.

William Yale Papers, Yale University, 2/11; 2/14; 2/19/2; 2/25.

CHAPTER 10: ICARUS FALLS FROM THE SKY

Adler, *Jacob H. Schiff*.

Barsley, *The Orient Express*.

Chernow, *The Warburgs*.

Fay, Sidney, *Origins of the World War*, vol. II Macmillan, 1930.

Fleming, *The Illusion of Victory*.

Gribbon, *Agents of Empire*.

James, *The Golden Warrior*.

Stewart, *T. E. Lawrence*.

Keynes, John Maynard, *The Economic Consequences of the Peace*, Macmillan, 1919.

Macmillan, Margaret, *Peacemakers: The Paris Conference of 1919 and Its Attempt to End War*, John Murray, 2001.

Morgenthau, *Ambassador Morgenthau's Story*.

Morgenthau, Henry Sr., letter to the editor, *New York Times*, Dec 11, 1917.

Morgenthau, *Mostly Morgenthaus*.

Nicolson, Harold, *Peacemaking: Paris 1919*, Constable, 1919.

Pound and Harmsworth, *Northcliffe*.

Temperley, Harold, *A History of the Peace Conference of Paris*, Oxford University Press, 1969.

Weber, *Eagles on the Crescent*.

Winstone, *The Illicit Adventure*.

Yergin, *The Prize*.

Zurcher, *Turkey*.

Aaron Aaronsohn diaries, February 1919.

Aaron Aaronsohn, "The Boundaries of Palestine," C.Z.A., Aaron Aaronsohn to Chaim Weizmann, Feb. 16, 1919; Weizmann Archive, Rehovot; Alex to Aaron and Frankfurter, May 6, 1919, Beit Aaronsohn.

C.Z.A. A264/7; Z4/1074, Aaron Aaronsohn Report, Nov. 5, 1918; Z3/371; A/262 and A/264/7, Szold to Frankfurter, April 27, 1919; 1074/A/264; A7/23/2; Flexner to Brumley, May 14, 1919.

Felix Frankfurter to Louis Brandeis, Mar. 1 and Mar. 3, 1919, also May 25, 1919; Frankfurter to Wilson, May 8, 1919; Wilson to Frankfurter, May 13, 1919; Frankfurter to Wilson, May 14, 1919; Wilson to Frankfurter, May 16, 1919, May 28, 1919, National Archives, Washington.

Le Telegramme and *Le France du Nord*, both of May 16, 1919. *The Barrovian*, June 1919, Isle of Man Municipal Library.

PRO FO 371/3057/251272, "Memorandum on Turkish Peace Overtures," FO 608/98/8858 of May 1, 1919; FO 608/9516; RO AIR 1/2400/286/1, RAF Flight Manifest; FO 371/4171/90899.

"R.A.F. Kenley," official history.

India Office Library, Curzon Papers, Eastern Committee Minutes, 40/2/12/1918.

Weizmann, Letters, Vol. IX, #38, #45, #85, #96, #114, #135, #136, note 8, #143 and notes, May 8, 1919; #147 to Julius Simon, Schmarya Levin and Victor Jacobson, May 17, 1919.

William Yale Papers, 6/19/2, Westermann to Bullitt, April 11, 1919, and telegram #230 of April 17, 1919, from the Office of the Secretary General to the
American Commission to Negotiate Peace; 2/11/12.

CHAPTER II: INCONVENIENT HEROES

Engle, *The NILI Spies*.

Farago, *Palestine at the Crossroads*.

Dorril, Stephen, *MI6: Inside the Covert World of Her Majesty's Secret Intelligence Service*, Free Press, 2000.

Halkin, *A Strange Death*.

James, *The Golden Warrior*.

Knightley, Phillip, and Simpson Colin, *The Secret Lives of Lawrence of Arabia*,
Panther, 1971.

Hart, Basil Liddell, *T. E. Lawrence: In Arabia and After*, Cape 1935.

Nutting, *Lawrence of Arabia*.

Shlaim, Avi, *The Iron Wall: Israel and the Arab World*, W. W. Norton, 2000.

Stewart, *T. E. Lawrence*.

Box 17, Zionist Central Organisation 17/1, War Office to Allenby, May 26, 1919;
Ruth Mack to Rivka Aaronsohn, 11 August 1919; Beit Aaronsohn; Ruth Mack
to Alex Aaronsohn, 9 November 1920; Ruth Mack to Rivka Aaronsohn, June
6, 1924; PRO FO 371/3180/ 18925/65; FO 371/23194 E 4645/3933/65, letter from Alexander Korda to Sir Robert Vansittart, 26 June 1939; FO ibid.,
Vansittart's reply; letter to author from Sebastian Cox, Head of Air Historical
Branch, RAF, 22 April 2004.

De Chair, Somerset, "The Identity of S.A." Knightley-Simpson, 6/389/D, Imperial War Museum; also 4/2830, June 18, 1968; Knightley-Simpson IWM
2/17/A, Robert Graves to Basil Liddell Hart, Feb. 19, 1954; Knightley Simpson IWM 2/35/A.

T. E. Lawrence Archive, 6752/79, Bodleian Library, Oxford. Interviews: Sebastian Cox, head of Air Historical Branch RAF, June 2004; Ran Aaronsohn,
Aaron's great-nephew and Israeli geographer, University of Chicago, May 18,
2005; Shmuel Katz, Likud historian and former Knesset member, Aug. 28,
2005, Tel Aviv; author visit to Dunkirk Town Cemetery, and interviews with
archivists of the Bureau Conservatoire, Michel DuBois, Marie-Paul Frederick, and Genevieve Panoy, Dec. 19, 2005.

The Barrovian, Nov. 1919; *Isle of Man Examiner*, Mar. 26, 1920; Journal "*Aux
Ecoutes*," Nice, April 9, 1948; Phillip Knightley and Colin Simpson, *Times* of
London, June 16, 1968; Graves, Robert, "S.A.," *Saturday Review*, June 15,
1963; *Life*, vol. 59, Oct. 15, 1965.

Hulbert, Jeffrey, and Richards, Jeffrey, "Censorship in Action: The Case of Law-rence of Arabia," *Journal of Contemporary History*, SAGE, London, Beverly Hills, and New Delhi, vol. 19,1984.

Shakespeare, William, *Romeo and Juliet*, Act IV, Sc. in.

CHAPTER 12: AARONSOHN'S ROAD MAP

De Villiers, Marq, *Water: The Fate of Our Most Precious Resource*, Houghton Mifflin, 2000.

Futehally, Ilmas," Preventing Water Wars: How to Build Bridges over Water Dis-putes," *The Guardian*, Sept. 30, 2014.

Garfinkle, Adam, *Water, War and Negotiation in the Middle East: The Case of the Palestine-Syria Border, 1916–1923*, Moshe Dayan Center for Middle East-ern and African Studies, Tel Aviv University, 1994.

Hillel, Daniel, *Rivers of Eden: The Struggle for Water and the Quest for Peace in the Middle East*, Oxford University Press, 1994.

Klare, Michael, *Resource Wars: The New Landscape of Global Conflict*, Metro-politan, 2001.

McCarthy, Justin, *The Population of Palestine: Population Statistics of the Late Ottoman Period and the Mandate*, Columbia University Press, 1990.

Milne, Seumas, "Now the Truth Emerges," *The Guardian*, June 3, 2015.

Naff, Thomas and Matson, Ruth, Eds., *Water in the Middle East: Conflict or Cooperation?*, Westview Press, 1984.

Oren, Michael, *Six Days of War: June 1967 and the Making of the Modern Middle East*, Ballantine, 2003.

Osman, Marwa, "Blue Peace in the Middle East," *Middle East Magazine*, June 2,2015.

Peres, Shimon, *Economic Cooperation at the Casablanca Conference*, Israeli Ministry for Foreign Affairs, 1997.

Pipes, Daniel, *Greater Syria: The History of an Ambition*, Oxford University Press, 1990.

Ra'anan-Frischwasser, Uri, *The Frontiers of a Nation: A Re-examination of the Forces Which Created the Palestine Mandate and Determined the Territorial Shape*, Hyperion Press, 1955.

Ross, Dennis, *The Missing Peace: The Inside Story of the Fight for Middle East Peace*, Norton, 2005.

Sacher, Howard, *A History of Israel*, vol. 1, Knopf, 1979.

Seale, Patrick, *Assad of Syria: The Struggle for the Middle East*, I. B. Tauris, 1988.

Siegel, Seth M., "Israeli Water, Mideast Peace?" *The New York Times*, February 17, 2014. Smith, Charles D., *Palestine and the Arab-Israeli Conflict: A History with Documents*, Bedford/St Martin's, 2001.

Soifer, Amon, *Rivers of Fire: The Conflict over Water in the Middle East*, Roman and Littlefield, 1999.

Starr, Joyce, and Stoll, Daniel, *The Politics of Scarcity: Water in the Middle East*, Westview, 1987.

Vidal, John, "Water Supply Key to Outcome of Conflicts in Iraq and Syria, Experts Warn," *The Guardian*, July 2, 2014.

Weizmann, Letters, vol. 9, introduction; #112, Weizmann to Gen. Wigram Money, Jan. 26, 1919, #220, #231 n. 3; Weizmann-Brandeis correspondence, C.Z.A.; vol. 22, April 6, 1945.

Wolf, Aaron, T., and Newton, Joshua T., "The Jordan River-Johnston Negotiations 1953-1955; Yarmuk Negotiations 1980s," www.transboundarywaters.orst.edu.

•◦• •◦• •◦•

Author interviews: Aaron Aaronsohn Jr., Aug. 30, 2005, Rishon-le-Zion; Dr. Imad Moustapha, Syrian ambassador to the United States, Oct. 13, 2006; official correspondence, office of Israeli Prime Minister Ehud Olmert.

Wolff, Aaron, "Water, War and Arab-Israeli Peace Negotiations," paper presented at Bloomington, Indiana, March 7-10, 1996; Stevens, Georgiana, "Jordan Water Partition," The Hoover Institution, Stanford, 1965; Cooley, John, "The War Over Water," Foreign Policy, spring 1984; Amaku, Konural, "Water-Related Cooperation between Turkey and Israel," undated, http://tsi.idc.ac.il/pamaku.html.

Tarnapolsky, Noga, *Forward*, Jan. 5, 1996; *MEED*, March 26, 1988, Jan. 19, 1990, July 17, 1981; *Sourcewatch*, Center for Media and Democracy (Web site), "Georgetown Media Profs" by Alison Muscatine, reprinted from the *Washington Post*, May 11, 1986; also "Programs and Activities," Center for Strategic and International Studies, 1987–88, re-printed from CSIS Publications, 1989; also Richard Lawrence from *Journal of Commerce*, undated; *New York Times*, Dec. 4, 1990, April 19 and 23, 1993, Stephen Pelletiere op-ed, Jan. 31, 2003.

Peres, Shimon, *Economic Cooperation at the Casablanca Conference*, Israeli Ministry for Foreign Affairs, 1997; *Facts about Turkey*, Republic of Turkey Directorate General of Press Information, 1998.

Index

Printed in the United States
by Baker & Taylor Publisher Services